Affirmation and Resistance in Spinoza

Spinoza Studies
Series editor: Filippo Del Lucchese, Alma mater studiorum, Università di Bologna

Seminal works devoted to Spinoza that challenge mainstream scholarship
This series aims to broaden the understanding of Spinoza in the Anglophone world by making some of the most important work by continental scholars available in English translation for the first time. Some of Spinoza's most important themes – that right is coextensive with power, that every political order is based on the power of the multitude, the critique of superstition and the rejection of the idea of providence – are explored by these philosophers in detail and in ways that will open up new possibilities for reading and interpreting Spinoza.

Editorial Advisory board
Saverio Ansaldi, Etienne Balibar, Chiara Bottici, Laurent Bove, Mariana de Gainza, Moira Gatens, Thomas Hippler, Susan James, Chantal Jaquet, Mogens Laerke, Beth Lord, Pierre Macherey, Nicola Marcucci, Alexandre Matheron (1926–2020), Dave Mesing, Warren Montag, Pierre-François Moreau, Vittorio Morfino, Antonio Negri, Susan Ruddick, Martin Saar, Pascal Sévérac, Hasana Sharp, Diego Tatián, Francesco Toto, Dimitris Vardoulakis, Lorenzo Vinciguerra, Stefano Visentin, Manfred Walther, Caroline Williams.

Books available
Affects, Actions and Passions in Spinoza: The Unity of Body and Mind, Chantal Jaquet, translated by Tatiana Reznichenko
The Spinoza-Machiavelli Encounter: Time and Occasion, Vittorio Morfino, translated by Dave Mesing
Politics, Ontology and Knowledge in Spinoza, Alexandre Matheron, translated and edited by Filippo Del Lucchese, David Maruzzella and Gil Morejón
Spinoza, the Epicurean: Authority and Utility in Materialism, Dimitris Vardoulakis
Experience and Eternity in Spinoza, Pierre-François Moreau, edited and translated by Robert Boncardo
Spinoza and the Politics of Freedom, Dan Taylor
Spinoza's Political Philosophy: The Factory of Imperium, Riccardo Caporali, translated by Fabio Gironi
Spinoza's Paradoxical Conservatism, François Zourabichvili, translated by Gil Morejón
Marx with Spinoza: Production, Alienation, History, Franck Fischbach, translated by Jason Read
Time, Duration and Eternity in Spinoza, Chantal Jaquet, translated by Eric Aldieri
Affirmation and Resistance in Spinoza: The Strategy of the Conatus, Laurent Bove, translated and edited by Émilie Filion-Donato and Hasana Sharp

Forthcoming
Spinoza and Contemporary Biology: Lectures on the Philosophy of Biology and Cognitivism, Henri Atlan, translated by Inja Stracenski and Robert Boncardo
Spinoza's Critique of Hobbes: Law, Power and Freedom, Christian Lazzeri, translated by Nils F. Schott
Spinoza and the Sign: The Logic of Imagination, Lorenzo Vinciguerra, translated by Alexander Reynolds
New Perspectives on Spinoza's Theologico-Political Treatise: *Politics, Power and the Imagination*, edited by Dan Taylor and Marie Wuth

Visit our website at www.edinburghuniversitypress.com/series/SPIN

Affirmation and Resistance in Spinoza

The Strategy of *Conatus*

Laurent Bove

Translated by Émilie Filion-Donato

Edited by Hasana Sharp and
Émilie Filion-Donato

EDINBURGH
University Press

Edinburgh University Press is one of the leading university presses in the UK. We publish academic books and journals in our selected subject areas across the humanities and social sciences, combining cutting-edge scholarship with high editorial and production values to produce academic works of lasting importance. For more information visit our website: edinburghuniversitypress.com

La stratégie du conatus. Affirmation et résistance chez Spinoza
© Librairie Philosophique J. Vrin, Paris, 1996
http://www.vrin.fr
© editorial matter and organisation Émilie Filion-Donato and Hasana Sharp, 2023, 2025
English translation © Émilie Filion-Donato

Edinburgh University Press Ltd
13 Infirmary Street
Edinburgh EH1 1LT

First published in hardback by Edinburgh University Press 2023

Typeset in 10/12 Goudy Old Style
by Cheshire Typesetting Ltd, Cuddington, Cheshire

A CIP record for this book is available from the British Library

ISBN 978 1 4744 3057 9 (hardback)
ISBN 978 1 4744 3058 6 (paperback)
ISBN 978 1 4744 3059 3 (webready PDF)
ISBN 978 1 4744 3060 9 (epub)

The right of Laurent Bove to be identified as the author of this work has been asserted in accordance with the Copyright, Designs and Patents Act 1988, and the Copyright and Related Rights Regulations 2003 (SI No. 2498).
The right of Émilie Filion-Donato and Hasana Sharp to be identified as the editor of this work has been asserted in accordance with the Copyright, Designs and Patents Act 1988, and the Copyright and Related Rights Regulations 2003 (SI No. 2498).

Published with the support of the University of Edinburgh Scholarly Publishing Initiatives Fund.

Contents

Translator's Note and Acknowledgements		vii
Abbreviations		ix
Introduction: Infinity and Strategy		1
1	The Strategic Logic of the Spinozist *Conatus*: The Stages of World Construction	12
	1 Habit as the Constituting Activity of Actual Existence	12
	2 *Conatus* as Joy Principle	25
	3 *Conatus* as Memory	31
2	The Constitution of the Strategic Subject	37
	1 The Object and its Recognition	37
	2 Recognition, Useful Inadequate Knowledge	46
	3 Theory of the Practical Subject	53
3	*Conatus* as a Strategy of Self-Love	63
	1 *Conatus* as Imitation and the Ambition for Domination	63
	2 Love of Self and Strategies of Self-Love	72
	3 Ostentation or Dissimulation? A Strategy of Appearance	83
4	*Hilaritas* and *acquiescentia in se ipso*: A Dynamic of Joy	89
	1 The Infant's Joyful Passion	90
	2 *Acquiescentia animi* and Adequate Knowledge	94
	3 Dynamic Equilibrium: Return and Productivity	97
5	Ethical Subjectivity and the Absolute Affirmation of Singular Existence: An Ethics of Resistance	106
	1 The Spiritual Automaton and the Practical Subject	106
	2 From the Practical Subject of Love to Ethical Subjectivity	110
	3 An Ethics of Resistance and Love	116

6	The Innocence of Reality and the Recursive Cycle	122
	1 *Causa sui* as the Real Movement of the Production of Reality	122
	2 Infinite Modes and Circular Necessity	130
	3 From the Identification of the Synthetic and Analytic Links to the Absolute Expression of the Univocity of Being (Singular Essence and Law of Production)	137
7	Why do People Fight for their Servitude as if it were Salvation?	147
	1 Servitude as a Paradoxical Object of Desire	147
	2 *Sed obtemperantia subditum facit*	157
	3 The Theocratic Solution: From the Order of Signs to the Political Order, a Rational Strategy for a Barbarian Nation	167
8	The Hebrew State: Elements for a Second Theory of the Imaginary Constitution of the Political Body	176
	1 From Habit (the Productive Activity of the Nation's Actual Existence) to the Self-Organisation of the *multitudinis ingenium* as the Practical Political Subject	177
	2 The Covenant: From the Joy Principle to the Establishment of a Temporality and Space for the 'Nation'	185
	3 The Institution of Freedom	194
9	The Strategy of the *multitudinis potentia:* The Political *Conatus*	204
	1 The Political Project of Autonomy as Absolute Sovereignty and/or the Collective Body's 'Absolutely Absolute' Affirmation	204
	2 Resistance Makes the Citizen	224
	3 Resistance as a Sovereign and Eternal Right	237
	3.1 The Ephors' Right of Resistance: From the Monarchomachs to the *Political Treatise*	237
	3.2 The Right of War and the Collective Body's Active Resistance Strategy	243
	3.3 Benevolence and Indignation: The 'Affects' of Resistance	248
	3.4 From the Resistance of the Best to the Indignation of All: Machiavelli, La Boétie, Spinoza	252
Conclusion: Strategy and Infinity		259
Index nominum		275

Translator's Note and Acknowledgements

In this translation of *La stratégie du conatus*, I have used Edwin Curley's translation for quotations taken directly from Spinoza: *The Collected Works of Spinoza*, trans. Edwin Curley (Princeton University Press, 1998). All other translations are my own. In the original work, Bove used Charles Appuhn's translation of Spinoza's work, with the exception of the *Tractatus Politicus*, for which he used P.-F. Moreau's translation. Bove sometimes adapted Appuhn's or Moreau's translations, however. When that change is not reflected in Curley's English translation, I have added a note to alert the reader.

With Bove's blessing, I have opted to challenge the common notion that Spinoza's *homine* ought to be translated using the masculine universal exclusively. Therefore, where 'homme(s)' refers to 'human beings', I use 'human beings'. When 'homme', 'il' and 'lui' refer to a specific individual, I favour female pronouns for Bove's text, and stick to male pronouns for Spinoza's text.

Hasana and I would like to thank Filippo Del Lucchese, dedicated editor of the Spinoza Studies series, for initiating this endeavour and for regular encouragement and guidance. Laurent Bove has also been a gracious and helpful advisor. We hope to have conveyed the creativity and passion with which his book was originally written. I am also grateful for the support I received from the research team LIS (Lettres, Idées, Savoirs - EA 4395) – Université Paris-Est Créteil as well as the CITL (Collège International des Traducteurs Littéraires). I want to thank Siarhei Blareishyk as well for convincing me to use 'infinite in acts' following Ruddick translation of Macherey's *Hegel or Spinoza*. I also thank him and his graduate students for their feedback on early versions of the translation. Hasana owes thanks to the Social Sciences and Humanities Research Council of Canada for supporting research on Spinoza's political thought during the gestation of this project.

Note from Laurent Bove

The following work is based on my doctoral thesis, defended in 1992 at the Université de Paris I Panthéon-Sorbonne. I particularly thank Professor Alexandre Matheron, whose comments and friendship have accompanied the history of this research. I also extend my thanks to Professors Geneviève Brykman and Pierre-François Moreau who kindly reviewed the manuscript and shared their observations with me.

Abbreviations

App.	appendix
Ax.	axiom
CM	*Cogitata metaphysica* (*Metaphysical Thoughts*)
Cor.	corollary
DA	definition of the affects
Def.	definition
Dem.	demonstration
Ep.	*Epistolae* (*Letters*)
Expl.	explanation
KV	*Korte Verhandeling van God, de Mensch, en des Zelfs Welstand* (*Short Treatise on God, Man and His Well-Being* = *Short Treatise*)
Lem.	lemma
Post.	postulate
Prop.	proposition
Schol.	scholium (i.e., a note, often containing an important digression from the main line of argument in the text)
TdIE	*Tractatus de intellectus emendatione* (*Treatise on the Emendation of the Intellect* = *Treatise on the Intellect*)
TP	*Tractatus politicus* (*Political Treatise*)
TTP	*Tractatus theologico-politicus* (*Theological-Political Treatise*)

Introduction
Infinity and Strategy

'By cause of itself I understand that whose essence involves existence, *or* that whose nature cannot be conceived except as existing.'[1] This is how the *Ethics* begins – with the affirmation (*affirmatio*) of an insight through which true thought and free life become possible. *Causa sui* is not an abstract principle and yet nothing can be derived from it; it is reality[2] – essence identical with its power (*puissance*)[3] – as 'absolute affirmation' or autonomy. Although Spinoza draws on a long tradition[4] by using this term, he rejects

---

[1] CWS I, 408. Translator's note. All references to the *Ethics*, the *Theological-Political Treatise* (*TTP*), the *Political Treatise* (*TP*) and the *Treatise on the Emendation of the Intellect* (*TdIE*) are taken from *The Collected Works of Spinoza*, trans. Edwin Curley, Princeton University Press, 1998 (CWS). Any amendments to Curley's translation are indicated by bracketing of the modified sections. All other translations are my own.

[2] Translator's note: Bove uses *le réel*, which I was tempted to translate as the Real, following Jacques Lacan. In discussion with Bove, however, he confirmed that he does not use *le réel* like Lacan and that the critical distinction, for him, is the one between *le réel* and *le Réel*, which I have rendered as reality and Reality.

[3] Translator's note: I am grateful to Gil Morejón and David Maruzzella for underlining and providing a solution to the problem of how best to deal with *pouvoir* and *puissance* in their translation of Alexandre Matheron's *Politics, Ontology and Knowledge in Spinoza*. They write 'these two French terms, which are broadly synonymous with Spinoza's Latin terms *potestas* and *potentia*, are really best rendered as "power" in English. (We considered, but ultimately rejected, alternatives such as "potency" and "capacity" for *potentia/puissance*.) Our general practice is to provide the original French in square brackets for the first appearance of either term in each chapter, and again whenever the other term appears or when the sense is at all ambiguous.' I follow their lead – with regular parentheses – in this translation.

[4] See S. Breton, 'Origine et principe de raison', *Revue des Sciences philosophiques et théologiques*, 58, 1974, pp. 41–57; and by the same author, 'Hegel ou Spinoza, réflexions sur l'enjeu d'une alternative', *Cahiers Spinoza*, 4, 1983, esp. pp. 66–71.

both its most immediate and its most remote legacy. He rejects interpretations inspired by either Aristotle's final cause[5] or Descartes' efficient cause. However,

> for each thing there must be assigned a cause, *or* reason, as much for its existence as for its nonexistence [. . .] But this reason, *or* cause, must either be contained in the nature of the thing, or be outside it.[6]

The expression, 'that whose essence involves existence', should thus help us to understand how much this inclusion of existence within essence emphasises the immanent presence of a cause *or* reason inherent in that essence. The presence is the infinite in acts, that is, the 'absolute affirmation of the existence of some nature'.[7] Infinity is thus known through the reason *or* cause that explains (develops and affirms) its presence. In other words, infinity is known through its inner cause; a cause that, when developed, explains everything about the harmony between the essence and existence of a thing. To be the cause of oneself is to affirm one's cause absolutely (perfectly or completely). *Causa sui* is the paradigm of the absolute affirmation of the cause (or reason). It is also the paradigm of infinity, freedom and eternity[8] – concepts that are both expressions of the power of the self-caused and characteristic features of Spinozist thought.

There are two major misconceptions that must be avoided by the reader of the *Ethics*. First, the idea that God or Nature (*Deus sive Natura*) is without cause or reason (which would reduce the ontological value of the mathematical model). Second, the notion that this cause, if it exists, somehow contains – in the absence of reason – the mystery of its own origin (this is the operational limit of the *Mathesis*).

Causa sui is by no means the basis for God's inscrutability. But, on the contrary, it is the paradigm through which Reality becomes fully intelligi-

---

[5] Aristotle, *Metaphysics*, trans. C. D. C. Reeve, Hackett, 2016, a 982, b 25–29. See also Thomas Aquinas's comment in *Commentary on the Gospel of John* (XV, 15), which emphasises the meeting of 'by itself' and 'for itself' (in *causa sui*) for the free human being. That is, as both the 'efficient and final cause of one's work'.

[6] *Ethics* I, 11 Dem. 2; *CWS* I, 417.

[7] *Ethics* I, 8 Schol. 1; *CWS* I, 412.

[8] On infinity, freedom, necessity and eternity, the 'indissoluble quadruplicity of *causa sui*', see Martial Gueroult, *Spinoza, I: Dieu*, Aubier, 1968, p. 75. To these 'virtually interchangeable' terms, Gueroult also adds 'truth' (p. 81); and 'the problem of infinity and that of self-caused existence are but one. . .' (p. 189).

ble. God affirms its[9] cause (or reason) absolutely in the infinite infinity of its effects and in each of its expressions. And so,

> whatever exists expresses the nature, or essence of God in a certain and determinate way (by P25C), i.e. (by P34), whatever exists expresses in a certain and determinate way the power of God, which is the cause of all things. So (by P16), from everything that exists some effect must follow.[10]

These last lines of *Ethics* I, 36 throw a radically Spinozist light on the traditional formulation of its first *definition*.

Nature affirms its cause absolutely, that is, its own power, in each of its singular affections, 'in a certain and determinate way'. Every determination is, *sub specie aeternitatis*, the absolute affirmation of substance in its affections, constitutive of this actual and productive singular essence that Spinoza calls *conatus*.[11] Thus, as suggested by *Ethics* III, 6, 'each thing, as far as it can by its own power [*puissance*], strives to persevere in its being'.[12] Each thing strives to affirm its existence absolutely, to express its cause fully (in the adequate idea, its reason), for 'the power by which singular things (and consequently, any man) preserve their being is the power itself of God, or Nature'.[13]

Spinoza's *Ethics* presents *causa sui* as its first definition. It does not, however, present substance as a principle. To affirm its cause absolutely is to think adequately, to think according to the self-production of Reality, to think according to the real movement of its becoming. Spinoza does not begin abstractly, with God as principle, but starts from the heart of thought, from the real movement of the 'absolute' and 'perfect' affirmation of the idea.[14] He thus invites the reader to think 'at once'. He invites her to follow this path without beginning or end, the path of the autonomous movement

---

[9] Translator's note: I decided to degender God for coherence and to stay closer to modern English usage. Nonetheless, if one is truly faithful to Bove's interpretation, some occurrences, particularly those found in the appendix, should present an anthropomorphic God by way of gendered pronouns. I refer the reader to the original text for more details.

[10] CWS I, 439. Translator's note.

[11] *Conatus, quo unaquaeque res in suo esse perseverare conatur nihil est praeter ipsius rei actualem essentiam*. Ethics III, 7.

[12] CWS I, 498. Translator's note.

[13] *Ethics* IV, 4 Dem.

[14] *Ethics* II, 34.

of the generation of reality, which is also the path of the generation of ideas that are true ideas only because they are real ideas: the path of reality itself as it is in and through the attribute of thought.

Reality derives its dynamism from the light of *causa sui* (or the position of self-caused existence). *Causa sui* enables people and societies to form adequate (that is, absolute and perfect) thoughts, in their minds and bodies 'in a certain and determinate way', and to lead their lives autonomously:

> Acting absolutely from virtue is nothing else in us but acting, living and preserving our being (these three signify the same thing) by the guidance of reason, from the foundation of seeking one's own advantage.[15]

Proposition 24 of *Ethics* IV, which applies to people and society, suggests that in the 'absolutely absolute' affirmation of its existence, society arrives by itself at the fullness of its own wisdom and freedom.[16]

The Spinozist significance and value of *causa sui* derive from their productive consequences in the political and ethical spheres. The causality according to which *causa sui* is essentially to be understood is not what is casually suggested by the second demonstration of proposition 11 of *Ethics* I. Rather, it is the principle of causality declared in the masterful climax of *Ethics* I: 'Nothing exists from whose nature some effect does not follow.'[17] This principle of causality and the expression of 'the power of God, which is the cause of all things', since it is the cause of itself, announce the meaning and value of *causa sui*: the absolute affirmation of power (*potentia*) in acts.[18]

---

[15] CWS I, 558. Translator's note.

[16] TP XI, 1; CWS II, 601–2. Spinoza comes from a time when the concept of *causa sui* was associated with a political and legal interpretation. Thus Aquinas, in his *Commentary on the Gospel of John*, XV, 15, identifies the state of the master with the autonomy conferred by *causa sui*, which is radically opposed to the status of the slave: *Servus prioprie est qui non est causa sui; liber vero qui est sui causa. Est ergo differentia inter operationes servi et liberi, quia servus operatur causa alterius; liber autem causa sui operatur et quantum ad causam finalem operis et quantum ad causam moventem, nam liber propter se operatur sicut propter finem et a se operatur quia propria voluntate movetur ad opus; sed servus nec propter se operatur sed propter dominum, nec a se sed a domini voluntate et quasi quadam coactione* (quoted by Breton, 'Origine et principe de raison', p. 45).

[17] *Ethics* I, 36; CWS I, 439. Translator's note.

[18] Contrary to common usage, Bove writes 'in acts' in the plural to emphasise that for Spinoza, the unity of substance lies in the plurality (the infinity) of its singular affirmations, as stated in Chapter 6 below. On materialist ontology, 'which no longer considers the principle of things that are beings, but Being qua being, that is, Being qua beings (the plural is not a lapse) in its inner structure', see Bernard Rousset, 'Le

But this circular movement by which the last proposition of *Ethics* I gives meaning and reality to its first definition – and which makes the *Ethics* the most extraordinary commentary on *causa sui* that philosophy has ever provided – is the expression, in thought, of the recursive cycle of true being.

Nature constitutes itself in and through its own affections. The perseverance of each of its modes (ideas, bodies, and the infinite infinity of modes and attributes we do not know) in their being is not merely an effect but the productive activity of Reality in its self-affirmation. This is how the imperative must be understood. One must strive to become what one is: an integral productivity of reality in and by oneself – a total actualisation of one's power (*puissance*) of being... *causa sui*!

Becoming God? A dream as absurd as it is chimerical, for it contradicts our human condition:

> It is impossible that a man should not be a part of Nature, and that he should be able to undergo no changes except those which can be understood through his own nature alone, and of which he is the adequate cause.[19]

It is possible to experience our infinity, eternity and freedom without ending or even accepting our finitude because it is already in and with us, *here and now*, at the heart of our own finite being and everything we do. This is all the more true if we do it with joy, since 'the greater the Joy with which we are affected, the greater the perfection to which we pass, that is, the more we must participate in the divine nature'.[20] We are in ourselves, like every mode, the 'absolute affirmation of the existence of some nature'[21] through which the 'infinite substance' is defined. It is indeed this – our – infinity, as the immanent presence of the cause in its effects, of the power (*puissance*) in acts, of infinity in the finite, that Spinoza asks us to reflect upon and fully become in the productive and full practice of our power to act. The adequate idea of our singular essence in the third kind of knowledge expresses the infinity that we are in a 'certain and determinate way'. To know oneself adequately in one's singularity as a finite mode is to understand oneself. This means knowing and understanding oneself, not from one's finitude or

---

problème du matérialisme dans le spinozisme', *L'Enseignement philosophique*, 5, May–June 1991, pp. 3–19.

[19] *Ethics* IV, 4; CWS I, 548.
[20] *Ethics* IV, 45 Cor. 2 Schol.; CWS I, 572.
[21] *Ethics* I, 8, Schol. 1; CWS I, 412. Translator's note.

from the limit that separates us from and confronts us with other modes, but according to the infinity of which we are made, from the way we proceed from eternity.[22] This is the core and most important idea of the *Mathesis* of being. For it is the idea of God itself, of the act by which substance affirms itself absolutely, *more geometrico*, in a singular affection in and through which it generates itself. It is precisely because the absolute affirmation of existence is at the heart of being, *is* this being *qua* absolute infinity, that there can be no arbitrariness and that we experience, in God, the absolute innocence without 'principle or end' of our eternal necessity, which is also our blessedness and freedom.[23]

To become God is absurd. But to bring forth in and through God (as Nature) the real, joyful and powerful movement through which a being generates itself absolutely autonomously... This is the meaning of the ethical project. And it is also Spinoza's political project.

The *Ethics* ends, however, by pointing out the extreme difficulty (and beauty) of this enterprise.[24] We already know from the second definition of *Ethics* I that each of our thoughts, like each of our actions, necessarily encounters another idea and body outside itself that stands in its way.[25] Spinoza defines the outer limit that characterises every finite thing according to the absolute affirmation of the inner cause that defines our freedom[26] and its fully effective development, our blessedness.[27] This outer limit is the horizon of servitude and death. The experience of obstacles and limits is the first – and constant – experience of every being. If an effect necessarily follows from the existence of any body – which has an inner necessity due to the absolute affirmation of the cause – we can also say that the affirmation of the

---

[22] See Pierre Macherey, *Hegel or Spinoza*, University of Minnesota Press, 2011, and Bernard Rousset 'L'Etre du fini dans l'infini selon l'*Ethique* de Spinoza', *Revue Philosophique*, 2, April–June 1986, pp. 223–47.

[23] *Ut ergo nullius finis causa existit, nullius etiam finis causa agit; sed ut existendi, sic & agendi principium, vel finem habet nullum*. Ethics IV, Praef.; CWS I, 544.

[24] 'If the way I have shown to lead to these things now seems very hard, still, it can be found. And of course, what is found so rarely must be hard. For if salvation were at hand, and could be found without great effort, how could nearly everyone neglect it? But all things excellent are as difficult as they are rare.' Ethics V, 42 Schol.; CWS I, 617.

[25] 'That thing is said to be finite in its own kind that can be limited by another of the same nature. For example, a body is called finite because we always conceive another that is greater. Thus, a thought is limited by another thought. But a body is not limited by a thought nor a thought by a body.' Ethics I, Def. 2; CWS I, 408.

[26] Ethics I, Def. 7.

[27] Ethics V, 42.

being (existence) of a particular body necessarily entails the affirmation of an infinity of other bodies. These are both immediate obstacles to its autonomous development, which, while they do not annihilate it completely, prescribe (in part) the necessary modes of its expression from without:

> Desire is the very essence, *or* nature, of each man insofar as it is conceived to be determined, by whatever constitution he has, to do something (see P9S). Therefore, as each man is affected by external causes with this or that species of Joy, Sadness, Love, Hate, etc. – that is, as his nature is constituted in one way or the other, so his Desires vary and the nature of one Desire must differ from the nature of the other as much as the affects from which each arises differ from one another.[28]

Desire is productivity, but it can only be understood in its specific content through the exchange (*commercium*)[29] between the body and the external world. This shows why autonomy – as absolute affirmation of the cause – is, within a necessarily unfavourable power dynamic, a struggle. From our birth, we are only in an extremely partial way the cause of what happens within us and of what we do.[30]

If we have referred to the principle of causality to understand the first definition, the second definition of the *Ethics*, interestingly, includes a principle of contradiction that is only explicitly affirmed in *Ethics* IV, 3. Within *natura naturata*, contradiction is the sign of the finitude of modal existence: 'The force by which a man perseveres in existing is limited, and infinitely surpassed by the power of external causes.'[31] The *conatus* of everything involves pure affirmation and can only be destroyed (in its extrinsic constitution) by an external cause.[32] By definition, 'things [that] are of a contrary nature . . . cannot be in the same subject, insofar as one can destroy the other'.[33] On the contrary, any thing is, by nature, 'opposed [*opponitur*] to everything which can take its existence away (by P5). Therefore, as far as it can, and it lies in itself, it strives to persevere in its being.'[34] And this perseverance in contradiction is the constitutive process of an individuality of a 'nature superior in power' capable of resistance.

---

[28] *Ethics* III, 56 Dem.; CWS I, 527.
[29] *Ethics* IV, 18 Schol.
[30] *Ethics* III, Def. 2.
[31] *Ethics* IV, 3; CWS I, 548. Itself prepared by *Ethics* IV Ax. and *Ethics* III, 4 and 5.
[32] *Ethics* III, 4.
[33] *Ethics* III, 5; CWS I, 498.
[34] *Ethics* III, 6 Dem.; CWS I, 499.

It is above all this dynamic between the active resistance of the *conatus* and its total exhaustion by external and more powerful forces that affirms existence as a strategy. Resistance is the root of all being. Resistance and strategy necessarily arise from the essence of every existing being, just as those things that 'necessarily promote [man's] preservation'[35] necessarily arise. The idea of strategy involves the idea of total causal action, and for every *conatus* – and at every moment – the essential question of life or death for the existing mode. All internal finality aside, the thesis of a strategy of *conatus* is rooted in the fully intelligible causality and immanence of absolute rationalism. As a singular force of affirmation and resistance, the Spinozist *conatus* is a strategic practice of decision with respect to problems and their solutions.[36] The concept of strategy, which comes from the vocabulary of warfare,[37] is not used metaphorically. The condition of bodies – even more than of societies – is total war, and no one will escape death in the end:

> There is no singular thing in nature than which there is not another more powerful and stronger. Whatever one is given, there is another more powerful by which the first can be destroyed.[38]

Danger is the permanent structure of the existing finite mode. To act is to put one's life in danger;[39] and we cannot abstain from acting, for our being is action.

The concept of strategy, then, refers first of all to the ability of a body to recognise and resolve a risky and depleting situation in which it is a victim. In and through habit, memory and recognition, the *conatus* finds the tools for its perseverance in the power of imagination. Bodies (like thoughts)

---

[35] *Ethics* III, 9 Schol.; CWS I, 500.
[36] Since what is at stake is the reality of the *activity* of finite things in their mutual articulation, the hypothesis of a strategy of *conatus* is diametrically opposed to an 'occasionalist' interpretation of extrinsic determinations between modes. This argument can be read, for example, in G. Huan, *Le Dieu de Spinoza*, Alcan, 1914, pp. 122–3.
[37] The term (from the Greek *stratêgos*, army commander) is found in Aristotle ('the goal of strategy is victory', *Nicomachean Ethics* I, ch. I, 3), but – although the term strategy did not yet exist – strategic thinking as a natural and necessary theory of warfare was only really born with Machiavelli to ensure the survival of the state: see Félix Gilbert, 'Machiavelli: la renaissance de l'art de la guerre', in *Les maîtres de la stratégie*, ed. Edward Mead Earle, vol. 1, 1943; French edition, Champs-Flammarion, 1980, with a preface by R. Aron, pp. 13–37.
[38] *Ethics* IV, Ax. 1; CWS I, 547.
[39] TTP XV; CWS II, 280.

struggle as soon as they are born, building and defending the space-time of their affirmation with the specific means of their own complexity. This *time* of the strategic productivity of finite modes, or the 'indefinite continuation of existing',[40] is what Spinoza calls 'duration'. And this *space* of finitude is the place where every thing that is 'finite in its own kind' is 'limited by another of the same nature'. What *Ethics* I Def. 2 highlights is that the problem of modal existence is above all a spatial problem – a problem of constructing, conquering, liberating, but also of defending space. The strategy of *conatus* is first a territorial conquest for both bodies and ideas. Ideas that are outside of us, like bodies, are systems of representation that immediately impose themselves on our minds and diminish their innate capacity to exercise their own power. Spinoza never stopped trying to conquer new territories for thought and freedom. This is as much an ideological as it is a political struggle because it is about constituting a public sphere that protects freedom of expression, the cornerstone of the constitutive dynamic of democracy.

The operating field of this strategy cannot be reduced to the realm of the individual or even to that of her survival. While survival is a pragmatic criterion for evaluating the strategic and adaptive abilities of a given individual, it cannot be the criterion by which the *conatus* (even the individual one) evaluates its ability to deal with the problems that arise in and through its efforts to realise itself. Only the 'adequate idea', as the reality of a true idea, gives an adequate answer to the problem of reality by starting from what is happening to someone (that is the affect, the object of the idea through which a body is affirmed, and thus the problem expressed through this encounter). This adequate idea implies a strategic position of power (of thought and action), and consequently of mastery over problems. It is the very movement of our plenitude, the one through which the mode conquers its autonomy: 'An affect which is a passion ceases to be a passion as soon as we form a clear and distinct idea of it.'[41] That is our path to freedom.

Every true idea (as adequate idea) will thus be a victory against the violence of the thoughtlessness of an 'epoch'. Its fulfilment according to the real movement of the dynamic constitution of Reality will be revolutionary, for it will create a new space-time, immanent in thought itself and new for all eternity. In and through such a project of liberation of thought and bodies, Spinoza initiates a strategy 'under the guidance of reason' in the real continuity of the spontaneous strategy of bodies' affirmation.[42] But it is

---

[40] *Ethics* II, Def. 5; CWS I, 447.
[41] *Ethics* V, 3; CWS I, 598.
[42] *Ethics* IV, 18 Schol., 24.

also, in part, against the extrinsic forms of the actualisation of this strategy which make people unbearable,[43] envious and loathsome to one another, when left to their own imaginative mechanism.[44] Having recognised the failure of a spontaneous logic of *conatus* within a heteronomous regime that favours the quasi-autonomous development of violence, a rational strategy becomes an indispensable necessity. The mathematical model becomes a tool to plough through these new spaces of the affirmation of thought and life, buried under prejudice and superstition and exploited by tyrants. For the obstacle becomes adversity in social life, and the fight becomes a political one.

But Spinoza does not leave behind the imperatives, questions and problems of the metaphysical or ontological realm. In both the political and ethical realms, we must understand the nature of strategy – and its ontological status – from the standpoint of the absolute affirmation of the cause (the real movement that defines the *causa sui*).

The political strategy of Spinozism is based on a theory of the immanent strategy of the collective body – or the political *conatus* – understood as the 'multitude' or, more precisely, the 'power of the multitude'. Like an individual body, the multitude tends in a strictly causal way towards the 'absolutely absolute' affirmation of its right. Spinoza calls the ability of a society to assert its power in an absolute way 'democracy'. Democracy is also the adequate idea (understood as an 'absolute' and 'perfect' idea) of human society in the sense of the real movement of the autonomous production of reality.

As wisdom is to the individual body, so democracy is to the social body the true movement of life in its affirmation, through which the disempowered and servile state of a particular being is ended. Spinoza's struggle based on true knowledge is involved in the construction of the objective conditions of this liberating movement.

After the collapse of Athenian democracy, Plato built a political philosophy centred on the exclusion of the multitude from political power. In contrast, after the failure of the free Republic of the United Provinces (1672), and despite the popular upheaval that drove him to despair – and which he vigorously condemned, *Ultimi barbarorum!* – Spinoza was the first philosopher, perhaps after Machiavelli, not to write a new private political *Weltanschauung* against the real movement of the 'masses'. Instead, he grounds his argument in the movement of absolute affirmation of the exist-

---

[43] *Ethics* III, 55 Schol.
[44] *Ethics* III, 31 Schol.

ence of *multitudinis potentia*.⁴⁵ This historical and ontological project begins in the *TTP* and is radicalised in the *TP*. We will thus see how the concept of resistance becomes politically and philosophically effective in the *TTP*, which he wrote from 1666–67 to 1670, while he was working on the *Ethics* (1662–75). Spinoza develops the constitution of popular sovereignty and the nature of citizenship and history from the activity of resistance. With him, political thought is no longer a matter of speculation about the best possible regime. Rather, it is a theory that asserts itself primarily as a strategy of the *conatus* of the collective body in its real process of 'absolute' self-organisation.

---

[45] On the 'point of view of the masses' adopted by Spinoza in his political and state theory, see Etienne Balibar, 'Spinoza, l'anti-Orwell. La crainte des masses', *Les Temps Modernes*, September 1985, pp. 353–94.

1
The Strategic Logic of the Spinozist *Conatus*: The Stages of World Construction

1 Habit as the Constituting Activity of Actual Existence

In the *Timaeus* (37 b ff.) Plato places the creation of time at the basis of the world's structure. Let me extend this demiurgic function to the Spinozist *conatus*, in the organisation of its own world, that is, that of its perseverance. Starting from an evaluation of the constitution of time, Spinoza leads us from his example in *Ethics* II, 44 Schol. via *Ethics* II, 18 finally to the discovery of the fundamental importance of the compositional activity proper to the *conatus* of the body – or to the body itself insofar as it strives to persevere in being. This leads us into the realm of Habit and the associative mechanisms that underlie memory and without which, Spinoza notes, the mind would be powerless.[1]

> Moreover, no one doubts but what we also imagine time, viz. from the fact that we imagine some bodies to move more slowly, or more quickly, or with the same speed.[2]

To imagine time is to imagine it simultaneously as outside and independent of us, while, at the same time, we imagine it as present to us, which is consistent with the definition of the mind's imaginative faculty.[3] To imagine time in this way is thus to objectify a mode of thinking that has a necessary reality only in the (relative) confrontation of humans and nature. This exteriority and presence, however, only has meaning in the (imagined) presence of coexisting things. For the reality of time exists only through the

---
[1] *Ethics* III, 2 Schol.
[2] *Ethics* II, 44 Schol.; *CWS* I, 480.
[3] *Ethics* II, 17 Schol.

relationship that the mind, when it imagines, establishes between bodies in motion:

> to determine this duration, we compare it with the duration of other things which have a certain and determinate motion. This comparison is called time. Time, therefore, is not an affection of things, but only a mere mode of thinking, or, as we have already said, a being of reason. For it is a mode of thinking that serves to explain duration. We should also note here – since it will be of use later, when we speak of eternity – that duration is conceived as being greater or lesser, and as composed of parts, and finally, that it is only an attribute of existence, and not of essence.[4]

Does this mean that time is produced solely by comparing the velocity between two or more bodies? It is true that we determine 'duration with the aid of some measure of movement, which is also done with the help of imagination',[5] but let us not jump to conclusions. This comparison – which is already the work of a mind capable of distinguishing bodies, thinking of relationships and even of mathematical proportions (greater, lesser, or equal) – is the result of a complex and hierarchised process sustained by a particular capacity of the body to connect its own affects. Indeed, at first it seems as if the body is subject to the 'accidental' nature of encounters,[6] as opposed to the intellect, which can 'direct and connect our clear and distinct perceptions' according to the necessary order of Nature. But the body is not entirely passive. Though burdened by the disparity of its affects, the body, in its effort to persist in being, establishes relationships and forms arrangements, continuities and unities. This is the work of Habit, which *Ethics* II, 18 Schol. presents as the basis of memory.

The example of *Ethics* II, 44 Schol. on the origin of time actually refers to *Ethics* II, 18, whose *scholium* defines memory as the associative mechanism of Habit. The *proposition* itself states:

> If the human Body has once been affected by two or more bodies at the same time, then when the Mind subsequently imagines one of them, it will immediately recollect the others also.[7]

---

[4] CM I, 4; CWS I, 310.
[5] TdIE, 83, note; CWS I, 36.
[6] Ep. XXXVII [to Johannes Bouwmeester]; CWS II, 32.
[7] CWS I [*Ethics* II, 18; CWS I, 465]. Translator's note.

The example given by *Ethics* II, 44 Schol., however, does not directly illustrate this *proposition*:

> Let us suppose, then, a child, who saw Peter for the first time yesterday, in the morning, but saw Paul at noon, and Simon in the evening, and today again saw Peter in the morning. It is clear from P18 that as soon as he sees the morning light, he will immediately imagine the sun taking the same course through the sky as he saw on the preceding day, or he will imagine the whole day, and Peter together with the morning, Paul with noon, and Simon with the evening. That is, he will imagine the existence of Paul and of Simon with a relation to future time. On the other hand, if he sees Simon in the evening, he will relate Paul and Peter to the time past, by imagining them together with past time. And he will do this more uniformly, the more often he has seen them in this same order.[8]

Let us note: *first*, that *Ethics* II, 18 starts from an image of simultaneously perceived bodies, whereas the example concerns the succession of three sequences of two simultaneous events. *More than that*, from the moment the child sees the morning light, the immediate image of the previous 'whole day' is re-presented in her mind. From this re-presented present, she reconstructs the actual 'unity' of the independent elements and, in a certain sense, their 'opposition', 'diversity' and 'complementarity': the 'order' of the different moments of the day and its different events.[9]

If Spinoza uses *Ethics* II, 18 as the basis for his example, it is because the successive events of the past day are now, in the child, simultaneously present *in* one and the same instant, present to herself, continuous and homogeneous; both the past and the future are only internal dimensions of this passing present. How is this total picture of the past 'whole day', from which the child thinks of a future or reproduces a past, composed in her mind? It all begins with the body in Habit.

Let us take events A (morning), B (noon), C (night) and events A' (appearance of Peter), B' (appearance of Paul) and C' (appearance of Simon). Let us imagine that these events are independent of each other, both in their order (A, B, C, or A', B', C') and in their simultaneity (A-A', B-B', C-C'), as the story in the example suggests.[10] Then take the sequences

---

[8] CWS I, 480–1. Translator's note.
[9] On the concepts of unity, opposition, etc., see CM I, 5, 6; CWS I, 311.
[10] In fact, this independence is itself the product of a separation from what we must first assume to be an arrangement in which everything is connected, from the fact that

A-A', B-B', C-C', repeated two or more times for the child. After the second time and at the first sign of repetition (appearance of the sun):

1. The child will expect the complete and identical repetition of the sequences A-A', B-B', C-C', both the simultaneity of the images (Peter in the morning, Paul at noon and Simon in the evening) and their order (Paul after Peter and before Simon).
2. The child will recognise the various events of the day without surprise or astonishment because of this expectation. It is morning, and here comes Peter; at noon Paul is here; in the evening – hello, Simon.

Expectation and recognition define the two levels of the process that lead to the construction of time.[11] However, both expectation and recognition presuppose a prior knowledge that is simultaneously determined by habit (in expectation) and by a certain kind of human reason, that is, recognition. So we can say that this repetition (the second day), which does not change things in themselves, presupposes a change in the child who witnesses it. From the first sign of repetition A, the child will expect A' and the sequences from the previous day, B-B' and then C-C', and, as Spinoza writes, 'in the same order'.[12] She therefore had to interpret the sign as the first element of a whole that will unfold again according to its homogeneous continuity, despite the *a priori* diversity of its elements. This is only possible because the child has taken in all the elements of her perception at once from day one. It is not the repetition that changes her. It is merely the realisation of the change that has arisen in and through her body from the first day. That is, A-A', B-B' and C-C' are connected in 'the same' continuous impression, even though they do not happen simultaneously but one after the other.

> the activity of the body forms relations that are consubstantial with its existence. For thought, however, what is always already connected necessarily presupposes a binding activity of elements that are *a priori* independent – even if these elements and their independence have only a theoretical existence. This does not make the binding activity of the body any less real. And no less real is the process of dissociation as a second step (that of memory and reflection) that distinguishes between the events that Habit makes possible based on what is always already connected.

[11] Translator's note: throughout this chapter Bove works on developing an understanding of time as temporality (but uses only time in the French). To keep with the unfolding of the demonstration, I have opted to keep 'time' at the beginning of the chapter, and then changed to 'temporality' once the argument is done. I then chose to use temporality throughout the rest of the book.

[12] *Ethics* II, 44 Schol.

In *Ethics* II, 18 Schol. it could still appear as if the remembering mind only passively repeats an apparently real contiguity of simultaneous events, going from one memory to the next, which it associates with the external reality of an objectively given situation. Association in this case could only be understood as a simple and passive impression of contiguities that already exist in reality and are reinforced in us by their repetition. *Ethics* II, 44 Schol. on the other hand, by introducing independent and non-simultaneous events and referring to *Ethics* II, 18, emphasises that associating images is a genuine organising activity of the body in its individuating effort to persist in being. The visiting 'order' of Peter, Paul and Simon exists only for and through the body of the child who imagines. That is, it exists because of the double mechanism that Habit sets in motion: first the contraction of simultaneous or successive affections, and then the reflexive reconstitution of events through memory and human reason. The child combines them simultaneously. That is, she assembles them into a singular block of duration, a singular individual, a singular homogeneous totality from which memory and human reason can work. It is necessary to recognise that the body has a power of composition and combination, and this power is that of Habit. This sequencing, which underlies the process of memorising and remembering, is constitutive of time as a 'continuous'[13] and homogeneous duration that varies the states of the body as much as its nature (its specific relationship of movement and rest) allows.[14]

Now if this connection is first established in the affected body by forming an 'order and connection of the affections'[15] – an individuating composition that expresses both the nature of the affected body and that of the external bodies – then the habit is also acquired in the mind, which sees the external bodies as present to it[16] through the connections of the body's images. Memory, according to Spinoza, is only a 'certain connection of ideas' that includes the nature of things outside the human body, a connection formed in the mind 'according to the order and connection of the affections of the human Body'. Since it does not connect things according to its own power (that of the intellect), the contemplative mind that acquires habit according to the connections of the body's affections is an essentially passive mind.[17]

---

[13] *TdIE*, 83; CWS I, 36.
[14] *Ethics* V, 39 Schol.
[15] *Ethics* II, 18 Schol.
[16] *Ethics* II, 17 Schol.
[17] *Ethics* III, Def. 2.

From this we clearly understand what Memory is. For it is nothing other than a certain connection of ideas involving the nature of things which are outside the human Body – a connection that is in the Mind according to the order and connection of the affections of the human Body. I say, first, that the connection is only of those ideas that involve the nature of things which are outside the human Body, but not of the ideas that explain the nature of the same things. For they are really (by P16) ideas of affections of the human Body which involve both its nature and that of external bodies. I say, second, that this connection happens according to the order and connection of the affections of the human Body in order to distinguish it from the connection of ideas which happens according to the order of the intellect, by which the Mind perceives things through their first causes, and which is the same in all men. And from this we clearly understand why the Mind, from the thought of one thing, immediately passes to the thought of another, which has no likeness to the first: as, for example, from the thought of the word *pomum* a Roman will immediately pass to the thought of the fruit [viz. an apple], which has no similarity to that articulate sound and nothing in common with it except that the Body of the same man has often been affected by these two [at the same time], i.e., that the man often heard the word *pomum* while he saw the fruit. And in this way, each of us will pass from one thought to another, as each one's association has ordered the images of things in the body.[18]

Habit, let it be said again, is not, as it seems, a behaviour acquired by the repetition of the same experience (by which we acquire habits), but the capacity (or spontaneous power) of the body, from the first experience, to combine two or many affects, whether simultaneous or successive.[19] This power is the very effort of the body to persevere in being, the sign of its inherent capacity to be autonomous, even if its mechanism for image combination, 'which

---

[18] *prout rerum imagines uniuscujusque consuetudo in corpore ordinavit*. *Ethics* II, 18 Schol.; CWS II, 179–80.

[19] For *succession*, see *Ethics* II, 44 Schol.; for *simultaneity*, *Ethics* II, 18. Reading *Ethics* II, 18 Dem. or *Ethics* II, 44 Cor. and Schol., one cannot help but think of the further development of these questions that will be found in the works of David Hume. Robert Misrahi points to this in *Le désir et la réflexion dans la philosophie de Spinoza*, Gordon & Breach, 1972, pp. 113ff., when he describes Spinoza's contribution through the unity of his critique of words, habit and imagination. For a systematic confrontation of Spinoza and Hume, see the major work of Gilbert Boss, *La différence des philosophies: Hume et Spinoza*, ed. du Grand Midi, 1982.

follow from the necessity of human nature',[20] is surpassed by the power of external causes in a regime of heteronomy (though still in the service of perseverance).

We must assume, however, that a body superior in power could relate its active affections, not according to a contingent order, but according to a necessity perceived by the mind, as the demonstrations and scholia of *Ethics* V, 10 and *Ethics* V, 39 suggest. Previously, *Ethics* II, 13 Schol. had made a connection between the autonomous power of the body and the capacity of the mind to understand: 'in proportion as the actions of a body depend more on itself alone . . . so its mind is more capable of understanding distinctly'.[21] In this case, it is a complete affirmation (*affirmatio*) of life, accompanied by the elimination of death.[22] Conversely, we can also assume that a suicidal tendency can be explained by a regime of almost complete heteronomy of the individuating encounters leading to a continuous depletion of active power. That is, largely negative encounters (ones that are incompatible with the perseverance of the individual) lead to a breakdown that allows for more and more depleting encounters . . . until death.[23] Death creeps in, it seems, in the same way that life perpetuates itself: through Habit and its individuating encounters, that follow necessarily from our nature. The depletion of active power can, in the worst case, even lead to a standstill of the associative process, which is itself a power. In this case, the mind of an exhausted body, crushed by external forces and unable to make new connections, contemplates the rigid image of its despair, its final sadness, in the process of the body's dissolution.[24] A fundamental postulate of Spinozism, however, is that 'nothing by its own nature seeks its own destruction',[25] so that no human being should ever desire to die or to be sad. One's fundamental objective is to resist depression and sadness,[26] even if this effort is often unsuccessful. We must therefore understand suicide as the breakdown of Desire, not as one of the paths that desire, even in its most perverted form, can take: death is never desired for its own sake.

In ordinary powerlessness, unable to perceive the affections of its body in the order of their necessity, the imagining mind acquires habits by the contingent association of actions driven by its own body. It can think *ret-*

---

[20] *TTP* IV; *CWS* II, 126.
[21] *CWS* I, 458. Translator's note.
[22] *Ethics* V, 38 Dem. and Schol.
[23] *Ethics* IV, 18 Schol.; 20 Schol.
[24] *Ethics* III, DA 15.
[25] *KV* II, xvii, 4; *CWS* I, 127.
[26] *Ethics* III, 37 Dem.

rospectively of the past or anticipate the future. The organisation of Habit thus takes place in the contemplating mind but is not directed by it, even though we must assume that the activity of the body is to some extent also an activity of the mind, which is the idea of the body.[27] That is to say, the organisation of Habit is the passive activity of a mind which is almost entirely governed by external causes.

This organisation, however, brings about a first constitution of time, namely, that of the lived duration, the 'passages'[28] of the body to a greater or lesser active power, to a greater or lesser perfection. This also has to do with the constitution of the sense of the continuity of its existence in the mind, that is, the existence of its own body.[29] Given that the states of the body (*constitutio*) are always-already in part the result of the body's own dealings with the world as an ensemble of connections, we can deduce that this first constitution of time gives human existence (not in imagination – as re-presentation[30] – but in the lived presentation of the variations of the power of one's own body) the existential ground, continuous and homogeneous, in and through which the effort to persevere in being can flourish.

The real identity of actual existence and duration has already been emphasised in the *Metaphysical Thoughts*: duration is

> an attribute under which we conceive the existence of created things insofar as they persevere in their actuality. From this it clearly follows that duration is only distinguished by reason from the whole existence of a thing.[31]

Without duration, which is associated with the body and contracted in the mind, eternal essence would not be an 'endeavour', that is, a lived temporality or continued existence. Habit, then, ensures the lived continuity of our being. By providing the lived present with a retained past and an anticipated future, Habit makes of time the very substance of our existence: lived time as the duration of our affects, or our affects as durations themselves, as 'passages', as Spinoza writes.[32]

---

[27] *Ethics* III, 28 Dem.
[28] CWS I, 531. Translator's note. Not cited but implied in Bove.
[29] *Ethics* II, Def. 5; *Ethics* II, 13 Cor.: *Hinc sequitur hominem Mente, & Corpore constare Corpus humanum, prout ipsum sentimus, existere.*
[30] CM I, 4; *TdIE*, 83 note; CWS I, 36; *Ep.* XII [to Lodewijk Meyer]; CWS I, 206; *Ethics* II, 44 Schol.
[31] CM I, 4; CWS I, 310.
[32] *Ethics* III, DA 3, Exp.; CWS I, 531.

Habit in acts explains (develops in temporality) the existence of all things: it is the figure of perseverance in being, our very habit of living. This spontaneously lived duration of Habit, which is intimately connected with actual existence,[33] must not be confused with the 'indivisible duration'[34] of the eternal, which can only be grasped 'by the third kind of knowledge entailed by the intellectual experience of eternity'.[35] Nevertheless, the duration of Habit is indeed a reality to which Spinoza devotes a definition.[36] Existential reality is temporal, and we can experience our eternity in time, when the existential continuity of our active affections expresses itself according to the same necessity as the order through which they are known by the intellect. This presupposes that the body, like the mind (its idea), attains an effective actuality of the absolute affirmation of existence: that is, a quasi-autonomy that enables the body to connect its affections according to the immanent necessity of its own affirmation, according to the real and substantial movement of its own production. In this affirmation, time does not disappear, but its meaning and value change. Time is no longer the sign of finitude that imposes an external order on humans (this external order being only the necessary objectification of an appearance). Nor is it any longer a 'measure of movement' subordinated to the movement of things to which a human being is related.[37] Liberated from empirical and relational content, time is the actual duration of substance in its affections; it is the duration of eternity.

In the third kind of knowledge, lived time is the real and absolute movement of the productivity of Nature. Time is no longer temporal, but an eternal, pure movement of substance, a change that remains the same. It is being (singular essence) in its absolute and perfect affirmation. The way to the sense of eternity (or the feeling of eternity)[38] is to develop a sensitivity to the form or manner (mode) through which we are produced and from which we produce ourselves. It is the sense of the singular essence, of our power as productivity of substance in act, which is nothing other than the 'certain and determinate way' in which we are and persevere in

---

[33] CM I, 4; CWS I, 310.

[34] Emile Brehier, *Etudes de philosophie antique*, PUF, 1955, p. 291. Bernard Rousset remarks that 'this indivisible duration is comparable to the indivisible extension invoked by Spinoza against Descartes and is opposed to discontinued duration and to the contingence of instants the latter engenders'. *La perspective finale de l'Ethique et le problème de la cohérence du spinozisme*, Vrin, 1968, p. 74, n. 33.

[35] Martial Gueroult, *Spinoza, II: L'Ame*, Aubier, 1974, p. 231.

[36] *Ethics* II, Def. 5

[37] CM I, 4; CWS I, 310.

[38] *At nihilominus sentimus experimurque, nos aeternos esse. Ethics* V, 23 Schol.

being.³⁹ The active affect (the feeling of eternity) is no longer defined by the animation of our active power, that is, by the experience of a transition from a state of lesser perfection of the body to a state of greater perfection, but by a fullness of existence in its absolute affirmation. The sense of eternity, the sense of the pure form of time as being in its affirmation, arises from the lived experience of this infinite duration (infinite because of the absolute affirmation of the body's existence that it expresses) that envelops the active affections.⁴⁰ The body's ability to connect its affects through the absolute infinite power of substance develops the existential continuity of a pure necessity of time, the indivisible duration of substance in act. Time as the inherent and eternal necessity of Nature *is* duration itself, indivisible and lived as existence of the third kind. If, in this wisdom, everything to do with memory and imagination is almost insignificant in comparison with what has to do with the capacity to understand,⁴¹ Habit as the capacity of the body to connect its affections remains a fundamental activity. Habit is, in acts, the expression of one's autonomy, of affirmative power, and in every human body the promise of great health regardless of its condition.

Indeed, the body, as an organic being (the first figure of Desire), strives from its birth to connect its affections despite its powerlessness, and to organise the world of its perseverance by itself, according to a minimally strategic logic of active resistance. The organisation of Habit is thus first experienced in the organism, which is the very production of Desire in its primary affirmation: 'all want to seek their own advantage'⁴² and the useful things are 'before anything else, those that can feed the body'.⁴³ The body, as longing-being, craves nourishment that is consistent with its nature. It yearns for the (desired) future of plenitude.

> By good here I understand, says Spinoza, every kind of Joy, and whatever leads to it, and especially what satisfies any kind of longing, whatever that may be. And by evil [I understand here] every kind of Sadness, and especially what frustrates longing.⁴⁴

---

³⁹ *Ethics* I, 25 Cor.; *Ethics* I, 36 Dem.; *Ethics* II, 10 Cor.
⁴⁰ *Ethics* I, 8 Schol. 1.
⁴¹ *Ethics* V, 39 Schol. Translator's note: *entendement* would normally be translated as 'understanding', but in this context I found 'capacity to understand' to be clearer.
⁴² *Ethics* I, App.; *CWS* I, 440.
⁴³ *Ethics* IV, App., ch. 27.
⁴⁴ *& praecipue id, quod desiderio, qualecunque illud sit, satisfacit. Per malum autem omne Tristitiae genus, & praecipue id, quod desiderium frustratur. Ethics* III, 39 Schol. See also *Ethics* III, 36 Schol. and *Ethics* III, DA 32.

There is necessarily always-ready longing in the pursuit of what is useful. But there is no longing without habit. In *Ethics* III, 2 Schol., we can read that 'we can do nothing from a decision of the mind unless we recollect it'.[45] This also applies to the 'determinations' of the body, which, as Spinoza tells us, are by nature 'one and the same' as the decisions of the mind. From this, we must conclude that the body could do nothing if it did not already have mnesic traces[46] by which its actions are determined.[47] So we are only ever waiting for what has already been acquired in a certain way. The same is true of continuous existence, which the body longs for, moment by moment, in the energy of its perseverance. This continuity of existence, however, could be either the spontaneously lived duration of Habit or the indivisible duration of the eternal, when the body, by its own power (its quasi-autonomy), assembles its active affections according to the same necessity as the order through which they are known to the mind. This hypothesis by no means excludes Habit but emphasises its fundamental role.

Does the assertion that there is no desire without habit and no body without desire (since the body is a memory), condemn us to inevitable pain, dissatisfaction and regret, even in wisdom, which presupposes a more powerful body?[48] Spinoza does not see it that way. In the mind *desiderium* is the sign of an *appetitus* which, though separated from what it can do, nevertheless affirms the perfection and power of *what it is capable of* in relation to the affections that actualise its corresponding capacity to be affected. Because essence is power, and because a body tends towards autonomy[49] by expanding its power, we must see something perfect, positive and active at the heart of *desiderium*, which removes pain and dissatisfaction at the height of its realisation.[50] Wisdom will not eliminate expectation, but will integrate it into a new regime of the quasi-autonomy of the connection of active affections according to their specific inner necessity. At the heart of the wise person's life (in body as well as in mind), life confidently expects itself. This expectation is not the sign of a lack of power, but rather the affirmation of

---

[45] CWS I, 497. Translator's note.
[46] *Ethics* II, 13 Post. 5 and Ax. 1 & 2, Lem. 3.
[47] On the always-already thereness of the traces or affections, see the wording of the demonstration of *Ethics* II, 17 Cor., *ut inde alio modo reflectantur, quam antea solebant*, which Curley translates as 'the fluid parts . . . are reflected from it in another way than they used to be before' (CWS I, 464). It is true that a body is already, in its relation to the world, a 'way of being', a habit.
[48] *Ethics* II, 14; *Ethics* IV, 38, 39 Dem.; *Ethics* V, 39 Schol.
[49] *Ethics* II, 13 Schol.; *Ethics* V, 39, 40.
[50] *Ethics* IV, 20.

the autonomous and indivisible continuity of existence in its fullness and the indefinite, creative repetition in the present. When the wise person anticipates, she is, so to speak, in a strain (*tension*) of existence (as affirmation) rather than in a tension towards existence (as aching). This state of anticipation is a power of being rather than an aching for being: *cupiditas* rather than *desiderium*. This expectant state is not only the constitution of a reflexive order of time. It is free of hopes and in harmony with the constant effort that expands and amplifies the time of its presence. For it is the time of the 'greatest satisfaction of Mind there can be',[51] the very present of eternity. Expecting, for the wise person, means actively waiting. Beyond the difficulties of language and the ordinary meaning of terms, then, we must see in the tendency of the more powerful body to repeat only those affections that increase her power of acting and bring joy to her soul a new regime of longing that *becomes* the constitutive dynamic of being when it is adequately realised.

But this constitutive dynamic at the heart of the more powerful body is indeed the dynamic, though limited, of all bodies. For it is the nature of every body not only to preserve itself but also to expand its being as far as possible. And this constitutive dynamic is explained (and develops itself) through the power of Habit.

On the one hand, the body is defined by a specific proportion of motion-and-rest (that corresponds to its unique essence) and correlates with a capacity to affect and to be affected (that corresponds to the same essence as degree of power). On the other hand, this proportion or capacity would remain abstract if Habit did not give it a specific content in actual existence. But what is Habit if not the activity of this capacity to be affected that constitutes the nature of a body, or, better still, the dynamic of the proportion of motion-and-rest that exceeds the parts of which it is made? The power of Habit to combine affections is the very power of the body that correlates with its unique essence. The essence, in existence, is constitutive of a particular 'state' of the body (*constitutionem corporis*),[52] according to the connections of Habit, of particular 'modes of being', of this specific 'disposition' of the brain mentioned in *Ethics* I, App.[53] that characterises an individual.[54] Habit is nothing other than our capacity to be affected

---

[51] *Ethics* V, 27 and Dem.; CWS I, 609.
[52] *Ethics* II, 17 Schol.
[53] *Quae omnia satis ostendunt, unumquemque pro dispositione cerebri de rebus judicasse, vel potius imaginationis affectiones pro rebus accepisse.* CWS I, 444.
[54] The term *ingenium* appears most frequently in Spinoza to refer to this 'disposition' of the individual, which thus refers to the primarily singular historical product of the contraction of the particular affections of a body. The term appears explicitly in

in actu, while the assembled affections are our habits, that is, the different 'modes of being' that constitute our individuality. Habits, as particular affections of the body,[55] and 'mode[s] that actually [exist and involve] the nature of the external body'[56] are thus one and the same. A unique capacity to be affected can have many ways of being affected 'at once': 'as a body is more capable than others of doing many things at once or being acted on in many ways at once', writes Spinoza in *Ethics* II, 13 Schol.[57] And these ways of being affected, which are themselves already affections or connections of affections, are the result of Habit. The capacity to be affected refers to a power, while the ways of being affected refer to the modalities of exercising this power. But just as we must distinguish the capacity from its modes of being, we must also distinguish Habit from habits. If Habit (as the exercise of this capacity) constitutes habits (as modes of being), the capacity to be affected cannot be completely reduced to Habit. For the former contains an eternal truth (the specific proportion of motion-and-rest) in which the parts of the body and the exercise of Habit are included. We see, then, how Habit can sometimes counteract our capacity to be affected, depleting it, but can also sometimes animate it, according to the same proportion of motion-and-rest that characterises the body. Conversely, the capacity to be affected can oppose Habit when the latter, through a certain connection of affections, depletes the proportion of motion-and-rest corresponding to its unique essence. The connections of Habit always depend on the proportion of motion-and-rest they favour or undermine. But the connections of specific affections that are constitutive of the organic body also express themselves as habits, depending on the proportion of motion-and-rest that characterises this body. If the proportion of motion-and-rest includes and exceeds the parts of which it is composed, which is the very activity of Habit, then we must see in Habit the basis of the organisation of bodies.

We acquired the habit of living from our very first instant, from the first connections of affects of the body that the cerebral *habitus* was prompted to repeat. This habit is strengthened by its very repetition, indefinitely, as long as the depleting exterior bodies do not trouble this beautiful dynamism that

Ethics III, 31 Schol.: *atque adeo videmus, unumquemque ex natura appetere ut reliqui ex ipsius ingenio vivant*; *CWS* I, 512. But it is already presupposed in *Ethics* I, App. in the 'dispositions' proper to each brain, or in *Ethics* II, 17 Schol. in the particular 'state' of each body. Only in the political analysis does the full meaning of *ingenium* unfold (see Chapters 8 and 9 below).

[55] *Ethics* II, 28 Dem.
[56] *Ethics* II, 17 Dem.; *CWS* I, 464. Translation modified.
[57] *CWS* I, 458. Translator's note.

puzzles and amazes the ignorant.[58] Can we then say that *conatus* is, before all else, Habit? If Habit is indeed this capacity to construct the continuity of actual existence in contingency (life of the first kind of knowledge) or necessity (according to the third kind of knowledge), then the answer must be yes. From the very depths of simple organic life – constituting and perpetuating itself according to the repeated connections of passive affections – up to the active affections of a more powerful human body, forged according to the intrinsic necessity of their adequate knowledge in the intellect, Habit comes forth as the fundamental affirmation of actual existence.

By connecting affections, Habit weaves the indefinitely continuous thread of an always-already-there fabric, without beginning or end, in and through which the imaginary constitution of reality is embroidered. The more complex activities of the human body will have to be understood from Habit, that is, memory, imagination and strategic reason of the second kind.

2 *Conatus* as Joy Principle

We have not yet considered the 'why' of repetition – as if the desire for the second were naturally implied by the first connection, which is itself guided by Habit. Certainly, for the least complex bodies, repetition of the same seems to be the general rule. For these bodies, to persevere in being is to repeat themselves. There is little room for them to change in a state so well adapted to external conditions, lest they be destroyed. The mere sensation of existing – outside joyful or sad affects – ensures the qualitative continuity of an almost undifferentiated existence. As a figure of the *conatus*, Habit is synonymous with pure preservative effort.[59] However, this does not apply to more complex beings and especially not to the human body (even if this body also contains some basic repetitions). The nature of memory – that is, the persistence of the physical traces or images of things we perceived in the past that are no longer present – is explained by the effort to preserve only that which increases our capacity to act and is thus accompanied by a joyful affect. In other words, we always strive to preserve what is 'useful' to, and in agreement with, our nature. First and foremost, we strive to preserve what satisfies our bodies.[60] So our endeavour is to keep reinvesting the image of an

---

[58] *Ethics* I, App.; CWS I, 443.
[59] For a systematic study of the nature of simple and complex bodies, and the logical passage from one to the other, see Alexandre Matheron, *Individu et communauté chez Spinoza*, Minuit, 1969, I, chs 2 and 3.
[60] *KV* II, xvii, 4.

object that has given us satisfaction in the past, and this endeavour defines memory.

Correlatively, under the pressure of present images that exclude the images of the past, we resist the ineluctable erasure of the image associated with Joy. This effort is a resistance to the destruction of a joyful affect (that is, resistance to Sadness), and tends to reactivate the intensity of the favourable image 'against' a reality of other images that deplete us. The point is to forget, to inhibit the depleting representation in favour of another one filled with a joyful affect.[61]

There is thus an objective criterion by which to explain repetition, the true joy (*laetitia*) principle according to which the desiring body perseveres in Joy (*gaudium*), and the conditions associated with it which strive to keep at bay everything that causes sadness.[62] In this strategy, which is no longer merely one of preservation but a tendency towards joyful repetition, memory becomes valuable as a matrix (condition of possibility), means and tool of Joy against Sadness. Joy and Sadness are the first strategic information that orients the dynamism of *conatus*.

But this orientation is not without danger since it reduces desire to longing and, doing so, programmes a 'privation' into desire that can never be fulfilled according to the same teleology. Indeed, the paradox of joy (*laetitia*) is that it can only be sought after since, even when we have it, while we are enjoying the desired object, our body acquires

> from this enjoyment a new constitution, by which it is differently determined, and other images of things are aroused in it; and at the

---

[61] *Ethics* III, 28.

[62] The pleasure principle: this concept, which we transfer from Freudianism to Spinoza's philosophy, is modified by this very transfer [here, in English, to the joy principle]. The essential difference we must emphasise is that for Freud the pleasure principle is subject to a principle of 'consistency' or stability, which leads to pleasure being explained by a decrease in tension, that is, a decrease in the amount of energy (whereas pain corresponds to an increase). For Spinoza, on the other hand, from an economic point of view, it is the 'transition' to a greater power (or perfection) that produces joy (*laetitia*). Sadness, on the other hand, always corresponds to a depletion of that same power (*puissance*). If one reduces perseverance in being to mere perseverance in one's 'state', then joy is indeed nothing other than the satisfaction of renewed rest, but in this case it is therefore a 'bad' joy (*Ethics* IV, 59 Dem.). On Freud, see the first pages of *Beyond the Pleasure Principle*. For Spinoza, 'titillation or elation' are Joys (*gaudium*) because they affect both the mind and the body (*Ethics* III, 11 Schol.), whether in a partial way (only a part of the body – titillation) or in a global way (elation). So the question of balance arises; see Chapter 4 below.

same time the Mind begins to imagine other things and desire other things.[63]

This perpetual displacement into the future of an enjoyment one craves causes anticipated and acquired joy to inscribe and maintain privation within desire.

Could one object that *conatus* as Habit is itself subordinated to the sought-after joy that Spinoza calls tickling sensation (*titillatio*) or elation (*hilaritas*)?[64] From a descriptive point of view, yes: human beings act according to that which is advantageous to them and, therefore, through the joy (*laetitia*) for which they long. This presents, however, a finalist explanation that reverses the real order of things. Joy, whether related to the entire being, as with elation, or only a part of it, as with titillation, if it is indeed a 'principle', is not a final cause. Indeed, 'we strive to further the occurrence of whatever we imagine will lead to Joy, and to avert or destroy what we imagine is contrary to it or will lead to Sadness'.[65]

If joy is the 'basis' of our actions, and the idea that gives rise to it is posited by consciousness as finality, it is paradoxically no less the consequence of a connection that the body itself establishes as the principle of repetition: a Habit. It is in and through the connections themselves (as organisations) that unique ways of being affected (ways of 'feeling') are produced. These are also, immediately, by the very arrangement of Habit and the Joy that accompany it, life-producing tendencies to preserve favourable traces (that is, memory) and desire for repetition and reproduction.[66] Through the very organisation of the body's affections (or the body itself as connected affections) and the singular determinations of its capacity to be affected, Joy becomes the empirical foundation of our bio-psychic life. As the principle of *conatus*'s strategy, Joy is appetite itself as the arrangement of Habit.

Of course, theoretically, one strives for joy. But this striving always proceeds from already connected affects, which, at the same time, trace the paths of joy *a priori*, in the repetition of the same (which can become tedious by changing the body through repetition).[67] This opens up a wide range of possibilities in which Desire – through 'resemblance' or simple

---

[63] *Ethics* III, 59 Schol.; CWS I, 530.
[64] *Ethics* III, 11 Schol. Translator's note: Curley translates *hilaritas* as cheerfulness, which neither Emilie nor Hasana felt rendered the full meaning of this Joy (*gaudium*) that affects all the parts of the mind and the body. We therefore use elation in this work.
[65] *Ethics* III, 28; CWS I, 509.
[66] *Ethics* III, 36.
[67] *Ethics* III, 59 Schol.

'correspondence', beyond any mastery of the subject and along specific associative paths – encounters the most peculiar and curious modes of satisfaction.[68] Spinoza, thus, does not reject the (admittedly theoretical) possibility of beings who could 'live better on the gallows than at [their] table' or who would 'enjoy a better and more perfect life or essence by being [knaves]'.[69]

Through Habit, the joyful affect becomes an empirical principle – as organised Desire – at the foundation of our efforts to persevere in being. This is despite the fact that this organisation is delirious and forces the individual to repeat 'bad'[70] joys that are obstacles to real fulfilment for both body and mind, as Spinoza's comments to Blijenbergh show. For this reason, Spinoza speaks of a '[perverse] human nature'.[71]

Although we are forced to reject the contradiction, in the ontological realm, of a *conatus* whose internal finality (as principle) is joy (*laetitia*), we are unable to make sense of the various figures of servitude without highlighting the close connection that binds desire to joy (for better or worse). Indeed, if the simpler bodies are incapable of joy or sadness, by virtue of the indistinctness of the (extremely limited) states that they undergo, there is already in some more complex animals devoid of memory (that is, of the connection of the image of the affecting object (cause) and the affect (effect)) an effort to maintain joyful stimulations and get rid of any sad ones. Beyond any representation of the object (cause of this satisfaction), this extension of satisfaction is explained by the absolutely positive nature of desire that can only desire (if we can put it this way) its own augmentation, for which joy is the sign. But from this very positivity, we must detect in joy the first possible form of servitude. Indeed, any joyful affect (*titillatio*) is not the fullness of joy or elation (*hilaritas*).[72] Its fragmented condition, attached only to one part of the body, leads any 'immoderate' joy to contradict an augmentation of active power, and tips the entire being over into sadness. This problem is exposed

---

[68] *Ethics* III, 14, 15 Schol., 16.
[69] *Ep.* XXIII [to Willem Van Blijenbergh]; *CWS* I, 390.
[70] *Ethics* IV, 59 Dem.
[71] *Nam scelera respectu istiusmodi naturae humanae perversae virtus essent. Ep.* XXIII [to Willem Van Blijenbergh]; *CWS* I, 390. Affirmation that does not suggest the existence of an external and transcendent norm from which *deviance* of desire would be judged. In a philosophy where the norm is never conceived as being exterior to its field of application, the correlative idea of perversion cannot have a pre-established character. See Pierre Macherey, who engages a Spinozist reflection on the topic in 'Pour une histoire naturelle des normes', in *Michel Foucault philosophe*, Seuil, 1989, pp. 203–21.
[72] *Ethics* III, 11 Schol.

even more clearly when memory, which allows one to 'recognise' the object-cause of her joy, lures her, according to the logic of love,[73] into making this object the very goal of all her efforts. To subject Desire to a strategy, from its focus on the conquest and possession of only one partial object, inevitably leads to an extreme depletion of life.

There is, however, a difference between, on the one hand, a neutral connection that neither activates nor depletes active power – and to which no sufficiently strong affect of Joy or Sadness is attached (that therefore concerns only the mechanism of memory itself)[74] – and, on the other hand, a connection that leads to Joy or to Sadness. In the first case, the affected body desires neither repetition nor avoidance. If an element of the connection is represented by the subject, however, the subject (according to the mind's consideration of the trace – or affection – imprinted in its brain)[75] will reconstitute the entire fabric of connection (as shown by the examples of *Ethics* II, 18 Schol.). If it concerns real events, the affected body will expect the unfolding of the whole established association, as with the example of the child in *Ethics* II, 44 Schol.

In the second case, the connection itself orients the behaviour of the subject towards a new corporeal and psychic disposition. Since the 'Mind, as far as it can, strives to imagine those things that increase or aid the body's power of acting',[76] it will also strive to remember what has given it Joy and even strive to provoke a repetition of the situation in and through which this Joy was produced:

> We strive to further the occurrence of whatever we imagine will lead to Joy, and to avert or destroy what we imagine is contrary to it or will lead to Sadness.[77]

In this second scenario, there is a true repetitive 'tendency': 'He who recollects a thing by which he was once pleased desires to possess it in the same circumstances as when he first was pleased by it.'[78] This tendency to repeat joy can thereby be understood as the very principle of our biopsychic existence.

---

[73] *Ethics* III, DA 6.
[74] *Ethics* II, 13 Post. 5; *Ethics* II, 17 Cor.
[75] *Ethics* II, 13 Post. 5; *Ethics* II, 17 Dem.
[76] *Ethics* III, 12; CWS I, 505.
[77] *Ethics* III, 28; CWS I, 509.
[78] *Ethics* III, 36.; CWS I, 515.

We thereby understand how depleting connections – which can lead even to suicide – by engaging a connective mechanism of strongly depleting images, are made possible in a heteronomous regime. But we also understand why the *conatus*, according to its joy principle, naturally 'resists' these depressive arrangements as much as it can.

A continual confrontation between depleting connective links resides in us, alongside connections that are favourable to our effort to persevere in being. Not only does Spinoza shed light on the existence of different groups of images (affections and ideas of affections) or relatively independent groups of connections (inside the mode of a same attribute) in our body and mind. At the same time, he affirms the dynamism of these associative series according to a mechanistic and determinist concept of memory. These groups of connections are also opposing forces whose equilibrium is always susceptible to change, depending on the situations (and power relations). In the subject, there is a dynamism of associative complexes whose forces find their source both in the external modes and in the individual himself. It would be misguided, however, to see here a struggle between the *conatus* striving for fulfilment (that is, towards Joy) and the depleting associations of images whose dynamism is of an exclusively external nature. Indeed, all connections, even depleting ones, come from the *conatus*, not insofar as they are depleting, but insofar as they express a dynamic connection between images. In this case, however, the *conatus* is in a global heteronomous regime, subjected to external forces in its very connective activity.

On the other hand, the *conatus* as joy principle, in opposition to connections that are contrary to it, can lead to a repetition of alienated joys that keep the mind from thinking. Connections that are only advantageous to the preservation of a being in its [current] 'state' can resist a higher affirmation (that is, passing to a higher perfection) if they fix the greater part of the *conatus*'s force upon persevering in this state, whether psychological or sociological. This is explained both by the relative independence of the associative circuits and by their own dynamism that nonetheless finds its source (quasi-totally or only partially) in one and the same *conatus*. A greater affirmation can be experienced as a depleting force and the *conatus* may resist such disordering, as the order of the present state, however liberating. . . The *conatus*, therefore, participates in all competing connections in the subject, including those that are contrary to it and those it resists. Beyond the mastery of the subject and his real interest (from the perspective of strategic reason), memories are a reservoir of forces favoured or dismissed by the present situation, according to the strategic logic (more or less rational, more or less blind) of the joy principle.

Indeed, when the Mind imagines those things that diminish or restrain the Body's power of acting, it strives, as far as it can, to recollect things that exclude their existence.[79]

The endeavour of a human being affected by Sadness[80] tends to be wholly focused on dispelling Sadness with the memory of a previous Joy desiring to repeat itself in the present. The mind thereby strives to 'imagine only those things that posit its power of acting'[81] and to repress anything that dismays it and, in so doing, depletes it. Every means, even the most illusory, is good for this action (even as passive, since this defence can also be used in a global regime of heteronomy with images presently favourable to *conatus*). The mind can, thus, strive to dispel Sadness with bad faith 'by wrongly interpreting his equal's actions'[82] or with an overestimation of the self[83] (*superbia*) 'by magnifying his own [actions] as much as [possible]',[84] etc.

The *conatus*'s action (even passive) consists in relentlessly guiding a being back to the Joy of existing (even in alienated ways) and, correlatively, in making one forget everything that can thwart this effort. This is how the ontological positivity of the *conatus*, the absolute affirmation of existence, expresses itself. The consequences of this demand can be paradoxical, however, since this alienated effort can also promote servitude against liberating truth. Liberating truth is too inconvenient when it is a force that dissolves the illusions from which an individual precisely strives, in his current state, to persevere in being.

3 *Conatus* as Memory

Let us come back to the distinction between the neutral connections and the connections that involve Joy or Sadness. In the two cases, *habitus* formed a neutral or active memory in relation to the Joy or Sadness of which it kept a trace. The memory contained in our desires constitutes those very desires. For what are our singular desires if not connected affections, which is to say, arrangements of Habit? Our desires affirm themselves according to the

---

[79] *Ethics* III, 13; CWS I, 502.
[80] *Ethics* III, 37 Dem.
[81] *Ethics* III, 54; CWS I, 525.
[82] *Ethics* III, 55 Schol.; CWS I, 525.
[83] Translator's note: Curley translates *superbia* as pride, but overestimation of the self is closer to Bove's text and to the Latin, and is my preference.
[84] *Ethics* III, 55 Schol.; CWS I, 525.

determinate laws of imagination. What we could call 'fate'[85] is woven into every being through repetition, through this process that connects our affections. It is through the mechanism of Habit – always necessarily confronted by specific situations– that we find our power (which, by itself, has no goal or object) fixed in a way-of-being-in-the-world, a way of projecting itself into it, that is, a destiny. The particularity of our loving and alienated history (always coupled with our hatreds) is defined in this way. Indeed, human action is always oriented towards some end: the good they desire, and the Joy or satisfaction accompanied by the idea of the desired object, which Spinoza calls love.[86] We find this loving structure of behaviour at the very heart of human reason.

We come into the world by the same power that allows us today to persevere in being. This power is acted upon according to a singular destiny linked to the fluctuations of individual history and particularly of childhood history, because the extreme powerlessness in which this state places us favours the stifling action of exterior causes. This existential situation – in which the body of the human-child, infinitely surpassed by exterior forces, is in a regime of quasi-total heteronomy – opens a privation at the heart of human existence. It is privation as need (and satisfaction), on which Desire illusorily models itself (but its necessity is ineluctable). When this privation – fundamental to the very constitution of the organic body[87] – becomes the (theoretical and practical) model of our Desire (as longing for an object, joy, love), we enter alienation. And we enter it necessarily, for what can the awareness (idea of the idea) of a powerless body bring but confusion about our essence? Yet the organic body and the psychic structure that accompanies it are figures of an absolutely positive Desire lacking nothing, since it has no end or object. But organic bodies, modes of the infinite and absolutely positive productivity of Nature, persevere in their being according to the mechanisms of Habit. For more complex bodies capable of memory, according to the psycho-biological joy principle, the mind experiences habit according to the finalist structure of love.

---

[85] In *Ep.* LVIII [to G. H. Schuller], Spinoza opposes the illusion of free will to fatal necessity (*fatali necessitate*, CWS II, 430). In *Ethics* III, 59 Schol., Spinoza writes: 'we are driven about in many ways by external causes, and . . . like waves on the sea, driven by contrary winds, we toss about, not knowing our outcome and fate' (*CWS* I, 530). See also the beginning of the preface of *Ethics* IV where Spinoza describes the strong power of 'fortune': *homo enim affectibus obnoxius sui juris non est, sed fortunae. . .* (*CWS* I, 543).
[86] *Ethics* III, DA 6.
[87] *Ethics* II, 13 Post. 4.

Whereas the mechanism of Habit conforms to the joy principle, the *conatus* does not yet have an object or a represented goal as such. In complex bodies and particularly in humans, memory allows both the designation of an object of desire and a goal. The causal connection of an experienced affect of joy together with an exterior object (as cause) introduces a problematic of love, which is to say, an interpretation of the world. From this new capacity to memorialise (or recollect) we are, indeed, led to a finalist structure of loving behaviour characteristic of human existence.[88]

There is indeed in humans a biopsychic structure of a teleological nature, even if the way this structure works must be understood strictly from the point of view of efficient causes (at the risk of totally slipping into the possible and almost inevitable finalist illusion that this structure effectively contains). In this problematic of love, desire becomes desire-of-something, that is, of an object that captures all our energy and attention because of the Joy that its presence brings us. It is this goal of loving intentionality that Spinoza names 'satisfaction'. It is 'in the lover on account of the presence of the thing loved, by which the lover's Joy is strengthened or at least encouraged'.[89]

According to the logic of the joy principle that gave it a memory, the *conatus*-Habit enters a teleological course that follows processes whose necessity (unconscious for the desiring subject) can only adequately be understood from the order of efficient causes.[90] This is the stage of conscious (illusory or adapted) strategies of the *conatus*, from which the specificity of 'human' reason can be understood. Human reason involves the mechanism of memory as such and its intrinsic relationship to the order of time.

Let us return to the example of *Ethics* II, 44 Schol. With the idea of recognition, this example recalls an action of the mind that (though it requires Habit) expresses a superior form of connection (a sign of the higher level of complexity of the body), which already contains, it seems, a determination of the intellect if we consider the activity of a reflected generality of the concept. We find ourselves at a turning point between imagination and reason in the constitution of time as representation. For the generalisation is also

---

[88] As Alexandre Matheron remarks, the teleological activity of humans is not merely of the realm of illusion or the fictitious interpretations that consciousness makes, after the fact, of this behaviour; it is a matter of fact: 'that is why Spinoza tells us that *we act* towards our ends and not simply that *it seems so to us*'. Matheron, *Individu et communauté*, p. 105, n. 67.
[89] *Ethics* III, DA 6, Exp.; CWS I, 533.
[90] *Ethics* III, 15 Cor. and Schol.; CWS I, 503.

a process of imagination[91] denounced by Spinoza. And deductive activity operates by virtue of this 'abstract' generality.[92]

The child (of *Ethics* II, 44 Schol.), because of her expectation, recognises the different events of the previous day when she recollects the past day. It is therefore based on a representation of the previous day (as passed) that the child recognises the events of the present and can also anticipate them in the future. In doing so, she uses both her memory and her intellect:

1. Her imagination/memory, not only as a connective activity (in habit), but also as an activity of the mind by which it recognises in the image, as a present sign ('sensation of impressions in the brain'),[93] events from a situated past (implying a relationship to time and to the process of reminiscence in the Aristotelian sense);[94]
2. Her imagination/intellect; in the activity of a mind that establishes new intelligible, logical or causal relations between its data the expectation of imagination is proportional to the number of similar distinct instances already observed and recalled by memory. The child who sees Simon at night will infer Peter's visit in the morning and Paul's visit at noon, just as she will infer from Peter's visit in the morning Paul's visit at noon and Simon's visit at night. (It does not matter whether these inferences turn out to be false in relationship to an aleatory reality. All that matters is that these conclusions are possible.)

Spinoza therefore presents the constitution of time no longer as the living present of experienced duration, but as reflected and determinate representations of this duration. A 'being of reason' is born of the synthesis of the relationships that the human intellect makes between images conceived 'distinctly', recognised and compared.[95] Time, so represented, is the first

---

[91] It is the case in the formation of *transcendentals* or of notions we call *general*, *Ethics* II, 40 Schol. 1.
[92] 'For we don't conceive things under numbers unless they have first been brought under a common genus. For example, someone who holds a penny and a dollar in his hand will not think of the number two unless he can call the penny and the dollar by one and the same name, either "coin" or "piece of money".' *Ep.* L [to Jarig Jelles]; *CWS* II, 406.
[93] *TdlE* 89; *CWS* I, 38.
[94] Ibid. As Wolfson rightly remarks, Spinoza's reference here is Aristotle, *On Memory and Reminiscence*. See Harry Wolfson, *The Philosophy of Spinoza. Unfolding the Latent Processes of his Reasoning*, Harvard University Press, 1983, vol. 2.
[95] *KV* I, x, 1.

system of order from which we imagine things distinctly and through which consciousness, by distinguishing between objects, differentiates itself from the object.

It is indeed the order of time (as representation) that is the condition:

First, of the appearance, for us, of the external object as such. By maintaining the image of a body in the present, memory makes of this body a being whose affiliation with the past renders it, in the present, independent of me and available for the future.[96] There are thus no representations of 'external' things outside temporality, which is itself made possible by memory based on the acquisitions of Habit.

Second, the order of temporality is also the condition of the separation of subject and object. According to the very logic of its appearance, the object is necessarily always a past object made present. The distinction between subject and object is itself a temporal differentiation, a product of the order of temporality.

The feeling of duration was until now only that of an immediate thought of the 'passages', augmentations or depletions of our power of acting that defined the rhythms through which we are made in the continuity of our existence. Temporality – which is the determinate re-presentation of duration experienced by the mind – implies a power of reflection, of presentiment, even, retrospectively, of deduction of past events. This reality belongs, to be sure, to a more complex body and, in the same way, to a higher level of Habit's connections in and through what we call memory. It is one whose full actuality is made possible only by the relay of the determination of duration in thought.

Memory enables both the anticipation of the future and the reconstruction of the past. However, this memory could be completely unconscious and produce nothing but reminiscence (in the Cartesian sense of reminiscence being unaware of itself as recollection) in the child of *Ethics* II, 44 Schol. The child does not have to know consciously that she saw Peter, Paul and Simon the day before in order to predict Paul's and Simon's visit after that of Peter. She could simply predict their appearance without knowing where she got that knowledge, according to a 'thought of a determinate duration',[97] without the memory of being aware of the series of events put together the day before (the process would of course be the same for retrospective reconstruction). The Roman from *Ethics* II, 18 Schol. does not have to consciously remember the day on which he acquired the conventional

---

[96] This is well understood by Matheron, *Individu et communauté*, p. 100.
[97] *TdIE*, 83; *CWS* I, 39.

connection between the word *pomum* and its referent, the fruit. He only knows that this fruit is an apple, without really knowing from where he got this knowledge, without knowledge of when he acquired the memory.

Yet memory itself cannot be simple non-reflective knowledge. Indeed, the knowledge of a child who does not remember 'when and where [the reported fact] happened'[98] – or even that she one day learned the thing she can today conjure (and even also from which she can eventually predict what is to come) – should not be taken for the full process of memory. The complete knowledge of memory arises from the imagination passing from the qualitative impression of Habit to its reflection in an orderly representation. For knowledge to become 'memory', it must combine with the conception (consciousness) of the 'determinate duration' of the affects through which it arose, the 'distinct' knowledge of the time (when) the events of which the subject has knowledge (which we call memory 1) unfolded.

When *Ethics* IV, 39 Schol. alludes to the story of the Spanish poet whose illness robbed him of his memories so that he no longer even recognised his own writings, Spinoza reveals memory as the ability to recognise a memory and locate it in the past. The poet retained the memory of his mother tongue, which, according to *Ethics* II, 18 Cor., is the mechanical association of words and affections evoked in us by the things to which they refer and which we have acquired through Habit. But the poet lost what constitutes memory as such, namely the consciousness of the past time and the consciousness of the self in that time.

If the child of *Ethics* II, 44 Schol. has 'perfect' memory (what we call memory 2),[99] and not just simple memory in the Cartesian sense (memory 1), then she must, in order to anticipate the events of the second day, remember that yesterday she saw (consciousness of time past and self-consciousness localised in temporality but extended to the present) how Peter passed in the morning, Paul at noon, and Simon at night (recognition and orderly localisation of beings and moments in a determinate temporality). Accordingly, the *TdIE* defines memory as the 'sensation of impressions on the brain, together with the thought of a determinate duration of the sensation'.[100]

---

[98] *TdIE*, 83, note; *CWS* I, 39.

[99] *TdIE*, 83, note d; *CWS* I, 39.

[100] *TdIE*, 83; *CWS* I, 39. For a synthesis of the different positions on this question, see R. Bordoli, who discusses the positions of Wolfson, de Deugd and Gueroult in chapter VII of his *Memoria e abitudine. Descartes, La Forge, Spinoza*, Guerini e Associati, 1994, pp. 93–7. See also Bernard Rousset's commentary in his translation of Spinoza's *Traité de la réforme de l'entendement*, Vrin, 1992, pp. 354–8.

2

The Constitution of the Strategic Subject

1 The Object and its Recognition

The represented order of time is the condition under which the external object can appear. Temporality makes both its separation from other objects and the very consciousness of which it is the object visible. This order of time is contingent on memory. In *Ethics* V, 29 Schol., Spinoza makes a clear distinction between the two types of 'things' our mind can conceive:

> We conceive things as actual in two ways: either insofar as we conceive them to exist in relation to a certain time and place, or insofar as we conceive them to be contained in God and to follow from the necessity of the divine nature.[1]

The constitution of things in relation to a 'certain time and place' is the central question of this chapter: that is, the constitution, for us, of the external object as such. This object is something external to us as much as it is our own body and mind (as paradoxical as this may seem). We know that

> [t]he idea of any mode in which the human Body is affected by external bodies must involve the nature of the human Body and at the same time the nature of the external body.[2]

The idea of the affection represents this affection (corporeal trace) and attributes its cause back to an external reality, that is, to the experienced affect (Joy or Sadness), which depends on the activation or depletion of

---

[1] CWS I, 610. Translator's note.
[2] *Ethics* II, 16; CWS I, 463.

one's power (*puissance*) to act. Imagination is the recognition of an object understood as external and real to which stable properties are attributed, such as being, form (more or less harmonious or beautiful), colour, consistency, quantity, temperature, etc., as if the idea were, in a mirroring fashion, the objective reflection of an independent reality. Granted, every thing can be grasped in its being. But we must not confuse the being that is its very essence (and which can only be known according to the third kind of knowledge) and the being attributed to an object 'in relation to a certain time and place'. In the second case, this being is the same 'genus' under which we place all individuals in Nature,[3] by convenience but also due to some confusion.[4]

The being of the imagined thing is, therefore, not a real thing, but only the expression of how we conceive external reality. The same is true of the 'form' of the object or its 'figure', which we imagine as a limit, that is, a negation.[5] It is true also of visibility and invisibility, of warmth and cold, of fluid and solid, which, as Spinoza explains to Oldenburg in *Ep*. VI, '[are] notions derived from ordinary usage . . . related to human sense perception'.[6] Colour itself is not a property of the object but a phenomenon constituted by the meeting of the eyes and external reality illuminated in a certain way.[7] We find a symptomatic example of this in *Ep*. IX [to Simon de Vries]: 'By flat I mean what reflects all rays of light without any change; I understand the same by white, except that it is called white in relation to a man looking at the flat [surface].'[8] Also, good and bad, useful and harmful, pleasant and unpleasant, order and confusion, beauty and ugliness, fragrant and foul, sweet and sour, hard and soft, rough and smooth, noisy and quiet, harmonious and cacophonous . . . are all products of the brain's dispositions or the ways of being of our imagination:[9] 'the ideas with we have of external bodies indicate the condition of our own body more than the nature of external bodies'.[10]

---

[3] *Ethics* IV, Praef.; CWS I, 545.
[4] *Ethics* II, 40 Schol. 1.
[5] *Ep*. L [to Jarig Jelles]; CWS II, 406–7.
[6] In the *Ethics*, however, hardness, softness and fluidity have objective definitions (*Ethics* II, 13, Ax. 3), in contrast to *Ep*. VI [to Oldenburg]; CWS I, 433. Translation modified.
[7] F. Mignini, in *Ars Imaginandi – Apparenza e rappresentazione in Spinoza*, ed. Scientifiche Italiane, 1981, p. 117, notes the relation between nature, the form and intensity of the luminous stimuli the eye receives, and the constitution of the form, colour, size, distance and position of the object.
[8] CWS I, 387.
[9] *Ethics* I, App.; CWS I, 443–6.
[10] *Ethics* II, 16 Cor. 2; CWS I, 463. Translation modified.

The object as a representation has its own reality only through the encounter of our body with the external world – a meeting of proportions composed and/or decomposed according to their specific combinations of motion-and-rest, of the speed and stillness of the infinity of particles that make them. In this encounter, a body affects other bodies or is affected by them according to the dual capacity to affect and be affected that bodies have – that is, according to the intensity of their power, which is also how Spinoza defines their singular essences. This multiplicity of encounters, combinations of powers, speeds and affects, is defined on an immanent plane, a reality that can only be conceived and lived in Habit, according to the active power's 'passages' to greater or lesser perfection. Represented within a process of organisation, this reality of the encounters of Habit, and leading to recognition of a world of objects for a subject, is unknown because of this very representation.

To think that Nature produces what our mind 'contemplates' (in the sense of 'imagining' according to *Ethics* II, 17, Schol.) independent of us is to believe that Nature itself 'imagines' what it produces. This, as Spinoza notes, is to attribute imagination to God.[11] Therefore, when Spinoza affirms in *Ethics* I, 16 that 'from the necessity of the divine nature there must follow infinitely many things in infinitely many modes (that is, everything which can fall under an 'infinite intellect'),[12] he is not speaking of those things that are in our imagination. Rather, he is referring to the infinite processes of dynamic individuation that can only be thought of outside the categories of 'object' and 'subject', and which are in fact 'beings of reason'.[13] These individuation processes, through their encounter with our bodies, are represented in temporality in the form of useful or harmful things, as objects we are used to seeing, using, consuming, loving or hating.[14] In the *Metaphysical Thoughts*,[15] Spinoza warns us not to confuse real beings and beings of reason. The latter are just ways of thinking (or more precisely, of imagining) that help us to retain, explain and imagine things more easily.[16] There is indeed 'no agreement between a real being and the objects of a being of reason'. And Spinoza stresses: 'For it is one thing to inquire into the nature of things,

---

[11] *Ethics* I App.; CWS I, 444.
[12] CWS I, 424. Translator's note.
[13] CM I, 1 and 5; CWS I, 299, 311.
[14] Martial Gueroult, *Spinoza, I: Dieu*, Aubier, 1968. On the radical difference between the thought-of (and real) body and the imagined body, see pp. 419–24 and more specifically, p. 419, n. 17.
[15] CM I, 1; CWS I, 301.
[16] CM I, 1; CWS I, 299.

and another to inquire into the modes by which things are perceived by us.'[17] There is therefore in Nature only substance and its modes that we must not confuse with the accidental qualities we attribute to things and that are, in fact, only *manners of thinking*,[18] such as opposition, order, agreement, difference, subject, complement,[19] but also beauty, colour, form, etc.

Our relationship to 'objects' is, moreover, never neutral. It is due to desire that we distinguish a thing to which we attribute our affect by separating it from its context. Since Joy is ignorant of its efficient causes, it is transferred, according to the affection's image (imaginative idea), to the object towards which the image is pointing. In its difference and vivacity, this image-object is only formed by the desire which drove me to it, or, more precisely, by this very movement, which is at the origin of its production. If, therefore, a thing is 'good' for me because I desire it,[20] it also simply becomes a 'thing' due to this very desire. To be sure, I do not desire all the things that make up the world around me, all of what are 'things' for me. Yet if these things make a world, it is precisely from the point of view of the order (or disorder) that my desire believes it discerns within it (under the figure of imagination). The world of the first kind (of knowledge) is a world of things, because it is also immediately a world of my desire. Desire must, therefore, be understood as a true process of making present (*présentification*). By singling out a thing among things, a being among beings, our *conatus* gives it a singular 'unity' *vis-à-vis* other beings or things. For the imaginative mind, the unity through which an object is 'targeted' can only be that of the connections of the affections of its own body. But this unity is itself just 'a mode of thinking through which we separate the thing from others which are like it or agree with it in some way'.[21]

Desire selects the beings with which we fall in love. This much is true. Yet this distinction supposes a prior unity resulting from our corporeal boundaries and the practical simplification of Habit that produces beings of reason (humans, for example). The main function of these beings of reason is to allow us to 'conceive of things distinctly',[22] even though this distinction is not attributable to the intellect, and even though it has only to do with imaginatively perceived and recognised things (by discrete quantity), as the

---

[17] CM I, 1; CWS I, 302.
[18] CM I, 1; CWS I, 302.
[19] CM I, 5.
[20] *Ethics* III, 9 Schol.
[21] CM I, 6; CWS I, 311.
[22] KV I, x; CWS I, 114.

Ethics highlights. Indeed, the discrete and discontinuous are introduced into Nature only via an ignorance of the intrinsic unity that makes any real separation between the modes impossible. If bodies really do exist, meet, join and oppose each other in Nature, our love only has to do with images (discrete quantities) constituted, for us, as distinct things, only according to a general idea. But one may ask, where does this general idea come from, if not from the simplification of reality produced by the epigenetic activity of *conatus*?

Let us return to recognition. To love is to attribute the cause of an affect (of Joy) to another being or a thing external to oneself. This movement towards the other, the cause of our Joy, is the very movement of loving desire (*désir amoureux*). Desire supposes, as its conditions of possibility, the joint activities of Habit, the joy principle and memory. The synthesis of recognition through loving desire relies on these arrangements and goes beyond the associated affects and their correlates, to the identification of an object which, by virtue of its qualities (its beauty, its colour...), is identified as the cause of our Joy and of our love. The process of recognition is therefore about relating Joy or Sadness to the connections of affections made by Habit (and preserved by memory, according to the Joy/Sadness principle). It is also about objectivising (*objectiver*) in reality the encounters of the body and of the idea of corporeal traces. Memory is, therefore, intrinsically connected to the recognition/constitution of the object.

The analysis of the recognition process seems, at first sight, to reveal a two-step movement: 1) relating the affect to the connections of affections; and 2) relating the connections of affections to an object in the process of making present. These two steps are, however, really one and the same movement (of loving desire): that of the very constitution of the loved (or hated) 'object' that transcends the connection of (subjective) affections towards an 'object' posited as real and present. This is the imaginative process Spinoza describes in *Ethics* II, 17 Schol.

The lover thinks she is attributing her Joy to a real object. In fact, she is attributing it to a (subjective) connection of affections that creates the object and which she, the loving subject, illusorily takes for real and for the cause of her Joy (when she is in fact ignorant of the efficient causes of her affections and of their connections). The object as imaginative idea of a being identical to itself, but endowed with its own attributes, does not therefore pre-date the desire that is directed towards it. It is only constituted according to the very movement of a complex body's desire seeking joy. In itself, it is true, desire is desire of nothing. It is productive force, affirmation (*affirmatio*) of existence. Joy (as principle) and its flip side, Sadness, however, are already orienting the process of their *conatus*, as beings capable of sensing differences between their affective states. Only under the influence of the loving representation of the world, which it nevertheless produces, does desire become desire for the object and a pursuit of joy, in and through the possession of the object. Loving desire divides up for us a world of objects, of things-to-love, and, at the same time, desire-for-some-thing. Desire's productivity becomes the production of fictions, of these useful or harmful, lovely or heinous image-things, that organise a representation of the world for and by the *conatus*.

Desire precedes love. In fact, it is because desire is – by the arrangements of Habit, the joy principle and memory – 'longing' that things and things-to-love can appear. Love, however, oppresses desire by subjecting it to its law, by imposing an object upon it to achieve its goal. Love reduces desire to a need by infusing it with a want – of an object, of joy, of love. Thus life, subject to the vicissitudes of external reality, becomes an eternal longing. It nonetheless remains bound to the *conatus* as joy principle. The represented real, far from being an obstacle to joy, is in fact its means. But it is a paradoxical means in that, by avoiding immediate appropriation, it makes a representation out of joy, an idea to realise in the future based on the models of the past. The ability to take reality into account is therefore correlative to the birth of a calculating reason, which, according to a more or less adapted strategy, will follow the joy principle's trend. This reality with which the *conatus* is confronted, however, is an immediate representation of reality, a conquest of reality within an always singular inscription of Desire.

We already mentioned that, beyond the literal signification of *Ethics* III, 9 Schol., not only does a thing become good for us because we desire it, but it becomes, simply, a 'thing' by this very desire. It is through desire that we recognise the thing we love, that we form it. The act of imagining the 'thing', correlative to the desire that draws me to it, affirms the present existence of the imagined thing. The positioning of any existence in relationship to a determinate time and place is the work of imagination. To perceive an object, or to remember it, is to posit its presence and existence according to a synthesis of recognition that relates the encounter of affections to an object, according to a process of making present. We already know all of this. But by underlining in the corollary of *Ethics* 17 that, 'although the external bodies by which the human body has once been affected neither exist nor are present, the mind will still be able to regard them as if they were present',[23] Spinoza identifies the process of perceiving external bodies with the process of hallucination. If we consider how making the external world present is not carried out in a neutral way but always from a singular desire, and that it

---

[23] CWS I, 464. Translator's note.

is from this point of view (symptomatic of a certain disposition of our body) that things appear to us as good or bad, beautiful or ugly, etc., it is possible to deduce that the very essence of our relationship with the external world is hallucinatory. Spinoza thereby invites us to understand sense knowledge from the point of view of fiction rather than from the habitual perception of objects.

It is legitimate, on the one hand, to read *Ethics* III, 9 Schol. in light of what Spinoza already develops in *Ethics* II, 17 Cor. and Schol. on the hallucinatory nature of the imaginative mind. On the other hand, it is also acceptable to define the synthesis of recognition as a constitutive synthesis of its object in its actual existence, temporally and spatially determined.

What makes possible Spinoza's definition of the idea? The nature of the idea consists in making the thing of which it is the idea appear to us as present: The mind, writes Spinoza, 'regards [non-existent things] as if they were present'.[24] In one and the same movement, the mind that imagines passes from the idea of a singular connection of affection to the idea of an actually (*in actu*) existing body, because it is one and the same idea. 'The human Mind perceives the nature of a great many bodies together with the nature of its own body.'[25] How do we distinguish a 'real' hallucination and an illusory hallucination?

In the first case, the process of making present 'represents' an actual external reality, even if it 'does not have adequate knowledge of it' (which is in itself impossible).[26] Hallucinatory perception is thus the product of an actual (*in actu*) encounter between the body and the bodies surrounding it.

In the second case, the process of making present does not represent anything externally actual but only images that, independent from actual external reality (that is, from a common hallucinatory perception), totally substitute themselves for it (as is shown by the example of hallucination described in *Ep.* XVII [to P. Balling]).[27] External causes are no longer what actualises the body's affections (or corporeal traces) and its idea (representative of an external body), but rather it is the movement of the animal spirits internal to the body. The illusory hallucination (*hallucination-fantasme*) is merely the product of an internal encounter of some mnemonic traces in the brain (soft parts of the body) and of the animal spirits (fluid parts) with

---

[24] *Ethics* II, 17 Cor. Schol.; CWS I, 465. Translation modified: Bove cited this as *Ethics* 49 Schol., but we could not find this quotation in that proposition.
[25] *Ethics* II, 16 Cor. 1; CWS I, 463. Translation modified.
[26] *Ethics* II, 26 Cor.; CWS I, 469.
[27] CWS I, 352.

spontaneous movements, that is, free of any immediate determination by external bodies.

In both cases, however, there remains an essentially hallucinatory process. Even in true perception, the perceived object is necessarily fabricated, even though it may be relatively common to all due to some common corporeal and psychic structures. Since imagination is a figure of desire, of our effort to persevere in being – and each being, due to its history, has singular desires – we must also note that there are as many species of objects as there are desires turned towards them. The same reality is thereby multiplied in proportion to its number of contenders. This is also necessarily true of the idea that Paul can have of Peter, but also the idea that Simon, Jacob, etc. can have of the same Peter. They are so different because the ideas say more about the state of Paul, Simon or Jacob's body than they do about the nature of Peter![28]

We, therefore, erect a world according to the objectified representation of our affective fluctuations. This epigenetic activity of the *conatus* is possible only from the relatively common material conditions of what a body can do, that is, its capacity to be affected. Though this power (*pouvoir*) varies in human beings, it is necessarily limited in each of us. And so, we are incapable of taking in the infinite depth of a reality that sweeps over and through us at every turn. We would surely be dazed, taken by vertigo and fainting spells[29] if – from this 'affective' confusion caused by the encounter with this infinite multiplicity and our limits – a certain clarity and apparent distinction between things did not paradoxically emerge in and through imagination. The very notions of 'being', 'thing' and 'something' are, in the mind, the universal results of this confusion.

> These terms arise from the fact that the human Body, being limited, is capable of forming distinctly only a certain number of images at the same time (I have explained what an image is in P17S). If that number is exceeded, the images will begin to be confused, and if the number of images the Body is capable of forming distinctly in itself at once is greatly

---

[28] *Ethics* II, 16 Cor. 2 and 17 Schol.; *CWS* I, 464.
[29] We use Leibnizian terms here (*Monadologie*, §§ 21, 25), even though the Spinozist problematic is quite different. For Leibniz, small unconscious perceptions integrated and surpassed in conscious apperception belong to the order of representation (or imagination-perception from the Spinozist point of view). Gottfried Leibniz, *New Essays on Human Understanding*, Cambridge University Press, 1996. For Spinoza, on the other hand, the encounters of bodies, according to the proportion of motion-and-rest, the capacity to affect and to be affected, take place outside any representation.

exceeded, they will all be completely confused with one another. Since this is so, it is evident from P17C and P18, that the human Mind will be able to imagine distinctly, at the same time, as many bodies as there can be images formed at the same time in its body. But when the images in the body are completely confused, the Mind also will imagine all the bodies confusedly, without any distinction, and comprehend them as if under one attribute, viz. under the attribute of Being, Thing, etc.[30]

How can the imaginative idea of a 'thing' arise in us given this limit? Spinoza answers that, from the confusion of the 'slight differences of the singular' and from the connection of affections that all agree among themselves, the mind, indeed, can

> imagine neither slight differences of the singular [men] (such as the colour and size of each one, etc.) nor their determinate number, and imagines distinctly only what they all agree in, insofar as they affect the body.[31]

In the case of Habit, we have underlined the extent to which the affected body is not totally passive but can compel connections. In an economical sense, reality would necessarily be traumatic if the living individual could not respond positively according to her own measure of resistance and mastery.[32]

In the constitution of an object, the capacity to be affected is both a limit and an activity (as affirmation). Confusion is therefore not merely the product of powerlessness. It is also an active simplification of reality that needs to be understood from the dynamic standpoint of a resisting *conatus* (by the mechanisms of Habit, the joy principle and memory). Spinoza often evokes this synthetic logic of simplification carried out by imagination and memory.[33] For, in the constitutive recognition of things, this simplifying activity is one of the fundamental laws of imaginative activity.[34]

On the side of the affecting reality, the constitution of the imaginative idea of the perceived 'thing' is composed by the differential multiplicity of modes. And on the side of the affected body, this constitution is born of the body's incapacity to fully take in this multiplicity, but also of its capacity

---

[30] *Ethics* II, 40 Schol. I; *CWS* I, 476.
[31] *Ethics* II, 40 Schol. I; *CWS* I, 477.
[32] We use the notion of trauma in its Freudian sense as used in *A General Introduction to Psychoanalysis*, trans. G. Stanley Hall, Boni and Liveright, 1922, ch. 18.
[33] CM V; *Ethics* I, App.; *Ethics* II, 40 Schol. 1.
[34] On this true principle of facility or economy, see the developments of CM I, 1 and V; *CWS* I, 299–301.

to make its affections meet and to actively resist the manifold flooding of reality. The object, therefore, appears to the mind's perception according to the double corporeal process of simplification-assimilation, by confusion and active simplification from the connection of affections. The connection of affections are not a practical ordering of confusion, but rather an ordering in and through confusion, since it is from confusion itself that the simple, clear and distinct imaginative idea emerges. It is according to this active simplification that loving desire selects, in an *a priori* undifferentiated situation, the cause of its Joy.

The passive–active confusion which results from our capacity to be affected and from the loving desire's selection expresses the process of imagination through which we adapt the world to us. Active, strategic adaptation is the effective means of our perseverance.

For how should we understand the formation of universal errors, constitutive of the reality in and through which we persevere in being – such as the belief in time, the existence of 'objects', identical or similar things, things good or beautiful in themselves, or even the belief in the liberty of our will – if not from the perspective of life in its effort to preserve itself, from the point of view of an elementary strategy of the *conatus*? Indeed, the *conatus*'s priority is to discover equivalences and similitudes, and to order them according to what is useful and harmful for the body's survival.[35] The incapacity to distinguish the multiple differentiations of reality is, paradoxically from the perspective of truth but obviously from the perspective of life, a true force. Simplifying reality to the point of reducing it to a single Being, common to all beings, is to avoid the hesitations, dispersals and doubts of the mind, which are all dangers when facing the murderous flood of Nature. To affirm a useful error rather than to suspend judgement is the vital imperative of the *conatus*. Life begins and preserves itself by misosophy.[36]

2 Recognition, Useful Inadequate Knowledge

A product of the epigenetic activity of the *conatus*, the world is not only one of the things conceived as external and independent of the self. Body

---

[35] *Ethics* IV, App. ch. 27.

[36] Both the nature and the origin of language should be understood according to the same process of practical confusion and simplification operated by a complex body, albeit always in a limited way given the multiplicity of reality. Moreover, it is in the sphere of recognition that language inscribes itself in our memory. For an analysis of this question, see Laurent Bove, 'La théorie du langage chez Spinoza', *L'Enseignement philosophique*, 4, March–April 1991, pp. 16–33.

and mind are also conceived by the imagination as objects of the world. The practical simplification that we perform under the pressure of the multiplicity of reality, and which we also resist, we also apply against ourselves, against our own body and mind (its idea). In *Ethics* II, 40 Schol., this process is explained from the point of view of the limits of the capacity to be affected. This limitation must also be understood as a constitutive activity (of active resistance). The synthesis of recognition as practical knowledge, which is useful but not adequate (not to be confused with inadequate ideas of external things), is affirmed precisely because of this resistance.[37]

Being 'part of the infinite intellect of God', the human mind's inadequate idea is a partial idea that God itself has, 'not only insofar as he constitutes the nature of the human mind, but insofar as he also has the idea of another thing together with the human Mind'.[38] But the mind, as far as it imagines, does not know itself, does not adequately know its own body and its parts, or external bodies. Not adequately knowing them does not mean, however, that it has an inadequate idea of them. Indeed, how can one have an inadequate idea of that which one does not even have an idea? The mind does not have an idea of itself,[39] its own body, the parts of this body,[40] or of the external objects[41] as such; it only has the idea of the affections of its body from which it imagines external bodies, parts of its body, its body and itself.

It is in this sense that the act of imagining is an attitude of the mind itself, a 'contemplation'[42] or the 'manner' in which the human mind finds itself when it considers external bodies as present, via the ideas of the affections of its own body.[43] This 'manner' being the condition of a being-in-the-world, imagination is thereby defined as a perspective, a relation to a particular world, a 'way'[44] of dealing with it, of knowing and recognising it in the (affirmative and resistant) practice of our perseverance in being.

---

[37] 'Inadequate' knowledge: Gueroult proposes to use this to refer to 'knowledge that is neither an adequate idea nor an inadequate idea. For it is not a part of the adequate idea, but rather knowledge that is alien to the adequate knowledge involved in the inadequate ideas.' Martial Gueroult, *Spinoza, II: L'Ame*, Aubier, 1974, p. 279. This term is equivalent, for us, to that of recognition even if one can say that inadequate knowledge is itself the product of a recognition process.

[38] *Ethics* II, 11 Cor.; CWS I, 456.

[39] *Ethics* II, 23 Dem.

[40] *Ethics* II, 24.

[41] *Ethics* II, 26 Cor.

[42] *Ethics* II, 17 Schol.

[43] *Ethics* II, 26 Cor. Dem.

[44] *alia ratione*, which Appuhn translates as 'd'autres conditions [other manner, CWS I, 468]', can also be translated as 'other way'.

Imagination allows us to recognise what is useful or harmful 'even if [it does] not reproduce the [external] figures of things'.[45] In this sense, imagination is knowledge of objects, even if they are only fictitiously made present, though this fiction is necessary in the process of our perseverance. This knowledge is inadequate without being an inadequate idea of external things themselves, since it is not part of the adequate knowledge that God has of these things.[46] Indeed, this inadequate knowledge of external objects, of the body's parts, and of the body and the mind is not the knowledge of something real of the affections of which God has the true idea, as is the case with the idea (adequate or inadequate). Rather, it is knowledge of a phenomenon produced from the connection of affections by Habit.[47] This does not mean that external bodies do not exist and that we cannot adequately know them. Instead, it means that bodies, as we imagine them, are constructions of the mind in its imaginative relationship to the world (these imaginative constructions being themselves expressions of the relation of the body with the external world).

This activity of the mind which Spinoza calls 'knowledge', while different from the (adequate or inadequate) idea, is the very process of recognition.[48] Recognition of objects is, in a certain way, knowledge (and useful knowledge in the practical realm of perseverance in being). But it is not an 'idea' of object, even if it involves the formation of the imaginative idea (and of the designation) of the external thing it claims to know. Recognition and adequate knowledge radically exclude each other. They do not have, we might say, the same object: 'Insofar as the Mind imagines external bodies, it does not have adequate knowledge of them',[49] nor, we add, does it have its inadequate idea. The object of common sense contemplated by the mind – and the product of this contemplation – is not the object of true and adequate knowledge. For the mind, knowing is identified with the idea when this knowledge is adequate, when it is no longer mere knowledge (or recognition) of something, but rather knowledge of the common properties in the second

---

[45] *Ethics* II, 17 Schol.; *CWS* I, 465. Translation modified.
[46] This inadequate knowledge is, however, *also* an inadequate idea of the affections of our body.
[47] Inadequate knowledge of the object dealing with an appearance is not, therefore, an inadequate idea either of the real external object as such or of the appearance of which it is the knowledge. But as reality (mode of the substance), appearance (object of recognition) is necessarily accompanied, in God, by its adequate idea (which then involves a theory of perception).
[48] *Ethics* II, 24, 25; *CWS* I, 431.
[49] *Ethics* II, 26 Cor.; *CWS* I, 470.

kind of knowledge or of singular essences (that are not objects) in the third kind of knowledge. Knowledge of something as an 'object' is but recognition, representation of a thing, in relationship to a determinate time and place.

We know that 'the human Mind does not know the human Body'[50] and that, therefore, it 'does not know itself'.[51] The mind is indeed the idea (or adequate knowledge) of the human body[52] defined according to a certain proportion of motion-and-rest or a capacity to be affected. But God 'has' this idea of the body insofar as it is affected by another idea of singular body, which is itself affected by another body, and so on, to infinity;[53] or insofar as God is affected by infinitely many bodies on which the very existence of the human body (of which the mind is the idea) depends.[54] Spinoza concludes from this that the knowledge God 'has' of the human body is not an idea that the mind – though idea of the body – 'has', and therefore the mind does not know the human body the way God knows it, but only according to this body's affections.[55]

The idea of the body by which it 'is' in God is nothing from the standpoint of the mind that only knows its own body, and itself, through some affections. If this idea is nothing for the mind, however, there is still in the mind a correlative activity to the body's capacity to be affected according to its specific proportion of motion-and-rest, its essence as an intensity of power (*puissance*). But this activity or capacity only makes sense in actions (*in actu*), for a mind that is also the idea, or more precisely the imaginative idea, of a living body (or the idea of the connection of affections operated by Habit). Indeed this connection is only possible under the specific proportion of motion-and-rest (known only to God), the mind can perceive its body empirically only according to the 'unity' of the confused image of the connection of affections. The connection of affections prompted by Habit and constitutive of the organic body, according to the very law of this individual body (its specific proportion of motion-and-rest), is thus perceived by the mind as a 'thing' or 'object'. The imaginative mind conveys the connection of the affections and the affects associated with this connection to its own body, just as it would do with a real, external and present object.[56] This action of the imaginative mind – applied to the mind's recognition of

---

[50] *Ethics* II, 19 Dem.; CWS I, 467.
[51] *Ethics* II, 23 Dem.; CWS I, 468.
[52] *Ethics* II, 13; CWS I, 457.
[53] *Ethics* II, 9; CWS I, 453.
[54] *Ethics* II, 13, Post. 4.
[55] *Ethics* II, 23 and Dem.
[56] *Ethics* II, 17 Schol.; CWS I, 465.

external bodies and of its own body as objects in the world – constitutes the synthesis of recognition.

This synthesis supposes a concordant operation of the associative activities of the subject on a reality that is presumed to be the same. This reality is identified as an object when every particular action (Habit, memory, causal intelligence) determines that its own data is identical to that of all the other actions concerning it. This concordant activity, which the tradition calls a 'faculty', is in fact nothing other than the ordering activity of the *conatus* in the mode of imagination.

Notice the different uses Spinoza makes of the terms 'knowledge' and 'idea' in *Ethics* II, 24 and 25. The 'knowledge' the mind 'has' is different from the 'idea' it has. The first is used by Spinoza to mean the mind's representation of a thing as an 'object', in recognition, without it having an 'idea' of this thing.[57] So, the mind represents its own body and external bodies as objects (imagined through the idea of affections connected to its own body), but does not know what they are in themselves. The mind therefore does not, in truth, perceive them. And neither does it have an idea of them, this idea being only in God.[58] The external body, represented as an object by the mind, cannot – and never will – be adequately known by it.[59] This is simply because the body is not the real object of which God has the idea and which the mind could know, according to its properties (in the second kind of knowledge) or according to its singular essence (in the third kind of knowledge). The object represented according to a determinate time and place, therefore, is not the object of knowledge, but only of practical recognition. This object does not, therefore, express reality as it is, but only as it appears to us. The object the mind represents and recognises, in sum, is not the one it can know. They are not the same objects, even if it is through the encounter with the real object that the mind is able to represent another object to itself, according to its capacity of recognition in the effort it makes to affirm the existence – and thereby the perseverance – of its own body.

What we can say of the external body as representation can also be said of our own body: 'The idea of any affection of the human body does not involve adequate knowledge of the human body itself'[60] but only, we add, its

---

[57] *Mens humana partium, Corpus humanum componentium adaequatam cognitionem non involvit. Ethics* II, 24; and *Ethics* II, 25: *Idea cujuscunque affectionis Corporis humani adaequatam corporis externi cognitionem non involvit.* CWS I, 468–9.

[58] Gueroult, *Spinoza, II: L'Ame*, esp. pp. 270–1.

[59] *Ethics* II, 26 Cor.

[60] *Ethics* II, 27; CWS I, 470.

'recognition'. The *body I* represented as an object by its mind is not the *body A* of which God has the idea.⁶¹ There is, properly speaking, no idea of *body I* since there is only: 1) an idea of *body A* that God 'has' and which the mind 'is'; 2) ideas of *body A*'s affections that the mind 'has'; 3) a feeling of *body A* that the mind 'has'.⁶² *Body I*, represented as an object by its mind, is, therefore, 'inadequate knowledge' without a corresponding 'idea' (other than the adequate one of the process of the production of appearance as such). This is so because *body I* exists only as a representation (even if this representation reveals the state of a real *body A*, of which we can have an idea, outside of any representation, through affections; then, however, it is a process other than that of inadequate knowledge or recognition). The represented body is not, properly speaking, the (adequate or inadequate) 'idea' of the real body. It is, rather, its sign or symptom (and the name given to this body will be the sign of a sign).

The knowledge I have of my body indicates its present state but does not express it necessarily. What difference is there, then, between the idea of Peter that constitutes the essence of Peter's mind and the knowledge Peter has of himself? The first idea expresses the essence of Peter's body directly and involves existence only as long as Peter exists. The knowledge that Peter has of himself, on the other hand, speaks to the state of Peter's body more than to the nature of Peter. Indeed, the idea that God 'has' of Peter adequately expresses the nature or essence of Peter (or of the body of Peter), whereas the knowledge that Peter 'has' of Peter only refers to the state of his own body. Peter is, in relationship to himself, or to his own body, therefore, in a position that is like Paul's in relationship to Peter's body.⁶³ For both, the idea of Peter's body is symptomatic of the state of the body from which this idea unfolds. The idea we have of our body is, therefore, intrinsically connected to the state of this body. This idea we have of our body is not the adequate knowledge of this state, which can only be elaborated according to another state of the body (superior in power). '[T]he cause why we have only a completely confused knowledge of our Body' is, Spinoza explains in *Ethics* II, 13 Schol., that the body, of which the mind is the idea, is globally in a heteronomous regime. On the contrary

> in proportion as a Body is more capable than others of doing many things at once, or being acted on in many ways at once, so its mind is more

---

⁶¹ *Ethics* II, 19 Dem.
⁶² *Ethics* II, 13 Ax. 4; *Ethics* II, 13 Cor.
⁶³ *Ethics* II, 17 Schol.; CWS I, 464–5.

capable than others of perceiving many things at once. And in proportion as the actions of a body depend more on itself alone, and as other bodies concur with it less in acting, so its mind is more capable of understanding distinctly.[64]

The only advantage Peter has over Paul is that Peter cannot be mistaken about the present and actual existence of his body. Whereas the existence of external things (despite their affirmation in the imaginative idea) remains problematic, the existence of one's own body is involved in the very perception of the mind's affects. The mind cannot perceive its affects without perceiving the body itself as existing. The existence of one's own body is therefore, for the mind, a feeling and 'the human Body exists as we are aware of it'.[65] This feeling that the mind has of its own body precedes any 'representation' of this body as an object. The sense we have of our own body therefore guarantees the existence of the object to a representation that remains, however, confused as to the nature of this object.

Another correlative consequence of the general law stated in *Ethics* II, 13 *Schol.*: the body's state in an autonomous regime would allow the mind to have an adequate idea of its affections (second kind of knowledge) or of its own singular essence (third kind of knowledge). In this case, the adequate idea expresses the nature or essence of the body, while indicating its state (here superior in power). In the third kind of knowledge, the state of the body tends to correspond to its nature (or essence), tends to become fully expressive and/or strategically perfect. This reveals the goal and means of the ethical project,

> [a striving especially such that] the infant's Body may change (as much as its nature allows and assists) into another, capable of a great many things and related to a Mind very much conscious of itself, of God, and of things. We strive, that is, that whatever is related to its memory or imagination is of hardly any moment in relation to the intellect.[66]

This is the path of transcending, through the adequate idea (and the active affection of extension to which it corresponds), the 'all too human' problematic of the recognition-constitution of the object.

---

[64] *Ethics* II, 13 Schol.; CWS I, 572.
[65] *Ethics* II, 13 Cor.; CWS I, 457.
[66] *Ethics* V, 39 Schol.; CWS I, 614.

3 Theory of the Practical Subject

We recognise external bodies, as well as our own bodies, as objects through the same process of recognition as inadequate knowledge, through the representation of an external object as present. But it is also from the same process that the mind has inadequate knowledge of itself. We can indeed read in Ethics II, 29:[67] 'The idea of the idea of any affection of the human body does not involve adequate knowledge of the human Mind.' We know that the knowledge the mind 'has' of its own body is not the adequate idea of this body as possessed by God. But we also know that this knowledge is only the recognition of the body as an object, in and through the mind's representation. The mind does not 'have' the (adequate or inadequate) idea that it 'is', but only inadequate knowledge of itself: it 'does not know itself' as Ethics II, 13 Schol. already stated. The mind is, therefore, only recognising itself as an object, according to a knowledge that is independent from its idea.

In relationship to external bodies or to one's own body, the recognised object benefits, in representation, from specific attributes that are those of a 'subject': she thinks, doubts, conceives, affirms, negates, imagines, senses, remembers, decides and wants. We must note, if we take Spinoza's text strictly literally, that the notion of a subject is reduced to the simple and very general imputative function: that is, the scholastic use of *subjectum* (*hupokeímenon*) in the sense of 'support' (*in eodem subjecto* as we can read in Ethics III, 5). A subject is but a 'simple mode of thinking' by which we 'compare things with one another', and whose only (pragmatic) use is to ease the indispensable work of imagination and memory, as we could already read in the *Cogitata Metaphysica*.[68] In the *Tractatus Theologico-Politicus*, the notion of a subject certainly has its own legitimate order of application: the political domain. In its semantic tension with 'citizen' (*civis*), a 'subject' (*subditius*), when we think of the questions of obedience and law, becomes a real theoretical concept in the field of political representation: *sed obtemperantia subditum facit*.[69] But this subject is not the one we are interested in here.

Reduced to a simple mode of imagining, or circumscribed by the realm of the political representation of obedience, at first the subject appears to play no major role in Spinozist philosophy. Yet the knowledge (even imaginative) that we have of ourselves is also immediately, in an experience, that of a subject capable of knowing and of knowing herself, and of judging of

---

[67] CWS I, 470. Translator's note.
[68] CM I, 5.
[69] TTP XVII; CWS II, 297.

what is useful to her. This acknowledgement of the self by the self would be pure abstraction if we did not understand ourselves, prior to anything else, as singular beings insofar as we desire something. But human beings, as beings of desires, always act towards an end: the useful thing they desire. And this teleology is, as we have already said, an effective structure of the human 'subject's' behaviour, even if it must itself be explained according to efficient causes. When Spinoza writes in *Ethics* I, App. that '[humans] act always on account of an end, viz. on account of their advantage, which they want',[70] he posits the existence of a telic and desiring structure for human activity. In so doing, he posits the form of an *in actu* subjectivity and its essentially practical nature – a form that is itself an effect since subjective teleology is explained in *Ethics* III by the loving logic whose causes are strictly efficient. Its essence is a practical one, since the final causes that the human subject pursues are affective, religious, aesthetic, moral, political and ethical. The subject is effect, which is to say, she is action. And, like every action, she is regulated by causes[71] that she ignores for the most part (which is why she believes in free will).[72]

What accounts for the particularity of subjective activity, however, is that it is determined, as effect, to unfold intentionally. And this, far from being an illusion, is a real modality of human nature and actions. God is the cause of human 'act and intention', as Spinoza writes to G. de Blijenbergh regarding crime and the *intentio Neronis*.[73] This subjective structure of action belongs to extraordinarily complex individuals[74] capable of memory and imagination; and this intentional process is immediately identified with the recognitive logic of loving desire, in which we find the very constitution of practical subjectivity and its own mode of knowledge as recognition. The subject acting according to an end is defined in the following way. On the one hand, it is defined by the two principles of association: contracting habits, forging memory and seeking joy (correlative to a principle of utility). On the other hand, she is also the one in and for whom these two principles operate, and also the one by whom they are used according to the problematic of means and ends (under the determination of causes that remain essentially hidden to her).

---

[70] CWS I, 440.
[71] *Ethics* I, 28.
[72] *Ethics* I, App.; CWS I, 440; *Ethics* III, 2 Schol.; CWS I, 496–7; *Ep.* LVIII [to G. H. Schuller]; CWS II, 428.
[73] *Ep.* XXIII [to Blijenbergh]; CWS I, 368.
[74] *Ethics* II, 17 Cor. Dem.; CWS I, 464.

We see, with this definition, that the notion of practical subject transcends the mind–body distinction, which the imaginative mind produces when it considers itself as a subject. The inadequate self-knowledge that the mind has of itself as a subject is entirely illusory when it attributes only to the intellect what is also an activity of the body. With this notion of the practical subject, we wish to underline the effect of perseverance in being, specific to a particular level of complexity of bodies. A human being who always acts according to her advantage – and consciously so[75] – also permanently strives to seize the law of image association to serve this end, by virtue of determinations of which she is not conscious. This striving, far from harming the law of her own nature, as Spinoza remarks in *TTP* IV,[76] gives it greater reach, illuminated by knowledge. The consciousness that humans have of their utility is admittedly largely illusory and dominated by inadequate ideas. Nevertheless, a practical subject who is essentially strategic is constituted according to the law of association. And this is as true of the ignorant as much as of the philosopher who strives to 'conceive [of] a correct principle of living, or sure maxims of life'.[77]

In imagination, ideas are connected by chance encounters, but always necessarily according to these three constant principles: contiguity, resemblance and causality (constancy or regularity, through which an individual can effectively persevere in being, or at least in its state). One could be surprised to see causality next to contiguity and resemblance, explicitly designated by Spinoza as the paths by which the law of association[78] is achieved. The reason for this is that the causal relation, as a law of association determined by reason, is itself the expression of the body in its effort to persevere in being at a higher complexity. How does this new type of connection of a causal nature come to be?

According to the necessity of the joy (or utility) principle, we know that a human being comes to love by joining her Joy to 'the idea of an external cause' (*Amor est Laetitia, concomitante idea causae externae*). The external thing, the object of our love, is, therefore, simultaneous with its discovery as a thing, a desirable thing, which is also acknowledged as the 'cause' of our 'satisfaction'. The world is made causal (*causalisé*) at the same time as it is thing-ified (*chosifié*) and given value (*valué*). The emergence of an external

---

[75] *Ethics* I App.; CWS I, 440.
[76] *TTP* IV; CWS II, 126.
[77] Translator's note: that she will commit to memory, along with their positive consequences. *Ethics* V, 10 Schol.; CWS I, 601.
[78] *Ethics* II, 18 and Schol.; *Ethics* III, 15 Schol., 16; *TTP* IV; CWS II, 149.

world of things is also, for us, an immediate temporal and anthropocentric order of determinations of these things. A 'cause' is intrinsically also a 'thing': a useful or harmful, lovable or detestable thing. But this presupposes an external thing (independent in space) that is anterior in temporality to the being on which it produces its effect. So, the causal relation attributes to our affects and actions a 'signification' constitutive of a world order. Because a thing is designated as the cause of a Joy (effect), always renewed and amplified by its presence,[79] we strive effectively to seek it out. That is, we make use of different means to this end. Thus, according to a truly causal principle (inherent in the temporal recognition-constitution of the object), our *conatus*, under the form of imagination, is determined as a loving subject who strives to seek the thing loved, through the same path. Indeed, the 'satisfaction in the lover on account of the presence of the thing loved' becomes the goal of the action as well as its motivation.[80]

In this appears the link between the subject's action (as necessarily finalised) and the causal relation. The latter is both constitutive of the subject as a determination of the imagination and the means of its own action. For the subject, to act is to arrange means towards an end, to generate 'causes' towards consequences presumed necessary. The causal relation is involved in every action we undertake in and on the world. But we undertake these actions because we seek goals that appear to be good and useful to our *conatus*. Through love (but, really, are any deeds not loving?) we want to 'join [ourselves] to the thing loved', to the thing that is useful to us ... and no matter whether this thing is really useful to us or not.

What we want to show here is that:

1. The subject, constituted by the joy principle and causation (involved in recognition), finds in love its teleological structure, and determines her goals and means by those same principles, and thereby commits herself to action.
2. The very unity of the subject in her teleological structure is constituted according to this necessary alliance between the joy principle in Habit and the causal principle in recognition.
3. This subject is essentially loving and also essentially strategic; the affect determines her intention and the development of her action.

---

[79] *Ethics* III, DA 6 Exp.
[80] *per voluntatem me Acquiescentiam intelligere, quae est in amante ob rei amatae praesentiam a qua Laetitia amantis corroboratur, aut saltem fovetur. Ethics* III, DA 6 Exp.; CWS I, 533.

4. The temporal differentiation of the subject and object allows the human subject to partly escape the 'appetite for joy' without 'regard for the future' (dominant in animals and 'barbarians').[81] In humans, the joy principle is thereby displaced in and by the subject's capacity to represent things (and herself) in time. These things are themselves evaluated only in this representation – and, at its core, according to the desire that draws us to them. For the human subject, the joy of representation dominates the immediate joy of the senses. And we can say, this tendency – according to which (as Spinoza also writes) animal and human Desire necessarily differ, even if they are both driven by a desire to procreate[82] – is characteristic of the desiring human subject. This primacy of representation allows us to distinguish an additional characteristic: compared with animals, naturally adjusted to what is useful to them (*a priori* adjustment that puzzles and amazes the ignorant), humans seem, on the contrary, naturally (natively) unadjusted (*in-ajusté*), 'powerless', Spinoza notes. This explains the multiplicity and versatility of the paths of adjustment in and through recognitive-representation through which human imagination moves, according to the singular histories and affective fluctuations specific to each.[83] There are, indeed, as many species of object as there are human desires that covet them. The same reality sees its figures multiplied according to its number of contenders, but also according to the *fluctuatio animi* of any one human. The capacity of the human subject to maintain an abundance of images is both a sign of the power of her singular imagination (at the origin of the difference in languages, laws, cultures and nations, as we learn in *TTP* XVII),[84] and a sign of the relative fragility of her perseverance. The reflexive strategy of the loving subject is condemned to fatal illusions: to chase the image of a good where there is evil and ultimately death. This is due to a relatively autonomous imagination *vis-à-vis* external reality that constitutes, for the subject, the object-cause of her desire in a hallucinatory way. Under these conditions (the primacy of representation, the existential un-adjustment of desire, the relative autonomy of imagination), the ethical project will be, first, under the imperative of reason, a project of disillusionment for the loving subject. But this supposes a better

---

[81] *TTP* V; *CWS* II, 143.
[82] *Ethics* III, 57 Schol.
[83] *Ethics* III, 57.
[84] *CWS* II, 316.

reflexivity that reflects on the nature of the reflexivity and on the volition of the practical subject, both of which are functional.
5. Finally, while it is the subject of recognition, the human subject is not a subject of knowledge. Although she is a practical subject, she is not the subject of praxis in that she only reflects, according to her own structures, an action of which she is herself only the result, and in relation to which, regarding this action's effects, she is on the receiving end. Essentially strategic (arranging means according to an end), the practical subject is herself the consequence of a strategy, without principle or end, which goes beyond and determines her: the strategy of the mathematical necessity of life, in its absolute affirmation in each of its singular affections.

The *conatus* – in the figure of imagination, determined by the body's associative principles (Habit, the joy principle, memory) and the mind's associative principles (recognition, causality)[85] – is 'human nature'. The strategic subject and human nature are, therefore, one and the same thing: a determined, desiring activity, that seeks Joy, that finds and applies means towards this end. Adequate knowledge (of which she is not the producer) is among the means the subject has. How is she led to make use of it? And under which conditions does the adequate idea generate a higher level of subjectivity?

As a strategic subject, the subject is compelled to think (though we should say that it is in fact thought that compels her, since the strategic subject takes shape as ethical subject through the pressures of a knowledge process that is different from that of recognition). As shown at the beginning of *TdIE*, the natural resistance she puts up against any and all sadness forces her to think, according to this minimal – but oh so precious – Joy (which is also resisting, though passively).[86] We find the real matters of life and death at the very heart of this active resistance. In and through her joyful resistance to sadness, the subject encounters the very affirmation of life. This affirmation forces her to think and gives thought its force. The strategic subject can become ethical subject through this vital necessity, by virtue of forces that go through her and follow a knowledge process that is different from that of recognition. The subject is, therefore, determined as ethico-strategic reason when her action comes from the true knowledge of relations or of proportions between things (which are different from the

---

[85] Translator's note: causality, causation and causal principle are used as synonyms.
[86] *Ethics* III, 37 Dem.; *Ethics* II, 13; CWS I, 515, 457.

objects identified by habitual perception): according to what Spinoza calls 'common notions'.[87]

According to the knowledge of the intrinsic relations between things (different from the extrinsic relations of the common order of Nature),[88] common notions express the very structure of reality and thereby make it possible to know what actually agrees with my body and mind. To be sure, because of the joy principle and according to imaginative information, the strategic subject was already striving to select and recognise the things whose encounters brought the most Joy. A strategic reason had already been recognised in this activity; but it was merely its (non-critical, unethical) reduction – functional, instrumental, calculating, in short, still animal. For, 'after we know the origin of the mind, we cannot in any way doubt that the lower animals feel things'.[89]

But, with our first common notions comes a practical displacement of our love, corresponding to the theoretical displacement of our knowledge of things. By striving to understand the agreement between our body and external bodies, we enter a territory yet unknown to our love: the territory of truth. When this happens, we experience other affects of Joy, which, adequately bound to truth as their cause, will make of truth the new object of our desire and, thus, of our love. We can even say, from the point of view of the subject, that truth – as object of desire – gives meaning and value to existence (meaning and value that it does not have, we must say, in itself, but only within the representation of the loving subject). As Spinoza writes in the beginning of *TdIE*, 'love toward the eternal and infinite thing feeds the mind with a joy entirely exempt from sadness. This is greatly to be desired, and to be sought with all our strength.'[90]

Thus begins another adventure, one that changes the very status of the subject involved. In recognition, the practical subject is defined according to a reflexivity and a will that are essentially functional – or at least that tend, according to the *conatus*'s strategy, towards a perfect functionality. The truth of the practical subject is its perfect automation or adaptation to its conditions of existence. Reflection, logical thinking, the search for causes are contained in the human subject's complete lack of knowledge about herself. By the very functionality of the practical subject, reason is reduced to instrumental use and to the calculation of probabilities. The subject is, thus, a

---

[87] *Ethics* II, 40 Schol. 2; CWS I, 478.
[88] *Ethics* II, 29 Schol.; CWS I, 471.
[89] *Ethics* III, 57 Schol.; CWS I, 528.
[90] CWS I, 9.

kind of automaton, and the consciousness she has of herself is a fundamental illusion (or unconsciousness). Reflexivity takes place in a strategic logic that is animal-like (in behaviour and in thought) and that is itself non-reflexive.

The constitutive reflexivity of ethical subjectivity, that is, a truly human subjectivity, is a reflection of this initial thoughtless functional thinking. It is a critical reflexivity that is only made possible through the change that the adequate knowledge of oneself as a practical and strategic subject allows. Ethical subjectivity *par excellence* arises from the adequate idea that one can have of herself, both as a power of imagination (constitutive of the world, in inadequate knowledge) and as an automaton-subject. This is really, at a greater level of complexity, only an extension of the animal logic of adaptation. By recognising the functional (and we will see later, social) automation of the animal in herself, the practical subject can lucidly become a strategic ethical subject (and the free subject of a free society). This implies a change in the meaning of recognitive activity. For the ethical subject, recognition, which is the constitutive imaginary activity of reality, is known as such. Recognition is known as a human being's creative ability to constitute its own world through representation. The capacity to imagine, through adequate knowledge of what it is and what it produces, can reach, in some areas of human activity (we will later see its importance in the political realm), an autonomy equivalent to the adequate idea to which it corresponds: 'absolute' and 'perfect'. Thus, Spinoza can write at the end of *Ethics* II, 17 Schol.:

> For if the Mind, while it imagined nonexistent things as present to it, at the same time knew that those things did not exist, it would, of course, attribute this power of imagining to a virtue of its nature, not to a vice – especially if this faculty of imagining depended only on its own nature, i.e. (by ID7), if the Mind's faculty of imagining were free.[91]

To conclude, let us emphasise that the strategic subject as human reason (desiring truth, loving truth) is nonetheless determined by the joy principle and the finalist structure behind it. In adequate knowledge, however, she circumvents recognition. Or rather, the production of true knowledge develops itself in her presence, even if, as a practical subject, she is determined to use adequate knowledge that she has not herself produced. This practical relationship of the subject to adequate knowledge is not without problems. The idea, even adequate, cut off from its production process and recognised as truth by the subject (according to the mechanisms of memory), is no

---

[91] CWS I, 465.

more than an imaginative idea or, more seriously, a dogma. The subject needs not only to guard herself against inadequate ideas and the inadequate knowledge that she takes from these inadequate ideas, but also against her inadequate knowledge of the adequate ideas themselves (thus transformed into inadequate ideas, conclusions without premises). In and through this caution, a specifically human subjectivity can be affirmed and maintained, a real reflection (which is not mere calculation) and an authentic project (ethical and, we will see, political) that is not merely our lust's chosen prey. For the human individual, this is the crux of the journey from automation to autonomy. We will return to these intrinsic difficulties of the human mind since, on the one hand, 'we can hardly understand anything of which the imagination does not form some image from a trace',[92] and since, on the other hand, the mind would be helpless without memory.[93]

As a subject, the strategic *conatus* is an effort which, by virtue of the joy (or utility) principle joined to an external cause, becomes a project, an organisation of means to an end. This behaviour, whose essence is love, is determined by two types of associative principles: *with the first kind of knowledge* (imaginative knowledge), associations of Habit or memory are extrinsic in nature and carried out practically, according to the rules of likeness, contiguity and causation; *with the second kind of knowledge* (following reason), associations are intrinsic in nature: they are true theoretical concepts through which the structures of reality are truly known.

In the first case, the practical behaviour of the subject is determined by inadequate knowledge (object recognition) and/or inadequate (truncated) ideas that are only clues, through the mediation of our own bodies, of our practice of existence. In the second case, the behaviour of the subject is determined by an adequate idea *of* the practice (that is, the encounters of one's body with other bodies). It is not determined by a symptom (not conscious of itself as a symptom) that indicates the state of the body in and through the encounter more than it explains the causes and effects of the conformities, differences or oppositions between bodies. From this point of view, there is only one (practical) dimension of the imaginative subject, but human reason has two aspects: *theoretical*, as adequate thought of the structures of reality; and *practical*, as action adjusted to the adequately known reality.

It is not knowledge, however, that urges us to act. We strive to know because we want the Joy we experienced through acting to continue, deepen and perfect itself. Passive joys alert us, by chance encounter, to our body's

---

[92] *Ep.* XVII [to P. Balling]; *CWS* I, 353; *CM* I, 1; *CWS* I, 300.
[93] *Ethics* III, 2 Schol.; *CWS* I, 497.

agreement with another body. They cause us to think of this agreement, and thus to discover the Joy of true knowledge and its consequences, which are useful and joyful when living under the command of reason. But human reason, as the desire for truth, is also the strategic use of this truth within the historical conditions of a determinate place and time: an 'epoch', as Spinoza writes in the last lines of the *Short Treatise*. Human reason combines truth and utility, the pursuit of one's own advantage.[94] Human reason is the *conatus* itself insofar as it has ideas that are both true and useful, true forces of and for perseverance, from the standpoint of the structure of the subject. The subject seeks the true idea as her advantage and makes it the object of her supreme desire and love. The joy principle, which discovered in truth the *optimum* object of satisfaction, becomes human reason.

The logic of the laws of imagination leads from Habit to recognition. But this logic still involves an abstraction, because it leaves aside the relationship, itself constitutive, that necessarily unites an individual to others according to the laws of imitation. Human reality is immediately collective reality, and the question of ethical strategy must be presented on this basis. This needs to be solved from a knowledge of the spontaneous strategy of the mode whose ethical strategy is both its ('adequate' or adjusted) pursuit of happiness (because everyone, whatever they do, wants to be happy) and radical criticism (due to the inevitable failure of the spontaneous strategy).

---

[94] *Ethics* IV, 24, 28, 68.

3

Conatus as a Strategy of Self Love

1 *Conatus* as Imitation and the Ambition for Domination

> If we imagine a thing like us, toward which we have had no affect, to be affected with some affect, we are thereby affected with a like affect.[1]

When we imagine the joy or sadness of those like us, the succession of images of their affections (induced by Habit) in (and through) our body is immediately 'our' joy or sadness, by virtue of the vitalising or depleting movement of active power (*puissance*) it provokes in us. Imitation is a real identification through which we immediately feel what we perceive in a quasi-osmotic way:

> If someone flees because he sees others flee or is timid because he sees others timid, or, because he sees that someone else has burned his hand, withdraws his own hand and moves his body as if his hand were burned, we shall say that he imitates the other's affect.[2]

We participate naturally (according to a true law of nature) in the feelings of others like us. Our body, by attuning to the nature of the thing it imagines, is spontaneously in unison with all its affective fluctuations, and thus becomes one and the same body with what it imagines. At this collective level of the constitution of humankind as a body, imitation plays a role in connecting affections that is equivalent to the role of Habit for the individual body.

---

[1] *Ethics* III, 27; CWS I, 508.
[2] *Ethics* III DA 33 Exp.; CWS I, 539.

The immediacy of imitation is, however, only apparent. There is always necessarily a difference (even if minimal) between the model and its imitation. The body of the imitator (which Spinoza also calls the emulator) could not do any particular thing if it did not have the mnesic trace of the model from which the action can be determined. The body is memory.[3] It is by virtue of Habit that the body's ability to be affected forms the connection of affections-images, their particular contents '[modes that actually exist. . .] that involve the nature of the external body'.[4] To imitate is to remember,[5] even if this memory, like the resulting imitation, is not recognised as such (as memories and imitations). For Spinoza, the dynamic of imitation is, short of being a representation, an activity of *conatus*-Habit, certainly, but one that is prior to any memory (understood as reflected consciousness of time) as well as to any object recognition. The dynamic of imitation can, however, be understood within the logic of the spontaneous strategy of the *conatus*, in that it is organisational in its consequences.

The dynamic of imitation is organisational in two senses: first, it always imposes an order (even if it is a decomposing order). To imagine is always to imagine an order, and so to imitate is always to imitate an order, a sequence of affections. But this order or sequence is imagined by us in as much as it consists of Habit's connections.[6] When we identify ourselves with something, therefore, it is only ever with some connections made by Habit. Identifying with Peter is, for example, to identify not with the nature of Peter, but with the state of our own body (the order and nature of its affections) corresponding to our encounter with Peter. Second, the dynamic of imitation is generative, due to the unity it creates between humans of a new individual that Spinoza calls 'humanity'. This dynamic grounds the constitution of a social body (which precedes the formation of a 'civil society', that is, governed by a common legal organisation)[7] – a *conatus* that has its own duration, its own depletion and vitalisation of power, its own joys and sorrows expressive of its constitution. Like Habit, it is not yet that of a reflected historical order of time, but one immediately felt in 'an indefinite continuation of existing'.[8] Despite its submission to the desires or feelings of others, imitation is also an activ-

---

[3] *Ethics* II, 13 Post. 5 and Ax. 1–2 Post. Lem 3.
[4] *Ethics* II, 17 Dem.; CWS I, 463.
[5] *Ethics* III, 2 Schol.; CWS I, 497.
[6] *Ethics* II, 17 Schol.
[7] *TP* III, 1.
[8] *Ethics* II, Def. 5; CWS I, 447. Translator's note.

ity of the bodies that tend to agree with each other when they imagine themselves as similar.

However, the spontaneous dynamic of imitation based on Habit's associations is independent from the joy principle. Any affect, even of sadness, is immediately imitated. If it involves a depletion of active power, it is also immediately fought by the *conatus* as the joy principle.[9] It is in this sense that joy – like sadness – provides the first strategic data that guide the dynamism of the *conatus*. The *conatus* goes towards an object to perpetuate, even amplify, a joy, or turns away from it if it causes it sadness. Proposition 29 introduces the mediation of the gaze of those like us whom we strive to please, which now structures desire in a triangular figuration whose points are the desiring subject, the object of satisfaction for other humans, the gaze of others.

> We shall strive [*etiam*] to do also whatever we imagine men to look on with Joy, and on the other hand, we shall be averse to doing what we imagine men are averse to.[10]

Though it introduces a new parameter for understanding the economy of human desire[11] based on the imitation of what is similar, this proposition nevertheless continues the logic of the joy principle set forth in proposition 28, realising paths already drawn out. In the quest for what is most useful to her, each naturally tends to conform to the models established by those like her. We strive to make present everything that we imagine leads to joy; we strive to do 'also' (*etiam*) everything we imagine humans will regard with joy. The individual *conatus* is thus determined by the global *conatus* of the social body in which it participates, building it through imitation. Like the constitution of the individual body through Habit, the joy principle steers the dynamism of the *conatus* as imitation for the social body, and

---

[9] See *Ethics* III, DA 18, 24, 25 and Prop. 27 Schol. Cor. 3.
[10] *Ethics* III, 29; CWS I, 510. Translator's note.
[11] 1) Because I imagine that something is like me, I feel what (I imagine) it experiences (even if that something is not a human being). 2) Because I imagine that something that is really like me (that is, another human being) experiences an affect, I feel what (I imagine) she experiences as a human being. Imagination, then, is always 'human' imagination, whether I am imagining the joy of an animal or that of another human being. But if it is really another human being, my imagination immediately adapts to the nature of what it imagines (Adam was certainly able to imitate animals by imagining them to be like him, *Ethics* IV, 68 Schol., but human lust is nevertheless different from that of the animal, *Ethics* III, 57 Schol.).

thereby subjects the multiple individual *conatus* to its models. In imitation, we immediately conform to those behaviours that cause joy to others and refrain from those that cause them sadness. Imitation is immediate, and yet it implies a reference to the object providing satisfaction to those who are like us, and thus the formation of a collective memory. A joy results from these actions, which, on the one hand, results from our active participation in the global *conatus* as an active power. On the other hand, our own joy results from the joy in our actions experienced by those we regard to be like us. We identify with this joy, even without consciousness of ourselves as its cause.[12]

In a passionate state, however, 'there is nothing [. . .] which, by the agreement of all, is good or evil'.[13] The only way to realise a joy common to all is through reason. Only through reason do humans agree in nature, such that they can be Gods to one another.[14] In a community of sages, the imitations of active affects (which correspond to the active connection of affects through Habit) essentially form the social body. The global *conatus* of this community and of the individuals who form it is, then, in an autonomous arrangement, in which each has become a true 'God' for the other: a source of life and supreme satisfaction that transcends the affirmation of one's power to live, understand and enjoy indefinitely.

In the ordinary condition of helplessness and ignorance, however, the imitating human can only imagine ways of fulfilling joy according to a necessarily restricted model, relative to a specific time and place. Common opinion forms this model, the particular prejudices of a nation and its particular 'mores'.[15] We thus imitate and strive to please the vulgar. Spinoza calls this desire 'ambition':

> This striving to do something (and also to omit doing something) solely to please [others] is called Ambition, especially when we strive so eagerly to please the people that we do or omit certain things to our own injury, or another's.[16]

The particular complexion of one's body, even in a powerless state, does not reduce a human to the satisfactions of partaking in a community, or of

---

[12] *Ethics* III DA 24.
[13] *Ethics* IV, 37 Schol. 2; CWS I, 567.
[14] *Ethics* IV, 35 Cor. 2 Schol.
[15] *TTP* XVII; CWS II, 316.
[16] *Ethics* III, 29 Schol.; CWS I, 510.

identifying with a common joy. She also recognises herself as cause of the joy of other humans, and hence, as first cause of her own satisfaction,[17] in the self-consciousness she comes to through the affections that determine her to act.[18] The subject discovers herself as self-loving by attributing her joy to herself as to an inner cause. Spinoza calls the feeling experienced in this love 'glory', when mediated by the praises of others. Conversely, when we imagine ourselves to be the cause of the blame and sadness of others, he calls it 'shame', which becomes our own sadness.[19] The ambition that spontaneously leads us to do what others consider with joy and to abstain from what they hate is, therefore, an ambition of glory.[20] Glory is, for Spinoza, self-love[21] (called *philautia* or *acquiescentia in se ipso* in Ethics III, 55 Schol.) when it is defined not solely by the consideration of our own active power, which already derives from a form of self-contentment,[22] but according to the signs of approval, or even love, of others like us. The joy of self-love is, in fact,

> more and more encouraged the more man imagines himself to be praised by others. For the more he imagines himself to be praised by others, the greater the Joy with which he imagines himself to affect others, a Joy accompanied by the idea of himself (by P29S). And so (by P27) he himself is affected with a greater Joy, accompanied by the idea of himself.[23]

However, it must be said that such love is the love of an image of the self. One must first understand the construction of its object (the ego), according to the same processes that explain the hallucinatory constitution of the object in general and of the object of love in particular. Let us recall these processes: a simplification-assimilation of affections by virtue of confusion and an active simplification through the connection of affections through habit.[24] This process of recognition binds the affect (joy) to the connection

---

[17] *Ethics* III, 30 Dem.
[18] *Ethics* II, 17, 23.
[19] *Ethics* III, 30 Schol.
[20] On ambition for glory and ambition for domination, see Alexandre Matheron, *Individu et communauté chez Spinoza*, Minuit, 1969, II, ch. 5, esp. pp. 218–21.
[21] Translator's note: Curley translates *acquiescentia in se ipso* as self esteem and *philautia* as self-love, though he notes that Elwe's self-approval could also work for the former (CWS I, 655).
[22] *Ethics* III, 53.
[23] *Ethics* III, 53 Cor.; CWS I, 524.
[24] *Ethics* II, 40 Schol. 1; CM V; CWS I, 477, 311.

of affections operated by habit (and preserved by memory according to the joy–sadness principle) by objectivising in reality what is in fact mere connections of the body and ideas of bodily traces. Memory is intrinsically related to the recognition-constitution of the object of love (ego) in self-love.[25] In self-love, one recognises herself as the cause of her own joy only 'inadequately'. We say according to inadequate knowledge, rather than according to an inadequate idea of herself,[26] because the mind does not have an idea of itself, its own body, the parts of that body,[27] or even of external bodies as such.[28] The mind has only the idea of the affections of its body from which it imagines external bodies, parts of its body, its body and itself. We recognise ourselves in our body, as well as our mind, and we enjoy this self-contentment (*acquiescentia in se ipso*) that Spinoza calls self-love by virtue of the same process of recognition involved in inadequate knowledge, by the hallucinatory representation of the presence of the ego-object.

In the first mention of the relationship to the self in *Ethics* III, Spinoza understands it immediately as both governed by the joy principle and the imaginary. On the one hand,

> we strive to affirm, concerning ourselves [. . .] whatever we imagine to affect ourselves with Joy [. . .] On the other hand, we strive to deny whatever we imagine affects ourselves with Sadness [. . .][29]

On the other hand, we are led to construct a positive fiction: the most favourable self-image possible for our effort to persevere in being. *Ethics* III, 51 Schol. reminds us that the things humans do for joy or to avert sadness 'are often only imaginary'. To love oneself is natural (and self-hatred is, conversely, against nature). Absolutely speaking, 'no one, out of hate, thinks less highly of himself than is just. Indeed, no one thinks less highly of himself than is just.'[30] On the contrary, we naturally always think 'too highly' of ourselves, and this excess appears to be constitutive of self-love in the

---

[25] *Ethics* II, 17 Schol.; CWS I, 464–5.
[26] *Ethics* II, 23 Dem.; CWS I, 468.
[27] *Ethics* II, 24; CWS I, 468.
[28] *Ethics* II, 26 Cor.; CWS I, 469.
[29] *Ethics* III, 25, which is based on III, 12; CWS I, 507. Translation modified.
[30] *Ethics* III DA 28 Exp.; CWS I, 537. Immediately following, Spinoza nuances this assertion by citing (while we 'attend to those things that depend only on opinion') cases of 'despondency'. But this affect is exceedingly rare and, when it exists, it is often in reality only the expression of ambitions and pent-up desires (*Ethics* III, DA 29 Exp.; CWS I, 538).

recognitive representation of our relationship to ourselves. That is why this love (or the self-contentment it involves independently of others' praise) is spontaneously blind. That is why the object of this love is also necessarily a fantasy, and why it is even more loved when 'men believe themselves free' (see *Ethics* III, 49).[31] Pride, a delusion, is the natural structure of self-love (*amour-propre*).[32] In *Ethics* II, Spinoza asked us to start from hallucination to think of ordinary perception. In *Ethics* III, he asks us to apprehend the relationship to self from the delusional hallucination that is pride. There is no self-love without excess, or pride, even when pride is disguised as humility, its putatively contrary affect.

One understands the reversal that takes place in ambition through the loving logic (in general) implied by self-love: the transition from the desire to satisfy the desire of others[33] to the desire to subject others to one's own desire.[34] The loving logic, by posing the object of love (ego) at the centre of the individual's every effort, subjugates active power (desire) to a centripetal law. As much as possible, therefore, all will strive to have others love what they love and hate what they themselves dislike.[35] But what everyone loves, above all, is themselves. All will act so that others love them as they love themselves. The ancient emulator therefore necessarily presents itself as model, and humans act only to be loved, admired and revered, according to the finalist structure of the practical subject brought on by the logic of love.

The loving logic of desire leads to the will to master and dominate the affections of others for the sole benefit of a narcissistic desire that demands of others a cult such as is given to Gods. That is the supreme fantasy of self-love. At this stage of the cognitive representation of the self, the logic of imitation, coupled with the joy principle, determines a behaviour that is both relational and teleological, following an efficient causality. This is a practical and strategic intersubjectivity. The practical subject desires this object (and not that other). She imagines, through its mediation, that she will win others' praises, even their admiration and veneration. One no longer seeks to satisfy[36] others only because she imitates their affects. It is for her own contentment that she wishes to satisfy others and receive their praise through imitation. As a result, there is a double movement of practical

---

[31] *Ethics* III, 51 Schol.; CWS I, 522–3.
[32] *Ethics* III, 26 Schol.; *Ethics* III, DA 28; CWS I, 508.
[33] *Ethics* III, 29; CWS I, 510.
[34] *Ethics* III, 31 Schol.
[35] *Ethics* III, 31 Cor.
[36] *Ethics* III, 29 Dem.

intersubjectivity. The subject wants to be praised by others, which is why she (the emulator) imitates their affects (and thus their values, prejudices, ideals, mores...). This imitation, then, satisfies the others' desire and directs her gaze to our merits, which fills us with glory.[37] This is the first stage of the development of self-love. This gaze makes us into the models that we strive to uphold, to bring self-contentment to its plenitude, through our awareness of it. The teleological structure of practical intersubjectivity, in actuality, reverses causal logic. The desire for the other's gaze motivates the practical subject's imitation. She is thus conscripted into the strategy of ambition for domination.

In this inversion of desire (from satisfying the other's desire to submitting to her), the two tendencies, seemingly opposed, persist together. The ambition for domination is an aspiration, at the same time, to rule the desires of others and to satisfy them. Even in tyranny, glory in self-contentment is sought. From the point of view of the ambition for glory, domination is only the passionate expression of a mimetic desire. This mimetic desire, when rooted in reason, becomes the desire to see others live under the determination of truth, that is, according to our own model of wisdom, which is a universal model. But under the determination of imagination, everyone wants to subject others to their particular preconceptions. This inversion tragically culminates when each one becomes the mortal enemy of all humankind. Each turns into their neighbour's tormentor, for whom she wants happiness, but only according to her own norms. *Ethics* III, 31 Schol. affirms this by drawing out the consequences of the 'vacillating' logic of ambition. The desire to please the crowd by adopting its values[38] leads to a 'mutual hatred', each wanting to impose the supremacy of their model. The utilitarianism which reduces others to a simple means of satisfaction, and which makes of reason an instrument of this desire, thus appears as the practical subject's illusion of intersubjectivity. The consequence is a reversal from a strategy for self-love (or strategy of the ambition to dominate) to the strategy of an ambition for glory. The individualistic strategy of self-love, based on imitation, severs any solidarity that this imitation first inspired. If political regulations did not modulate its spiralling dynamic, this logic of selfish calculation would tear apart the social body, or even lead to perfect 'inhumanity'.[39]

---

[37] *Ethics* III, 30 Schol.
[38] *Ethics* III, 29 Schol.
[39] The logic of imitation explains 1) humanity and the dehumanisation of relations between humans; and 2) solidarity and the manipulation of others who are under the command of selfish calculation and without pity: 'For one who is moved to aid others

We must here consider some difficulties of *Ethics* III, 53:

> When the Mind considers itself and its power of acting, it rejoices, and does so the more, the more distinctly it imagines itself and its power of acting.[40]

As the demonstration emphasises, one only knows herself through the affections of her body and their ideas, according to the effective expressions of her power to act.[41] This knowledge can be adequate or inadequate. *Ethics* III, 53 is an example of the inadequate knowledge of our affections which extends into inadequate knowledge of ourselves. The subject of *Ethics* III, 53 considers her power to act from the point of view of imagination. She can only know herself inadequately, according to the structure of the object and the qualities that can be attributed to it, its 'facts, actions, forces', according to *Ethics* III, 55 Schol. The causal relation (from the point of view of the first kind of knowledge) is, therefore, also connected to a process of objectification. As the cause of our joy, power to act will appear to us as an object. But the more we distinguish it from similar objects, the more joy it will give us. *Ethics* III, 53, thus, considers not only the relation of the subject to herself, but also the existence of other objects (other causes) from which we must distinguish ourselves to be able to imagine our own causal power more 'clearly'. As for inadequate knowledge, *Ethics* III, 55 Schol. clarifies proposition 53. However, this proposition is partially elaborated in *Ethics* IV, 52 (and Dem.) by presenting the relationship to the self as one that transcends the recognitive structure of the practical subject, and thus frees the power to act (as a cause) from objectification. Let us also consider an inadequate recognition of the self (an image) in one who otherwise has an adequate, rational idea of herself. We can think of this as the self-love of the wise, not as a sage but as a practical subject. Beyond the representation (adequate or inadequate) and the interpretation of reality that it implies (by virtue of its application of the causal relation), *Ethics* III, 53 gestures towards an immediate self-contentment. The consideration of one's power to act eludes the recognitive structure. Unlike the *acquiescentia in se ipso* of adequate representation, this immediate self-contentment has no opposite. For, as we have seen, it is not sadness but rather joy that is inherently attached to being in its affirmation.

---

neither by reason nor by pity is rightly called inhuman. For (by IIIP27) he seems to be unlike a [human].' *Ethics* IV, 50 Cor. Schol.; CWS I, 799. Translation modified.

[40] CWS I, 524. Translator's note.
[41] *Ethics* II, 19, 23.

2 Love of Self and Strategies of Self-Love

The love every being has for itself is not reducible either to its representation in self-love or to the logic of ambition for domination, the strategic axis of such love. The pure humanity of the immediacy of imitation is non-representative. It correlates to a love of oneself (*philautia* and *acquiescentia in se ipso*) that does not yet imply a self-recognition that passes through the recognition of others. It is a love prior to any memory, any thoughtful representation of temporality and of the self in it. Thus, it precedes the constitution of a subject–object pair, and the existence of practical intersubjectivity. Yet this 'natural'[42] awareness one has of oneself is also an awareness of time, though immediate, without a reflective consciousness of the past or the future, in the pure present activity of the present that endures. The lived duration of Habit encounters the love for a being (or for the perfection of the being) before the longing (*desiderium*), hope and fear of time-constrained desire creeps in. This difference – between the feeling of the immediate and actual presence that a being has of herself (her duration in the affect of the self by the self) and the consciousness that she has of being-in-time – distinguishes love for oneself from self-love, an implicit distinction in the Spinozist text.[43]

---

[42] KV App. II, 6.

[43] In highlighting the role of love of oneself in Spinoza, one cannot help but recall (albeit briefly) the important tradition of this concept going back to Aristotle (*Nicomachean Ethics* 1166 a 1) and the Stoics (see Cicero, *De finibus bonorum et malorum* III, 5). In Christianity, love of oneself is considered the prototype of all love, the very experience of inwardness, our intimate relationship with God (see Paul's Letter to the Galatians 5:14 and Letter to the Romans 13:8). Thomas Aquinas, drawing on Aristotle and Augustine (perhaps also Bernard de Clairvaux), clearly makes love of oneself a principle that grounds, first, our access to God as the proper human good (whose 'cause' is in God and 'effect' in us) and, second, our access to our neighbour on the basis of our likeness (*Commentary on the Sentences*, III, distinctions 27, 28, 29). To love oneself is to recognise in the 'self' the identification of being with the Good: its essentially desirable nature (*Summa Theologica, prima pars*, question 60, art. 3). And therefore natural love for oneself is not a mere passage (to God and/or others) destined to be surpassed; it affirms itself in the heart of charity and glory (*Summa Theologica* II, II, question 25, art. 4). But to make of love of oneself a path to the good is also to recognise the good, upright nature, which by nature tends to the good. From this tradition, Spinoza gains a loving (ethical) subjectivity that he liberates from theological dualism and the problem of (teleological) order, meaning and value, by embedding the process of self-love (in and through intellectual love of God) in an ontology of the radical immanence of the self-causation/constitution of the substance in the infinite infinity of its expressions: *Amor sui sive causa sui. . .*

At some level of physical and mental complexity, every being can feel that it has an immediate (more or less obscure) 'consciousness' of its life (or activity). Nature's individuals 'are all endowed with minds [*animata*] though to varying degrees', Spinoza writes.[44] And this union of mind and body in every being is a 'natural love'[45] 'founded' in the body.[46] For every mind spontaneously has a more or less confused knowledge of its body. This knowledge is also a form of love: 'the knowledge we have of the body we do not know it as it is, or perfectly. And yet, what a union! what a love!'[47] This love (which the *KV* opposes to the love of God) or 'enjoyment'[48] immediately attached to a being through the 'consciousness' one spontaneously has of her activity is the love the mind has for the body of which it is the idea.[49] And the knowledge of the mind, as well as its love, will be all the greater and more magnificent as the body's power of acting is greater:[50] 'The excellence of ideas and the actual power of thinking are measured by the excellence of the object.'[51] Yet 'the Mind's striving, or power of thinking, is equal to and one in nature with the body's striving, or power of acting'.[52] Therefore, what each being loves, first and immediately, is her own power to act: 'When the Mind considers itself and its power of acting, it rejoices'; this is completely true.[53]

Love of oneself (an affect of the self by the self), intrinsic to the existence of each being, is confused with the feeling we have of our own body:[54] the feeling of an 'indefinite continuation of existing'[55] by which Spinoza also defines duration. Through this love, we feel our essence itself, a power to act (determined as indefinite perseverance in being).[56] That is why the love for oneself is, above all, love of the reality of the power in us, which differs

---

[44] *Ethics* II, 13 Schol.; CWS I, 458.
[45] *KV* App. II, 6; CWS I, 153.
[46] *KV* II, xxiii, 2; CWS I, 111.
[47] *KV* II, xxii, 2; CWS I, 139.
[48] *KV* II, v, 4; CWS I, 105.
[49] *Ethics* II, 11, 12, 13 Dem. Cor. and Schol.; CWS I, 456–62.
[50] *KV* II, v, 1; *Ethics* II, 13 Schol.; CWS I, 104, 457–8.
[51] *Ethics* III, DA Exp; CWS I, 543. Translator's note: Shirley's translation (p. 319) used here because this sentence does not appear in Curley's translation. Baruch Spinoza, *Complete Works*, ed. Michael L. Morgan, trans. Samuel Shirley, Hackett, 2002.
[52] *Ethics* III, 28 Dem; CWS I, 432.
[53] *Ethics* III, 53 and DA 25; CWS I, 524, 536.
[54] *Ethics* II, 13 Cor.; CWS I, 457.
[55] *Ethics* II, Def. 5; CWS I, 447.
[56] Robert Misrahi rightly states that 'love of oneself is *conatus* itself'. *Spinoza. Un itinéraire du bonheur par la joie*, J. Grancher, 1992, p. 203.

from the self-love that is mere love of an image. We also love Nature's power, of which we are only a part,[57] through this love. Far from folding us back on to ourselves, love of oneself opens us up to the love of a life that exceeds us from all sides, and it is no stretch to say that this love brings us to love ourselves outside of ourselves as well. Unlike the centripetal logic of self-love, the love for oneself unfolds as a centrifugal and radiant force. The imitation of the feelings and desires of those like us can, therefore, be understood as an extension of love of oneself. Through imitation, the union of the mind with its body becomes a union with all the bodies imagined as like ours in the present. In self-love, being flourishes only by distinguishing itself, as much as possible, from others according to a logic of oppositional identification. With love of self, being amplifies itself by extending its love beyond itself over all the similar bodies, according to a logic of fusional identification. This love through identification is lived to its highest degree in the bond that spontaneously attaches children to their parents, such that the very possibility of parricide seems to contradict (as does suicide) human nature.[58]

A dual reading of the *Short Treatise* and the *Ethics* can lead us to the expansive logic of the love for oneself in humanity (the ethical process itself), which is the natural love of one's own body, expanded into a universal love of all similar bodies. The *Ethics*, which addresses the problem of inter-human relations already, essentially, in their intersubjective (and so representative) aspect, only assumes the logic of love for oneself-as-humankind by making it a support of the practical figures of self-love and ambition. This is how *Ethics* III, 55 Schol. describes the objectification of power to act in the game of comparisons, made possible by the process of recognition:

> Joy arising from considering ourselves, is called Self-love or self approval. And since this is renewed as often as a man considers his virtues, or his power of acting, it also happens that everyone is anxious to tell his own

---

[57] *Ethics* IV, 4 Dem.; CWS I, 448–9.

[58] Of course, we must nuance this because, in fact, according to their history, the particular circumstances of their lives and/or their present affections, some 'necessarily' kill their parents just as others (or the same people) end their lives. It is in the context of reflecting on the right of the political body over its subjects that *TP* III, 8 sets out the commandments that cannot really be followed by obedience when they demand actions 'which human nature so abhors that it considers them worse than any other evil, as that a man should act as a witness against himself, that he should torture himself, that he should kill his parents, that he should not strive to avoid death, and the like, which no one can be induced to do by rewards or threats' (CWS II, 520).

deeds, and show off his powers, both of body and of mind – and that men, for this reason, are troublesome to one another.[59]

Self-love is the love of an image of the self (as an object of love), which, to constitute itself, assumes the structure of the practical subject. Self-love is reinforced in three ways. First, using the auxiliaries of imagination, particularly with comparison, applied to the connections of Habit, memory and according to the recognition process. Second, self-love is reinforced through the use of transcendentals and universals (particularly with the general notion of human), for a prior unity (here that of human beings) establishes that 'we separate the thing from others which are like it' on the basis of a judgement of similarity.[60] Finally, it is reinforced by the illusion of freedom because 'love toward a thing will be greater if we imagine the thing to be free than if we imagine it to be necessary. And similarly, for Hate.'[61] Self-love reaches its own truth in delirious pride at the supreme stage of the illusion of freedom, and this truth is the desire to be God.

Let us go back to *Ethics* III, 55 Schol.:

> For whenever anyone imagines his own actions, he is affected with Joy (by P53), and with a greater Joy, the more his actions express perfection, and the more distinctly he imagines them, i.e. (by IIP40S1), the more he can distinguish them from others and consider them as singular things. So, everyone will have the greatest gladness from considering himself, when he considers something in himself which he denies concerning others. But if he relates what he affirms of himself to the universal idea of men or animal, he will not be so greatly gladdened. And on the other hand, if he imagines that his own actions are weaker, compared to others' actions, he will be saddened.[62]

There is a desire to distinguish oneself through self-love, to differentiate oneself, to be singularised, because a longer, more constant, more exclusive affection arises from a singularity than from properties that are common to other objects.[63] This feeling is further reinforced by two factors, one being the consequence of the other: the spontaneous illusion we have of our

---

[59] CWS I, 525. Translator's note.
[60] CM I, 6; CWS I, 311–12.
[61] *Ethics* III, 49; CWS I, 521.
[62] CWS I, 525. Translator's note.
[63] *Ethics* III, 52 Dem. and Schol.; CWS I, 523–4.

freedom and the ease with which we think of ourselves 'simply', ignorant of the other causes that determine us to act.[64] For we imagine that a thing is free when it can 'be perceived through itself, without others'.[65] If this is a valid definition,[66] it is one which, when used to differentiate between things and self through habitual perception, only legitimises the atomistic illusion of free will and thus amplifies the love we have for ourself[67] to the point of seeing oneself, through pride, as a God. The delusional truth of self-love leads one to think of herself as God. One who, in the affirmation of his supreme singularity separates himself from the human condition, 'dreams, with open eyes, that he can do all those things which he achieves only in his imagination',[68] and thus imagines that his own active power, as well as his power (*pouvoir*) over the world and humans, is infinite. For this, he demands veneration and fervour[69] of the kind that some monarchs took full advantage of.[70]

The very existence of self-love is thus, in practice, the affirmation of difference (to the point of divinisation) and a radical rejection of imitation. But this is misleading. Paradoxically, mimesis affirms the aspiration for singularity and difference of self-love. In the representational logic of loving desire, the immediate and real imitation of another's desire, something to which everyone is naturally led, changes course by the amplification of singular differentiation. There is therefore a paradox in self-love: it only lives off that which it ostensibly rejects; and the singularisation to which it leads is the symptom of a servile imitation. No one is in truth more subjected to another than the creature of self-love. Self-love is only the alienated extension of spontaneous imitation and of wanting to satisfy another's desire. This prolongation is alienated because it flips the logic of humanity and benevolence[71] into a logic of ambition that is both self-constraining and oppressive to others. It is also alienated by the fact that the more forcefully self-love affirms its singularity, the more it masks its consubstantial alterity (the 'ego' of self-love appears according to the constitution of the external object). It is finally also alienated, in its contents, since it is essentially envy (of what the other possesses and is) that fuels the dynamic of ambition and

---

[64] *Ethics* V, 5 and Dem.; CWS I, 599.
[65] *Ethics* III, 49 Dem.; CWS I, 521.
[66] *Ethics* I, Def. 7; CWS I, 409.
[67] *Ethics* III, 51 Schol.; CWS I, 522–3.
[68] *Ethics* III, 26 Schol.; CWS I, 508.
[69] *Ethics* III, 52 Schol.; CWS I, 523–4.
[70] *TTP* XVII; CWS II, 299–301.
[71] *Ethics* III, 27 Schol.; CWS I, 509.

difference. It is delusional when, from pride, self-love comes across the fantasy of total independence and omnipotence ... but only to make us the slaves of others. Because, 'by the foul crime of bondage, or by treachery [no] one is more taken in by flattery than the proud, who wish to be first and are not'.[72]

Self-love is therefore also a servile love, and an admission of powerlessness. There is something abject in the desire to be loved by the same love through which we love ourselves,[73] when we know that this love is only love of a flattering image, which, when necessary, relies on bad faith.[74] In its effort to perpetuate itself, existence gets rid of inconvenient truths. Self-love and the correlative love we seek from others (which strengthens self-love) are there to reassure and give us (even from the greatest illusion) the confidence and quieting of the mind without which life would be unbearable, except for the wise. But this psychological state is unstable. All it takes is for the lover not to be greeted by flatterers or by 'the thing he loves ... with the same countenance as [it] used to offer him'[75] or in general, that fortune should change, for one to fall back into misery and powerlessness.[76] Pushed into the shadow and into solitude, Jealousy and Envy then dominate one's relationships to others. Love of oneself, by imitation, naturally develops into a love of what is different from the self (because we nevertheless imagine it to be similar). Now, however, self-love (still in the realm of the same), through imitation and comparison, develops into hatred of everything that is different, more perfect (we imagine), happier and envied, because we imagine it to be in the way of our own happiness.

Ambition is first characterised by imitation of the vulgar, accompanied by the desire to satisfy them, and later by a strategy of self-love according to a logic of loving desire. We must recognise in envy the driving force of a new dynamic of the strategy of the ambition for domination (driving force as an efficient cause, and not as an end, which remains self-contentment in glory):

> For the most part human nature is so constituted that [humans] pity the unfortunate and envy the fortunate, and (by P32) [envy them] with greater hate the more they love the thing they imagine the other to possess. We see, then, that from the same property of human nature from

---

[72] *Ethics* IV, App. 21; *CWS* I, 591.
[73] *Ethics* III, 31 Cor.; *CWS* I, 512.
[74] *Ethics* III, 55 Schol.; *CWS* I, 525–6.
[75] *Ethics* III, 35 Schol.; *CWS* I, 472.
[76] *qui animo impotentes sunt*. *Ethics* V, 10 Schol.; *CWS* I, 602.

which it follows that [humans] are compassionate, it also follows that the same [humans] are envious and ambitious.[77]

This property is, of course, imitation, but here it is determined by the joy principle. The joy principle resists the destructive consequences of imitation (by responding with benevolence to the sadness of commiseration or mercy, for example) and determines us to envy those we imagine to be happy (obviously, we do not envy misfortune or sadness). So imitation alone does not explain envy. However, starting from there, under the determination of the joy principle, we can follow the destructive logic of envy.

By affirming in DA 33, Exp. that the cause of imitation is emulation, Spinoza makes the definition of emulation the true genetic definition of imitation:

Emulation is a Desire for a thing which is generated in us because we imagine that others have the same Desire.[78]

Spinoza, after linking this affect to envy (*Ethics* III, 32 and Schol.), explains envy through the cyclical and contingent situation in which the emulator is placed when she is unable to appropriate what she desires, on another's model, other than by destroying this model. This is explained by the singular nature of the desired thing, which can only be possessed by a single individual:

If we imagine that someone enjoys some thing that only one can possess, we shall strive to bring it about that he does not possess it.[79]

This restriction having to do with the nature of the object does not seem to be entirely determinate. For, if the desiring subject constitutes the object of her own desire (or the image of the desired thing), this object is always singular, as are the affections of the body that form desire. As *Ethics* III 32, Schol. reminds us, 'the images of things are the very affections of the human Body'[80] and these can only be particular. There are, therefore, as many species of objects as there are desires attached to them. If

---

[77] *Ethics* III, 32 Schol.; CWS I, 513.
[78] *Ethics* III, DA 33; *Ethics* III, 27 Schol.; CWS I, 539, 508.
[79] *Ethics* III, 32; CWS I, 513.
[80] CWS I, 513. Translator's note.

> different men can be affected differently by one and the same object [then] one and the same man can be affected differently at different times by one and the same object.[81]

Is this object really the 'same' if its reality x (which can only be thought of) has reality, for us, only in usual perception, through the images of our affections, and which we recognise as object y (and not as a x) through inadequate knowledge? I do not think so. In this sense,

> from the mere fact that we imagine someone to enjoy something (by P27 and P27C1), we shall love that thing and desire to enjoy it. But (by hypothesis) we imagine his enjoyment of this thing as an obstacle to our Joy.[82]

At least on first analysis, the rivalry seems to come from the real singularity of the desired object (and thus its rarity). Yet it is desire itself, in certain conditions, which makes of the coveted thing something singularly desirable, according to a double determination: particular desire in its autonomy (though theoretical), and desire of the other which the first desire naturally tends to imitate. In the second case (which also includes the first), emulation generates envy and this makes the model imitated by the desiring subject the essential obstacle to her own contentment. If envy does not explain ambition, it becomes its main driving force in the strategy of self-love.

Immediately after *Ethics* III, 31 Schol., which explained rivalry and violence by the mutual ambition to dominate, the self-love standoff, *Ethics* III, 32 explains this rivalry by emulation and by the singular nature of the desired object. These two levels of explanation meet in the logic of pride, which is both the natural matrix of self-love and consubstantial with desire: 'the proud man must be envious'.[83] The proud believer in her superiority over others cannot bear the glory of others. She 'hate[s most those] who are most praised for their virtues',[84] and her effort will go towards diminishing their merits and flaunting her own perfection.[85] In imagination and, if she can, in reality, through the dynamic of emulation, the proud will endeavour

---

[81] *Ethics* III, 51; CWS I, 522. Translation modified.
[82] *Ethics* III, 32 Dem.; CWS I, 513.
[83] *Ethics* IV, 57 Schol.; CWS I, 577.
[84] *Ethics* IV, 57 Schol.; CWS I, 577. Translation modified.
[85] *Ethics* III, 55 Schol.

to undermine the glory of her competitors in order to keep for herself, and herself alone, the praise of her equals.

Envy, it is true, implies a desire directed towards objects. Yet it is, above all, envy of the singular joy[86] of another, and not simply envy of a thing. The envy that brings the rivalry between equals to its height[87] indicates, paradoxically (in the desire for the other's death implied in hatred),[88] the ultimate point of imitation. Identification with the rival/equal necessarily leads to a desire to 'avert or destroy' her, a desire to take her place. Or, if this is impossible, we may strive to frustrate her *vis-à-vis* what she has, even by destroying what we ourselves love, so as to no longer face her unbearable satisfaction. The hatred that leads us to destroy what we desire so that we can harm another is a sign of the primacy of the mimetic logic over the mere competitive desire for an object. Beyond the conquest of the real object that becomes desirable only because it pleases another, envy leads to a direct confrontation, the goal of which is the death of the other, or at least her sadness. This is the meaning of the negative statement of *Ethics* III, 32: 'we shall strive to bring it about that [our rival] does not possess it': we strive to hurt her directly. This culmination of the mimetic dynamism, which is originally constitutive of sociability, signals its failure. Spinoza answers to this failed strategy of *conatus* in two ways (and the second assumes the realisation of the first): the need to organise a political society and the need for a knowledge of affects, corresponding to the ethical project.

Mimetic logic, the basis of the autonomous constitution of the social body, has paradoxically produced a heteronomous individual and collective body, torn by a violence that is quasi-autonomous. To counter this savage and murderous autonomy of violence, Spinoza rejects the idea of the constitution of the political autonomy of the social body whose purpose (as the State) is the citizens' freedom, as well as the idea of the constitution of an ethical autonomy based on the transformative power (*puissance*) of reason and active affects.

Democracy and generosity: two adequate ideas and active affects by which the social individual (the social body) and the human individual can respond effectively to the deadly logic of violence (in relation to the conditions that meet their ability to be affected). For both individuals and societies, the solutions chosen are always necessarily those that an individual has been able to produce by virtue of the more or less powerful way in

---

[86] *Ethics* III, 56.
[87] *Ethics* III, 55 Cor. and Dem.
[88] *Ethics* III, 39 Dem.

which it has made clear the problem of its survival and its absolute and perfect affirmation, or of its absolute absolutism (as Spinoza writes of a society in *TP* VIII, 3–4). The political organisation of the social body is the desire of the social body itself, which has reached a certain level of complexity (a greater capacity to be affected), that now enables it to pose the problem of its survival as a collective. Democracy is the highest level of this desire, as an absolute affirmation of the existence of the social body (the absolute enjoyment of its right).[89] The adequate idea ('absolute' and 'perfect') of the social body, when society can produce such an idea and/or desire, can also change its conditions of existence into a new active liaison of its members, and thereby achieve its absolute absolutism.

We cannot abstractly isolate (through an individualistic reading) the Spinozist analysis of the passions of *Ethics* III, first, from the discovery of the organisational and constitutive power of sociability that the affects involve, or, second, from the political consequences that necessarily arise from this discovery and allow Spinoza to break with any utopian and artificialist conception of the State. On the one hand, the passional logic of passive affective imitation forms a social body (of a heteronomous nature, dominated by the violence of its contradictions, which ultimately leads to its loss). On the other hand, the same mimetic logic, but of active affects, forms a perfect, rational and autonomous sociability: the sociability of the sages. But this community of friends who know no division has no political reality (and cannot have one, since it has no need for politics). It has only a very fragmented, ethical, relational reality, within an already constituted political society. This society of beings led by reason, without State or power (*pouvoir*), would be a fantasy and a utopia if we thought it could include all human beings as they ordinarily and necessarily are: dominated by passions (the *multitudo*, according to the expression of *TTP* XVII,[90] often taken up in the *Political Treatise*). This community of sages might be called pure political activity, for it establishes concord and peace without sovereignty or power.

> Still, it rarely happens that men live according to the guidance of reason. Instead, their lives are so constituted that they are usually envious and burdensome to one another. They can hardly, however, live a solitary life; hence, that definition which makes man a social animal.[91]

---

[89] *TP* V, 2.
[90] *CWS* II, 298.
[91] *Ethics* IV, 35 Schol. of Cor. 2.; *CWS* I, 564.

Thus, the heteronomous social body expresses the actual and common reality of the paradoxical relations through which humans, at the same time, get close to and destroy each other. The question of a specifically political organisation, the question of 'civil society' and the State, arises from this first concrete organisation of sociability and its contradictions.[92]

The community of sages, therefore, cannot serve as a political model (except for idealists):

> those who persuade themselves that a multitude, which may be divided over public affairs [*publicis negotiis distrahuntur*], can be induced to live only according to the prescription of reason, those people are dreaming of the golden age of the Poets. They're captive to a myth.[93]

Yet Spinoza does not give up what is essential to this: the autonomy of the collective, corresponding to the autonomy of the individuals who make up this society. Individual as well as State autonomy is the expression of the natural and necessary effort every being makes to persevere. This effort is inseparable from strategy. There is a political strategy that is not only technical, the conquest and conservation of power. It is the strategy of the *conatus* of the social body itself, which tends towards its own adequacy: the absolute exercise of its right.

The constitutive strategy of the heteronomous social body is *conatus*-imitation when the mimetic logic is the imitation of the passive affects. This strategy is doomed to fail. From this failure emerges the political question, the question of a higher organisation of the social body's desire. There is, therefore, a political objective analogous to the ethical one: to find an autonomous logic of life's fulfilment for heteronomous processes that lead to death. This is no polity for fictitious or exceptional humans, but only one that starts from humans as they really are. It begins from the passionate and mimetic logic in which they are necessarily caught, and, from there, finds clear paths towards harmony and peace. This is the role of the State, which is nothing other than the desire of the social body when it has reached a certain degree of complexity. For the social body's *conatus*, the political question and the question of its autonomy are one and the same question, which can all the better be asked and resolved when the social body as a whole is faced with the same problem: the desire for society to pass to a greater organisation. For Spinoza, the 'supreme desire' of the social body can

---

[92] *TP* III, 1; *CWS* II, 517.
[93] *TP* I, 5; *CWS* II, 506.

only be democracy. This is so because, as with reason for the individual,[94] it constitutes the most adequate strategy for the absolute and perfect (that is, autonomous) affirmation of a social body that has become political: a rigorously absolute authority, if it can exist, held by the mass as a whole.[95]

3 Ostentation or Dissimulation? A Strategy of Appearance

The strategic logic of the practical subject of intersubjectivity envelops and links emulation, ambition for glory, self-love and pride, ambition for domination and envy. The practical subject, as self-loving subject (through self-love), is determined by circumstances to one of two types of behaviour (tactics) imposed by the structure of imagination, two types of relational existence according to the first kind of knowledge: ostentation or dissimulation. Both are strategies of pride. Ostentation is an explicitly affirmed and deployed strategy of pride. Dissimulation is a strategy of pride, but masked as its opposite: humility and modesty.

These two adaptive tactics must be understood, at their level, from within a utilitarian logic (although they are not reducible to it). The one who is 'necessarily always subject to passions, [follows] and obeys the common order of Nature and accommodates himself to it as much as the nature of things requires'.[96]

The capacity for adaptation is a paradoxical positivity since the subject with inadequate ideas finds a way to persevere in being (or rather in her state) necessarily through passive activity. Despite the imaginary nature of its object, and the powerlessness and servitude it involves, self-love is thus both a dynamic and a protective adaptive structure whereby a complex being, under given conditions, strives to persevere in being. In self-love, one loves herself, and acts to preserve, expand and defend her being. It is the refracted expression, in self-representation, of the 'natural love, which is in each thing' and which defines the *conatus* in the *Short Treatise*.[97] When defined only by comparison with (and differentiation from) her equals, this being is reduced to a mere (psychological and social) state and to her interest in preserving that state, or in modifying it within a given relational and social system. Such is the context of the *conatus*'s dynamism within the ambition for domination, developed, paradoxically even when successful,

---

[94] *Ethics* IV, App. 4.
[95] *TP* VIII, 3.
[96] *Ethics* IV, 4 Cor.; *CWS* I, 549. Translation modified.
[97] *KV* App. II, 6; *CWS* I, 156.

at our and others' expense.[98] Ambition appears (within the sociability to which it contributes) as the inevitable strategy of the relational and social being's *conatus*, through ostentation or dissimulation. The immediate love we have of ourselves has no opposite. For in this love, the essence of the mind affirms itself, and affirms 'only what the mind is and can do, not what it is not and cannot do'.[99] Self-respect in self-love can follow both from of its power (*puissance*) and its powerlessness.[100] The praise or blame of others amplifies the joy or sadness that follows from this self-respect.[101]

Self-love's opposite is humility, which is the sadness that accompanies the idea of our powerlessness.[102] Humility turns into shame when it is amplified by the blame of others,[103] and into repentance when we believe we have done freely the action which now causes us sadness, with or without shame.[104] Humility, however, is not a natural virtue. A being's entire effort is,[105] even in bad faith,[106] to get rid of the sadness involved in the consideration of one's powerlessness. Absolutely speaking, humility – like the self-hatred to which it leads – is unnatural, and only when 'we attend to those things that depend only on opinion [are] we be able to conceive of it as possible that a man thinks less highly of himself than is just'.[107]

And we must beware of appearances! We oppose the affects of pride and humility because we are accustomed to considering them from the point of view of 'their effects', or their manifestations. The proud person is ostentatious, while the humble person is self-effacing:

> We usually call him proud who exults too much at being esteemed (see P30S), who tells of nothing but his own virtues, and the vices of others, who wishes to be given precedence over all others, and finally who proceeds with the gravity and attire usually adopted by others who are placed far above him. On the other hand, we call him humble who quite often blushes, who confesses his own vices and tells the virtues of others, who

---

[98] *Ethics* III, 29 Schol.; CWS I, 510.
[99] *Ethics* III, 54 Dem.; CWS I, 525.
[100] *Ethics* III, 55; CWS I, 525.
[101] *Ethics* III, 53 Cor., 55 Cor.; CWS I, 524–5.
[102] *Ethics* III, 55 Schol.; *Ethics* III, DA 26; CWS I, 525–6, 536.
[103] *Ethics* III, 30 Schol.; *Ethics* III, DA 31; CWS I, 511, 538.
[104] *Ethics* III, 30 Schol.; *Ethics* III, DA 27; CWS I, 511, 536.
[105] *Ethics* III, 13, 54; CWS I, 502, 525.
[106] *Ethics* III, 55 Schol.; CWS I, 525.
[107] *Ethics* III DA 28; CWS I, 537. Translation modified and translator's note.

yields to all, and finally, who walks with head bowed, and neglects to adorn himself.[108]

But ostentation and self-effacement are two faces of the same strategy, the strategy of an ambitious and envious *conatus*:

> These affects – Humility and Despondency – are very rare. For human nature, considered in itself, strains against them, as far as it can (see P13 and P54). So those who are believed to be most despondent and humble are usually most ambitious and envious.[109]

The self-effacement of humility, as well as the ostentation of pride, belong to a strategy that unfolds in the realm of appearances. Humble people, Spinoza writes, 'praise only Despondency, and exult over it – but in such a way that they still seem despondent'.[110] Humility and pride share some core elements, which are the drives that determine them. The despondent – like the proud – only lives to compare herself to the vices and virtues of her equals; and because of the sadness that dominates her, one can even say that the despondent is even more sensitive to ambition and envy than the proud, who already savours, in part, her perfection.[111] We can here anticipate the analysis Spinoza could make of puritan moralism, the refuge of repressed envy: 'no one is more prone to Envy than the despondent man is, and why they strive especially to observe men's deeds, more for the sake of finding fault than to improve them...'[112]

This adaptive strategy by means of appearance, which Spinoza reveals in passing (in an explanation of a definition or a *scholium*), is not without some historical resonance. Is Spinoza not describing the strategic choices of his contemporaries, reduced to the functions and illusions of practical and utilitarian subjects? Reading some historical analysis gives some weight to the hypothesis.[113] Yet Spinoza is no Hobbes: to enjoy one's assent, in the last instance, to glory (the immoderate exaltation of self-love), the ambitious person strives to subject human relationships to a strategic imperative of

---

[108] *Ethics* III, DA 29 Exp.; CWS I, 538.
[109] *Ethics* III, DA 29 Exp.; CWS I, 538.
[110] *Ethics* IV, 57 Schol.; CWS I, 578.
[111] Ibid.
[112] Ibid.
[113] Charles Wilson, *Dutch Republic and the Civilizations of the 17th Century*, Littlehampton Book Services, 1968, and Max Weber, *The Protestant Ethic and the Spirit of Capitalism*, Dover Publications, 2003.

dissimulation, thus reducing human relations to manipulation, and her equals to instruments of her ambition.

But the object of ambition is vain when glory is a 'self-esteem that is encouraged only by the opinion of the multitude'.[114] Spinoza's denunciation of the vanity of glory is not moralistic. He clearly says that such glory is 'nothing', since the contentment it seeks and hopes for is based on a contradiction that makes its existence impossible. This object is a delusion, which, like any object, constitutes itself in relation to the affects of those who pursue and recognise it, just like the freedom and the mastery of all things that the proud person thinks she has, which necessarily includes vainglory. Vainglory is the hallucinatory object *par excellence*. One can never really possess it, because of the inconstancy of those whose satisfaction it depends on: 'he who exults at being esteemed by the multitude is made anxious daily, strives, sacrifices, and schemes, in order to preserve his reputation'.[115] The expected self-satisfaction, the 'highest thing we can hope for',[116] is cancelled out by the fear of losing it as soon as we believe we possess it. It is, in reality, never reached. It is impossible to know through this path. And the creature of vainglory finds only a substitute enjoyment through the humiliations that, out of fear and hatred, she inflicts upon her perpetual rivals:

> Indeed, because everyone desires to secure the applause of the multitude, each one willingly puts down the reputation of the other. And since the struggle is over a good thought to be the highest, this gives rise to a monstrous lust of each to crush the other in any way possible. The one who at last emerges as victor exults more in having harmed the other than in having benefited himself. This love of esteem, or self-love, then, is really empty, because it is nothing.[117]

The self-contentment that one expects from the crowd is only ever imagined but never experienced. No one ever possesses it, because it has no more reality than the freedom it imagines having to favour its thriving (delirium). But the emulator does not know that. For her, proof that the glory, fuelled by the opinion of the crowd, is very real lies in the (imagined) pride and enjoyment among those who have her favours because they work hard to win them. What should reveal the masquerade paradoxically strengthens

---

[114] *Ethics* IV, 58 Schol.; CWS I, 578.
[115] Ibid.
[116] *Ethics* IV, 52 Schol.; CWS I, 575.
[117] *Ethics* IV, 58 Schol.; CWS I, 579.

it and pushes the emulator to rival those whom she desires to imitate. This only accentuates the illusory reality and value of the coveted object, and thus the violence of the 'struggle for what is esteemed as the supreme good'. In 'vainglory', we imagine that at least one other already possesses what we desire, which justifies our desire (even if this desire does not come from envy but only finds in envy a new dynamism).

By refusing the moralising explanation of a 'vice of human nature'[118] – which is, like God's will, the refuge of ignorance – Spinoza reveals the causal chain of a specifically human violence beyond any political constitution of society. The effort of each to persevere in being, under the necessary determinations of the joy principle and the dynamic of imitation of the vulgar's affects, leads to a war of all against all, exacerbated by the dynamic of envy, 'the reversal' of self-love and the vainglory it involves and desires. Even in the sadness of murderous delirium, the other's consent and the joy she involves remain 'the highest thing we can hope for'.[119] This is why the autonomy of human violence (which casts humans and fragments of always-already-constituted societies into a regime of total heteronomy and servitude) calls for the ethical and political response of humanity and liberty. It does not require the relinquishing of natural rights for the sake of security and peace, as Hobbes demands. The individual's and the multitude's *conatus* aspire to the autonomy of plenitude rather than to the autonomy of violence: political society and reason must strive to answer to this demand. If there is a specifically human violence born of imitation (in the sense that there is also a specificity of human appetites in relation to animal appetites...),[120] it points to the lowest degree of humanity and freedom of which humans are capable. Children are, for Spinoza, an excellent example of this.

The child, who 'has a Body capable of very few things, and very heavily dependent on external causes',[121] is ruled by passive affects, and thus lives in a state of quasi-total heteronomy with respect to the world and her parents. Spinoza refers the reader to the experience of early childhood, to its desiring and mimetic relations, and to its dynamics of ambition overdetermined by an education based on the incentives of honour and envy,[122] which adults model for their children. But in truth, for Spinoza, the (epistemological)

---

[118] *Ethics* III, Praef.; CWS I, 491.
[119] *Ethics* IV, 52 Schol.; CWS I, 575.
[120] *Ethics* III, 57 Schol.; CWS I, 528.
[121] *Ethics* V, 39 Schol.; CWS I, 614. Translator's note.
[122] *Ethics* III, 55 Schol., 32 Schol.; *Ethics* III, DA 27 Exp.; CWS I, 525–6, 513, 537.

model of human behaviour (of the *vulgus*) is the child herself! The hidden child continues to live in adult passions, and the educational function ultimately only amplifies and orients a dynamic of desire, which is already structured by specific values. We are led to a logic of hatred, both by the dynamism of ambition (subject to passive affections) and by the guidance of education. The logic of hatred is the logic of the destruction of the other.[123] The ethical project must, therefore, break with childhood as well as with the educational principles of adults. It must break with powerlessness to truly expand life's potential for humanity, knowledge and liberty.

> And really, he who, like an infant or child, has a Body capable of very few things, and very heavily dependent on external causes, has a mind which considered solely in itself is conscious of almost nothing of itself, or of God, or of things. On the other hand, he who has a Body capable of a great many things, has a mind which considered only in itself is very much conscious of itself, and of God, and of things. In this life, then, we strive especially that the infant's Body may change (as much as its nature allows and assists) into another, capable of a great many things and related to a mind very much conscious of itself, of God, and of things. We strive, that is, that whatever is related to its memory or imagination is of hardly any moment in relation to the intellect.[124]

Spinoza, however, has a positive perception of childhood as well, understood from an ethical perspective.

---

[123] *Ethics* III, 28, 39 Dem.; CWS I, 509, 516.
[124] *Ethics* V, 39 Schol.; CWS I, 614.

4

Hilaritas and *acquiescentia in se ipso*: A Dynamic of Joy

Hilaritas (elation or cheerfulness), for Spinoza, is a joy that expresses a perfect affective equilibrium of the body's parts (and, indeed, of all the parts of our being), which are identically or equally affected with this affect.[1] He promptly adds in *Ethics* IV, 44 Schol., however, that *hilaritas* 'is more easily conceived of than observed'.[2] Yet Spinoza also endeavours to convince us that:

1. While this joyful affect, indeed, only occurs very rarely or fleetingly in practice, it is an adequate expression of the necessary structure of all existence insofar as it is wrapped up in the essential love for oneself and/or the *conatus* itself, which it develops and affirms in a certain proportion of motion-and-rest.
2. *Hilaritas* points to a direct, practical and affective path (of balanced joy) for the formation of adequate ideas. This is the way to our freedom, since it implies a dynamic passage from passive to active affects.
3. Therefore, *hilaritas* is also, and above all, the adequate expression of the necessary ethical existence *par excellence*, namely, of *acquiescentia in se ipso*. *Acquiescentia* finds its origin in reason, and the essential equilibrium this 'contentment' implies is, by *Ethics* IV, 52 Schol., 'the highest good we can hope for'.[3] As per *Ethics* IV App. 4, it is also 'the ultimate end of the man who is led by reason, i.e., his highest Desire, by which he strives to moderate all the others, is that by which he is led to conceive adequately both himself and all things that can fall under his understanding'.[4]

---

[1] *Ethics* IV, 42 Dem.; CWS I, 570.
[2] CWS I, 571. Translator's note.
[3] CWS I, 575. Translator's note.
[4] CWS I, 588. Translator's note.

4. Lastly, found at the very heart of *Ethics* IV, *hilaritas* announces that the ethical end is, as much as possible, *acquiescentia in se ipso*. It is the complete agreement of a human being with herself, equally and positively affected in all the parts of her body and mind.

To address the question of the structural underpinnings of reason and human freedom, therefore, we shall follow the dynamism and vital balance that *hilaritas* assumes and expresses in *Ethics* IV. Even if experience shows us how rare this vital balance is, reason and Spinozist philosophy nevertheless presuppose its necessary and immanent presence in any activity, especially in the practice of ethics.

1 The Infant's Joyful Passion

Why, then, does Spinoza say that *hilaritas* 'is more easily conceived of than observed'? *Ethics* IV, 42 states that there can be no excess of elation, but that it is always good. In *Ethics* III, 11 Schol., Spinoza defines elation as a joyful affect that pertains to both the mind and the body, when all the parts of a human being are equally affected. And *Ethics* IV, 42 Dem. further specifies that, in this affect:

> The body's power [*puissance*] of acting is increased or aided, so that all of its parts maintain the same proportion of motion-and-rest to one another. And so (by P39), [elation] is always good, and cannot be excessive.[5]

With this, we understand the rarity, the transience, of *hilaritas*: a state that presupposes a perfect equilibrium of our whole being. It is a balance that, at first, is not due to the being's own power. Since *hilaritas* is a passive joy, this equilibrium is rather due to 'fortune', to favourable circumstances. In fact, to create this perfect affective equilibrium, those fluctuating yet favourable external causes need to affect the body and mind at the same time. Meaning that, under *hilaritas*, we are but 'partial' causes of our affect.[6] And as with all passive affects, the 'force' and 'growth' of *hilaritas* 'must be defined not by human power, but by the power of things that are outside us'.[7] From *Ethics* IV Ax., *Ethics* IV, 2–4, *Ethics* IV, 4 Dem. Cor. and *Ethics* IV App. 30, we learn how rare this equilibrium is in a being which is both endowed with

---

[5] CWS I, 570. Translation modified.
[6] *Ethics* III Def. 1; *Ethics* IV, 2 Dem.
[7] *Ethics* IV App. 2; *Ethics* IV, 5; CWS I, 588.

many capacities for being affected and in constant commerce (*commercium*)[8] with an external world in which 'things do not act in order to affect us with Joy, and their power of acting is not regulated by our advantage'.[9] If this affect is rare, however, it is not impossible. We could even perhaps say that we have all already experienced it. It is, after all, Spinoza's ethico-political project to (re)arrange external circumstances such that as many as possible experience *hilaritas*, for this is the way to freedom.

Let us then return, first, to *Ethics* III, 57 Schol.:

> Therefore, though each individual lives content with her own nature, by which she is constituted, and is glad of it, nevertheless that life with which each one is content, and that gladness, are nothing but the idea, or soul, of the individual. And so the gladness of the one differs in nature from the gladness of the other as much as the essence of the one differs from the essence of the other.[10]

Consider the case of a child. Indeed, her capacities to affect and to be affected are limited, since she 'cannot talk, walk, or reason'.[11] For a long time, the child's soul has 'practically no consciousness of itself, of God, or of things'[12] and only yearns for her mother's milk, and the physical and affective warmth of her environment. Her native weakness and 'very small number of capacities' to affect and be affected places her in an extremely unstable 'equilibrium', depending almost completely on the fluctuations of external causes.[13] That said, this equilibrium is easily achievable once her needs for nourishment, well-being and love are satisfied.[14] Accordingly, a child will experience an elation that will last as long as circumstances meet her needs and so long, also, as these needs are easy to meet. But this elation is experienced within a dynamic of *appetitus*, in a regimen of quasi-total heteronomy. We can thus say of the newborn what Spinoza says of the ignorant: namely, that as soon as she ceases to be passive (in sadness or in joy), she ceases to be.[15]

---

[8] *Ethics* IV, 18 Schol.; CWS I, 555.
[9] *Ethics* IV, App. 30; CWS I, 593.
[10] CWS I, 538. Translation modified. Translator's note.
[11] *Ethics* V, 6 Schol.; CWS I, 600.
[12] *Ethics* V, 39 Schol.; CWS I, 614.
[13] *Ethics* V, 39 Schol.; CWS I, 614. Spinoza also speaks of the mimetic joy of children's laughter in *Ethics* III, 32 Schol.
[14] *Ethics* III, 32 Schol.; CWS I, 513.
[15] *Ethics* V, 42 Schol.; CWS I, 616.

If the body's equilibrium is indeed actualised through external conditions, Spinoza also says in *Ethics* IV, 42 Dem. that the defining characteristic of *hilaritas* is that it maintains the same proportion of motion-and-rest between the parts of the body. This proportion of motion-and-rest through which one experiences a certain measure of plenitude is not created by external causes even if it is aided by favourable ones.[16] On the other hand, if elation is always good and cannot be excessive, it is because the proportion of motion and rest maintained in this affect is already itself, and by itself, beneficial, balanced, good and without excess. What makes elation possible, therefore, is not the preservation, for its own sake, of the same proportions, but the preservation of a good equilibrium between all parts of our being. Indeed, let us suppose a proportion of motion-and-rest that would bring about a joyful imbalance, which can occur in the case of *titillatio*, defined by Spinoza in *Ethics* IV, 43 Dem.:

> Pleasure is a Joy which, insofar as it is related to the body, consists in this, that one (or several) of its parts are affected more than the others (see its Def. in IIIP11S). The power of this affect can be so great that it surpasses the other actions of the Body (by P6), remains stubbornly fixed in the Body, and so prevents the Body from being capable of being affected in a great many other ways.[17]

Let us imagine a joyful imbalance in a body whose power to act would nevertheless be increased in all its parts. This increase in power to act could not, however, produce *hilaritas*. Because of the prior structural imbalance (even if this imbalance were maintained in all its proportions), such an increase in power to act would always produce *titillatio*, albeit with a higher degree of power to act.

Elation already supposes, therefore, a state of equilibrium, and a specific affect (and/or desire) without excess, linked to the state of equilibrium belonging to our body and our whole being. This affect is not, however, the expression of the transition of our body's power to act from a lesser to a greater perfection. It is a joy, 'if we may still use this term', as Spinoza will say of blessedness in *Ethics* V, 36 Schol., that is, to speak like the Epicureans, a tranquil joy.[18] But it is constitutive, active, and so of the same type as the

---

[16] *Ethics* IV, 39; CWS I, 568.

[17] CWS I, 570. Translator's note.

[18] Translator's note: the usual translation for 'ataraxy' is 'tranquil pleasure' but I have chosen 'tranquil joy' for reasons that will become apparent later in the text.

feeling of freedom, love or glory experienced in the third kind of knowledge. In fact, this restful affect that accompanies the idea of the self (however unconscious it may be) is already this very blessedness. It is blessedness, however, not yet adequately understood or lived in an autonomous regime of desire. Love of the self is the first and fundamental form of agreement, of balanced affect of self, by the self, and is necessarily implied in the *conatus*. It is the minimum reflexivity that is the singular self-determination of nature's affirmation (*affirmatio*) in and through us. Since it affirms our singular essence through our existence (and *is* this affirmed essence itself), it is a 'natural love',[19] necessarily balanced and without excesses. This love affirms the characteristic proportion of motion-and-rest, in and through which a singular essence actualises itself. And this restful equilibrium of the love for oneself is immanent to the power to act itself, immanent to the real movement of Reality in its productive affirmation. It is an active and fruitful stillness.

Let us return to the case of the child. There is in her a contentment, a sense of well-being specific to her nature, specific to her singular proportion of motion-and-rest. This condition of plenitude, of alignment with herself, expresses itself perfectly in the equilibrium of her affects in her body as well as in her mind. Spinoza has distinguished elation and melancholy from titillation (or pleasure) and pain. He further tells us that these two affects concern human beings only when all the parts of their beings are 'equally affected'. Even though Spinoza deals with elation and melancholy symmetrically, in *Ethics* III, 11 Schol. and *Ethics* IV, 42, but contrary to the usual reading, these two affects are not actually symmetrical or equivalent. Indeed, elation is an affect of equilibrium that is by nature without excess, and always good, whereas melancholy, despite the maintained equilibrium of the body's parts in the depressive movement, is by nature unbalanced and excessive. In that sense, melancholy is rather the opposite of a *titillation*, likewise increased in each of the body's parts. So understood, melancholy is an excessive pain to which all parts of the body are radically subjected. This subjection decreases the power to act of our whole being as well as that of all its parts, such that no further resistance is possible. The sadness of melancholy, by becoming constitutive in this way – and this is the limit of life and of its possibility – becomes a veritable death instinct. In contrast, the joy of *hilaritas* is positively constitutive. It is linked not only to the increase of the power to act but also, and above all, to the active rest immanent to the very movement of affirmation. This essential rest is the preservation of the same proportional equilibrium in this increase of power, the preservation of the

---

[19] KV App. 2, 6.

same balanced proportion of being in its affirmation. It is, therefore, without excess by nature, like the love that accompanies it. And here is, already, the joy of blessedness.

2 Acquiescentia animi and Adequate Knowledge

The path from balanced love for oneself to blessedness is direct. And *hilaritas* is, to a certain extent, the practical linchpin of this journey, a practical condition of the transition. If *hilaritas* is admittedly shaped by external causes, organised and supported by favourable encounters (as in the case of the child), it nevertheless presupposes an essential equilibrium, an equilibrium of the essence itself expressed in a specific proportion of motion-and-rest. Meaning that, with *hilaritas*, if the intervention of favourable external causes is necessary (and this is our passivity), this alone does not explain the originality and power of this affect. That is, these favourable external causes must also meet our actual essential activity: the *conatus*. Indeed, at a certain degree of perfection of our being (when our body can affect and be affected in many ways), this essential activity will make the occasion of a veritable constitution of internal contentment whose origin will be reason out of these fortunate circumstances. Indeed, 'the force of a Desire that arises from Joy must be defined by human power and the power of an external cause'.[20] This is the example *par excellence* of *hilaritas* in which forces combine. The dynamic of *hilaritas* is, therefore, the direct and royal route of an *acquiescentia in se ipso* that takes its origin and solid equilibrium from reason itself, that is, from the autonomous power of a singular life. For if elation is a passive joy, it is also the expression of a powerful joy of living fully in all our actions, of *acquiescentia animi*, an agreement with the self and with life. It is also the expression of a fundamental trust. When accompanied by the idea of God as its cause, with the second and third kinds of knowledge, it will become an active affect, blessedness.

The dynamic of the joy of elation, as activity that is nevertheless still passive, however, can lead us to adequate knowledge, as indicated by *Ethics* IV, 45 Cor. 2 Schol., *Ethics* IV, App. 31, and *Ethics* IV, 59 Dem. 1.

Consider *Ethics* IV, 45 Cor. 2 Schol.:

The greater the Joy with which we are affected, the greater the perfection to which we pass, i.e., the more we must participate in the divine nature. To use things, therefore, and take pleasure in them as far as possible – not,

---

[20] *Ethics* IV, 18 Dem.; CWS I, 555.

of course, to the point where we are disgusted with them, for there is no pleasure in that – this is the part of a wise man [. . .] For the human Body is composed of a great many parts of different natures, which constantly require new and varied nourishment, so that the whole Body may be equally capable of all the things which can follow from its nature, and hence, so that the mind also may be equally capable of understanding many things.[21]

And *Ethics* IV, 59 Dem. 1:

Insofar as Joy is good, it agrees with reason (for it consists in this, that a man's power of acting is increased or aided) and is not a passion except insofar as the man's power of acting is not increased to the point where he conceives himself and his actions adequately. So if a man affected with Joy were led to such a great perfection that he conceived himself and his actions adequately, he would be capable – indeed more capable – of the same actions to which he is now determined from affects which are passions.[22]

And so, elation – which is always good and never excessive – is the passive affect *par excellence* that agrees adequately with reason. Reason may begin to express itself through this affect. It does so through the very self-arranging process of life. It is a process of composition and organisation, which is also the very process of reason-affirming joy and actively resisting external forces that together tend to suppress a state of elation, suppressing the perfect affective equilibrium between all parts of our being. It is a dynamic of ascending reason through joy as well as a dynamic of perfection. It is

moved not by Fear or aversion, but only by an affect of Joy, [men] may strive to live as far as they can according to the rule of reason.[23]

And

we must always (by IVP63C and IIIP59) attend to those things which are good in each thing so that in this way we are always determined to act from an affect of Joy.[24]

[21] CWS I, 572. Translator's note.
[22] CWS I, 579. Translator's note.
[23] *Ethics* IV, App. 25; CWS I, 592. Translation modified. Translator's note.
[24] *Ethics* V, 10 Schol.; CWS I, 602. Translator's note.

But from this dynamic self-arrangement, which only really brings about autonomy when accompanied by the idea of God as the cause of our affects, cannot result any passivity or decrease in power. Even if the augmentation is extrinsically passive, in the sense that a human being's power to act has not yet increased the critical point or threshold where he may conceive of himself and of his own affects appropriately, elation is not essentially passive. Its relative passivity is, in some way, a passive activity, since its dynamism leads only to activity rather than to passivity, both of the body and mind. If elation is not obliterated by unfavourable external causes, then it is the active, immanent route to produce adequate ideas and common notions. Why is elation, in practice, a power productive of common notions?

Elation is, due to the equilibrium and the equality it entails, simultaneously an affection of each of the body's parts, and the idea of this affection. Now, at a certain stage of perfection (fullness of the ability to affect and to be affected), the human body in its numerous parts is equally affected by external causes, as with elation. This means that the body begins to affect itself, because it is also affected by something common both to its parts and to all other bodies. Its extrinsic passivity is therefore immediately correlative with an activity that is, absolutely speaking, that of reason. This is where reason truly begins, since 'that which is total in the thing' – that is, the plenitude itself of the affection – 'is *ipso facto* total (or adequate) in the idea'.[25] Per *Ethics* II, 37, however, 'those things that are common to all things and are equally in the part as in the whole, can be conceived only adequately'.[26] Because they allow singular beings to agree, the affections must also be considered in terms of their activity. These affections express the common properties that are derived from the very essence of these particular bodies. Thus, *Ethics* II, 39 reads:

> If something is common to, and peculiar to, the human body and certain external bodies by which the human Body is usually affected, and is equally in the part and in the whole of each of them, its idea will also be adequate in the Mind.[27]

And the corollary reads: 'From this it follows that the mind is more capable of perceiving many things adequately as its Body has many things in

---

[25] Martial Gueroult, *Spinoza, II: L'Ame*, Aubier, 1974, p. 336.
[26] CWS I, 474.
[27] CWS I, 474. Translator's note.

common with other bodies.'[28] Knowing, as *Ethics* IV, 32 Dem. reminds us, that things that agree in nature agree in power, and do not agree in weakness or negation, we find in *Ethics* II, 37, 38 and 39 the justification of this ethics of quantity, which is found in *Ethics* IV, 38, in *Ethics* IV, 45 Schol., in *Ethics* IV, App. 27, and in *Ethics* V, 24, 26 and 39 Schol.

Hilaritas, which denotes a process in which no affect contradicts our nature[29] and hinders our thinking,[30] expresses a dynamic in which clear and distinct ideas are formed and deduced from one another.[31] Consequently, according to *Ethics* V, 1 and 10 Dem., as long as *hilaritas* is maintained or increased, 'we have (by P1) the power [*pouvoir*] of ordering and connecting the affections of the Body according to the order of the intellect'.[32] Our entire development presupposes, of course, that the dynamic of *hilaritas* either remains unaffected by external forces or that it is already able to resist their interference. It also presupposes that this dynamic of perfection, both in body and mind, can organise itself in an autonomous, rational way. For the active immobility of *hilaritas* is *cupiditas*. It is the very essence of human beings, insofar as it is balanced and without excess by nature,[33] and insofar as it makes possible an autonomous and rational conduct of life in one's ethical striving. As Spinoza states in *Ethics* IV, 21 Dem., 'the desire to live blessedly . . . is the very essence of man'.[34] External causes are thus only the attendant causes of the fortunate manifestation of *hilaritas*. But the intensity of this manifestation is an activity, the activity of *cupiditas*. And it can, at a certain stage of perfection of being, bring forth clear and distinct ideas and thus transform *hilaritas* into *beatitudo*.

3 Dynamic Equilibrium: Return and Productivity

We must insist on the fact that Spinoza, like the materialists of antiquity, has always thought that 'one will not triumph over internal enemies before having vanquished the enemies from outside'.[35] Blessedness, thus, has as its precondition a material arrangement of the conditions of existence, conditions which are necessary, albeit not sufficient, for its establishment. This is

---

[28] CWS I, 474.
[29] *Ethics* IV, 30.
[30] *Ethics* IV, 26, 27.
[31] *Ethics* II, 40 Schol. 2, 47 Schol.
[32] CWS I, 601.
[33] *Ethics* IV, 61 Dem.
[34] CWS I, 557.
[35] Paul Nizan, *Les matérialistes de l'antiquité*, Maspéro, 1965, pp. 17–18.

what the first pages of the *Tractatus de intellectus emendatione* were already declaring. The demands of adulthood are certainly much greater than those of childhood, but the problem is the same for both. The ethical-political project is to make space for *hilaritas*, as lucidly as one can.

To form a human 'nature much stronger than ... his own',[36] it is also necessary to 'form a society of the kind that is desirable, so that as many as possible may attain it as easily and surely as possible'.[37] If it will be necessary, as suggested by *Ethics* V, 39 Dem. Schol., to direct the body's perpetual changes towards the ethical end, it is also necessary to direct the panoply of social institutions having to do with bodies and their internal and mutual equilibrium towards that same end. From this point of view, we can better appreciate Spinoza's political programme in the *TdIE* and its necessity:

> Attention must be paid to Moral Philosophy and to Instruction concerning the Education of children. Because Health is no small means to achieving this end, fourthly, the whole of Medicine must be worked out. And because many difficult things are rendered easy by ingenuity, and we can gain much time and convenience in this life, fifthly, Mechanics is in no way to be despised.[38]

The school (moral philosophy and educational science), the health system (medicine) and the world of work (mechanics) are three institutions that directly affect and accompany the life and death of human beings, the very existence of the *conatus*. More precisely, these institutions concern bodies, their 'equilibrium' and the 'agreement of life'. With this, the sociohistorical determination of these 'corporeal capacities' is better understood. Indeed, Spinoza gives them a key role in that they are the basis of the mind's modification in practical life and, in the same movement of affirmation, the basis of the production of true ideas. Not to mention the love or friendship that other human beings can have towards each other, be it under the guidance of reason or of 'true faith', and which are (as for the child) sources of equilibrium and well-being. For they are real effective remedies against passive affects before one has embarked on the path of reason.[39] But we also understand that other people and external causes in general are not always favourable to us. And we understand that for this reason we are subject to

---

[36] *TdIE*, 13; CWS I, 10.
[37] *TdIE*, 14; CWS I, 11.
[38] Ibid. *TdIE*, 15.
[39] *Ethics* IV, 46 Schol.; *Ethics* IV, App. 11. See also *TTP*, particularly chs XI–XIV.

violent contestations for hegemony between our affections themselves, as well as between our reason and our affections. The same logic of affects is at work in both the hegemony of one affection over another (as in *titillatio*) and in the hegemony that reason exercises over the affections.

Reason is, thus, represented in *Ethics* IV in the form of an *imperium* and its dictates (*dictamina*). But this *imperium* dictates only what nature already asserts in and through its self-organisation, but which we cannot directly achieve because of our weakness and/or because of the passive affects of the body subject to external forces. The first rule that reason prescribes, then, is love for oneself.[40]

It should be noted that love for oneself (*amour de soi*), and the essential equilibrium it involves, is not the same as self-love (*amour-propre*). Self-love implies a structural imbalance, since it is necessarily both imaginary and tainted by pride or false modesty. Love for oneself is, on the contrary, balanced like nature itself. It is balanced like a 'desire considered absolutely', which could not exceed itself in its affirmation since it is an affection of the self by the self, a positive and intrinsic determination of Nature in and through us:

> So if this desire could be excessive, human nature, considered in itself alone, could exceed itself, or could do more than it can. This is a manifest contradiction.[41]

Thus, when Spinoza presents love for oneself as the first principle of the dictates of reason, which 'demand nothing contrary to nature' in *Ethics* IV, 18 Schol., he is essentially thinking of this love for oneself as a balanced love of

---

[40] *Ethics* IV, 18 Schol. In his Sixteenth Lecture on the Fine Arts, Alain makes a very clear connection between the Spinozist theme of the singular essence, its 'formula of equilibrium', to use that expression, and the logic of love for oneself: 'For every man, whether Peter or John, Spinoza says, there is necessarily in God an idea or essence, a formula of equilibrium, of movements, of connected functions, which is his soul and which is the same as his body... [And] it is necessary not to believe that this essential architecture could ever become sick, end, wear out, or die by its own doing... The tide of existence does not cease to beat against our cliffs; but Spinoza energetically declares, a man cannot possibly kill himself, or even point a dagger at his own breast, unless another hand, stronger than his, twists his. Here, in this austere philosophy, we find the kernel of hope and courage, and the true foundation of love for oneself.' Alain, 'Vingt leçons sur les Beaux-Arts', in *Spinoza*, Gallimard, 1968, pp. 171–2. A kernel of hope and of courage, or kernel of resistance to anything that hinders our self-affirmation or threatens to destroy us, is explained in *Ethics* III, 6 Dem.

[41] *Ethics* IV, 61 Dem.; CWS I, 581.

a being, of its perfection. He is not thinking of self-love, a necessarily unbalanced love of an image of the self. The ethical project – to conduct oneself 'according to the dictates of reason' – is presented as being within the real continuity of a spontaneous strategy of affirmation of bodies, or of the centrifugal dynamics of the immediate love for oneself (*Ethics* IV). Yet it is also presented as partly against this strategy. More precisely, the project is against its forms of actualisation which have made of each human being, left to their own imaginary mechanisms, the worst of enemies for herself and her fellows.

In the dynamic continuation of the balanced love for oneself, the ethical enterprise presents itself as a strategy using a double movement: *first*, as a movement back to an equilibrated state, regulated by the essential proportion of motion-and-rest. This is a strategy of resistance proper to the double meaning of the 're-' prefix of 'resist'. It expresses a return to the self, an insistence but also a repetition of being-there, its persistence and perseverance. But this resistance is an active resistance, for our being dynamically opposes (*opponere*) what undermines our essential proportion of motion-and-rest, and which, in so doing, severs the presumed equilibrium of a fundamental and essential *hilaritas*. Meaning that, if there is indeed a 'return', nostalgia (sadness, pain) is not its catalyst. *Second*, and consequently, it is also a movement of the dynamic and productive affirmation (rest is active!) of new desires, new joys and new ideas. This way the proportion can positively regulate itself by increasing the capacity of our body and mind to affect and to be affected. This self-regulation of the proportion, therefore, defines not only the radical change of condition from childhood to adulthood ('is this even the same human being?' Spinoza asks in *Ethics* IV, 39 Schol.). It also defines the ethical project, as an ethics of accumulation,[42] quantity[43] and indefinite productivity.[44] Let us consider these two aspects of the ethical strategy of *conatus*.

The logic formulated by our first point about a 'return' is not a retreat to an *a priori* order or principle, since the norm is itself susceptible to modifications within an actively relational existence. One can even say that the *conatus* forms its own norm of action through its relational activity, as is clearly the case in the transition from childhood to adulthood, or from a state of ignorance to a state of wisdom. Spinoza's philosophy, therefore, is one of the real movement of Reality in its autonomy. The Spinozist ethical (and political) imperative is a 'return to the principle'. But it is not a con-

---

[42] *Ethics* IV, 20.
[43] *Ethics* IV, 38.
[44] End of *Ethics* V, 39 Schol.

servative return to an order postulated as 'natural', nor is it a return to a life that has organised its materiality prior to modality. Rather, it is a return to order as a real movement of the Real, the movement of nature balanced in its autonomy and immanence. This self-organising and auto-normative movement is without excess or deficiency. It is the law of nature realised as the power (*puissance*) of the idea, of bodies or of the multitude. Due to our finite condition and to 'human weakness and inconsistency',[45] this logic of return also supposes a conjectured state of imbalance. This also means that it is a dynamic of active resistance of the parts of our being that suffer from the dominion (the real *imperium*) of one of its parts, as in *titillatio*. Indeed, by subjecting the individual in its entirety, this dominion tends also to threaten the individual's life. In this state, the oppressed parts resist this hegemony with their particular *conatus* and in solidarity with one another. Thus, an affect is said to be evil insofar as it prevents both the mind from thinking and all parts of the body from performing their function.[46] In short, it resembles an 'evil joy' insofar as it prevents human beings 'from being rendered more capable'.[47] The pain endured by the oppressed parts of our body as they resist the dominion of another part is, then, good, in some way. That is, insofar as it is able 'to restrain Pleasure [*or titillatio*] so that it is not excessive, and to thereby prevent the body from being rendered less capable'.[48] One can make a similar argument in the case of excessive pain, which other parts of the body resist, as much as they do exclusive pleasure.

But in melancholy, because all parts of our body are equally affected by sadness, nothing allows us to resist it inwardly when depression itself is in equilibrium. The entire defence system is neutralised and put in the service of depression in a true suicidal dynamic. An external cause could unbalance this global depression through a joyful affect and allow the *conatus* of one part of our body to resist the other depressed parts. But apart from this external intervention, the individual in melancholy is logically and inevitably doomed to destruction. The love for oneself, the active core of resistance, is otherwise completely neutralised by it. Thus, we must *melancholiam expellere*. To expel melancholy, to resist it with all our might, is an important categorical imperative in Spinoza's *Ethics*. And as far as the individual *conatus* is concerned, *Ethics* III, 37 Dem., has already underlined the necessary active resistance to sadness:

---

[45] *Ethics* IV, 18 Schol.
[46] *Ethics* IV, 26, 27.
[47] *Ethics* IV, 59 Dem., 65; CWS I, 579.
[48] *Ethics* IV, 43 Dem.; CWS I, 570–1.

> All a man affected by Sadness strives for is to remove Sadness. But [. . .] the greater the Sadness, the greater is the part of the man's power of acting to which it is necessarily opposed. Therefore, the greater the Sadness, the greater the power of acting with which the man will strive to remove the Sadness.[49]

And in *Ethics* IV, 45 Cor. 2, Schol., Spinoza firmly says, in a personal intervention too rare in the geometric order to be overlooked:[50] 'Why is it less fitting to drive away melancholy than to dispel hunger and thirst? Th[is] principle . . . guides me and shapes my attitude in life.'[51] Indeed, melancholy is the main adversary. Through neutralisation, paralysis or the reversal of its life forces into forces of death, melancholy can completely overcome the *conatus*. Death creeps in through the same dynamic of associations (harmful ones) through which life could otherwise affirm itself and be deployed.

The second aspect of the strategy, as a dynamic power of affirmation, underlines the productivity of the *conatus* itself. This strategy would be absolutely and always favourable to the preservation of the individual, if she did not meet external obstacles to her affirmation. So, the abstract idea of a perfect strategy can be causally deduced, without any teleology, from the definition of 'man's essence, from the nature of which there necessarily follow those things that tend to his preservation'.[52] To posit the essence of a finite mode is necessarily to deduce actions that are useful to its preservation. And if the finite mode, by some exceptional destiny, could think according to the norm of the adequate and given idea, corresponding to the real activity of the body whose affections would hence be actively ordered, it would develop a perfect strategy of absolute affirmation of existence. But this rarely or never happens.[53] *Ethics* IV, 19, 24 Dem., 61 Dem. and App. 6 highlight the identity between perfect strategy and autonomy. This was already assumed in the opening of *Ethics* IV, Praef., which introduced the opposition between *sui juris* (a human being who relies only on himself and hence preserves herself adequately) and one pushed around by external causes, and therefore completely dependent on 'fortune'. *Ethics* IV Ax. and *Ethics* IV,

---

[49] CWS I, 515. Translator's note.
[50] This personal intervention becomes even more vibrant knowing that it borrows the words of Terence without naming him. See *Adelphi*, v. 68: *Mea sic est ratio et sic animum induco meum*. Spinoza writes: *Mea haec est ratio, et sic animum induxi meum* (*Ethics* IV, 45 Cor. 2 Schol.).
[51] CWS I, 572. Translator's note.
[52] *Ethics* III, 9 Schol.
[53] *TdIE*, 44; CWS I, 21.

Def. 8 successively posit the intrinsic infinity of the mode in its 'power [*pouvoir*] to bring about that which can be understood solely through the laws of her own nature'[54] – her power (*puissance*) of autonomy – and its extrinsic finitude in the power struggles between finite things. These passages emphasise the existential connection between the power of autonomy and the necessary, active resistance, in which autonomous affirmation must engage when faced with external challenges. Thus, the *conatus* is inextricably, in its very productivity, both a power of affirmation and a power of resistance. For the *conatus* not only resists. It also builds and is constitutive through its very resistance as affirmation. And the ethical enterprise is entirely in this process of autonomous self-organisation, of active resistance of the singular modality. This tendency to return to the essential equilibrium, which is first experienced in *hilaritas* and which is, in the same movement, at a certain level of perfection, is a production of new desires and new joys together with new adequate ideas: *acquiescentia in se ipso*, love for oneself adequately conceived.

This spiralling process through which we can find equilibrium, but always at different levels of perfection, has no model, purpose or limit. It is a dynamic of infinite perfection. It is, in some way, Epicureanism multiplied and put in endless motion. But for Spinoza, as for the Epicureans (according to a strategy of the indefinite productivity of desire or according to the Epicurean strategy of 'natural and necessary' tranquil joy), it is indeed the same project of return to an equilibrium that makes living as a wise person possible – to live as a God for other humans,[55] or, as per the final expression of the *Letter to Menoeceus*, as 'a God among [humans]'.[56] For that to which the best of us can aspire, as will be demonstrated by *Ethics* V, is to replace an object of affection, which affects us in different and often contradictory ways, with a new object. The best we can hope for is to replace an object of affection that throws us into perpetual change[57] and makes us enemies to ourselves and to other humans, with one that would affect us 'with a continuous and supreme joy for all eternity',[58] 'equally' for all human beings[59] and in all parts of our body and mind. We seek an object that would offer

---

[54] CWS I, 547. Translator's note.
[55] *Ethics* IV, 35 Cor. 2 Schol.
[56] Epicurus, *Letters and Sayings*, in *Epicurus: The Extant Remains*, ed. Cyril Bailey, 1926, Facsimile Publisher, 2015, p. 93. For a comparison of the two philosophiers, see Laurent Bove, 'Epicurisme et spinozisme: l'éthique', *Archives de philosophie*, July–September, 1994, pp. 471–84.
[57] *Ethics* IV, 33 Dem.; CWS I, 562.
[58] *TdIE*, 1; CWS I, 7.
[59] *Ethics* IV, 36; CWS I, 564.

us a tranquil joy of the type already found in *hilaritas*. But, if the matter is left to happenstance with *hilaritas*, the idea here, in contrast, is to 'command fortune' as much as possible, in the words of *Ethics* IV, 47 Schol.

The new object, if I can still call it that, is God or Nature. And, as stated by *Ethics* V, 39 Dem., which relies on *Ethics* IV, 38 and *Ethics* IV, 30, we can only aspire to the knowledge and love of God (or Nature) when our body possesses many capacities to be affected and to affect. Let us turn to *Ethics* V, 39 Dem.:

> He who has a Body capable of doing a great many things is least troubled by evil affects (by IVP38), i.e. (by IVP30), by affects contrary to our nature. So (by P10) he has a power [*pouvoir*] of ordering and connecting the affections of his Body according to the order of the intellect, and consequently (by P14), of bringing it about that all the affections of the Body are related to the idea of God. The result (by P15) is that it is affected with a Love of God, which (by P16) must occupy, or constitute the greatest part of the Mind. Therefore (by P33), he has a Mind whose greatest part is eternal.[60]

Through this knowledge of God and of our affects, *hilaritas* becomes *beatitudo*. It is a blessedness of our whole being, of a human being in her totality. Spinoza speaks of a 'whole man' (*totius hominis*),[61] of all the parts of his body and mind, and not only of 'that part of us which is defined by understanding, i.e. the better part of us'.[62] Based only on this last affirmation, one might believe that fortune, a necessary if circumstantial, occasional cause of *hilaritas*, may ultimately do more for human happiness than one's own reason or virtue. The *Short Treatise* had already declared that one who seeks and finally 'rests in that good which is all good, and in which there is the fullness of all Joy and satisfaction',[63] finds a 'love' that is 'unlimited, [that is] the more it increases, the more excellent it becomes, since it falls on an object that is infinite. That is why it can always increase.'[64] And the more we live in and off this complete and integral love, the less we will need of 'fortune's help'.[65]

---

[60] CWS I, 614. Translator's note.
[61] *Ethics* IV, 60 Schol.; CWS I, 581. Translator's note.
[62] *Ethics* IV, App. 32; CWS I, 594. Translator's note.
[63] KV II, vii, 3; CWS I, 110.
[64] KV II, xiv, 4; CWS I, 112.
[65] *Ethics* IV, 46 Schol.; CWS I, 573.

The definition of *hilaritas*, therefore, reveals both the very meaning, in a fleeting experience, of blessedness, and the dynamic and autonomous route, at a certain degree of perfection, of its access. Through this joy by which we come to 'know' a fundamental good,[66] we can come to the knowledge of God and of ourselves. We can find, in the highest degree of perfection or virtue, this tranquillity in oneself that we have already experienced as an infant. Easily contented by fortune, then, we had been (even if very temporarily) in blessedness. *Ethics* IV and *Ethics* V summons us to develop and rediscover this free offering of blessedness, in agreement with the dynamics of our own virtue, the very laws of our nature.[67] *Hilaritas* is both a vehicle and an invaluable guide for this undertaking of and to *acquiescentia in se ipso*.

The question of strategy has, thus, moved from the domain of representation to that of the production of adequate ideas. The first is the domain of the practical and ethical subject, under the determination of reason, which seeks out means according to an end. Whereas the second, by following the order of affections identical in the body as well as in the mind, shares in the very order by which nature produces and affirms itself in its absolute plenitude through the sequence of active affects. And this new logic – which is in reality eternal – is the very logic of essence in its actualisation, the logic of existence in its absolute and perfect affirmation. Without some abstract model of mediation for means and purpose, this is the perfect strategy for the mode. It is perfect in that it is here and now, in the deployment of the mode's autonomy, in the real mastery of the problems faced by its efforts to align itself with reality, its efforts to align with itself. Human beings enter the real movement of the active affects through adequate ideas. Wisdom is this real movement that abolishes the present state of servitude. Wisdom is the struggle of the strategic subject who can participate in the construction of the objective conditions of this movement on the basis of true knowledge.

---

[66] *Ethics* IV, 8; CWS I, 550.
[67] *Ethics* IV, Def. 8; *Ethics* IV, 24; CWS I, 547, 558.

5
Ethical Subjectivity and the Absolute Affirmation of Singular Existence: An Ethics of Resistance

1 The Spiritual Automaton and the Practical Subject

'Every idea that in us is absolute, or adequate and perfect, is true', says *Ethics* II, 34. The adequate idea as absolute idea affirms absolutely (or perfectly) what it is as an idea (as a mode of the attribute of thought): infinity in act.[1] In and through it, the unity of substance intensively expresses itself in its complete actuality. Insofar as it has adequate ideas, the mind can be understood as a 'spiritual automaton', following the expression from the *TdIE*, 85.[2] This formulation must be reserved to describe the spontaneity of the mind, its productive activity rather than its passivity. When the mind is forced into action by the automatism of Habit, memory and imagination, it loses its status as an automaton, that is, its autonomy.[3] This spontaneity is not that of a freely willing subject. It is a 'free necessity' by which the mind, insofar as God is its essence, produces ideas according to its own intensity. The adequate idea expresses a power (*puissance*) of thought, identical in us and in God. It expresses a way of thinking (a mode of production of ideas) that is identical with that of God. The standpoint of adequation and identification, in us and in God, of the productive force and the mode of production it involves, clarifies the relationship between truth and essence in the third

---

[1] *Ethics* I, 8 Schol.
[2] CWS I, 37.
[3] Mathematical intellection is exemplary since it expresses the complete autonomy of mind (*TdIE* 70–1; CWS I, 31–3). We can only understand what we do autonomously. This statement, which for Hobbes was true only in the ethical and political spheres (*De Corpore* I, ch. I, 8), is valid for Spinoza in all spheres of activity, and especially in metaphysics. Notice that the *TdIE* does not yet consider the possibility of an autonomy of the imagining mind, as will *Ethics* II, 17 Schol.

kind of knowledge (according to *Ethics* II, 40 Schol. 2). Yet Spinoza thinks of an idea of the second kind of knowledge (a 'common notion' is an idea of the bodies' properties and therefore not of its essence) as an absolute and perfectly adequate idea. In which sense, then, does a common notion also constitute a spiritual automaton?

The 'spiritual automaton', in the *TdIE*, is intrinsically linked to the specific laws of production of the true idea as it is conceived through the fourth type of perception.[4] It is possible to keep the formulation of the spiritual automaton for the *Ethics* (which does not use it again), not only in relationship to 'intuitive Science' but also to reason, knowledge of the 'second kind'. In fact, although the common notions do not express the singular essence of a thing, they express properties that are truly common to two, several or all bodies. For this reason, in God, this idea (as a common property) is deduced from the adequate idea of bodies' essences, considered through the common notion only in terms of their properties.

The common notion (like the adequate idea of the third kind of knowledge) is identical in the human mind and in God. The mind does not arrive at this knowledge, however, by the same deductive path it took in the second kind of knowledge. In the mind, an adequate idea of the second kind is identical with the idea in God, with respect of the knowledge of truly common properties of bodies, but also 'less perfect'. It does not know these properties according to the bodies' essences, but only intellectually, based on the experience of 'agreements, differences, and oppositions'[5] between things. An idea of the second kind is thus the absolute and perfect affirmation (*affirmatio*) of the reason that produced it. For it expresses every notion from the most general one to the most particular notion of common properties between this and that body, the genetic order *more geometrico* of its deduction. Yet this geometric order – also found in the *Ethics* – is not the one through which we acquire, through imagination, our first common notions.

If the *more geometrico* must be understood as a radical weapon against the finalist bias and its ideological forms of theologico-political expression, the (existential) genesis of the common notion must be understood as part of the logic of the strategy of the Spinozist *conatus*. This means that we can understand it as one of the solutions that the *conatus*, in its effort to persevere in being, came up with in the face of the dangerous complexity of reality. From the point of view of its consequences, the strategy of the *conatus* appears to be the resolution of the problems that the body encounters in

---

[4] *TdIE* 19; CWS I, 12–13.
[5] *Ethics* II, 29 Schol.; CWS I, 434.

and through its effort to persevere in being. Although it has this operative effect, we must not confuse the cause with its effects, or explain one through the other.

Regarding the formation of common notions, the efficient cause is our body encountering other bodies, which always necessarily results in the conservation, activation or depletion of our power to act. These fluctuations, as we know, are accompanied by an affect of joy or sadness that our body will strive to preserve or diminish. This natural law leads the *conatus* to resist sadness actively and to conserve and amplify joy. The dynamic traces of memory[6] determine the *conatus* to seek bodies with which it agrees and to think of how and why some bodies agree with it and others do not. This is thinkable only if the *conatus* has the strength. The strength – from the active-resistance to sadness, towards the constitution of an autonomous ethical subject – has its concrete conditions of possibility which are already those of the interrelation of bodies, which are also power struggles. It is an always-already-there of traces of the affections of a singular body in its relations with the world.[7] According to this necessity (a singular vital necessity involved in the universal necessity of power struggles), the *conatus*, in and through its strategic logic of active resistance, develops as 'reason'. It does so according to forces in and through which it grasps what is true, according to a process other than that of recognition.

Access to the common notions is explained by the logic of Habit, the utility principle and memory. In its indefinite effort to persevere in joy, the vital consequence of access to the common notions is an effective adjustment of the *conatus* to reality. We must distinguish the adequate idea of the second kind of knowledge, however, from the experience and process of recognition that is at the basis of its elaboration. The end of *Ethics* II, 29 Schol. indeed states:

> so long as it is determined internally, from the fact that it regards a number of things at once, to understand their agreements, differences, and oppositions. For so often as it is disposed internally, in this or another way, then it regards things clearly and distinctly.[8]

---

[6] *Ethics* III, Post. 2.
[7] With Wim Klever, then, we can speak of 'Spinozist ethics as a human physics'; *La ética de Spinoza. Fundamentos y significado*, ed. Atilano Dominguez, Universidad de Castilla-La Mancha, 1992, pp. 29–36.
[8] CWS I, 471. Translator's note.

We know, from *Ethics* II, 17 Schol., that this contemplation (of the first kind of knowledge) is the imaginative way the mind represents external things to itself as present, even if its representations 'don't reproduce the figures of things'.[9] The mind first perceives the external world and the things in it through the process of practical recognition (or of inadequate knowledge), but it does not understand them through this process.

To transition to adequate ideas, then, is to pass from extrinsic determinations to an intrinsic determination, from passivity to activity:

> Our Mind does certain things [acts] and undergoes other things, viz. insofar as it has adequate ideas, it necessarily does certain things, and insofar as it has inadequate ideas, it necessarily undergoes other things.[10]

There is continuity, however, behind this rupture from one kind of knowledge to another: that of the very principle of the *conatus* that perseveres in its effort, through its imaginary associations (according to likeness, contiguity or causality), and through the real understanding of the internal associations between things (common notions).[11] The demonstration of *Ethics* IV, 59 was already considering the advent of reason as a cause, with the strategy of a continuous amplification of joy alone – a passing to an ever-greater perfection, an ever-greater degree of individual organisation and composition. *Ethics* V, 10 Schol. answers to the same dynamic:

> in ordering our thoughts and images, we must always (by IVP63C and IIIP59) attend to those things which are good in each thing so that in this way we are always determined to acting from an affect of Joy.[12]

The quest for 'true' ideas thus belongs to the global strategy of the *conatus*. Seeking what is useful to herself, a subject makes the truth the object of her desire and love. It is the continuation, by other means, of the natural inclination for joy. Absolutely speaking, in Reality's actual movement, the adequate idea is the idea (in thought) of an active affection of extension. The spiritual automaton's expression corresponds to an autonomous strategy of corporeality, an increasingly recurring theme from *Ethics* II, 13 Schol. to *Ethics* V, 39 Schol.

---

[9] *CWS* I, 465. Translator's note.
[10] *Ethics* III, 1; *CWS* I, 493.
[11] *Ethics* III, 9; *CWS* I, 499.
[12] *Ethics* V, 10; *CWS* I, 602.

2 From the Practical Subject of Love to Ethical Subjectivity

For the theory of the practical subject, the legitimate use of the notion of subject was confined: first, to the temporal differentiation of the subject from its object; second, to its teleological (and/or loving) structure; third, to its specific process of knowledge as recognition (or inadequate knowledge); fourth, to its status of 'effect'. At some level of complex modal reality, this describes a simply given subject-form. It is a matrix from which the concrete subjectivity of the individual as 'effect' expresses itself in acts (in its choice of objects and/or its intentionality), informed both by the particular and conjectural determinations of the organic and social body and under the guidance of knowledge. How shall we understand the *Ethics* IV, 47 Schol.'s identification of life under the guidance of reason with the power (*pouvoir*) to 'force destiny', that is, to be the subject – Spinoza says 'adequate cause'[13] – of its actions? Even activated – that is, under the determination of the adequate idea and according to the adjusted use she makes of the true idea according to her ethical purpose – the strategic ethical subject (in her practical form) remains an 'effect'. This concept of the subject operates only at the level of reality that is taken into consideration: the temporal differentiation of the subject and its object. This approach does not completely subsume the dynamic reality of (ethical) subjectivity in its becoming-cause. The ethical subject can be considered not only as an 'effect' but as an efficient cause of the good conduct of life, according to the real movement of the absolute expression of the singular existence with which it is identified.

It is paradoxical to use, as I have done, 'subject' to mean an entity that is reduced to a result or a product. It is to conceive of the subject only as subjected even if, while freed from any illusion, 'she' ethically, 'actively' acts. Spinoza represents the specific action of the loving subject (grounded in the search for one's own advantage) in the Schol. of proposition 18 of *Ethics* IV – before that subject is understood to be determined by truth – as a 'principle' (*principium*) or 'foundation' (*fundamentum*) of virtue and morality. *Ethics* IV, 24 confirms this. Loving logic gives the ethical subject the matrix of its action: it is intentional and rests on the foundation of seeking one's own advantage as well as on the model of 'morality', that is, a practice of relational composition. We compose 'human' relations[14] either by the laws of imitation or by the laws of reason, both of which direct us to be of help to others. It is, however, in reason, in truth, that the subject 'absolutely'

---

[13] *Ethics* III, Def. 1 and 2.
[14] *Ethics* IV, 50 Cor. Schol.

finds her fundamental ethical determination (*ex virtute absolute agere...*). Rid of the illusions of the loving subject through 'adequate' knowledge of the causes of her action (of her own affects), the subject is defined by the 'desire to do good generated in us by our living according to the guidance of reason'.[15] Rational intention is desire finding its origin in reason and thereby affirming its cause. It is, for Spinoza, ethical conduct in its radically philosophical sense.[16]

But the relationship between the (practical) subject and truth is not without problems. Indeed, the structure of the practical subject develops outside any theoretical preoccupation, simply as the result of the efforts to persevere in being of the complex individual. This makes truth an extrinsic fact or a simple means to a possible utility whose effects in spatio-temporal reality are even more contingent and problematic because it is divorced from the forces that might give it some efficacy. The production of adequate ideas of our affects[17] is the only immediate strategic position of mastery for the subject in her ethical problematisation of reality. In its productivity, this strategic position provokes a crisis of the instrumental and abstract problems of the use of truth.

While true knowledge of good and evil (specific to the practical subject) is contingent since it depends on fortuitous connections of passive affections, the adequate idea of our affects is indeed immediately a real ethical event. The adequate idea of our affects is a power (*puissance*) in act of humanity and love. The active affect is a direct and necessary practice of morality. The subject no longer strives to act under the guidance of an external and abstract reason, incapable of regulating desires by herself. Rather, she is this very reason herself as desire and the 'highest Desire [*summa cupiditas*], by which he strives [*studet*] to moderate all the others'.[18] The Desire, that is to say the appetite (or the combined 'effort' of mind and body), with self-awareness[19] 'is related to us insofar as we understand, or (by P1) insofar as we act'.[20] Intentional and rational action affirms the self as an ethical subject by virtue of the perfect unity of mind (adequate idea) and body (active

---

[15] *Ethics* IV, 37 Schol. 1; CWS I, 564.

[16] In *Le Christ et le salut des ignorants*, Aubier, 1971, Alexandre Matheron writes that the morality of Spinoza is a 'morality of intention' (p. 108); see also pp. 77–9: the 'psychological conditioning', in the believer, replaces the full consent of the rational mind.

[17] *Ethics* V, 3.

[18] *Ethics* IV, App. ch. 4; CWS I, 588. Translation modified.

[19] *Ethics* III, 9 Schol.; CWS I, 500.

[20] *Ethics* III, 58 Dem.; CWS I, 529.

affection), which are 'one and the same thing'[21] in the real (substantial) movement of the absolute and perfect assertion of Reality. This ethical unity is the strict sense of the realisation of reason as '*humanae rationis*'[22] and of the subject as adequate cause of her actions. To understand this better, we must return to the necessary connection between the subjects' rational activity and the efficient causality of the actual affections of which a body is capable.

The actual power of the body and the specific laws of its assertion are at the root of subjectivity, intent and action: first and foremost, the capacity of each body to connect its own affections. This, we already know, is the function of Habit. The connection of affections is mostly passive, for the body connects its affections of 'chance' encounters with external bodies. In contrast, the intellect can 'direct and link our clear and distinct perceptions' according to the necessary order of Nature.[23] This passivity, because of the singular and dynamic essence of any reality (*conatus*), necessarily always takes place against a background of activity which, despite the heteronomy in which one finds oneself, expresses the singular capacity of each body to self-organise in its strategy of active resistance. The ethical unity of the subject is built in this capacity of the body to connect its affections (which expresses its tendency towards autonomy), that is, active unity as the power of a singular being to understand and act. For, 'in proportion as the actions of a body depend more on itself alone ... so its mind is more capable of understanding distinctly'.[24] 'Acting absolutely from virtue' is, therefore, to assert the subject's ethical unity, and to assert its power or autonomy 'absolutely'. For virtue is one's own power or essence 'insofar as he has the power of bringing about certain things, which can be understood through the laws of his nature alone'.[25]

Virtue, then, leads us to power, which leads us to autonomy. It begins with Habit, the capacity – however minimal and passive – that each body has to connect its affections and, by doing so, to actively resist depleting external forces and death. Habit is one's own power of affirmation. The subject is therefore both power of affirmation and power of resistance. In either case (passive activity or active activity of the body connecting its affections), Habit (the foundation of memory)[26] proceeds, at the root of subjectivity,

---

[21] *Ethics* II, 21 Schol.; *CWS* I, 467.
[22] *TP* II, 8; *CWS* II, 511.
[23] *Ep.* XXXVII [to J. Bouwmeester]; *CWS* II, 32.
[24] *Ethics* II, 13 Schol.; *CWS* I, 558.
[25] *Ethics* IV, Def. 8; *CWS* I, 547.
[26] *Ethics* II, 18 Schol.; *CWS* I, 465–6.

to an initial constitution of time as the lived duration of 'transitions' from greater to lesser power of acting, to a greater or lesser perfection. Beyond any (or any retention of this or that particular event) particular memory, Habit is that fundamental memory through which temporality constitutes itself (as essential duration) and through which life perpetuates itself as a repetitive necessity (habit of living). The *conatus* is, therefore, a fundamental memory that does not remember anything except itself (even if, strictly speaking, it does not have an object). It is action by itself, in itself and for itself. Memory is the very process of self-causality.

This activity of the *conatus*, which indicates a 'minimum of reflexivity',[27] does not reintroduce in any way the myths of interiority or internal finality that Spinoza rejects. The 'in itself' is also the absolute outside of the self. And the 'for oneself' is openness to an infinite internal communication with all that is not oneself. For each singular being, Habit is the absolute memory of Nature, universal communication and universal necessity. As a singular being's capacity, memory is a process of subjectivation, for it 'is' absolute assertion of the cause (as singular causality or essence). Memory is, thus, in every individual, the singular power by which one is adequate cause of one's actions. Fundamental memory (as the *conatus*) is both temporality and life itself (which are the same thing). It is the actual causal process, the actualising 'singular essence'. It is the subjectivation process in and through which each being affects itself. Memory is minimal, essential and singular at once, involved in all perseverance *in suo esse*. If existence in each of its singular affirmations is singular auto-affection, it is because subjectivity (as a vital process) is 'duration', or *affectus*. Except in blessedness, *affectus* is a variation, a *transitio a minore ad majorem* (or *a majore ad minorem*) *perfectionem*. . .[28] The subject is this very variation, in and through which she is composed or, at the limits of modal heteronomy, decomposed. Becoming-subject is a project – the human project *par excellence* – and not the natural destiny of human nature. It is only its ethical possibility.

At its foundation, a subject is a singular duration,[29] the very movement of *affectus*, *affectus* itself as life's *more geometrico* movement. Because of the connected affections' tendency to repeat, at the foundation of subjective intention is also a 'longing', a tension and thus already an orientation. The first notions of good and evil arise from this longing in the practical subject

---

[27] S. Breton, 'Hegel ou Spinoza, réflexions sur l'enjeu d'une alternative', *Cahiers Spinoza*, 4, 1983, p. 73.
[28] *Ethics* III, DA 2, 3.
[29] *Ethics* II, Def. 5.

(generated by the passive connection of passive affections). When the body's actions 'depend more on itself alone' by virtue of the active connection of the affections, longing asserts, beyond good and evil, the very tension of existence in the continuation of its plenitude, as well as the ethical unity of the subject. The meaning and value of time have changed (time understood as representation/comparison of moving bodies, that is, as 'simple way of thinking') through this assertion.[30] This is no longer a sign of the finitude that subjects human beings to an external order of representation, or of the uncertainty and imperfection of the action and intention of the subject.[31] Freed from empirical and relational content,[32] temporality is the very duration of substance in its affections. It is being itself (singular essence) in its absolute and perfect assertion; it is eternity's duration. The perfect correlation of *affectus*, singular duration and essence, thus, asserts itself in the ethical process of subjectivation. The ethical subject is a process. It is the very productivity of reality in its human singularity. The separation of the means from the end is, thus, erased for the subject, but also that of the means and the force that made it possible to attain that end. For there is no more end. There is only the tension and force of a singular and subjective existence that is no longer an effect but, for the most part, an adequate cause of its affects. It is the active affect itself as real movement of *causa sui*: by itself, in itself and for itself.

The subject's becoming-efficient-cause is, therefore, at the heart of nature's immanent plan, the real movement of the absolute assertion of existence. Before going into the Spinozist ontology of *Ethics* I, and to make sure that we closely follow the logic of force affirmation in its relationship to the practical subject-form (before the 'absolute' association of active affection – in body and in mind – and the subjective process of *affectus* is carried out), let us turn to two points.

Ethics V, 10 Schol. rules out any idealist assimilation of the ethical problem that would understand it in terms of a greater or lesser distance to be bridged between the practical subject and the proposed 'model of human nature' (according to *Ethics* IV, Praef.).[33] The *scholium* concerns giving, through the true knowledge of our own advantage and based on the laws of human nature, a real efficacity to the ethical intention when it doesn't directly express the real movement of the active affection (and/or the adequate idea of its own affects). This happens by mastering the associative laws

---

[30] CM I, 4; *CWS* I, 310.
[31] *Ethics* IV, 62 Schol.; *CWS* I, 581. Translation modified.
[32] CM I, 4; *CWS* I, 310.
[33] *CWS* I, 545.

of the body through which the subject develops *habitus*, enabling the true expansion of life. This strategy, under the guidance of a subject that knows her purpose through reason, is a mnemotechnic that draws on a dynamic of affects whose origin is nevertheless not reason. The dynamic of the pursuit of joy, represented as the 'true advantage', becomes the principle (even if accompanied by the individualist illusion of self-love) of a utilitarian strategy, itself a useful phase of moral education. Confrontation with reality therefore correlates with the birth of calculative reason, which, according to a subjective strategy, follows the *élan* of the principle of the pursuit of one's own advantage.

In service to the ethical goal, affects themselves become means:

> For example, if someone sees that he pursues esteem too much, he should think of its correct use [*ejus recto*], the end [*finem*] for which it ought to be pursued, and the means [*mediis*] by which it can be acquired.[34]

By considering our 'true advantage', or from the 'love of liberty', the (desiring) subject endeavours to master her affects and appetites so that, through the conditioning of associations, she can adjust to any situation (under the guidance of the principle of one's own advantage involved in the acquired imagination of a good and highly desirable 'rule for living'). While we do not yet have perfect knowledge of our affects, this transformation belongs to the global strategy of the ethical subject, presented in *Ethics* V, 39 Schol. In the perfect combination of the adequate idea and the active affection of the body, memory and imagination's initial decisive role fades, whereas the activity of Habit (fundamental memory), as the body's capacity to connect its affections, remains the true foundation of the ethical subject and of her unity.

The subject, first constrained to chance encounters and associations, progressively transforms herself into a machine able to use not only acquired but also new associations, strategically formed according to her own advantage. She can, thus, escape the illusions and deadlocks of 'practical science', which the subjective position necessarily includes with inadequate knowledge.[35] Under the universal principle of the search for one's own advantage, before the rational strategy even comes to be, a subject is always already a habit, which is both particular and common, a singular and shared longing.

---

[34] *Ethics* V, 10 Schol.; CWS I, 602. Translator's note.
[35] See André Tosel, 'La théorie de la pratique et la fonction de l'opinion publique dans la philosophie de Spinoza', *Studia Spinozana*, 1, 1985, pp. 183–206.

Because of our relationships to others, the first values born of longing belong to a particular collective body, a family, a nation, a culture:[36] 'finally, because men everywhere, whether barbarians or civilised, combine their practices [*consuetudines*] and form some sort of civil order', a subject is also already a collectivity, a 'practice', a history.[37] The collective and always particular history is, first, the very constitution of a human being's 'humanity' in and through the spontaneous ties of imitation.[38] Spinoza locates the matrix of morality in imitation. This is where we find the first 'human' processes of subjectivation, by virtue of which the ethical subject develops. We could not understand how this 'humanity' is an ethical matrix, however, without seeing in it more than the dynamic of imitation and thus the extrinsic loving relations, mediated by images. This 'more' is the resistance that each being exerts against its own destruction.

3 An Ethics of Resistance and Love

We find at the core of mimetic logic (in its *humanitas*), before the ambition for domination perverts it, the formation of a subject that wishes to bring joy to others (and, through this, to enjoy their gratitude and love).[39] The subject's pursuit of joy and resistance to sadness (and destruction) in this mimetic logic explain the formation of an affect that can be understood as the affect at the root of morality: benevolence (*benevolentia*).

From the natural resistance through which each being opposes 'everything which can take its existence away' to the full development of blessedness,[40] it is the same affirmation of the compositional power and the organisation of bodies generate the real continuity of virtue from benevolence to generosity. The systematic order of reason is expressed in this power. The benevolence through which we strive to free an other from her suffering is a desire born out of pity,[41] but from the point of view of the dynamic of resistance to sadness, which Spinoza explains in *Ethics* III, 27 Schol. Cor. 3. The demonstration of *Ethics* III, 13 clearly states that we act to help others, to recompose life in ourselves, in and with others, because of a dynamic of resistance to sadness (in ourselves and in the other with whom we identify).

---

[36] *Ethics* III, DA 27 Exp.; CWS I, 537.
[37] TP I, 7; CWS II, 506.
[38] *Ethics* III, 29 Schol.; CWS I, 471.
[39] *Ethics* III, 29 and Schol.; CWS I, 471.
[40] *Ethics* V, 42.
[41] *Ethics* III, Def. 35; CWS I, 539.

Resistance is an effort to reorganise life, an effort of bodies to self-organise against the depleting process of which sadness is the sign: 'insofar as a thing is affected with Sadness, it is destroyed'.[42] 'Natural' and fundamental love for oneself – self-affection,[43] the *conatus* itself – is found in benevolence and the resistance to destruction. The life-affirming power of resistance explains action in contrast to the depleting pity that benevolence rejects. An ethics of resistance is at the root of the Spinozist ethics of similitude. The dynamics of ethical subjectivity as process develops through this resistance.

That human nature is irreducible to sadness and destruction is the first lesson of morality and virtue that the experience of life provides. This does not presuppose a moral order of Nature (a good nature of Nature) in the sense of harmony or happy finality. It presupposes only the mathematical necessity of a law of physical determination, that is, a causal rather than a natural moral law (according to which a right of resistance would be legitimated, for example).[44] Physical or logical necessity is the only objective feature of the resistance process: Life's aversion to sadness is a fact that has no meaning or value in itself, but this fact is nevertheless at the root of morality. We can say that the truth of all ethics is expressed through it: affirmation of life over death, of composition over depletion, of joy over sadness; and, in the benevolence that follows, affirmation of love over hate, of solidarity over solitude. Human existence has no prescribed direction, but there is a 'human' orientation, which, in and through the subject, is indicated by resistance, taken in its largest and most profound sense.[45]

---

[42] *Ethics* III, 21 Dem.; CWS I, 506.

[43] KV, App. II, 6; CWS I, 153.

[44] I cannot write this without evoking the memory of Jean Cavaillès, 'philosopher, mathematician' and 'resistant *by logic*' (according to Georges Canguilhem). 'I am a Spinozist, J. Cavaillès told Raymond Aron in 1943, I believe that everywhere we grasp what is necessary. The necessary sequences of mathematics, even the necessary stages of mathematical science, and this necessary war we are waging...'; R. Aron, 'Jean Cavaillès', *Terre des hommes*, 12, 1945, quoted by G. Canguilhem, *Vie et mort de Jean Cavaillès*, Les Carnets de Baudasser, ed. P. Laleur, Ambialet, 1976, p. 31. On the (logical and moral) relationship between the Spinozism of Cavaillès and his resistance to National Socialism, read the beautiful text by André Comte-Sponville, 'Jean Cavaillès ou l'héroïsme de la raison', in *Une éducation philosophique*, PUF, 1989, pp. 287–308.

[45] To resist is to desire, and to desire is to invent value. For in the sense of *Ethics* III, 9 Schol., we do not resist sadness because we consider sadness and oppression to be an evil. Rather, we make sadness and oppression evils because we resist them. Strictly speaking, we do not resist evil. We create evil by resisting it.

In desiring benevolence, the subjective intention does not come from a rational decision. But neither does it come from pity, which is only the opportunity for action. The benevolent intention is the expression of our active power in its rational self-organisation. In its fight against sadness, benevolence apportions the strength of its active resistance according to the intensity of the experienced destruction. As a real movement of resistance and love, benevolence is, at the same time, at the very heart of a condition of servitude and at the centre of liberty and virtue. The singular life's power of self-organisation is affirmed in and through benevolence. It is the active longing for a unity of the subject – in the making – that directly expresses this generosity and this love in (and through) which morality resides and affirms itself absolutely.

We find the origin of the ethical subject's unity (the same unity of virtue, body and reason) in the body's capacity to actively connect its own affections (that is, to mobilise actions that 'depend on itself alone').[46] This capacity to be autonomous correlates with a logic of accumulation of strength and the amplification of joy in the process of continuous transformation belonging to a child's body.[47] The subject finds the strength of her own action, however, in the practice of morality. She is all the stronger (in her means) and better adapted (to her ends) when the exercise of morality belongs to a logic of continuous amplification of joy and power:

> The more each one strives, and is able, to seek his own advantage, i.e., to preserve his being, the more he is endowed with virtue; conversely, insofar as each one neglects his own advantage, i.e., neglects to preserve his being, he lacks power.[48]

Ethics IV, 20 presents, in the process of morality, a recursion by which action (the intention of the ethical subject) becomes an efficient cause by itself. If we first conceived the (desiring) subject as an effect, the logic of the subject in the ethical project is now a becoming-cause. This becoming is the very movement by which essence and existence become adequate in the intellectual love of God. If we first understood subjectivity 'in relation to a certain time and place', the ethical subject must finally be thought of as a singular affirmation 'of the necessity of divine nature'.[49] Subjectivity is a singular

---

[46] *Ethics* II, 13 Schol.
[47] *Ethics* V, 39 Schol.
[48] *Ethics* IV, 20; CWS I, 557. Translator's note.
[49] *Ethics* V, 29 Schol.; CWS I, 610.

affirmation of the 'necessity of divine nature', but also, through this affirmation, a constitutive power of substantial existence in its eternal continuity. This means that it is in the 'free necessity'[50] of the real movement of *causa sui* that our subjectivity changes; it is amplified, or it disappears.

According to the recursive necessity of virtue, the efficient cause of tenacity and generosity[51] is the firm and generous action itself. It is the active affect (and an adequate idea) that, strictly speaking, has no cause other than itself. For it is, in the fully actualised activity of the present that passes, and *sub specie aeternitatis*, the real movement of reality in its absolute affirmation. This movement has no end either. This does not mean that the sage's human activity always involves an intention for ends, even disillusioned ones. The power of the mind over the affects consists not only in the adequate knowledge of these affects but also 'in the fact that it separates the affects from the thought of an external cause, which we imagine confusedly' as an end.[52] The subject is fully in this intention, this rational action (*intendo*)[53] based on no model, pursuing no end. She nevertheless affirms her joy and causes absolutely (and thus asserts in the present, with her love) the formal possession of her power of action and constitution. The loving intentionality (or the 'will' of the loving subject)[54] that defines the ethical subject is the dynamic of joy itself, which amplifies into blessedness. Blessedness is the enjoyment of virtue or the mind's satisfaction in action.[55] It is the fullness of this natural love for oneself already found in resistance (and developed through it). This is what Spinoza means when he says that reason asks for nothing that is against Nature: reason 'thus asks that each love himself...'[56] A position and a real mastery of problems is found in this love (which is a singular relation to the self as singularity), as well as the advent of an intention and of an action according to which life is produced in the fullness of sociability, happiness and liberty.

Acquiescentia in se ipso, in which the perfect unity of the subject is expressed, is the highest thing we can hope for: it is the human project *par excellence*. No one 'strives to persevere in being for the sake of any end'.[57] The ethical subject is, therefore, a longing without hope, an intention without end,

---

[50] *Ep.* LVIII [to G. H. Schuller]; CWS II, 427.
[51] *Ethics* III, 59 Schol.; CWS I, 529–30.
[52] *Ethics* V, 20 Schol.; *Ethics* V, 2 and 4 Schol.; *Ethics* III, 48; CWS I, 605, 597, 598, 520.
[53] *Ethics* III, 59 Schol.; CWS I, 529–30.
[54] *Ethics* III, DA 6 Exp.; CWS I, 533.
[55] *Ethics* V, 36 Dem.; CWS I, 612.
[56] *Ethics* IV, 18 Schol.; CWS I, 555. Translator's note.
[57] *Ethics* IV, 52 Schol.; CWS I, 575.

perfection without a model. It is the very tension of singular existence in its absolute and productive affirmation, a power of being rather than absence of being: it is *cupiditas* and not *desiderium*. The wise person's morality is the 'free necessity' constitutive of an existent. In 'morality' a singular existent, in its absolute affirmation, becomes a 'subject'. Nevertheless, this subject is an affective process of the infinite expansion of love for oneself (and/or the intellectual love of God). In the reflective order of time, loving subjectivity first develops as an effect, which supports the strategic ethical subject and her intermediate strategies, in the separation of means from ends. Beyond this, a loving and rational intention, which defines human subjectivity at its highest stage (*summa cupiditas*) as causality (singular actualising essence), is wholly within the continuous effort that constitutes, prolongs and amplifies the temporality of presence to self and other. This is the temporality of the highest satisfaction of the mind there can be.[58] This temporality is the very present of eternity.

This implies that the simply given form of the practical subject (as effect) is a process of causality, of the free necessity of an essence that tends (in the ethical project) to constitute, 'absolutely', the singular existent as subject. The subjectivation process is a becoming-cause. In this process is a resistance to the destructive violence of other modes, but also to the practical subject's workings. It is a salutary violence that forces her to doubt, to question and to seek to make sense of problems.[59] Ethical subjectivity is preceded and accompanied by a critical subjectivity provoked by the strength of resistance. It is critical reflection specific to the human subject on her own workings, on the nature and value of her goals . . . of which the beginning of the *TdIE* provides an example. This questioning is already a symptom of a becoming-subject. It is never-ending, for it is the power of a critical mind. This art of questioning and calculating reason is characteristic of the human

---

[58] *Ethics* V, 27 and Dem.

[59] To stick to the letter of the *Ethics* (II, 44 Schol.; III, 17 Dem. and Schol.) and as Victor Delbos (to remember him with regret) points out, in Spinoza 'doubt and deliberation are inferior states, states of powerlessness, which dominate and suppress clear thinking and decisive action in us'. *Le problème moral dans la philosophie de Spinoza et dans l'histoire du spinozisme*, F. Alcan 1893, repr. Presses de l'Université de Paris Sorbonne, 1990, p. 544. See also p. 83. It does not contradict the spirit of Spinozism, however, to think that, in the gradual self-transformation (of the mind and body in childhood) implied by the ethical project, doubt, questioning and deliberation have a positive role to play as real powers. That said, Spinoza sees deliberation, interrogation and the suspension of judgement as positive activities in the pursuit of decision making (and/or just action) (*TP* IX, 14).

mind as such. Despite its intelligence and efficiency, it is, at various levels of consciousness and complexity, shared by many living beings with their own survival strategy. It is different from the possession of the adequate idea, or of the mind as 'spiritual automaton', through which humans identify themselves with God (God does not question or doubt).

The point of view of the practical subject, however, despite its humanity, is an abstract point of view. This is even more so as she departs from the singular and real point of view of the underlying process of subjectivation, and even more abstract as the process of becoming-subject is constantly halted, in a context of dependency and fluctuating affect. The ethical project is, therefore, to rediscover, in the lucidity of truth, the singular relationship of trust and love that envelops and develops each life in its essential affirmation. Trust was there from the start. This is the heart of Spinozism. For Spinoza, the truth of life is not apprehended from the 'abstract' (non-) point of view of God or of reason, by some ascetic division from singular subjectivity, as a guarantee of objectivity. On the contrary, the truth of life is apprehended from the point of view of the singular necessity of desiring subjectivity. It is the point of view of natural love for oneself, the real relationship to reality through which we exist and think according to one and the same movement of affirmation, which is first the affection of the self by the self. This is the point of view of Desire (*cupiditas*), which is always-already a singular relationship to the world and to the self, the absolute confidence of Reality in itself.[60] This is the real standpoint of the strategy of the *conatus*. The entirety of the *Ethics* I – that is, the true conception of Nature or God – must be read as opening the possibility of the absolute affirmation of this ethical singularity that is both necessary and free. Spinoza had to radically question the 'unity' of reality. He went from the oppressive unity to the liberating unity that frees the infinite multiplicity of strategies in and through which substance constitutes itself.

---

[60] Contrary to a still widespread interpretation – which was well summed by Alexander Kojève's 'God alone can be a Spinozist' – Spinozism is not the point of view of God, but that of a being who affirms its singular existence absolutely. For Kojève on Spinoza, see his *Introduction to the Reading of Hegel*, trans. J. Nichols, Cornell University Press, 1980, and Laurent Bove, 'Spinoza dans le cours d'Alexandre Kojève', in *Spinoza au XXème siècle*, ed. Olivier Bloch, PUF, 1993, pp. 177–202.

6

The Innocence of Reality and the Recursive Cycle

1 *Causa sui* as the Real Movement of the Production of Reality

For Spinoza, the problem of the unity of Nature is the problem of immanent causality. God is productive force, and this force is life itself. This is quite different from how Renaissance thinkers defined life: an irrational and obscure *élan vital* that necessarily implies contingency.[1] Spinoza cannot accept this definition, since, for him, 'things could have been produced by God in no other way, and in no other order than they have been produced'.[2] This argument is based on the identity of God's power and essence, already implied in the identification of God, cause of all things, with God, cause of itself:

> from the given divine nature, both the essence and existence of things must necessarily be inferred. In a word, God must be called the cause of all things in the same sense in which he is called the cause of himself.[3]

The problems of a self-caused existence and infinity, or indetermination, are the same.[4] Both are the absolute expression of an existence that includes the production of particular things. God cannot be the absolute expression of existence without also being the absolute expression of the existence of singular things. Precisely because 'the absolute affirmation [*affirmatio*] of existence' is at the root of being (real Being itself as absolutely infinite),

---

[1] As shown by the essential work of S. Zac, *L'idée de vie dans la philosophie de Spinoza*, PUF, 1963.
[2] *Ethics* I, 33; CWS I, 436.
[3] *Ethics* I, 25 Schol.; CWS I, 431.
[4] *Ep.* XXXVI [to Hudde]; CWS II, 29.

there can be no chance; only this world could have ever existed. It is also why only this rationality can exist, which finds its *raison d'être* and necessity in the absolute affirmation of existence itself, in God's absolutely infinite nature. This explains how Spinoza can write to Hugo Boxel that 'the world is a necessary effect of the divine nature and was not made by chance'.[5] By 'chance' (*fortuito*), Spinoza means some failure to reach a goal, a deviation from the projected and originally pursued end. Chance refers to the unintended and unwanted effect of an action, a discrepancy between the pursued goal and the obtained result. In a teleological conception of the production of things, the notion of chance has the negative connotation of a deviation. Boxel defines chance in the following way: 'something is said to have been made by chance when it does not originate from the agent's intention'.[6] Spinoza uses the notion comparably: 'in creating the world God had one goal, and [yet] he went completely outside the goal he had'.[7] In *Ep.* LIV and *Ep.* LVI, however, Spinoza presumes that no one could think that 'the world was made by chance'. Still, the same *Ep.* LVI ends with a eulogy of Epicurus, Democritus and Lucretius, who, we know, championed this very notion.[8]

Atomists are certainly praised by Spinoza in these letters, but not for their conception of chance and necessity. This discussion of the question of chance and of the 'champions of atoms' in the same letter, however, is not trivial. By asking: 'Tell me if you have never seen or read of Philosophers who think the world has been made by chance', Spinoza, who praises the Atomists a few lines later, is implicitly saying that their conception of *clinamen* is different from that of the Epicureans, though I can only speculate on this point since Spinoza never directly addresses it.

---

[5] *Ep.* LIV [to Boxel]; *CSW* II, 414.
[6] *Ep.* LV [to Boxel]; *CSW* II, 417.
[7] *Ep.* LVI [to Boxel]; *CSW* II, 420. Like the idea of 'chance', the idea of 'contingency', which Spinoza seems to oppose to the 'necessity' perceived by reason in *Ethics* II, 44 Cor. 1 and 2, is in fact the other face of the repetitive order that imagination 'expects' in nature. The real opposition, which belongs to the realm of imagination, is between 'contingency' and 'imaginative order'. If it is in the nature of reason to perceive things as necessary and as having a certain kind of eternity, it is in the nature of imagination, determined by the associations of Habit, to conceive of things as immutable and according to a repetitive order whose alteration always provokes wonder. *KV* II, iii, 2 and note 1; *Ethics* III, DA 4: 'Wonder [*admiratio*] is an imagination of a thing in which the mind remains fixed because this singular imagination has no connection with the others. (See P52 and P52s.).' The reader of the *Ethics* must think of the eternal and infinite necessity of Nature beyond the imaginary couple formed by the images of the (repetitive) order and of its correlative, contingency (as breakdown of order).
[8] *CWS* II, 421–2.

In a study of Lucretius, Gilles Deleuze shows that the *clinamen* is not a simple deviation of the atom from its perpendicular fall – as we too often try to explain it – which would miraculously introduce pure contingency into necessity. If this were the case, the world would indeed be 'a chance product'. With Deleuze, we learn that, on the contrary, the *clinamen* is, from all eternity, 'the original determination of the direction of the movement of the atom. It is a kind of *conatus* – a differential of matter and, by the same token, a differential of thought.'[9] There is, thus, a positive conception of chance that is independent of a teleological one. If the *clinamen* is an intrinsic positive determination and, therefore, a 'necessity', the Epicurean affirmation of chance is the affirmation of the infinitely many differential necessities. We can assume that this positive conception of chance, which does not contradict universal causation, is what Spinoza understood from his reading of Lucretius.[10] Is there anything equivalent to this in the Spinozist system?

The multiplicity of first causes unencumbered by an architect-will indeed resembles 'this opinion, which subjects all things to a certain indifferent will of God, and makes all things depend on his good pleasure'.[11] In both cases, the result is that the determinations are not totalised (due to reality or to some shortcoming of a directing will). In the first case, the result comes from distinctive affirmations of the differences, due to the real absence of a First Cause at the root of the formal unity of all beings. In the second case, the result comes from a similar expression of different determinations; but here, it is due to the versatility or arbitrariness of the cause's decrees, not to its absence. God would have created the world according to its 'good pleasure' and not by chance, which is absurd. For Spinoza, this second thesis has, however, a certain positivity:

> [It] is nearer [to] the truth than those who maintain that God does all things for the sake of the good. For they seem to place something outside God, which does not depend on God, which God regards as a model in

---

[9] Gilles Deleuze, *The Logic of Sense*, trans. M. Lester and C. Stivale, ed. C. V. Boundas, Athlone, 1990, Appendix II.

[10] The intuition of the identity of chance (Epicurus) and necessity (Spinoza) was first discovered by the opponents of spinozism. Jean La Placette writes: 'I am convinced that what Epicurus called chance and what Spinoza called necessity are the same thing.' *Eclaircissements sur quelques difficultés qui naissent de la liberté nécessaire pour agir moralement avec une Addition où l'on prouve contre Spinoza que nous sommes libres*, Etienne Roger, 1709, p. 317; cited by P. Vernière, *Spinoza et la pensée française avant la Révolution*, PUF, 1954, p. 71, note.

[11] *Ethics* I, 33 Schol. 2; CWS I, 438.

what he does, and at which he aims as at a certain goal. This is simply to subject God to fate. Nothing more absurd can be maintained about God, whom we have shown to be the first and only free cause, both of the essence of all things, and of their existence.[12]

To subject God to 'fate' is to force its action, power and thereby its production into a 'model' that is 'outside' of it. This 'outside', however, is also the inside, since even in God, this model would compel its power according to an end, an order, something the divine essence absolutely excludes. What would the action of this 'model' be? It would direct the action of God via the formal and totalising unity of the project. Each decree would be no more than the determined and subsumed expression of a single (unique) and self-same (united) design. The Stoics taught us that destiny is the expression of the unity of causes, or the unity of decrees subsumed under one and the same decree. Yet Spinoza refuses both the Cartesian thesis of the arbitrary will of God (the 'good pleasure' of an 'indifferent divine will' or of a mischievous God) and the moral thesis of a will acting according to an order, an (external or internal) unifying formal model – a thesis defended both by the Stoics and by Leibniz. But by affirming his preference for the first conception of a world created by chance (which is closer to the truth), Spinoza forces us to take a better look at the Epicurean thesis.

The Epicureans can reject destiny, which haunts the Stoics' cosmos, because they refuse the formal unity of the causes 'between them' and thereby the idea of a First Cause, which remains an extrinsic form of the determination of beings, though internal to Nature. Against this formal unity imposed by destiny, the Epicureans offer a multiplicity of differential determinations, both intrinsic and positive. Chance is the expression of this multiplicity. This thesis, in this positive sense, encounters in Spinoza the absolutely positive infinity, that is, 'the absolute affirmation of existence' and/or of existences. In the *Ethics*, however, the self-causation of infinity, which is the very necessity of this affirmation, is not an affirmation of chance or contingency, but of necessity. This necessity has the same meaning for everything about which it is said.[13] This unique and differential necessity excludes any model and formalism. It is 'without principle or end', as innocent and real

---

[12] Ibid.

[13] *Ex qua enim naturae necessitate existit, ex eadem ipsum agere ostendimus* (Prop. 16 p. I). *Ratio igitur, seu causa, cur Deus, seu Natura agit, & cur existit, una, eademque est. Ut ergo nullius finis causa existit, nullius etiam finis causa agit; sed ut existendi, sic & agendi principium, vel finem habet nullum*. Ethics IV, App.; CWS I, 544.

(since the real movement is independent of any formal or abstract logic) as Epicurean chance. Spinoza was already alluding to this innocence, this a-morality, this reality of necessity, in the letter XXXVI to Hudde, when he wrote about 'the indeterminacy' of substance. Indeterminacy is another word for actual infinity or affirmation. Indeterminacy must be understood positively; the arbitrary (the indifferent will of God) is the negative point of view. We know, however, that the arbitrary (a world created by chance) is closer to the truth than moral necessity (a world based on a model). But affirmation exceeds these two antagonistic theses: in affirmation, both arbitrary and formal orders are abolished. In their positive sense, chance and necessity, multiplicity and unity, are different names for one and the same Reality: Nature 'without principle nor end' in its absolute affirmation; 'physis is an outburst in all directions'.[14]

The absolute affirmation of existence – absolutely infinite power – is what is constitutive (as *causa sui*) of Being in its essential, structural unity. Since God is the cause of all things in the same sense that it is the cause of itself,[15] the absolute affirmation of existence determines the differential elements (attributes) of the structure and the singular determinations that 'express the nature or essence [power] of God in a certain and determinate way'.[16]

In his understanding of Nature, Spinoza combines two ideas that seemed incompatible: the ideas of structure and genesis. They seemed incompatible because the first involved the idea of order in the formal, hence closed, fixity

---

[14] Léon Robin, quoted by Paul Nizan in *Les matérialistes de l'antiquité*, Maspéro, 1965, p. 27. Since Spinoza takes infinity 'seriously' in its actual affirmation, we must also see the dynamic and constitutive unity of chance and necessity at the heart of his philosophy. This is part of his anti-teleological radicalism that characterises (from Democritus to Lucretius, and within the atomist structure that Spinoza rejects) ancient materialism in its opposition to any finalist doctrine. Olivier Bloch writes of Democritus: 'Thus the emergence of things, like that of worlds, occurs exclusively by "chance" and "necessity": chance encounters, which means that no plan, no intention, nothing resembling a purpose, governs their production. This chance is at the same time a necessity, since this production is entirely determined by the mechanical process of collisions, intertwinings, unions and divisions of atoms according to their dimensions, their forms, their position, their movement, and their direction.' Olivier Bloch, *Le Matérialisme*, PUF coll. Que sais-je?, 1985, p. 40. See also, on Epicureanism, the 'play of infinity and limit that . . . serves as the basis for the immanent structuring of a universe in which nothing resembling thought or intention intervenes' (ibid., pp. 45–6). For a comparison of the physics of Spinoza and Epicurus, see Pierre-François Moreau, 'Epicure et Spinoza: la physique', *Archives de Philosophie*, July–September 1994, pp. 459–69.

[15] *Ethics* I, 25 Schol.

[16] *Ethics* I, 36 Dem.; *CWS* I, 439.

of the physical system and of mathematical reasoning, whereas the second involved the idea of movement, the temporal change of form. To understand the originality of this combination, it is enough to understand that genesis must not be grasped in terms of a temporal representation of passing from one term (substance-attribute-mode) to another. Indeed, 'in eternity, there is neither *when*, nor *before*, nor *after*', Spinoza insists.[17] This necessary genesis must be regarded as the atemporal passage from the constitution of a structure to its actualisation, from the conditions of its production to the production that encompasses and realises these conditions absolutely, infinitely and necessarily, in existential relationships. These are, for us, the necessary relationships among ideas in the intellect and among bodies in extension. The structure is not an internal spiritual principle or a virtuality. It is the same process of absolute affirmation of substance's absolutely infinite power of existence and is explained 'in a certain and determinate way' in everything that exists.[18] It is the innocent necessity, without principle or end, the real movement of the production of Reality, the absolute and eternal movement of the self-creation of substance and its modes: the very duration of eternity, the conception of the immanent cause understood through self-causality.

This self-creation is the (same) immanent cause of any dynamic 'effect' in duration. Efficient causality is itself only adequately explained from the point of view of immanent causation, which is the (absolute) necessity of all necessities in the order of temporal existence.

> Efficient causality offers us nothing but extrinsic denominations, relations, or at most, circumstances, all of which are far from the inmost essence of things.[19]

Absolutely speaking, however, this discrepancy between essence and existence is nothing; there is nothing behind surface causality. The immanent cause is not a backstage world, but the very necessity of this world in its unfolding and affirmation. Again, every being is in the closest vicinity to Being, in all its being.[20] *Causa sui* is the very movement of substance's self-affirmation through its acts. Immanent causation expresses the 'free necessity' of Nature's absolutely infinite power, of which all existing things

---

[17] *Ethics* I, 33 Schol. 2; CWS I, 437.
[18] *Ethics* I, 36 Dem.; CWS I, 439.
[19] *TdIE* 101; CWS I, 41.
[20] *Ethics* I, 28 Schol.

are, in the last instance, the necessary effect. Nature immediately gives all things the power that constitutes and characterises their essences in existence in and through the attributes. Yet the attributes that constitute the very essence of the substance, the infinite structure in and through which substance produces itself, are the necessary conditions of the modes' production (whose essence, however, is not constituted by the attributes). Through its self-production, Nature immediately produces the power of singular things in and through the attributes that form (by virtue of the free non-causal necessity of their relations of production) the essence of the substance.

As the very first lines of the *Ethics* show, where *causa sui* is defined, the immanent cause develops the life of God-Nature, its power in acts. God, therefore, is never presented as a person precisely because he is not one. Spinoza negates God as Being-Substance-Subject by the universality of the affirmation of its infinite, absolute power (its universal freedom). He considers the imaginative concept of equivocal and eminent Being to be an abstraction, which he places in the category of transcendentals.[21] This is a criticism of Aristotelian and Cartesian conceptions of Being, that see, in unity, the simplicity of a transcendent whole that subsumes the diversity of Reality. On the one hand, this (moral and religious) *a priori* makes difficult the understanding of infinite multiplicity and how it is structured, that is, the specific unity of the infinity of parts and of an absolutely infinite whole. On the other hand, when it comes to the singular essences of modes, it makes understanding the genesis of the multiple as independent of an *a priori* rule of internal resemblance impossible. The attributes are not, in fact, parts of a totality. Since they are infinite, they evade the (imaginative) numeral category, as well as the enumeration and (imaginary) totalisation towards infinity that it entails.[22] The infinity of attributes is not cumulative. The

---

[21] *Ethics* II, 40 Schol.; *Ethics* IV, Praef.

[22] Spinoza thus avoids the Kantian criticism of the improper use of the category of totality. By bringing forth the idea of an absolutely infinite and untotalisable whole, a structural-genetic nature that has no principle or goal, Spinoza avoids a spatial and mechanistic conception of totality (as later found in P. S. Laplace, *Essai Philosophique sur les probabilités*, in *Oeuvres*, Gauthier Villars, 1886, vol. VII, 1, pp. 6–7). He also avoids an implicit reintroduction of immanent finality which, as Bachelard showed, necessarily involves a mechanistic ideology of universal determinism. Gaston Bachelard, *L'expérience de l'espace dans la physique contemporaine*, PUF, 1951; *L'activité rationaliste dans la physique contemporaine*, PUF, 1965, pp. 211–12, 214, 216, 219. The Laplace of Spinoza, still present in the conception of the spatial totality of the *KV*, with which the *Ethics* had to break, is Maimonides. For the latter, God both operates the unity between the causes and has absolute knowledge of the infinity of specific

unity of substance cannot be thought of as a simple arithmetical unity, but as *the* absolute affirmation of itself, in and through its infinite differences. The unique substance affirms itself absolutely in and through its infinite attributes and in each of its acts.

Spinoza transforms the difference between each attribute and between each singular essence into the affirmation of the equality of each. Substance affirms itself absolutely in each of the attributes as well as in all its modes, without restriction or division such that, 'if one part of matter were annihilated, the whole of Extension would also vanish at the same time'.[23] This allows us to grasp a kind of unity and identity of substance from the essential point of view of its 'absolutely infinite' affirmation. From this point of view, there is no need for a justification of unity (from a necessarily arbitrary and formal moral principle). The attributes are intrinsically different with respect to their expression (thought, extension etc.). They share, however, a universal and common necessity in and through their free relationship of production, which constitutes the very essence of substance as affirmation. This relation is outside any preordained harmony and any end, both external and internal, imposed by the production process. Spinoza refuses to give his interlocutors an explanation according to the good nature of the attributes, or according to 'common sense', which Oldenburg, Hudde or Tschirnhaus expected. Spinoza refuses to subsume the differences – which are constitutive of Being – under a totalising unity. In his letters, Spinoza defends the position of an irreligious conception of Nature against the theological interpretation of his Christian interlocutors. Universal necessity, the very freedom of substance, defines the actual order of production and self-production of Nature and its modes. The real unity of the production of modes, in and through the infinity of attributes (the order and connection of ideas being the same as the order and connection of things), defines the unity of substance, in and through its absolute affirmation.

To think of the immanent causality of substance, cause of all things and cause of itself, as an open and unlimited genetic structure, is to make the difference between the unity of the Spinozist substance and the problem of order, which was the problem of the *Short Treatise*, into the originality of the Spinozist take on substance. It locates its originality in its difference from classical transcendental unity (Platonic, Aristotelian, Cartesian or Leibnizian), which is a formal unity whose essentially moral function

---

causal series *a priori*. See *Guide for the Perplexed*, I.1 and III.17, where Epicurus is contrasted with the authority of Aristotle.

[23] *Ep.* IV [to Oldenburg]; CWS I, 171.

suppresses difference as such for the benefit of a transcendent identity and an imaginary principle of internal resemblance. The sort of unity that Spinoza produces is an entirely new epistemological concept. This explains his interlocutors' and interpreters' difficulty in understanding (and accepting) its originality.[24] Strictly speaking, it is an untraceable unity. Since the unity is neither a totalisation nor a substance-subject, it never appears in person (indeed, we must rule out any mystical or religious interpretation of the third kind of knowledge). It exists only in the infinity of its expressions.[25] The genetic structure is always and only in act, and its acts are its necessary and actual effects, modifications of thought and extension.

2 Infinite Modes and Circular Necessity

The 'passage' from the absolute to the relative, from the infinite to the finite, from the absolutely infinite and indeterminate substance to its determinations, is *at first* the matter, in *Ethics* I, 21, 22, 23 and 28 Schol., of a theory of mediations that is not without ambiguity. This theory allows for a Neoplatonist interpretation, because of the hierarchical conception of Being (and beings) to which these propositions can lead. Yet the study of infinite modes leads us to a better understanding of autogenesis, a new logic of Being that is unquestionably at the heart of Spinozist philosophy.

Spinoza, like Philo, *seems to* introduce intermediaries in between the absolutely infinite substance and its finite modes: the infinite and eternal, immediate and mediate modes. E. Amado Levy-Valensi sees in this procession of modes the progressive alienation of the self-contained universe of Spinozism. 'Natured Nature (*natura naturata*) is less perfect than naturing Nature (*natura naturans*).' And 'at the lowest limit of the created world' – finite modes – there is a level of being where substance is no longer really involved.[26] Yet from his very first writings – and in the explanations he gives to his interlocutors – Spinoza affirms the substance's participation

---

[24] 'Self-sufficient attributes, however, express substance. What exactly do they express? They express its strength; we understand that. They express its power, its eternity, its infinity; we understand that too. But the attributes should also express its unity. And we do not understand that, because how can different attributes express one substance?' Ferdinand Alquié, *Nature et Vérité dans la philosophie de Spinoza*, CDU, 1971, p. 62.

[25] *Ethics* I, 17 Schol.

[26] E. Amado Levy-Valensi, *Les niveaux de l'être. La connaissance et le mal*, PUF, 1962, ch. 3, 'De la mystique juive à l'intellectualisme de Spinoza', pp. 183, 188.

in the slightest parcel of *natura naturata*, in the finite modes.[27] This is an essential consequence of *Ethics* I, 13: because of its 'indivisibility', substance is necessarily present as a whole in each of its acts or modes, be they infinite or finite. This is also true of 'finite' modes whose limits are only existential, that is, due to external causes. Apart from the constricting exteriority of the world, the mode is 'infinite through its cause'.[28] Through God's causation, constitutive of its very essence – the *conatus* – a mode affirms an indefinite power to persevere in being.[29]

The text of *Ethics* I on the theory of infinite modes is certainly even more perplexing. The very fact that there are 'infinite' modes excludes the separation or even opposition between those two kinds of orders in relation to their essential and exclusive property, that is, infinity for substance and finitude for modes. In *Ethics* I, 28 Schol., the infinite modes seem to be presented as 'intermediaries' between infinite substance and its finite modes:

> certain things had to be produced by God immediately, viz. those which follow necessarily from his absolute nature, and others (which nevertheless can neither be nor be conceived without God) had to be produced by the mediation of these first things.

Yet to save us from a dead end regarding these 'intermediaries', Spinoza immediately stresses that God can only 'properly be called the remote cause of singular things' due to some flaw of language that makes distinctions for the sake of analysis (and, what is more, it is quite an abstract language since it includes the imaginary representation of that to which it refers). The function of the intermediary, however, seems to be reinforced by Spinoza's distinction between the immediate infinite modes, which follow 'from the absolute nature of any of God's attributes' and express it directly,[30] and the intermediate infinite modes, which follow 'from some [necessary and infinite] attribute of God insofar as it is affected by a modification' that is necessary and infinite.[31] The reader is, thus, confronted with a theory of mediations which, if one is quite inattentive, can be understood as a hierarchical neoplatonic conception of representations.

---

[27] See *Ep*. IV [to Oldenburg], of 1661; CWS I, 171.
[28] *Ep*. XII [to Meyer]; CWS I, 203.
[29] *Ethics* III, 6, 7, 8.
[30] *Ethics* I, 21; CWS I, 429.
[31] *Ethics* I, 22; CWS I, 430.

When Schuller asks for 'examples of things produced immediately by God and of things produced by the mediation of some infinite modification',[32] Spinoza answers:

> examples of the first kind [that is, of things produced immediately by God] are, in Thought, absolutely infinite intellect, and in Extension, motion and rest; an example of the second kind [that is, of those produced by the mediation of some infinite modification] is the face of the whole Universe, which, however much it may vary in infinite ways, nevertheless always remains the same. On this, see L7S before II P14.[33]

Let us take the example of the attribute of extension about which Spinoza gives the most detail. In this case, the relationship between the absolute and the relative can be explained according to the following distinctions: extension/substantial attribute; motion and rest / immediate infinite mode; *facies totius universi* / mediate infinite mode; singular bodies / finite modes. But what does it mean for motion and rest to be presented as the immediate infinite mode of extension? It means the absolute expression of the substantial reality of extension in the proportion of motion-and-rest, without depletion or loss, since the relationship of motion-and-rest *is* absolute extension in act as the intellect perceives it. The demonstration *ad absurdum* of *Ethics* I, 21 (about the infinity and eternity of the immediately produced mode) is meant to show that the attribute cannot be without the existence of its immediate mode. The attribute that produces its immediate mode in a necessary way (according to *Ethics* I, 16) 'cannot be without it; in this sense, the latter is as eternal and infinite as the attribute'.[34] The attribute cannot be without its mode (just as the triangle cannot be without its properties), something the KV already proved (II, 19, 8):

> When we consider extension alone, we perceive nothing else in it except motion and rest, from which we find that all its effects derive. And such are these two modes in body, that there can be no other thing which can change them, except themselves.[35]

---

[32] *Ep.* LXIII [from Schuller]; CWS II, 437.
[33] *Ep.* LXIV [to Schuller]; CWS II, 439.
[34] Martial Gueroult, *Spinoza, I: Dieu*, Aubier, 1968, p. 310.
[35] CWS I, 131. Translator's note.

The *Ethics* confirms this[36] by demonstrating the absolute compatibility of extension with the laws of nature:

> All bodies agree in that they involve the concept of one and the same attribute (by D1), and in that they can move now more slowly, now more quickly, and absolutely, that now they move, now they are at rest.[37]

The laws of nature, which express the proportion of motion-and-rest, derive immediately from substance. If they regulate the conditions of existence in extension, these laws are in themselves – like the substance from which they come – strictly speaking, unconditioned. Because of its status as mode, an infinite mode belongs to the realm of determination, but it is also, because of its infinity, unassignable. How, then, can a mode express the indeterminate?

The answer lies in Spinoza's absolutely positive conception of substance. Any determination, even finite, is also the positive and intrinsic expression of substance. Determination implies no privation, no essential lack in its being; it is pure positivity. The Spinozist universe excludes any idea of essential finitude, even in finite modes, whose very being is precisely constituted by this infinite dimension. Any finite determination is, at the same time, infinite through the infinite power of its immanent cause (substance) and through the infinite multiplicity of its transitive causes (whose efficient necessity is the extrinsic figure of immanent causation). But *Ethics* I, 21 Dem. also applies to all singular essences, infinite and eternal, in that they follow from God's nature (taken absolutely). This raises a fundamental question about the Spinozist conception of causation. But we will return to it, after we finish analysing the problem introduced by the infinite modes of the attribute of thought. The immediate infinite mode, to be anything other than an abstraction, must assume the existence of singular essences and their forces. If the forces of these singular essences precede the immediate infinite mode, can we then say that the latter is the mere modal expression of their total intensive interplay?

Let us return to our example to understand what is different about the 'mediate infinite mode' or *facies totius universi*. The latter corresponds, according to *Ep.* LXIV, to the constancy of a universe that changes only according to fixed and eternal laws. Everything that happens in Nature always happens according to the same necessity. The present task, therefore, is to show, as we have done for the immediate infinite mode, that the attribute

---

[36] *Ethics* II, 13 Lem. 2.
[37] *Ethics* II, 13 Lem. 2 Dem.

is absolutely expressed in its mediate infinite mode. We must demonstrate that the existence of the attribute is necessarily linked to the very existence of the mediate infinite mode, and that it, therefore, undergoes, both in relation to its attribute as well as in relation to the immediate infinite mode, no depletion (or loss of being) in this *apparent* procession of Being.

The permanence that *facies universi totius* expresses, which the order of a living individual[38] may suggest by metaphor, is, however, not an immanent finality, the harmony (in the Augustinian sense) that Spinoza criticises.[39] The 'order' of Nature in extension is not the 'order' wanted by God (internally finalised), found in the Cartesian extension. It is an aimless and lawless necessity whose innocence we have already emphasised. Thus, the Spinozist universal determination is absolutely indeterminate. It does not find its *raison d'être* in a whole or a subject which, external or internal, would give it order or sense. The reason for its existence is the very existence of the absolutely infinite and indeterminate substance, identical to its essence.[40] The mediate infinite mode, like the immediate infinite mode, really has, *in a certain way*, no cause at all. It is itself the reason, or the cause, of its consequences: the laws of nature are the matrix, in itself indeterminate, of any scientific explanation of natural phenomena. Substance, as cause, is also immediately and totally in the mediate infinite mode, as it is in the immediate infinite mode, and, in the same way, it cannot exist without it. Indeed, how can we grasp Nature without its laws?

An assessment of the infinite mode in the attribute of extension cannot lead us to a hierarchical vision of the order of Nature. It even seems as though this hierarchy, whose legitimacy is already challenged by our analysis, is curiously reversed and subverted when we realise that the so-called 'inferior' levels are necessary for the existence of the 'superior' levels. A sort of reversal of causality is here outlined whose logic we can carry into an analysis of the infinite modes in the attribute of thought. Already, however, we can conclude that there is no conception of the degradation of the absolute into the relative, of the infinite into the finite in the Spinozist theory, as Neoplatonism presupposes (and which comes from imagination). In reality, the finite is absolutely identified with infinity; one is nothing without the other.[41] The infinite is nothing but the intensive infinity of

---

[38] *Ethics* II, 13 Lem. 7.
[39] *Ethics* I, App.; CWS I, 444.
[40] *Ethics* I, 20.
[41] This thesis is remarkably explained, in other ways, by Bernard Rousset in 'L'être du fini dans l'infini selon l'*Ethique* de Spinoza', *Revue Philosophique*, 2, 1986, pp. 223–47.

modes that express it, and the finite is nothing but the infinite in actuality: this is Spinoza's thesis.

Let us take the case of modes in the attribute of thought: thinking / substantial attribute; absolutely infinite intellection / immediate infinite mode; . . . / mediate infinite mode; singular ideas / finite modes. Note, first, that *Ep.* LXIV does not give us the modal equivalent, in thought, of the *facies totius universi* in extension. This omission is already symptomatic. It points to the difficulty of separating the absolutely infinite intellect from the entirety of the ideal relations that rule in thought, the determinations of ideas as ideas of existing modes. Spinoza himself suggests, by a surprising shortcut, and from the very first dialogue of the *KV*, that intellect, the immanent cause of its ideas, can also be understood as 'a *whole* for it is composed of its ideas'[42] – a whole that would be nothing other than a 'being of reason'[43] without its parts, or an 'absurdity'.[44] God, on the other hand, does not think, and does not think of itself, by virtue of our 'common notions'. God thinks – and thinks of itself – only through the adequate idea of its own essence, or through the infinite 'entirety' of adequate ideas of singular essences, elements of the infinite whole that the absolutely infinite intellect, the immediate infinite mode, forms.[45] Thus, there is no absolutely infinite intellect except in act. To separate intellect from its ideas is as absurd as wanting to think of a triangle without its properties. If absolutely infinite intellect is nowhere else than in its ideas, how can we think of an 'intermediate' mediate infinite mode 'between' the absolutely infinite intellect and ideas (as finite modes)? Spinoza seems to reject the ontological implications of this question both in *Ethics* I, 30 and in *Ethics* II, 4, where he *de facto* identifies the immediate infinite mode and the mediate infinite mode by referring to both as 'infinite intellect in acts', or 'idea of God'. If one can, as we believe, attribute the 'common notions' to the mediate infinite mode, this distinction becomes purely epistemological. Moreover, it exists for human reason alone, and no longer for the absolutely infinite intellect of God, which this reason nevertheless objectively explains, with both common notions and adequate ideas of singular essences.

The divine intellect cannot be separated from its ideas, from 'the very action of knowing', any more than the attribute of thought can be

---

[42] *KV*, end of first dialogue; *CWS* I, 76.
[43] *KV* I, ii, 19; *CWS* I, 71.
[44] *Ethics* I, 12 Dem.; *CWS* I, 419.
[45] *Ethics* V, 40 Schol.

abstractly separated from the absolutely infinite intellect[46] that expresses it, absolutely without depletion or loss. The idea of an intellect in *potentia* (*entendement en puissance*) is foreign to Spinozism.[47] It thus seems that,

> The power of the Attribute invests itself *fully* in the immediate mode. The latter, produced by the infinite power with which the attribute fills it, and because of its infinity, is equal to the Attribute. Further, it expresses the infinite power of the absolute nature of the Attribute as fully as the Attribute does.[48]

On the other hand, if the infinite power of each attribute is also expressed completely in each of its finite modes, as Spinoza compellingly states in *Ep.* IV, the proportion of motion-and-rest of extension and the absolutely infinite intellection of thought also necessarily express the eternal and infinite interplay of active forces, through the infinite set of finite modes from which they cannot be separated. These are the 'certain and determinate modes' of the expression of God's power.[49] What is the infinite power of the attribute if not the infinite set of singular forces (or essences) it involves? (Spinoza says the same thing of the power of Nature which 'is nothing but the power of all individuals together'.)[50] Detached from matter, or from the totality of existing and determinate bodies outside of which it cannot exist, the proportion of motion-and-rest of extension could only have an abstract existence (as a being of reason). This immediate infinite mode, therefore, implies the existence of eternal singular forces. It expresses the full interplay of these forces, since it also implies the very substantiality of extension – that is, the existence of determinate matter – or all extended bodies – through which this expression takes form: reality. The universal laws of nature are not forms that extrinsically subsume their content but are rather the expressions of the intrinsic necessity of these material contents in their determination, expressions of the eternal interplay of Nature's internal affirmative forces.

Far from finding a hierarchical conception of Being in the theory of the infinite modes, we find the circular necessity that binds the finite to the

---

[46] *Ethics* I, 21 Dem.
[47] *Ethics* I, 31 Schol.
[48] As stated by Gueroult, *Spinoza, I: Dieu*, p. 313.
[49] *Ethics* I, 36 Dem.
[50] TTP XVI; CWS II, 282; and already also KV II, xxi, 3.

infinite, the determinate to the indeterminate, the singular to the universal, within this full being without fissure or hierarchy that is the Spinozist substance. On the one hand, the attribute expresses itself fully in its immediate infinite mode. The latter invests itself fully in its mediate infinite mode, which in turn expresses itself absolutely in each finite mode. On the other hand, we may also say that everything begins in the absolutely infinite expression of the physical universe of singular essences, the universe of active forces whose intensive multiplicity 'is' the absolutely infinite power of substance itself. We find that the attribute whose productive force is the force of the entirety of its own affections – or determinations (singular essences) – would not exist without its modes – through which this power is in act. The immediate infinite mode, allegedly 'immediately' produced, needs the mediate infinite mode to become real. And the mediate infinite mode is only the expression of the interplay of the active and actual forces of finite modes existing in act.

That the universal laws of nature as we perceive them are 1) the expression of the constitutive singular forces of concrete modality as much as they are 2) the action of these same forces (and what they necessarily produce), the effect of these same laws, makes us discover a new paradigm of rationality in the *Ethics*. The paradigm is a paradoxical logic that can be called recursive in that, through its causal logic, the effect circles back to its own cause, which is also the case with the determinate with the indeterminate, and the singular with the universal.

3 From the Identification of the Synthetic and Analytic Links to the Absolute Expression of the Univocity of Being (Singular Essence and Law of Production)

The *Ethics* begins with the conventional expression of substance's priority over its affections.[51] The logic of precedence is causal, deduced from Def. 3 ('by substance I understand what is in itself and is conceived through itself, i.e., that whose concept does not require the concept of another thing, from which it must be formed'),[52] and Def. 5 ('by mode I understand the affections of a substance, or that which is in another through which it is also conceived').[53] God is cause of the essence and existence of the modes, from which he nevertheless differs in essence and existence.

---

[51] 'A substance is by nature prior to its affections.' *Ethics* I, 1; CWS I, 410.
[52] CWS I, 408. Translator's note.
[53] CWS I, 409. Translator's note.

Hence the problem that Schuller presents to Spinoza in 1675:

> since God's intellect differs from our intellect both in Essence and in existence, it will have nothing in common with our intellect, and therefore, by I P3, God's intellect cannot be the cause of our intellect.[54]

Leaving aside Schuller's misconception of the incommensurability of human intellect and the divine mind, which, of course, is not in the *Ethics*, Spinoza goes to the essential by reformulating the question in general philosophical terms:

> [can one thing] be produced by another from which it differs, both in its essence and in its existence [?] For things which differ in this way from one another seem to have nothing in common. But since all singular things, except those produced by their likes, differ from their causes, both in their essence and in their existence, I do not see any reason for doubt here.[55]

This answer is ambiguous. On the one hand, it affirms the thesis of incommensurability based on logical (scholastic) evidence. On the other hand, it refers Schuller back to the experience or knowledge of the first kind that seems to prove the opposite. Spinoza does not directly answer, he only suggests. But what is he suggesting that is so dangerous that it cannot be written about openly?

Let us go back to September 1661. The *KV* was surely already largely written by then, and Spinoza simply sent Oldenburg – with whom, in Rijnsburg, he had the opportunity to speak 'as if through a lattice and only in passing' of matters as important as those of 'God, [infinite] Extension and Thought, [the] difference and agreement of these attributes...'[56] – a more rigorous argument, *more geometrico*, presumably closer to the Geometrical Appendix of the *KV*. In his reply, Oldenburg asks Spinoza about the fourth axiom:

> [the fact that things that] *have nothing in common with one another cannot be the cause of the other* [is] not so evident to my dull intellect that it does not need more light shed on it. Surely God has nothing formally in common with created things, yet nearly all of us regard him as their cause.[57]

---

[54] *Ep.* LXIII [from Schuller]; CWS II, 436–7.
[55] *Ep.* LXIV [to Schuller]; CWS II, 439. Translation modified.
[56] *Ep.* I [from Oldenburg]; CWS I, 169. Translation modified.
[57] *Ep.* III [from Oldenburg]; CWS I, 168.

Spinoza answers:

> As for your contention that God has nothing formally in common with created things, etc., I have maintained the complete opposite of this in my definition. For I have said that God is a Being consisting of infinite attributes, of which each is infinite, or supremely perfect in its kind.[58]

Plainly said, Spinoza does not answer Oldenburg's question. He curiously seems to take the attributes for 'created things', when Oldenburg was in fact asking about finite modes.[59]

However, the rest of the letter, which distinguishes between 'created being' and 'generated beings', is more enlightening:

> I ask you, my friend, to consider that men are not created, but only generated and that their bodies already existed before, though formed differently. It may, indeed, be inferred, as I cheerfully acknowledge, that if one part of matter were annihilated, the whole of Extension would also vanish at the same time.[60]

It is really the response to Oldenburg's objection to the first proposition that answers the question of the fourth axiom. The 'matter' that Oldenburg doubtless takes for a 'created thing' is consubstantial with God in that the existence of God is linked to the existence of a created thing *sub specie aeternitatis*. However, by 'matter' Spinoza must necessarily mean something 'infinite'[61] that cannot be composed of separate parts. If it were composed of parts, one could conceive that, while some of its parts would be destroyed, it would subsist,[62] which is contradictory to what Spinoza 'expressly professes'.

---

[58] *Ep.* IV [to Oldenburg]; *CWS* I, 172.
[59] This answer is all the more curious because the Cor. of Prop. 4 of the Geometrical Appendix of *KV* states: 'Nature is known through itself and not through any other thing. It consists of infinite attributes, each of which is infinite and perfect in its kind. Existence belongs to its essence, so that outside it there is no essence or being. Hence it agrees exactly with the essence of God, who alone is magnificent and blessed' (*CWS* I, 152). *Ep.* IV, which answers as if the attributes were created things, stops at the sovereign perfection of the attributes without proclaiming, as the appendix does, that their essence involves existence. From this we must conclude that the final draft of the appendix of *KV* follows this letter of October 1661 (remember that the *KV* had not yet granted the attributes the power to cause themselves, I, ii, 17 and note 5).
[60] *Ep.* IV [to Oldenburg]; *CWS* I, 172.
[61] *KV* I, ii, 19 note 6.
[62] *KV* I, ii, 20.

Matter must be understood as the substance of the extension attribute, just as thought is the substance of the thought attribute. The attribute of extension without matter is, therefore, as contradictory and absurd as the attribute of thought without thought.

What is Spinoza saying to Schuller in *Ep.* LXIV? With the off-handedness of his response, his almost provocative irony ('I do not see any difficulty') and the ambiguity of his wording (*nam quae ab invicem ita differunt nihil commune habere videntur*), Spinoza is saying the opposite of what he seems at first to be suggesting.

In *Ep.* LXIV and in the *Ethics*, the essence–existence distinction, like the cause–effect relation, must be interpreted with a quite different mindset than the one with which one approaches common seventeenth-century philosophical language. Which path must one follow in this endeavour? The one indicated by *Ethics* I, 16 Dem.: namely, the identification of the synthetic relation of cause–effects with the analytic one of essence–properties. In what way does this first correspondence require us to read it with a totally different mindset? To what extent is this identification subversive? And to what extent does it set the tone for another subversive identification – of the analytic relation with the genetic power–acts relation – that reveals the deepest insight of the *Ethics*, against the (scholastic) language with which it must wrestle and the false interpretations that this language can impose on thought?

Let us look at *Ethics* I, 16:

> From the necessity of the divine nature there must follow infinitely many things in infinitely many modes, (i.e., everything which can fall under an infinite intellect).[63]

And its *demonstration*:

> This Proposition must be plain to anyone, provided he attends to the fact that the intellect infers from the given definition of any thing, a number of properties that really do follow necessarily from it (i.e., from the very essence of the thing); and that it infers more properties the more the definition of the thing expresses reality, i.e., the more reality the essence of the defined thing involves. But since the divine nature has absolutely infinite attributes (by D6), each of which also expresses an essence infinite in its own kind, from its necessity there must follow

---

[63] CWS I, 424. Translator's note.

infinitely many things in infinite modes (i.e., everything which can fall under an infinite intellect).[64]

First, a problem of translation: *infinitis modis*, generally translated as 'infinite modes', which is confusing. The effective modes (that is, the ideas and the bodies, like the infinity of other modes belonging to the attributes which are unknown to us) produced by the divine nature, Spinoza calls 'things'. For this reason, *infinitis modis* is better understood as 'infinite number of ways' (as many as there are attributes, this is the real distinction) by which God produces its modes. Or, better yet, 'infinity of modes' of production of these 'things' (which *are* modes). *Modis* would therefore not mean that which is 'caused', that is, the product – called 'thing' here – but the specific 'causality' by which divine nature produces the modes in each of its attributes and maintains them in their existence in a 'certain and determinate manner', as *Ethics* I, 25 Schol. Cor. specifies. This translation, however, is also an interpretation. What is the specific 'causality' by which God produces each thing and maintains it in its existence if not the singular and actualising essence of this thing, or the law of its production?

Singular essence as a law of production is the very movement of the productive power of God or Nature 'in its full presence' to use the *TP*'s formulation:

> Any natural thing whatever can be conceived adequately, whether it exists or not. So just as the beginning of a natural thing's existence can't be inferred from its definition, neither can its perseverance in existing. For the ideal essence of these things is the same after they've begun to exist as it was before. Just as their beginning to exist can't follow from their essence, neither can their perseverance in existing. The same power they require to begin to exist, they also require to continue to exist. From this it follows that the power by which natural things exist, and so by which they have effects, can't be anything but the eternal power of God itself. For if it were any other created power, it couldn't preserve itself, and so couldn't preserve natural things. The same power it requires to be created, it also requires to persevere in existing. From the fact that the power of natural things, by which they exist and have effects, is the very power of God, we easily understand what the Right of nature is.[65]

---

[64] CWS I, 425. Translator's note.
[65] *TP* II, 2, 3; CWS II, 507.

It is the logic of the production of Being (or beings) as a productive force. Its production – as law – corresponds to what Spinoza calls 'singular essences' and their products are 'things' or 'modes'. Before we continue, we must return to the source of the Spinozist identification between essence and causation (law of production), which is paradoxically scholastic. That is, we must return to the *Short Treatise* (KV).

The audacity of the *KV* is to identify the '*emanative or productive* cause' with the '*active or efficient* cause':

> We say that God is an emanative or productive cause of his actions, and an active or efficient cause with respect to the action taking place. We treat this as one thing, because they involve each other reciprocally.[66]

Adriaan Heereboord, who inspired chapter III of the *KV* I,[67] defines the 'emanative cause' as that from which the thing 'immediately' follows (for example, heat from the fire); the 'active cause', in contrast, produces the thing through the 'intermediate' of an action (for example, heat applied to an object). There are two terms in the emanative cause that are really one: the cause and the caused – the cause's existence is identical to its causation. With an active cause, there are three distinct terms: cause, caused and causation. It follows that, whereas the emanative cause necessarily involves its effect, the active cause does not necessarily produce its effect, since the cause's action can be prevented from producing its effect without ceasing to be as a cause.[68] By identifying 'emanative cause' and 'active cause', Spinoza introduces the caused into the cause. By keeping the activity, however, he also introduces 'causation' – which is the action of the cause – in the caused.

We thus find in the *KV* the source of 1) the identification between a 'singular essence' and 'causation'; God is not the cause of what makes things persevere in existence, but the direct cause 'that makes' them persevere in their being; 2) the subversive identification between the synthetic relation of cause–effects and the analytic essence–properties relation. God as triangle:

> I think I have shown clearly enough (see P16) that from God's supreme power, or infinite nature, infinitely many things in infinitely many modes,

---

[66] *KV* I, iii, 2; *CWS* I, 79.
[67] On the relations of the synoptic table of Franco Burgersdijk and the re-edition of Adriaan Heereboord, his student, see Gueroult, *Spinoza, I: Dieu*, p. 245, n. 7.
[68] We repeat here note 8 of Gueroult, *Spinoza, I: Dieu*, p. 246, but draw different conclusions from it.

i.e., all things, have necessarily flowed, or always follow, by the same necessity and in the same way as from the nature of a triangle it follows, from eternity and to eternity, that its three angles are equal to two right angles.[69]

Here, Spinoza confirms the radicalism of immanent causation. With traditional, scholastic or even Cartesian formulations of his time, Spinoza gradually unveils the unique existential Reality of all things: Nature's power in acts (*puissance en actes*). The 'infinite nature' of God is its 'sovereign power' in acts. This sets the stage for *Ethics* I, 34, the 'culminating point of *Ethics* I', which equates in a single 'absolute affirmation of existence' 'the power of God with his essence'.[70] *Ethics* I, 36 Dem. draws, according to two forms of language, the consequences of this dual identification: 1) the power of God is expressed in a certain and determinate way in everything that exists; 2) the power of God is the cause of everything that exists, so all things must be understood as the effects of this power.

Spinoza introduced the caused in the cause and causation in the caused. However, in fact, the language of expression rather than of causality is adequate, since causality intrinsically signifies a certain distance of the cause with respect to its effects. Everything that exists expresses in a certain and determinate way the power of God in acts, a Nature that exists only in its expressions. This affirms the radicalism of the immanent cause. The existence of Nature is the absolute expression of the modes' existence, as 'infinite'. From the first to the 34th proposition of *Ethics* I, then, the separation of essence and existence, of substance and the essence and existence of modes, is only a matter of metaphysical language, which, through the progress of the logic of *potentia*, tends to allow for the expression of a Reality that is fully described only by its expressions. The phenomenological language of the cause, which at first entails the ontological incommensurability of substance and its modes, is gradually deprived of its meaning until the distinction of the poles cause–effect is abolished in the pair power–act. This pair affirms the absolute uniqueness of being, that is, the ontological commensurability of substance and its modes, as expressed in the correspondence of God and the triangle. The sum of the angles of a triangle can no more be separated from the triangle than the modes can be separated from Nature. The modes, 'from eternity to

---

[69] *Ethics* I, 17 Schol.; CWS I, 426.
[70] CWS I, 439. Translator's note.

eternity',[71] result from the essence or power of God. God without modes would no more exist than a fire without heat, or a triangle without its properties.

The identification of the active and the emanative, thus, has the diabolical consequence of 'enclosing' God in the universe of things. This is the absolute limit of any theology, even of the most immanent, for it points to a passage from the highest tolerable spirituality (God is in everything)[72] to that which, entirely beyond, is called (from weakness, even of the best minds) pure atheism. There is an obvious gap between Schuller's reasoning and Spinoza's philosophy (over which he had, by 1676, full mastery). This gap makes us better understand the caution and flippant irony of Spinoza's response which, though sensitive to the philosophical initiation of his correspondent, suggests, if he can read it, that they should be cautious that the metaphysical and scholastic language in which they write to each other does not mask reality.

We must also make note of another language, used by Spinoza, to talk about the relation of the cause to its effects, of the thing to its properties, or even of power to its acts; that of the relation of the whole to its parts. We know in fact that, starting in the *KV*, Spinoza identifies the intellect ('cause' of its ideas) with 'a whole composed of its ideas'.[73] Without its parts, this whole would be nothing but a 'being of reason'[74] or an 'absurdity'.[75] *Ethics* IV, 4 Dem. reads: 'man's power, therefore, insofar as it is explained through his actual essence, is part of God or Nature's infinite power, i.e. (by IP34), of its essence'.[76] This confirms that the essence of God (that is, the existence of substance)[77] really constitutes itself (ontologically) in and through the attributes in act. Negating these acts (that is, the modes) would negate the attribute itself and, in doing so, negate God. We add that 'actual essence [. . .] part of the infinite power' corresponds to the notion of essence as 'causality', the activity of the cause in the caused, and of the radicalism of immanent causation. Essence is indeed thought of here as productive power. Yet

---

[71] *Ethics* I, 17.
[72] Saint Augustine: 'God fills up all that he has created. And yet I do not mean that they enclose him. . . He is whole in all things and all things in him.' *Enchiridion*, 2, 'Of the unspeakable knowledge of God'.
[73] *KV* I, first dialogue, 12; *CWS* I, 75.
[74] *KV* I, ii, 19; *CWS* I, 71.
[75] *Ethics* I, 12 Dem.; *CWS* I, 419.
[76] *CWS* I, 548–9. Translator's note.
[77] *Ethics* I, 20; *CWS* I, 428.

God's power is nothing except God's active essence [*essentia actuosa*]. And so it is as impossible for us to conceive that God does not act as it is to conceive that he does not exist.[78]

To erase God's activity, that is, singular essences, is to erase God, for, as *TTP* XVI emphasises: 'the universal power of the whole of nature is nothing but the power of all individuals together'.[79]

In what sense are these singular essences 'parts' of God's power? *Ethics* I, 36 Dem. has already explained: the singular essences of modes express God's power according to 'a certain and determinate mode'. This 'determination' is what allows us to define essence as a determinate quantity of power, and so as a 'part' of the absolutely infinite power of Nature.[80] Far from expressing 'the extreme remoteness'[81] of the part from the whole, *pars* expresses on the contrary the common measure of the part with this whole composed of the infinite set of parts. If we take this composition for something other than a mere tabulation or sum that would produce the infinite by mere accumulation of finitude, then we can say, unambiguously, that the whole–parts couple is the very idiom of the absolute intelligibility of Being, and of the autonomous affirmation of singular essences through which this Being constitutes itself.

We conclude that the self-genesis of substance (as cause, thing, power, whole) is carried out in the infinitely many diverse geneses specific to each thing, as 'certain and determinate modes' of their production. Further, the infinitely many diverse geneses specific to each singular thing necessarily produce effects, which are also properties, acts, parts and ideas in thought, and, existing or non-existing, bodies in extension. These 'certain and determinate modes' of production follow from, and in, the self-genesis of substance ... which is, however, performed in and through them. The affirmation of substance is, thus, realised in a certain and determinate manner in and through the infinitely many individual strategies. There are only strategies of individuation within reality. Reality is strategies. We are thus left with this looping effect, the process of an aimless and lawless circular causation in which the effect, as a part, composes and thereby participates in the production of its cause. This thesis is both absurd for classical (scholastic

---

[78] *Ethics* II, 3 Schol.; CWS I, 449.
[79] *TTP* XVI; CWS II, 282.
[80] *Ethics* IV, 4 Dem.; CWS I, 549.
[81] A. Malet, *Le Traité Théologico-politique de Spinoza et la pensée biblique*, Les Belles Lettres, 1966, p. 31, n. 1.

or Cartesian) rationalism and heretical for theology, insofar as it suggests that humans participate in the production of God, whose creatures they nevertheless remain, through their existence in act.

Hence the ethical, but also the political, consequence: each mode (more particularly, the human individual or the totality of the collective body) can affirm its life (its power) as much as it is able, bearing in mind that this 'as much' is not to be read as any limitation or 'boundary' to its freedom, even in the case of the finite modes. This is because singular necessity is free and productive. By returning to its cause, each mode participates in its own production. The more this mode experiences 'active' affections, the more it is giving itself the strength to amplify its expression. The paradigm of Nature's self-constitutive recursive cycle applies to each mode, each strategy, and, more particularly, to the ethical logic of the accumulation of power (*puissance*) as well as to the political logic of the 'absolutely absolute' self-organisation of the collective body.

7

Why do People Fight for their Servitude as if it were Salvation?

1 Servitude as a Paradoxical Object of Desire

Why are humans attracted to prejudice and superstition? Why do they fight for their servitude as if it were their salvation? Why does the desire for life so often turn into its opposite, a desire for oppression? This question is only implicit in Spinoza's work. The phrase that humans 'fight for [their servitude] as they would for their salvation'[1] is found in a long passage of the Preface to the *TTP* in which Spinoza contrasts the main interest of a monarchical regime with that of a free Republic, from the point of view of freedom of judgement. To the implicit 'why' of the above question we find only a superficial answer: humans have been deceived. The weight of the question,[2] however, demands a more comprehensive explanation – one that relates to the very constitution of human beings, namely desire (*cupiditas*). *Ethics* I, App. and *Ethics* III, 9 Schol. provide us with some elements of this explanation.

'Appetite, therefore, is nothing but the very essence of [human beings]' and we therefore 'judge something to be good because we strive for it, will it, and desire it'. The appendix also says that all are

---

[1] *TTP*, Praef.; *CWS* II, 68.
[2] The question that Etienne de La Boétie asked first in relation to monarchy; Etienne de La Boétie, *The Politics of Obedience: The Discourse of Voluntary Servitude*, trans. Harry Kurz, Ludwig von Mises Institute, 2015. La Boétie's text was published in the Netherlands in a condensed version in the *Réveille-Matin des Français et de leurs voisins* under the title *Der Francoysen ende haerder nagebueren Morghenwaecker*, attributed to Eusebious Cosmopolitan Philadelphus (Dordrecht, 1574 and 1575). Simone Goyard-Fabre cites the French version of this fragment (first published in Edinburgh in 1574) in the Garnier-Flammarion edition of the *Discours de la servitude volontaire*, 1983, pp. 175–85.

born ignorant of the causes of things and seek their advantage, something they are conscious of. From this it follows, first, that humans think of themselves as free, because they are conscious of their volitions and appetites, and do not think, even in their dreams, of the causes by which they are disposed to desiring and willing, because they are ignorant of those causes. It follows, second, that humans act always on account of an end, viz. on account of their advantage, which they desire. Hence they seek to know only the final causes of what has been done, and when they have heard them, they are satisfied, because they have no reason to doubt further.[3]

The definition of human beings as desire (*cupiditas*), the immediate illusion of their freedom (as free will) and their spontaneous finalist behaviour towards the pursuit of their own advantage are the three points of entry into the problem of servitude.

The illusion of freedom – which Spinoza maintains as an immediate fact of consciousness – and the spontaneous finalist behaviour with respect to one's own advantage necessarily determines the orientation of the *conatus* towards the teleological fiction. Because of her native powerlessness,[4] the subject is fundamentally fearful, worried, gravely concerned by the universe's chaos and fragmentation. The fiction is thus devised to resist and respond to this 'concern', so it may alleviate the anxiety, and so that humans may stay calm, to follow Spinoza's idea. Spinoza thus diverts representation (here, the fiction) from its traditional function of knowledge (true or false) to understand it as the existential/imaginary relationship humans have to reality, by virtue of a natural necessity owed to their powerlessness.[5] We note, however, that in its development, the representation of finality as fiction deepens and perpetuates the initial misunderstanding, without truly addressing the anxiety except by plunging headlong deeper into it. 'Men are moved more by opinion than by true reason';[6] but if the influence of what is true can rid us of illusion and fiction (by substitution), the absence of doubt that belief involves – and which takes, for the ignorant, the place of certainty – sustains illusion and fiction and makes them ever more real. The reality of the (illusory and fictitious) representation thus becomes more and more pronounced and alienating in that it separates humans from their own

---

[3] *Ethics* I, App.; *CWS* I, 440. Translator's note and citation.
[4] *Ethics* IV, 3.
[5] See Louis Althusser, *Essays in Self-Criticism*, Verso, 1976, pp. 135–7.
[6] *Ethics* IV, 17 Schol.; *CWS* I, 554.

essence or power (*puissance*), from their desire (*cupiditas*) as affirmation of life. The teleological fiction becomes a veritable system, the structure from which all humans live and think, and whose idea of a personal God is both the Foundation, the Origin and the End.

In *Ethics* I, App., Spinoza produces a theory of the imaginary relationship that humans have to their quotidian reality, that is, a theory of representation understood as a set of signs that provide unity, order[7] and meaning. Its essential characteristics are as follows. Its imaginary reality: the finalist fiction is real, or rather it is in its image that the existent accesses reality. Its internal inversion: the finalist doctrine 'turns nature completely upside down' Spinoza writes, 'for what is really a cause, it considers as an effect, and conversely'.[8] This reversal in the imaginary is the delusion. Its centre is the anthropocentric illusion of the free-ego subject. Its foundation is the anthropomorphic God-person, master of nature. And its practical consequence is the morality of universal order, or widespread alienation.

What is at stake is the strategic unveiling (insofar as it is the explanation of any human phenomenon) of a structure that is never quite present in anyone, but always covered (and thereby partially transformed) by its forms of actualisation: the cultures or prejudices belonging to each nation. The transition from the state of nature to the civil state is but the institution of the State that imposes specific laws and customs, the transition from a universal bias (that of finality) to particular biases that are the modified and specific forms of its actualisation according to historical conditions. The finalist bias expresses itself as a universal structure of thinking (or, more precisely, of imagining), through different forms in each nation's culture, in the ordinary discourses of the vulgar, the oracle, the prophet, the priest, the theologian and even the non-Spinozist philosopher. Spinoza therefore distinguishes between the finalist bias (which is the representation's universally shared essential structure) and the national cultures that are its specific iterations, determined by given historical conditions.

What does freedom mean within this finalist ordering of the world? The natural freedom that humans spontaneously recognise for themselves has a paradoxical meaning within the finalist system when it comes to its proper use. The proper use of freedom is to serve God. In other words, the proper exercise of freedom is submission, or voluntary servitude. For it is with

---

[7] 'Order' is one of the 'modes of thinking by which we retain or imagine the things themselves more easily'. *Metaphysical Thoughts*, I 5; CWS I, 311. On 'unity', see CM I, 6.

[8] *Ethics* I, App.; CWS I, 442. Translator's note.

religion that this prejudice becomes superstition and takes root in the soul.[9] It is through this transition from the simple representation of bias to a practice of intervening into this reality-representation that humans enter the ecosystem of superstition. The effect of the finalist fiction is therefore to impose a necessary orientation upon the *conatus*, such that freedom is necessarily the pursuit of one's own advantage, or a necessary orientation towards one's own health. 'Whatever conduces to health and the worship of God, they have called good; but what is contrary to these, evil.'[10] The finalist fiction imposes upon the *conatus* an image of one's own health that is intrinsically tied to submission to God through worship. Yet from the point of view of the affirmation of desire (*cupiditas*), such health is the disease itself, the progressive and inevitable poisoning of the power to act.

The religious and political powers (*pouvoir*) will be sure to exploit this self-submission and self-poisoning of desire (*cupiditas*) for their own benefit, and the theologians are the tinkerers of the fiction that makes this exploitation possible. But the role of religious and political powers comes after the fact. They are inserted into and called for by the system that humans build in their imaginary. The master is born out of the slave.

Ethics I, App. shows how the finalist bias, with the introduction of worship, inevitably turns into superstition. In the *TTP*'s preface, Spinoza emphasises the necessary connection between superstition and fear.

> Men are tormented by superstition only so long as they are afraid. All of the things they have ever worshipped in illusory religion have been nothing but apparitions, the delusions of a sad and fearful mind.[11]

Superstition is prejudice plus fear, which manifests itself as soon as we experience nature's hostile, dream-crushing chaos. We desperately seek a cure and worship the *rectores naturae* to convince them to change their plans for us.

Superstition is therefore complete in its kind. Rooted in weakness and fear, it is comprised of two elements: a theoretical element consisting of beliefs and myths, and a practical element consisting of worship and rites. Each involves, envelops, sustains and deepens the other. Through the finalist bias of which it is a necessary outcome, superstition reveals that this representation of the world is not only a system of imaginary ideas in the

---

[9] *Ethics* I, App.; CWS I, 441.
[10] *Ethics* I, App.; CWS I, 444. Translator's note.
[11] *TTP*, Praef.; CWS II, 67.

heads of humans and determined by the constitution of their organic bodies. Representation, it shows us, is also a set of practices, a way of acting implied by these ideas, themselves exploited, or in some way remodelled and over-determined, according to the oppressive social body in and through which they develop.

We must answer the question from this dual Spinozist theory of the affects and of the signs that represent and express them. Why is it so easy to take humans in with prejudice and superstition? Why do they want what destroys them?

Both at the collective and individual levels, superstition, after representing itself as a remedy, leads desire to its own loss. To save themselves, everyone deepens their own servitude. Superstition becomes a true culture of the death instinct. Yet, since the origins of humanity, humans have continued to hold on to their prejudices and superstitions, to fight and die for them. How do we explain this seemingly contradictory and absurd attitude? What do they really want from this? What is the actual object of their desire when they seek servitude as if their survival depended on it? How can the servitude that belongs to superstition be desirable? How can it be advantageous to a desire (*cupiditas*) which, according to its essence, can only desire its affirmation? The only Spinozist hypothesis is that in superstition, as overwhelming object of desire, there must be another object at which desire aims. It must be that desire, paradoxically, can only get to its affirmation through the object of servitude. We must uncover in the Spinozist text this other positive object of desire – as desired[12] – at the centre of the negativity of servitude.

Spinoza's very formulation is illuminating and must guide us: humans do not seek servitude for its own sake, the negation of their desire in order to negate their desire; there must be something in servitude, in this negation, that belongs to the order of salvation, and thus to the affirmation of life. Humans fight for servitude with a zeal equal to that with which they fight for their salvation because they seek salvation in servitude. It is this appalling paradox that we must come to terms with; servitude is a paradoxical object in that it involves, in its negativity, something that is desired naturally.

We know that humans strive to persevere in their being,[13] when they have clear and distinct ideas as well as when they have confused ideas. Even through prejudices and superstition (that is, poisons), the *conatus* stubbornly tends towards the affirmation of life. Is this not the theoretical affirmation,

---

[12] *Ethics* III, 9 Schol.
[13] *Ethics* III, 9, 12, 54; CWS I, 499, 502, 525.

practically legitimated by *Ethics* I, App., of the vital necessity of the code that gives meaning and therefore reality to our actions? Doesn't the deep primal concern born of our powerlessness demand codification, a tidying up, to be satisfied? Is it not this fundamental fact that Spinoza recognises and describes in the appendix? The code is a necessity called upon by the vital process itself, by the conatus as a power (*puissance*) of resistance, an effort to persevere in our being. The epigenetics of the finalist bias answers this need that we must understand as 'properties which pertain to human nature in the same way heat, cold, storms, thunder, etc., pertain to the nature of the air'.[14] What is negative and criticisable from the point of view of reason plays a positive and effective role from the point of view of life, in its effort to perpetuate itself. To be accepted, reality covers itself over with an image of itself that becomes real to us. Isn't that the affirmation of the vital necessity of representation? For Spinoza, the idea, or mental representation, always correlates with the mind's affects such as love, desire, etc.[15] The idea of order is tied to the mind's affect of joy and security, just as the idea of disorder is tied to the affects of fear and sadness. On the other hand, in the idea or representation, there is necessarily always something positive, which is the very activity of the mind.[16]

So the finalist bias in the mind translates the effort of all the instincts of our organism in order to appropriate the chaos of a disturbingly strange reality, which only effectively becomes a world for us (a coherence and a unity) after the demiurgic work of the *conatus* gives it order and meaning. We must recognise the ordering nature of the *conatus*. Because of passive affections, the original powerlessness to simply be what we are, an absolute and joyous affirmation of our existence, the existential impossibility of accepting existence in its raw state necessarily results in the formation of an illusory consciousness, an inverted reading of reality. The code from which everything takes on meaning, far from being the reproduction in thought of the actual order of Nature, is nothing other than a combination of signs expressing, through our imagination, the diverse dispositions of our body that vary according to chance encounters: 'each [judges] things according to the disposition of his brain',[17] from the point of view of the state of the organic body and the basic principle of joy and sadness. The mind's decisions are nothing other than the appetites themselves, which change according

---

[14] *TP* I, 4; *CWS* II, 505.
[15] *Ethics* II, Ax. 3; *CWS* I, 448.
[16] *Ethics* II, Def. 3 and Expl.; *CWS* I, 447.
[17] *Ethics* I, App.; *CWS* I, 445.

to the variable dispositions of the body.[18] The code as vital imperative is therefore perverted from the beginning, reduced to the illusions and fictions of our imagination. Our representation of the world and of ourselves is spontaneously imaginary (identical for all in its finalist structure): the castration of desire is original and universal.

Although necessary from a vital point of view, the code is arbitrary from a logical point of view. From this, we understand the self-poisoning: the vital necessity that binds humans to that which destroys them. Although the two moments are necessarily linked, it is precisely because one can analytically separate the vital necessity of a code (the representation) from its ideological perversion in the fiction that the superstitious system can be dismantled (and not only for the philosopher), for Spinoza. Beyond the true and adequate conception – or conceptualisation – of philosophy, but not in contradiction to it, there is indeed a right, 'sound' or just side to the imaginary representation that does not lead to universal servitude to superstition. (Spinoza speaks of a 'sound concept of God', which is not necessarily identical to the true and adequate idea of God.) The correct aspect of imaginary representation makes the process of liberation possible. It is the 'right' side of religion, implicitly taught by the Old Testament and explicitly by Christ and the Apostles, a message studied by the central chapters of the *TTP* (XI–XIV).

It is extremely important to understand the difference between the vital necessity of the code and its perversion in fiction to appreciate how everyone's liberation is possible for Spinoza. To sum up: on the one hand, the code seems to be a requirement and an effect of the *conatus*'s ordering nature. On the other hand, the expression of this requirement is necessarily determined by the structures of the organic body, and then overdetermined by the structures of the social body. In *Ethics* I, App., however, Spinoza emphasises the relationship between the body's 'health' as an organism (he speaks of 'the motion the nerves receive')[19] and the affections that fulfil its capacity to be affected. One then finds that it is not necessarily the truth, or what is genuinely good (advantageous), that brings 'health' in the first place (truthfully, a minimal health if we are talking about the 'ordinary'[20] human type), but also the finalist and anthropocentric illusions that reason rejects. Still in the appendix, the conceptual pair 'order and confusion' speaks to a relative bias compared to the main teleological bias. Spinoza's point is that

---

[18] *Ethics* III, 2 Schol.
[19] *Ethics* I, App.; CWS I, 445.
[20] *TdIE* I; CWS I, 7.

humans 'prefer order to confusion'.[21] So they necessarily want, for their own 'health', to perceive an order in nature that is satisfactory (to their organs), rather than confusion, because the latter plunges them into 'anxiety' and insecurity, sadness and fear. When imagination represents things in a way that is simple and easy to remember (memory and not intellect have an essential role), we are pleasantly affected and say that things are 'well-ordered'. If, on the contrary, we have a hard time understanding things, we say that 'they are confused'.[22]

Let us take the problem from the point of view of the last instance: desire. If we acknowledge, with Spinoza, that everything that is 'bad' for us is measured by the depletion of our acting power and everything that is 'good' by the increase of that power, and that humans find order 'more pleasurable' than disorder and therefore experience Joy (which necessarily follows from an increase in power), then one must realise that this relationship humans have with the image of order increases power and life. Humans who judge that 'what is most important in each thing is what is most useful to them, [rate] as most excellent all those things by which they were most pleased'.[23] Order is an example of such a 'useful' object of desire. What feeling would be more useful to the *conatus* than the security it experiences with the image of order?

'Security' is certainly the sign of an interior 'lack of power',[24] but it is also the object of an 'honourable' or 'reasonable'[25] desire which causes Joy, though this Joy still presupposes that 'a Sadness has preceded [it], viz. Hope and Fear'.[26] On the other hand, in *Ethics* III, DA 14, Spinoza defines security as 'a Joy born of the idea of a future or past thing, concerning which the cause of doubting has been removed'.[27] We therefore understand 1) that those who wish not to doubt to preserve their security and peace of mind do not take into account the permanent dead ends of the finalist bias; 2) that this vital prejudice – the image of order it involves, which guarantees the feeling of security – is virtually ineradicable; and 3) that the feeling of security that leads to the 'sluggishness' and 'laziness' of the body and

---

[21] *Ethics* I, App.; *CWS* I, 444.
[22] Ibid.
[23] *Ethics* I, App.; *CWS* I, 444.
[24] *Ethics* IV, 47 Schol.; *CWS* I, 573.
[25] *TTP* III; *CWS* II, 113. Reading the *TTP* from the point of view of the quasi-permanent state of insecurity in which Jewish people live, Geneviève Brykman has underlined the importance Spinoza gives to 'security', *La Judéité de Spinoza*, Vrin, 1972.
[26] *Ethics* IV, 47 Schol.; *CWS* I, 573.
[27] *CWS* I, 534. Translator's note.

mind[28] contributes to inertia, to fixing desire. The joy that stems from it must be called an improper Joy (like the 'ordinary' joy of the basic health of the ordinary human), in that it is an 'obstacle' to a real and meaningful fulfilment of life. On the one hand, there is an increase of the power to act, and so a (passive) joy. But, on the other hand, this passive joy 'fixes' the subject in a state of servitude and blindness that poisons her, diminishing and getting in the way of her power to act.

The study of the two concepts, 'order and confusion', confirms the thesis according to which the order (what orders if not a code?) is required by the vital process but nonetheless turns against it. Here, Spinoza explicitly differentiates between 'order' as vital necessity (increase in our power to act, and whose meeting – or production – provokes joy) and 'order' as it is at the origin. This 'order' is necessarily mystifying, and therefore a perversion of our power to act. The order (and therefore also the code) as vital requirement is summoned by the very structures of our organism. The organic body suffers from disorder in the same way it can suffer from an excess that challenges its structural and vital balance between motion and rest. It is symptomatic that the 'hot and cold' pair immediately follows, in the appendix, the 'order–disorder' pair in the exposition of the secondary biases derived from the finalist bias. Since there is an objectivity of the representation of the sensation for our body beyond any ideological deceit, there is an objectivity of the desire for order anchored in the structures of the organic body before any ideological constitution of this order: the code. The code is therefore universal and necessary as it is required by the vital process itself. It is, however, also arbitrary, since it is the product of imagination; it is a requirement of the organic *conatus*, a requirement of the rule as rule. We now understand better why the mystification of prejudices and superstitions 'takes' so well in individuals. Ideological mystification, not as such, that is, not as mystification but 'as code', is necessary to the life it nevertheless contributes to destroying. Thus, the body, powerless in its desire for order, necessarily and paradoxically creates an order that distorts desire. The body against desire: the oppression starts here, in the necessary contradiction between the organic body and the desiring body that nevertheless constitutes it. This contradiction may be mitigated by knowledge of the structure of the organic body and a life-practice that gradually reduces the organic body to desire. The latter, turned into reason, creates a new way of feeling for the subject (including the feeling of eternity).[29] The conflict is

---

[28] *TP* X, 4–6.
[29] *Ethics* V, 23 Schol.

thus resolved by wisdom, in the perfect unity of the mind (adequate idea) and of the body (active affections) that are 'one and the same thing' in the becoming-adequate-cause-subject.

There is thus a contradiction that can be found both in the body and in the intellect. In the body, the contradiction lies between the absolute affirmation of existence and the contingent preservation of the organism in which it is necessarily fixed by a strategy of survival. In the intellect, it lies between the intrinsic and affirmative logic of the adequate idea and that of the human mind whose logical necessity – the law of the association of ideas – is unsurpassable because it is proper to human nature. These systems (of preservation in the organic body and of association of ideas in the mind) are systems that are not – at least in theory – in contradiction with the affirmation of the life they express (in the body and in the intellect). In practice, however, they necessarily set the affirmation in the passive joys because of the powerlessness of the human condition. In fact, the body, like the mind, finds the mechanisms of its own passivity in itself, and so it cannot simply be explained by external causes. The whole point of the *Ethics* is to put these mechanisms at the service of the full and complete affirmation of life by giving them an intrinsic necessity, internal to human nature and to its spontaneous affirmation. We thus do not negate these mechanisms, even though they are normally governed by external forces.

If superstition works so well, if it is, as Spinoza says, so deeply rooted in our souls, it is precisely because the representative order that underlies it is not caused by the representation itself but by the *conatus*, by the very life that requires and produces it. The deepest secret of the force and authority of superstition is the very force or power of the *conatus*. The mystifying and poisonous representation is not the very necessity of the representation as order. It is but its malignant and arbitrary growth (but also its necessary sustenance because of human weakness). Let humans find another symbolic support (a system of signs or of adequate images) that adequately answers their vital requirement for a code, and the system of superstition will be broken. This adequate code, a path to salvation for all, is found in the Scriptures, and, more specifically, in the teachings of Christ. However, as long as these words of salvation are not taken in (well interpreted) by the ignorant, the actual and vital existence of the code will, through its development, paradoxically introduce a separation from reality, life, other and self. This introduces the universal misfortune of humans who can only access reality, their reality, through the inverted mirror of a false (and from a practical point of view, bad) consciousness. In this case, the code from which everything acquires meaning, value and reality can only ever render that which it has become:

a fiction. Necessary, though arbitrary in its content, without logical reason or justification, its vital function – although necessarily always there – is inverted/perverted into an oppressive function. The arbitrary code usually and naturally submits everything in its grasp (its producers but also its victims) to the arbitrary domination of its moral, religious and political laws. It does so in the name of order, truth and the good. The most adequate theological-political expression of this state of affairs (that is, the least appropriate to vital necessity) is the tyrannical monarchical system.

2 *Sed obtemperantia subditum facit*

Entry into the structure of superstition is therefore characterised by two criteria: the affect of fear and the practice of a cult. This practice itself involves a double aspect: submission to a transcendent order that holds common meanings; but also, and within this very submission, a certain activity, a space of pseudo-freedom, room for intervention in this order that the superstitious subject believes she possesses as her own power (*pouvoir*) (which is how she explains her freedom). The system of superstition forms an obedient subject who, within actual servitude, has some individual (and/or collective) latitude with respect to the order and power to which she is subjugated. Political obedience rests on the ambivalence of this imaginary structure.

Obedience is not, however, consubstantially linked to superstition or subjugation. As for the (unwritten) code whose vital and positive necessity must be distinguished from its content (developed in religion and superstition whose commandments may be written, as is the case in the Jewish and Christian traditions), we must differentiate between superstitious obedience to the content of the law (or to the person embodying this law) and obedience to the common representation of the law as a vital connection between humans that gives unity, order and meaning to their actions. If the content of the law is the expression of the power relations and interests peculiar to a given society, the existence of a common law in its contradictions expresses the unity and identity of that society.[30] This distinction between the function and the content of the law allows us to think of the status of a citizen in

---

[30] My distinction between the law as such and its content is based on *TTP* IV; *CWS* II, 126, where Spinoza writes *verus finis legum*, an expression that captures the possibility of an internal tension between the 'true end' of the law (its vital function, that is, to ensure security, concord and peace) and the insurgencies that it nonetheless, by its particular content, causes. An example: the Mosaic Law, by making the Levites the guardians of the sacred instead of the firstborn of each family, is responsible for the Hebrews' misfortunes (*TTP* XVII; *CWS* II, 318).

a free republic, who is free both to abide by the law and to question its content, to debate it and even to propose to the sovereign power (*puissance*) that it be changed, even abolished, in favour of laws more suited to the actual conditions of society and reason.[31] The capacity to resist is an expression of the right (power) of a free republic to criticise and contradict within the limits of language, education and reason. Its very existence is a sign of the mind's capacity to be autonomous (at least *vis-à-vis* the content of the law or hegemonic meanings). This resistance, in its most primal form, supports the imaginary structure of obedience at its origin. By demanding the obedience of the will it seeks to suppress, the law opens up the very space in which it can be questioned.

The critically obedient subject, citizen of a free republic, free from superstitious subjection to the law, is undoubtedly the product of humanity's long history of liberation from the 'remnants of [its] ancient servitude'.[32] Although the first challenges to law accompanied the emergence of law itself, they were limited by the particular terrain of superstition they confronted. Historically, political obedience and the resulting political dissent were forged on the basis of superstition, fear and submission. Superstition provides a solid foundation because it is formed by a strict and internalised order of meanings. But it is also a fragile foundation, for it is subject to that doubtful human freedom which they suppose can change the will of the Gods according to their desires and actions. This often creates a sense of dissatisfaction or even injustice and then anger and rebellion when people feel they have been betrayed in their loyalty or love. For this touches them at the core of the imaginary economic-affective exchange relationship they enter into with the divine subjects they imagine to be as free as they believe they are themselves. This pseudo-freedom that underlies the system of superstition is determined by fear and the hope that results from it and is extremely dangerous for the stability and longevity of the superstition in question. People do indeed forge 'innumerable fictions' according to the needs of the moment. Superstition is therefore

> very fluctuating and inconstant; and [. . .] protected only by hope, hate, anger, and deception, because it arises, not from reason, but only from the most powerful affects. As easy, then, as it is to take men in with any superstition whatever, it's still just as difficult to make them persist in one and the same superstition. The common people always remain equally

[31] *TTP* XX; CWS II, 346.
[32] *TTP*, Praef.; CWS II, 68.

wretched and are never satisfied for long. What pleases them is what is new and has not yet deceived them.[33]

Spinoza draws the political consequences:

This inconstancy has been the cause of many uprisings and bloody wars. As is evident from what we have just said, and as Curtius aptly noted, 'nothing governs the multitude more effectively than superstition' (Quintus Curtius, IV, x, 7). That's why they are easily led, under the pretext of religion, now to worship their Kings as Gods, and now to curse and loathe them as the common plague of the human race.[34]

From this follows the political and, in this first sense, instrumental function of religion. It must stabilise superstition, and in order to do this it packages a particular superstition into an apparatus that can give it as much power as possible in the imagination of the common people. In order to rule the minds of the people with the greatest possible efficiency, the State must impose a single superstition. From this point of view, we can distinguish superstitions according to the degree of their effectiveness, with monotheism proving much more politically successful than polytheism.[35] The space of freedom and subversion associated with the practice of worship is strictly controlled and codified, so that worship is subject to submission to a single faith, and 'so that everyone will always worship it with the utmost deference'.[36]

The vital requirement of the law is alloyed with its content. Doubt and even any 'discussion' are banished from the relationship with the law, from which follows complete and constant obedience. This is the dream of a tyrannical authority. The political subject, subjected to constant obedience to the established juridico-political order ('obedience makes the subject'),[37] is shaped by the semiosis of mass religious organisation, the realm of established superstition. Religious discipline conditions political discipline.[38]

Spinoza explains that the arbitrariness of monarchical power (*pouvoir*) can only find its meaning and legitimacy through the rule of organised

---

[33] *TTP*, Praef.; *CWS* II, 68.
[34] *TTP*, Praef.; *CWS* II, 68.
[35] On this, see Alexandre Matheron's comment in *Le Christ et le salut des ignorants*, Aubier, 1971, pp. 17ff.
[36] *TTP*, Praef.; *CWS* II, 67.
[37] *TTP* XVII.; *CWS* II, 297.
[38] *TTP*, Praef.; *Ep.* LXXVI [to Albert Burgh]; *CWS* II, 67–8, 473–8.

religion (that is, through the Church). The role of the religious orders, the priest, the rabbi and the theologian is therefore essential. They are the builders of an arbitrary but vital code which they adapt to the control of thought rather than to the crucial function of life.

There must be an identity between the ruler and the deity, *first*, so that religion does not turn against the king's power; *second*, so that it can appropriate that part in each subject which is still free (so that obedience becomes the only possible way of life); and *third*, so that submission becomes a genuine self-surrender to the king. Only then can the State, through religion, gain total control over its subjects, who become perfect automatons: slaves.[39] To get what they want, kings try to pass themselves off either as Gods or as their descendants, or – an imperfect solution – as their earthly representatives. This mystification is certainly much easier to carry out with 'barbarians', who are victims of superstition and fear and therefore very gullible by nature. It is more difficult with the less devout peoples, and therefore the strategy of divine representation is preferred. However, this mystification is always difficult to accept, not because the theological-political imaginary of the people is hard to reach, but because, due to the instability and changing nature of superstition, they may begin to suspect the ruler of being a fraud. Therefore, to get what he wants, the monarch is forced to move from indirect to direct forms of violence, which only widens the gap between him and the people. From the Gods (or half-Gods) that they were, the kings become the mortal enemies of humankind . . . and other despots then take their place, as long as the causes that enable tyranny are not changed.[40] How can this circular, catastrophic necessity be avoided? In the case of the monarchical or tyrannical states of the seventeenth century, there is no answer in the *TTP*. They seem condemned to a servitude whose lesser evil is to continue in their usual form, namely the 'right of the legitimate king'. This seems to be the lesson Spinoza draws from the English example.

Apart from this historical impasse in which nations accustomed to monarchical power are stuck (according to the *TTP*), the *TTP* continues to insist on the democratic question. Can humanity escape the monarchical fate imposed on it by its imaginary, systematised by a few and still shackling so many? Some nations, thanks to their 'fortune', have indeed escaped this fate (Spinoza gives the example of the States of Holland, which 'never had

---

[39] He uses the notion of 'automaton' to express the condition of humans subjected to the absolute 'domination' of the state in *TTP* XX; *CWS* II, 346: *Non, inquam, finis Reipublicae est homines ex rationalibus bestias, vel automata facere*. . .

[40] *TTP* XVIII; *CWS* II, 328–9.

a king').⁴¹ But apart from the historical coincidences that have led one nation to freedom and another to servitude, we can imagine two theoretical assumptions by which people might have escaped the logic of the imaginary: 1) either people are able to live under the command of reason, but then the State becomes superfluous, so this cannot be a political hypothesis; or 2) people are able to establish a democracy, but in that case how could they escape the laws of the teleological imaginary and the superstition that follows from it?

From this perspective, *TTP* V[42] expresses the aporia into which Spinoza was led by the fundamental logic of the political constitution of the imaginary, the origin of which is set out in the Appendix to *Ethics* I. If imagination is always already constitutive of politics and is itself already erected on the search for final causes, then people are necessarily always driven by superstition towards monarchy. This happens through the work of codifiers, mystifiers and tyrants and those who serve tyrants. Hence the inescapable importance of superstition, which is indeed, in this constitutive logic, the mediator of the political institution. From this also emerges the importance of servile obedience: the believing subject who obeys without discussion clears the way for the passive political subject. Whether we look at it from the transcendent, instrumental and mystifying point of view of the tyrant (and this deceptive practice is, as we know, 'the great secret of the monarchical regime')[43] or from the immanent and vital point of view of the desire that guides the common representation-signification of the world by the multitude, the problem of superstitious mediation is found even in the study of the Hebrew State.[44]

To better understand this theoretical impasse, let us take up the parallel demonstrations of *TTP* V, *TTP* XVI and *TTP* XVII.

1) Spinoza first establishes an ideal condition which, if implemented, would render the State useless:

> If nature had so constituted men that they desired nothing except what true reason teaches them to desire, then of course a society could exist without laws; in that case it would be completely sufficient to teach men

---

[41] *TTP* XVIII; CWS II, 329–30.
[42] *TTP* V; CWS II, 143–4.
[43] CWS II, 315–16. Translator's note.
[44] By persuading the people of 'his divine virtue', did not Moses introduce religion into the state so that the Hebrews could be governed by devotion rather than fear? (*TTP* V; CWS II, 145–6).

true moral lessons, so that they would do voluntarily, wholeheartedly, and in a manner worthy of free men, what is really useful.[45]

If this condition were fulfilled, an associative alliance would suffice, rendering the coercive force of the State superfluous:

> If all men could easily be led just by the guidance of reason, and could recognize the supreme utility and necessity of the Republic, there would be no one who would not absolutely detest deceptions. With the utmost good faith, everyone would stand by their contracts completely, out of a desire for this supreme good, the preservation of the Republic. Above all else, they would maintain trust, the chief protection of the Republic.[46]

2) Reality, however, contradicts this ideal condition on a daily basis. Indeed,

> human nature is not constituted like that at all. It's true that everyone seeks his own advantage – but people want things and judge them useful, not by the dictates of sound reason, but for the most part only from immoderate desire and because they are carried away by affects of mind which take no account of the future and of other things.[47]

> [I]t's far from true that everyone can always be easily led just by the guidance of reason. Everyone is drawn by his own joy. Most of the time the mind is so filled with greed, love of esteem, envy, anger, etc., that there's no room for reason.[48]

> Those who've experienced how changeable the mentality of the multitude is almost despair about it. They're governed only by affects, not by reason.[49]

The security of the State is thus threatened less by external enemies than by its own citizens.

---

[45] *TTP* V; *CWS* II, 143.
[46] *TTP* XVI; *CWS* II, 285.
[47] *TTP* V; *CWS* II, 143.
[48] *TTP* XVI; *CWS* II, 285.
[49] *TTP* XVII; *CWS* II, 298.

3) Hence the necessity of violence, since

> no society can continue in existence without authority and force, and hence, laws which moderate and restrain men's immoderate desires and unchecked impulses.[50]

To the 'promise' to rule by the dictates of reason alone, to curb our own appetites, and to do to no one what we do not want others to do to us, we must 'add something else': A 'sovereign power [that can] compel everyone by force and restrain them by fear of the supreme punishment (which everyone, without exception, fears)'.[51]

4) But force keeps the multitude in check only with difficulty because: a)

> the hardest thing for them to endure is being subservient to and governed by their equals;[52]

> from love of esteem, each disdains their equals, and will not put up with being ruled by them;[53]

and b) nothing is more difficult than to take freedom away from men once it has been granted.[54] 'All beings are born' into this 'natural freedom', according to *TTP* XVI,[55] and they do not let go of it so easily. For no one is obliged by natural law to live according to the temperament of another, since 'each [is] the defender of his own freedom'.[56]

5) The political problem that arises, then, is the organisation of the multitude: 'How [must the subjects] be led so that they constantly maintain their loyalty and virtue?'[57] We must

> establish the State so that there's no place for fraud – [establish] things so that everyone, whatever his mentality, prefers the public right to private advantage, this is the task, this is our concern.[58]

---

[50] *TTP* V; *CWS* II, 143–4.
[51] *TTP* XVI; *CWS* II, 285. Translation modified.
[52] *TTP* V; *CWS* II, 144.
[53] *TTP* XVII; *CWS* II, 298.
[54] *TTP* V; *CWS* II, 144.
[55] *TTP* XVI; *CWS* II, 292.
[56] *TTP*, Praef.; *CWS* II, 73. Translation modified.
[57] *TTP* XVII; *CWS* II, 298.
[58] *TTP* XVII; *CWS* II, 298.

6) There are three solutions: monarchical, democratic and (for those who live 'barbarically') theocratic.[59] The *monarchical* solution can only be maintained by mystification, for this is the only way to resolve the contradiction between the nature of monarchy and the laws of human affect, which do not tolerate being ruled by an equal. Without religious mystification, kings could only be hated. So if power belongs to a single person, he 'ought to have something above ordinary human nature. If he does not surpass ordinary human nature, he at least must strive with all his might to persuade the common people of this.'[60] That is why 'when Kings assumed the rule in earlier times, to make themselves secure they tried to persuade people that they were descended from the immortal Gods'.[61]

The *democratic* solution solves the political problem naturally, without being supported by illusions. Society is the continuation of natural freedom and equality by other means and under other conditions.

> If possible, the whole society should hold sovereignty as a body, so that everyone is bound to be subject of himself, and no one is bound to be subject to his equal;[62]

> This, then, is the way [i] a social order can be formed consistently with natural right, and [ii] every contract can always be preserved with the utmost good faith. If each person transfers all their power [*puissance*] to the social order, which alone retains the supreme right of nature over all things. That is, the social order alone will have sovereignty, and each person will be bound to obey it, either freely, or from fear of the supreme punishment. The right of such a social order is called Democracy. This is defined, then, as a [corporate body] of men which has, as a body, the supreme right over everything in its power [*pouvoir*].[63]

---

[59] Aristocracy is an intermediate solution (between monarchy and democracy) that we will not look into here because it is not an original solution to the problem at hand. I have analysed aristocracy as a possible transitional structure to democracy in 'Enseignement du Christ et résistance dans le *T.T.P.*', in *La Bible et ses raisons*, Jean Monet University, Saint-Etienne, 1996.

[60] *TTP* V; *CWS* II, 144.

[61] *TTP* XVII; *CWS* II, 300.

[62] *TTP* V; *CWS* II, 144.

[63] *TTP* XVI; *CWS* II, 287. Translation modified.

This State indeed seems to be

> the most natural state, and the one which approached most nearly the freedom nature concedes to everyone. In [democracy] no one so transfers his natural right to another that in the future there is no consultation with him. Instead he transfers it to the greater part of the whole Society, of which he makes one part. In this way everyone remains equal, as they were before, in the state of nature.[64]

Amid the tension created by the contrast between the most mystifying and the most natural regime, Spinoza in *TTP* V refuses to use the concept of obedience[65] to characterise the citizen's position within the democratic regime:

> since obedience consists in someone's carrying out a command solely on the authority of the person who commands it, it follows that obedience has no place in a social order where sovereignty is in the hands of everyone and laws are enacted by common consent.

This explains the absence of resistance to sovereignty in a democracy, which allows an increase or decrease in the number of laws with the full consent of a people who 'nevertheless remain equally free'. In contrast, the sovereignty of a monarchical power, which is supposed to be absolute, is in fact quite limited when confronted with a rebellious multitude: 'it will be difficult for [the king] to institute new laws when it is necessary, and to take away a freedom once it has been granted to the people'.[66] There is thus a radical contrast between the question of 'rule' as the goal of a monarchical State (in complete contradiction to human nature and the natural function of the State in general) and democracy, whose goal is 'freedom'.[67] In democracy, 'natural freedom'[68] ultimately prevails. That is, the effective preservation of 'the natural right to exist and act without harming oneself or others'[69] takes precedence. In contrast, in a monarchy, natural law is opposed.[70] In order to produce obedience, which is nothing other than submission and servitude, this regime must condition its subjects from the beginning and

---

[64] *TTP* XVI; *CWS* II, 289.
[65] Contrary to *TTP* XVI; *CWS* II, 286.
[66] *TTP* V; *CWS* II, 145.
[67] *TTP* XX; *CWS* II, 346.
[68] *TTP* XVI; *CWS* II, 293.
[69] *TTP* XX; *CWS* II, 346.
[70] *TTP* XVI; *CWS* II, 286. Translation modified.

make them fight for their servitude through illusions, as if it were a matter of their salvation.

In the texts that run through the *TTP*, the complex of obedience, conditioning and imagination seems specific to the monarchical State, whose relative stability (that is, the subjugation of subjects) can only be achieved through 'certain ruses'.[71] Democracy, which is the continuation of the state of nature under different conditions (that is, for Spinoza, the State that 'comes closest to the state of nature'),[72] would not know what to do with obedience, conditioning and imagination: its natural basis thus guarantees its excellence.

Based on this observation, Spinoza would be described as a thinker of natural law who bases democracy's legitimate claim to be the best system on a theory of natural freedom and equality. The most innovative thesis of *TTP* – namely, that of the imaginary formation of the body politic, which first takes an ambiguous form in the analysis of monarchy and then takes a more radical form in the analysis of Hebrew theocracy (an analysis that leads to the conclusions of *TTP* V as much as that of XVII, which we have just looked at) – would thus be refuted by the idealist and abstract thesis of natural law. To say that Spinoza distances himself completely from this position in the *TTP* would be an exaggeration. The very wording of the texts indicates its presence. In *TTP* V, Spinoza contrasts the abstract logic of normative reason with the real political productivity of the imagination, as he must, but which nevertheless does not seem to be a real political alternative to the combined forces of the superstitions of the multitude and the cunning and efficient techniques of tyrants. There is an emphasis, at least in the language Spinoza uses in the *TTP* for the *jus naturale*, which comes up against a notion of the political imaginary as its other (but also as its counterpart), which at first sight seems to be valued by monarchy for its power (*puissance*) of illusion and mystification. We must add, however, that these very real surface effects cannot stand up to the core ideas of the *TTP*, namely:

1. The radical identification of right and power,[73] which presents the state of nature as a state of complete dependence and its corresponding right as theoretical rather than real.

---

[71] *TTP* XX; CWS II, 345.

[72] *TTP* XX; CWS II, 351.

[73] Edwin Curley stressed the presence of the right–power identity encountered as early as *TTP* IV: 'L'état naturel et sa loi chez Hobbes et Spinoza', in *La ética de Spinoza. Fundamentos y significado*, ed. Atilano Dominguez, Universidad de Castilla-La Mancha, 1992, pp. 355–60.

2. The encounter – the result of a particular historical context on which Spinoza draws and whose whole aspiration is the realisation of progressive possibilities – of the rise of scientific and technological rationality and the emergence of a new imaginary embracing a practical of faith freed from the Church and the theologians, in a free republic full of promise for the future.[74]
3. The study of the Hebrew State, its foundations and its history, which produces both the elements of a new political philosophy and, in the context of the Dutch Republic in the second half of the seventeenth century, gives Spinoza the weapons to shift the aims of his fight from the defence of the freedom to philosophise to a more radical struggle for the democratisation of the collective body.

3 The Theocratic Solution: From the Order of Signs to the Political Order, a Rational Strategy for a Barbarian Nation

The Hebrew nation chooses a unique God as king, a political principle essential for the stability of the State. This solution reverses the strategy of the monarchical regime: not to deify the king (something that can always be contested), but to make God king. In this sense, and only in this sense, the identity of the sovereign and the deity is truly effective for the stability of the State. The stability in this case can even be considered eternal.

Moses offers the perfect political solution to the problem of governing a barbarian people. This solution transforms historical contingency (this institution, this law) into an absolute necessity that completely erases arbitrariness. To understand this last point, let us return to the distinction already mentioned in Spinoza's text. On the one hand, the code appears as a vital requirement. On the other hand, this requirement is immediately perverted in the fiction of an arbitrary code. The actual operation of the original code (the finalist bias) inevitably leads to the catastrophe that is superstition and to its political realisation: a tyrannical monarchy. Superstition (under the guise of religion) and tyranny (under the guise of the divine right of kings) poison the individual *conatus* and are powerless to control the political rebellions they cause by their very existence. There is a contradiction between the necessity of the code and its arbitrary expressions, which inevitably lead

---

[74] A historical conjuncture particularly studied by André Tosel in *Spinoza ou le crépuscule de la servitude*, Aubier, 1984. See also L. Mugnier-Pollet, *La philosophie politique de Spinoza*, Vrin, 1976; J. Huizinga, *La civiltà olandese del Seicento*, Einaudi, 1967; and J.-T. Desanti, *Introduction à l'histoire de la philosophie*, La Nouvelle Critique, 1956.

the *conatus* of the State (and the individuals who constitute it) to a death that can only be postponed.

There is a way – albeit paradoxical – to avoid this catastrophic development. It consists in radically institutionalising superstition (by unifying it, which is the task of religion). It must be elevated to the rank of an inviolable political law, to make superstition in its peculiarities (which are absurd to anyone to whom they are alien) something vital; to make it the very meaning and value of existence, both for the individual subject and for the whole community. This is the paradox: superstition, a poison, becomes a cure for its own evil through its institutionalisation.

When this happens, the contradiction between the necessity and the arbitrariness of the code is actually negated. It is the code, which has become political law insofar as it is arbitrary – but not known as such and absolutely revered and respected by all as the law of God – that ensures the preservation of life and happiness. So it is precisely the perversion of the vital code reflected in the law of the divine king that ensures the preservation and reproduction of a happy life. The point is, on the one hand, to institutionalise superstition so that it becomes law and, on the other, to extend it to every aspect of daily life so that it embodies the specificity of mores. Superstition is a sacred order that is the same for everyone, a system of indicative and imperative signs that supports the life of the nation. It is a symbolic support through which life can find itself (which is the necessity and vital function of the code). It is this symbolic order that identifies God with the law of the nation that enables the Hebrews to escape the instability of the State, the fluctuations of superstition and the consequent inevitable self-destruction of the *conatus* (the nation and the individual).

To reduce the symbolic order of the Hebrew State to the mere political technique of a great legislator, as some of Spinoza's remarks would have us believe (*Moses . . . Divino religionem in Rempublicam introduxit*), would be to ignore all the richness of the analysis of the collective imagination that pervades the *TTP*. We already know by the necessary logic that forms the finalist bias how people are led to imagine and ultimately believe that they are loved by God 'above all others' and that God alone can direct all of nature for their benefit. The Jewish people, however, have made this fiction (that of the Appendix of *Ethics* I, presented as universal) the sole calling of their nation: to be the chosen people of God for all eternity. This belief gradually takes shape and is inscribed in their souls long before they realise it politically and historically through their pact with God. In contrast to the *Ethics*, Spinoza writes in the *TTP* that the finalist and anthropocentric bias (in its ethnocentric form) is originally an invention of the ancient Jewish people, later adopted by practically all humanity.⁷⁵ Thus, after the transfer of their right of nature to God, the Hebrews are naturally and historically led to believe that

> their kingdom was God's kingdom, that they alone were God's children, and that the other nations were God's enemies. As a result, they felt the most savage hatred toward the other nations – a hatred they also believed to be pious (see *Psalm* 139:21–22).⁷⁶

The Hebrews thus define their identity in imagination by giving themselves exclusively the name of *filios Dei*. This identity is that of a people, the mythical history of a nation that, beyond the mortal individuals that compose it, expresses itself in its imaginary substance as indestructible and eternal.

The Jewish people have constituted their being, which is immediately identified in imagination with their collective existence, according to a belief which, as Spinoza writes, 'comes from envy and a bad heart – if it is not mere childishness'.⁷⁷ This is not a moralistic judgement. Collective life involves a diversity of habits, customs (*consuetudines*), usages, languages and laws, and each lives according to their own prejudices and their own particular universe of meanings and values. This diversity is inherent in nations, character and unique mentality,⁷⁸ the origin of which (even if Spinoza does not explicitly say so) is explained by the laws of imitation highlighted in *Ethics* III. The particular focus of the Hebrew nation on the belief in its unique election must be understood through the 'childishness' of that nation⁷⁹ and through the laws of imitation that enslave it even more because of its condition as 'children who lack all reason'.⁸⁰ The result is a delusional

---

⁷⁵ '[To convince] the Gentiles of their time [that] worshipped visible Gods, such as the Sun, the Moon, the Earth, Water, Air, etc., to prove them wrong and to show them that those Gods were weak and inconstant, or changeable, and under the rule of an invisible God, the Jews related their miracles, by which they tried to show that the whole of nature was directed only for their advantage, by the command of the God they worshipped. This was so pleasing to men that to this day they haven't ceased to feign miracles, so that they might believe themselves to be dearer to God than the rest, and the final cause on account of which God has created, and continually directs, all things.' *TTP* VI; *CWS* II, 153.
⁷⁶ *TTP* XVII; *CWS* II, 313.
⁷⁷ *TTP* III; *CWS* II, 111.
⁷⁸ *TTP* XVII; *CWS* II, 317.
⁷⁹ *TTP* III and XII; *CWS* II, 112, 249.
⁸⁰ *TTP* II; *CWS* II, 107.

self-love rooted in the claim to be 'superior to all others',[81] and accompanied by a hatred of everything that is not itself, the genesis of which can be schematically reconstructed as follows: the desire to be different,[82] reinforced by the imagination of one's own freedom and the simplicity of the causes of one's action,[83] leads to delusional pride[84] and the supreme illusion of being divine, chosen by God, the Son of God, to the exclusion all others... From this mimetic and comparative unconscious basis follows the radical rejection of imitation and any comparison. The Pharisees consider the idea that the omens and soothsayers among the gentiles could also be 'true prophets' as sacrilege and an insult. The 'divine gift' of prediction is reserved for their own people, so they dismiss as devilish those outside Israel who claim to know the future.[85] The delirium of self-love naturally turns into hatred of all that is different (and, paradoxically, all that is too similar...).[86] Spinoza does not give in the *TTP* the mimetic explanatory matrix he provides in *Ethics* III. He does, however, show how the imitation of affects and desires within the nation is the best source and cement of national identity and the quasi-organic unity of the community, if institutions know how to limit their harmful counter-effects. The Hebrew example is that of a State in which the identification of each with all and all with the nation is practically complete. This is due to the still barbaric nature of its citizens and to the idiosyncratic tendency of this form of government to turn individuals into perfect automatons through habituation.[87]

Thus, by studying the Hebrew State, one can fully understand the Spinozist thesis of the constitution of the body politic according to a system of imaginary meanings. For like all individuals, every society must define its identity (that is, its own image) in and through its difference from other societies by representation. It must also define the meaning of its existence (which is the same thing), its relationship to the world, to others (which

---

[81] *TTP* I; CWS II, 91.
[82] *Ethics* III, 55 Schol.
[83] *Ethics* III, 49 Dem., 51 Schol.; *Ethics* V, 5 and Dem.
[84] *Ethics* III, 26 Schol.
[85] *TTP* III; CWS II, 120.
[86] Spinoza visibly enjoys underlining in this chapter of the *TTP* everything in Scripture that calls into question the relevance of the difference between Jews and Gentiles: other peoples had a kingdom and special laws through a government independent of God; God was also known to other peoples through miracles; and at the time of Malachi (Genesis 1:10–11), when God, ignoring the Jews, performed miracles for other peoples, the Jews ironically regained their kingdom partly without miracles (*TTP* III; CWS II, 114–15).
[87] ... *sine ulla rationis consultatione obtemperare debebant.* TTP XVII; CWS II, 316.

must also be named) and also its relationship to itself, to its needs and desires (the relationship of people within that society and all to a common symbolic order that connects each citizen to an entity that transcends him or her and in which all the threads of the logic of imaginary meanings and identification are interwoven). This mythical entity is 'the nation' and its power is such that it can survive even after the dissolution of the State.

The greatest strength of the Hebrew State is the unity of its institutions and the meaning of life they regulate. It is the lived and known usefulness of the commandments and the identity of obedience and reward from which necessarily follows the benefit of all:

> the most important factor to prevent its citizens from thinking of defection or wanting to desert their country is the principle of advantage, the mainstay and life of all human actions. That force was exceptionally strong in this state.[88]

In a true democracy we find the same force under different conditions. By defining the advantage of the people and introducing the means of satisfying it, the Hebrew State, given its historical circumstances, was able to develop into a genuine rational strategy based on particular causes which we cannot understand. Note the extraordinary coherence of Hebrew legislation in its concern for eternity, which follows the strict logic of the imaginary that produced this type of State. Indeed, according to the logic of 'opinion' that underlay the first covenant with God, Moses did not choose a successor who could take over the entire administration of the State on their own, even though he had the authority to do so. He would have chosen a monarch and thus changed the originally democratic meaning of the people's covenant with God.

> But Moses chose no such successor. Instead he left the state to be administered by his successors in such a way that it couldn't be called either popular, aristocratic, or monarchical, but only Theocratic. For one person had the right of interpreting the laws and communicating God's replies, and another had the right and power [*pouvoir*] to administer the state according to the laws already explained and the replies already communicated.[89]

---

[88] *TTP* XVII; *CWS* II, 315
[89] *TTP* XVII; *CWS* II, 305.

Under the leadership of Moses, the power (*puissance*) of the theocratic imagination causes the Hebrew people to protect themselves from a monarchical development (with its disastrous consequences) by establishing, after the death of their leader, a functional balance between the legislative and executive powers (*pouvoirs*) that is specifically theocratic. Moses thus introduces an administrative structure of the State that, *first*, leaves no room for a dominant ruler of the State;[90]

> These things didn't all depend on the decision of one man, one council, or the people. Some were administered by one tribe, and others by the other tribes, with equal right for each one. From this it follows most clearly that, after Moses' death, the state was neither monarchical, nor aristocratic, nor popular, but, as we have said, Theocratic.[91]

And *second*, it prevents the ruled from becoming rebels.

Spinoza shows how the Hebrew theocracy, in its democratic character, succeeded in building a double inner resistance to the logic of power. Theocracy enables resistance against the rebellious power of the multitude, but also and above all against the tyrannical power of the leaders. Theocracy is thus governed by these opposing forces, which lie both in the interpretation of the law reserved to the pontiff and in the supervision of an armed people trained in the law, attached to the law and inclined to indignation. Thus they are inclined to defend the law when it is violated. Finally, they fear a new prophet commissioned by God to judge the leader's actions or misinterpretation of the law.[92] Freed from its archaic and mystical matrix, the logic of the counter-powers deployed by the Hebrew State expresses the very logic of the institution of freedom.

What Moses was able to achieve thanks to his divine virtue – namely, that he knew how to pose the real problems within Hebrew society and give the most appropriate answers – becomes what Hebrew society after him can achieve in and through its institutions. It is the tribal leaders, the commanders of the troops, the supreme council, or other qualified persons,[93] undoubtedly the elders, Spinoza supposes,[94] who, because of their advanced age, the lessons of the past and their closeness to immediate reality, can

---

[90] *TTP* XVII; *CWS* II, 306.
[91] *TTP* XVII; *CWS* II, 310.
[92] *TTP* XVII; *CWS* II, 310–13.
[93] *TTP* XVII; *CWS* II, 306–8.
[94] *TTP* XVII; *CWS* II, 310.

best formulate the problems that arise within their own social structure. Every tribe is made up of families whose leaders are chosen from the elders of the family, and of course the leader of the tribe is himself the elder of these elders. They understand best the actual relationships that make up their society. Yet they cannot provide an answer to the problems they raise. What is a strength when it comes to raising problems is a weakness when it comes to solutions. This is due to the strong selfish interests of the individual tribes, with their own land, their own militia and generally the 'unbridled lust of the Leaders'.[95] Therefore, the great pontiff, who like his entire tribe has no property rights, has 'the right to interpret the laws and transmit God's answers'.[96] We move from the actual conditions of the problems to their solutions, which are answers that reflect those conditions without being directly in them. The status of the Levites, who are responsible for the law before the whole people, guarantees greater objectivity (rationality) in the answers that the great pontiff (representing the whole people) can give to the questions specific to each tribe. 'This makes it clear that he took a great opportunity for crimes away from the Hebrew leaders.'[97]

By modifying the specific arrangement of the Hebrew collective body through the particular expressions of problematic questions and the particular modalities of their answers, Spinoza outlines a strategy specific to the *conatus* of the self-organisation of the body politic, which he will develop for each type of State in the *Political Treatise*. The genetic logic – which leads from the conditions of the problems (how a society poses its problems for itself) to the cases of solutions (which are more or less well adapted to the collective body in question) – is the logic of historical reality, the logic of self-affirmation of the collective body. It is also the problem of the strategic realisation of a singular being that develops in this theoretical crucible: the historical-political analysis of the essence of the Hebrew State as an individual. If we stay with this first analysis, this realisation had to be perfect for the Hebrews.

Everything seemed to be directed towards obtaining the eternal blessing of the Hebrew State, which, it seems, succeeded where all other monarchical regimes have failed (or will fail). Through the operation of an immanent and constitutive power, the Hebrew State succeeded in exorcising the imaginary of the rule of the people by the people in favour of a complete submission to nothing other than the whole of society in its functioning. Because,

---

[95] *TTP* XVII; *CWS* II, 311.
[96] *TTP* XVII; *CWS* II, 306.
[97] *TTP* XVII; *CWS* II, 311.

even if these [hearts are not under] the direct command of the supreme power [*puissance*], (*Adeoque etsi haec non directo mandato summae potestatis fiant*) still experience abundantly testifies that they often happen by the authority of its power and by its guidance, i.e., by its right.[98]

Spinoza clearly distinguishes here between the sovereign's explicit (direct) power of command and an implicit (indirect) power that is no less his own, and that tends to transform subjects into true automata.[99] Therefore, without any logical contradiction, we can conceive of humans entirely subject to the sovereign but who do not feel constrained. The perfect Hebraic theocracy, thus, comes closest to the theoretical model of a society led by reason evoked in *TTP* V – obedience, which implies a relationship of the will to an external command, disappears to the benefit of total agreement between the behaviour of the citizen and the law. When fully internalised, the law merges with the immanent essence of everyone's activity. It is in this sense that Spinoza can talk about a confusion between servitude and freedom among the Hebrews.[100]

If, however, this immanent power had actually been absolute, if it had actually formed subjects wholly subordinate to divine sovereignty, the Hebrews would automatically and forever have reproduced the theocratic form of their government. There would have been no history of the Jewish people except for the circumstances of its defence against external enemies to preserve its non-historical continuity, its unchanging identity. The Hebrew State, however, disappeared after a long history – not only of wars with external enemies, but also of internal contradictions, revolts and insurrections, which give the State a real historicity . . . and gave Spinozism a true theoretical concept of history.[101]

The study of the Hebrew State has not yet yielded all its fruit. Before the political function of the imaginary signification from which an initial theory of the imaginary constitution of society could develop, which goes from one formed imaginary (religious) to another (political), it is possible to identify the elements of a more radical theory of the constitution of the political body, elaborated fully in the *Political Treatise*. We are no longer thinking

---

[98] . . . *fiunt tamen saepe* [. . .] *ex authoritate ipsius potentiae, & ipsius directione, id est, ex ipsius jure.* TTP XVII; CWS II, 297.

[99] TTP XX; CWS II, 346.

[100] TTP XVII; CWS II, 315.

[101] On the reasons that led Moses to change his first aim of entrusting the sacred ministry to the firstborn to introducing causes for discord in the Hebrew State, see *TTP* VI; *TTP* XVII; CWS II, 159, 316.

of a constitution of the political understood as the political realisation of a 'referential imaginary' (the product of the quest for final causes and theological craftwork). Rather, we are thinking of the political as the actualisation of an essential imaginary that merges with the very *conatus* of the political body, its singular actualising essence. The question is then no longer about moving from a political conception based on domination and deception to the imaginary constitution of society. It is a matter of proceeding from an initial conception of the imaginary constitution of the political body (still connected to the mediation of the constituted religious imaginary) to a new, more radical theory of the political institution on the exclusive basis of the laws of the imagination through which the multitude transforms itself into a political body.

8

The Hebrew State: Elements for a Second Theory of the Imaginary Constitution of the Political Body

We now turn to the philosophical consequences of the pages devoted to the Hebrew theocracy in the *TTP*. In these pages, Spinoza develops the following:

First, he elaborates the idea of an individuality proper to the collective body in the form of the 'nation'. If Spinoza generally identifies the nation with the State, under certain conditions the nation can precede and outlast the constitution of State. The same concept (*ingenium*) is also used to define the particular 'complexion' of human individuals and of nations. National complexions are not only the abstract arithmetical sum of individuals but express their singularity through 'differences of language, laws and accepted customs'.[1]

Second, we learn that a nation's individuality has similar requirements for its effort to persevere in its being to those of human individuals (including the essential requirement of representation-signification, which is needed to attain its own imaginary reality).

Third, he shows that collective individuality affirms itself in and through its power (*puissance*) to pose problems and identify solutions adequate to its own perseverance.

Fourth, we find that collective individuality is formed according to the same principles as human individuality. The politico-social (laws), cultural (language, customs) and historical nature of the nation, just like human nature, establishes and remains in its own identity according to the laws of Habit, the joy principle, memory and recognitive imagination.

---

[1] *TTP* XVII; CWS II, 316. On the question of whether the 'state should be thought of as an individual in the strict sense', see Lee C. Rice's review of the different positions in 'Individual and Community in Spinoza's Social Psychology', in *Spinoza. Issues and Directions*, ed. E. Curley and P.-F. Moreau, Brill, 1990, p. 279.

And *fifth*, this isomorphism suggests a strategy for the collective body as such, a strategy of the *multitudinis potentia* (as per Spinoza's expression in the *Political Treatise*). Spinoza proposes, correlatively, that we understand any strategy of the *conatus* on the political model of posing and resolving problems.

1 From Habit (the Productive Activity of the Nation's Actual Existence) to the Self-Organisation of the *multitudinis ingenium* as the Practical Political Subject

In Chapter XVII – along with many other passages of the *TTP* – Spinoza attributes the main 'strength' of the Hebrew people to the power of habituation (habit), whose value depends on 'opinion' alone. Opinions, however, are formed by 'acquired habit'.[2] It is by virtue of these habits and opinions that the Hebrews were led to their first covenant with God. When the Hebrews transferred their natural right to God on Moses' advice, they were only acting on an old political belief according to which God is a legislator and a king. They were perpetuating what past generations passed on to them and were accustomed to believing. The only difference from these past generations, admittedly a big one whose consequences the Hebrews did not anticipate, was the following: being their political king, they expected clear commandments from God to guide their behaviour in their new city. But they heard God's word on this matter with alarm.[3] Terrified, they thought their last hour had come.

What was the reason for this alarm? First, this new situation caused a brutal and unexpected fracture in the structure of habit. Spinoza writes in the *KV*:

[Wonder, *verwondering*] is found in one who knows the thing in the first way [that is, through opinion].[4]

it also occurs [that] we tacitly presume that the thing is so, and not different from the way we are used to seeing, hearing, or understanding it.[5]

Wonder [*admiratio*] is an imagination of a thing in which the Mind remains fixed because this singular imagination has no connection with the others.[6]

---

[2] *TTP* VI; CWS II, 152.
[3] *Deum loquentem adeo attoniti audiverunt*. *TTP* XVII; CWS II, 302.
[4] *KV* II, iii, 2; CWS I, 99.
[5] *KV* II, iii, 2, note 1; CWS I, 99.
[6] *Ethics* III, DA 4; CWS I, 532.

Spinoza refers us to *Ethics* II, 18, which discusses the order and connection of images. He then refers us to *Ethics* III, 52 and Schol., which defines singularity as a thing that preoccupies the mind 'by itself', separate from any connection. The Hebrews' wonder can, therefore, be explained by their panicked powerlessness that made them unable to integrate and interpret this new, singular and distressing image of God, so foreign to them and, therefore, so frightening. They brought this new and unprecedented situation upon themselves by making a political covenant with God, which was meant to be a simple extension of their habits, but which also exposed them to a radical strangeness. The covenant mandates God (that is, in fact, the Hebrews' very imagination) to provide solutions to their problems, which the imagination was not accustomed to posing, let alone resolving. This explains the panicked fear, which is due to the real trauma the Hebrew nation experienced. The situation they face goes beyond the limits of their tradition, memory[7] and connections formed by habit. It exceeds what is possible by virtue of their prior experience.

There is no way, however, to draw the Hebrews away from this unintelligible God, despite their incomprehensible experience of horror. On the contrary, the more unusual God's actions are, and the more they exceed the Hebrews' 'power of understanding', the more brilliant he appears in their eyes and the more they are 'amazed'.[8] This becomes part of their mental habits,[9] because the Hebrew people, like the common people, *tum Dei potentiam & providentiam quam clarissime constare putat, cum aliquid in natura insolitum, & contra opinionem, quam ex consuetudine de natura habet, contingere videt.*[10]

> Nevertheless, [the Hebrews] were quite incapable of establishing legislation wisely and keeping the sovereignty in their own hands, as a body. Almost all of them were unsophisticated in their mentality and weakened by wretched bondage. Therefore, the sovereignty had to remain in the hands of one person only, who would command the others, compel them by force, and finally, who would prescribe laws and afterward interpret

---

[7] *TTP* VI; *CWS* II, 155.
[8] *TTP* I; *CWS* II, 87.
[9] 'Though the voice the Israelites heard could not give them any philosophical *or* mathematical certainty about God's existence, still, it was enough to make them wonder at God, insofar as they had previously known him, and to motivate them to obedience.' *TTP* XIV; *CWS* II, 270.
[10] 'For the common people think God's power [*puissance*] and providence are established most clearly when they see something unusual happen in nature, which is contrary to the opinion they have of nature from custom.' *TTP* VI; *CWS* II, 152.

them. But Moses was easily able to retain this sovereignty, because he excelled the others in divine power [*vertu*], persuaded the people that he had it, and showed this by a great deal of evidence.[11]

This explains the second covenant, which arose from the impossible situation created by the first. With this second covenant, the Hebrews return to what they are accustomed to, namely, complete submission to the commandments of a peer, namely Moses, in whom they had 'the greatest confidence' because of his virtue and their habit of obeying him.[12] With this second covenant, the Hebrews combine the imaginary dimension of their desire (or the opinion that they made God their king) with the capacity to self-organise through the mediation of a human leader, Moses, who, in this situation, was able to lean on acquired habits to illuminate the future paths. The Hebrews, therefore, articulated two logics through which they were habituated. First, the logic of an imaginary ancestry, which was elevated to the rank of a political conception. Second, the logic of their actual practice of civil obedience. Obedience takes the form of total servitude, which is the result of a timeworn mentality overdetermined by their long state of slavery in Egypt. It requires the absolute authority of a leader who subjects them to thoroughly codified activities through specific commandments.

The genius of Moses – who is in quasi-total osmosis with his people's mind, whose prejudices he shares – was to prescribe only what was not in contradiction with the Hebrews' habits but which, on the contrary, gave those habits full political actuality for the material well-being of the nation. Moses imagines what the Hebrew nation (the matrix of customs and acquired habits) was unable to imagine without him: stable institutions for a new State. Moses is the productive imagination of the Hebrew nation's body, one through which this body attains a greater complexity. His is not the mind of a body that would lead it from the outside but the mind of the collective body at a greater level of perfection, a greater state of power (*puissance*). Through the mechanisms of habit, imitation or the joy principle, the social body, like that of a simple animal in this respect, does not yet have an object or purpose: it remains in a pre-political condition. At this lower level of complexity, the Hebrew nation – like an individual in a state of great powerlessness – becomes dizzy and suffers from fainting spells, when it is confronted with the immensity of a reality that it has no way to control. But, with Moses, who talks to God 'as a companion and is not terrified',

---

[11] *TTP* V; *CWS* II, 145.
[12] *TTP* XVII; *CWS* II, 301.

the nation's body is capable of a higher synthesis.[13] Thus, the nation's body is similar to a more complex body that is capable of feeling joy or sadness, by virtue of its capacity (its *habitus* or its power) to connect its affections according to the laws of resemblance or contiguity (the *conatus* as habit involves the *conatus* as imitation). This body is also capable of representing and recognising the 'cause' of this affect (and thereby of experiencing 'love' or 'hatred'). It is consequently capable of leading a life according to what is useful to it, in agreement with what it imagines its end to be,[14] and thus according to a teleological (and in the last instance, loving) logic.

When it comes to the history of the Hebrew nation, the *conatus* as Habit of the collective body enters a teleologicl mode with Moses (according to the logic of joy that, as for the human individual, gave it a memory). For the collective body, teleology implies a political direction, the creation of an *imperium*. It is the stage of conscious strategies (illusory or adjusted) through which a being (individual or collective) reaches a higher level of organisation: the practical subject.[15] The Hebrew social body, therefore, becomes a legislative subject thanks to Moses. It becomes able to 'vividly' imagine a law of self-organisation, to anticipate its effects and benefits. It is a law of self-organisation because it comes from the habits of a people who cannot but consent to it. On God's laws or the commandments described in Exodus from chapter 22 v. 22 to chapter 24, Spinoza notes that:

> as soon as Moses understood the people's intention to enter into a covenant with God, he immediately wrote down God's pronouncements and laws. Then in the morning light, after he had performed certain ceremonies, he read out to the whole assembly the conditions of entering into the covenant. Once these conditions had been read out, and without doubt grasped by all the ordinary people, they bound themselves with full consent.[16]

Beyond Spinoza's 'Machiavellian' formulations (in the traditional sense), we must understand the example of the Hebraic society in terms of the self-organisation of the State, because the real movement of the constitution

---

[13] *TTP* I; CWS II, 83.

[14] *Ethics* III, 12, 13 and Schol.

[15] The teleological nature of human law is underlined many times at the beginning of *TTP* IV: 'law is generally taken to be a principle of living prescribed to men by the command of others' (CWS II, 127).

[16] *TTP* VIII; CWS II, 198.

is immanent. The Hebrew nation is the cause of the belief in its own election, the cause of the Hebrew language, habits, opinions and customs. Without those, the law pronounced by Moses would not speak to them. Even if the Hebrew nation was unable to hear God's law during the first covenant (to prophesy), it nonetheless authors this law and its constellation of meanings. The covenant expresses the common life of the nation, of its *consuetudines*,[17] and answers this social body's desire to attain a higher level of organisation and to form a political body, for its own security. Spinoza's entire analysis of the Prophets insists on the osmosis between the prophetic and the common people's imaginations. In *TTP* I, Spinoza notes that God speaks to Moses 'without obscure symbols ... [or] enigmatic sayings',[18] thus distinguishing Moses from the other prophets. But beyond this distinction, the entirety of his prophetic activity can be understood as the expression of the Hebrew nation's imagination (its opinions and prejudices). The 'mind' and 'thought' of the prophets is the same as the 'mind' and 'thought' (that is, imagination) of the Hebrew people themselves. Therefore, 'all [their] visions agree completely with the vulgar ways of imagining God and Spirits'.[19] Moses is no exception: his 'revelations ... were accommodated to these opinions'.[20] But with Moses, the imagination of the Hebrew nation becomes politically actualised. This is due to the schematising power that the Hebrews' imagination finds in Moses (his 'divine virtue'). The whole social body, through the mediation of its leader and his dynamic of active simplification (God speaks to Moses 'without obscure symbols ... [or] enigmatic sayings'),[21] controls and organises its own multiplicity. We have already said this about the individual body, which does this according to a real strategic logic of active

---

[17] *Consuetudo*: three times the notion expresses the dynamic and constitutive nature of the collective body: *Hominibus apprime utile est, consuetudines jungere, seseque iis vinculis astringere, quibus aptius de se omnibus unum efficiant; & absolute ea agere, quae firmandis amicitiis inserviunt* (Ethics IV, App. 12; CWS I, 589); *Praeter homines nihil singulare in natura novimus, cujus Mente gaudere, & quod nobis amicitia, aut aliquo consuetudinis genere jungere possumus* (Ethics IV, App. 26; CWS I, 592); *Denique quia omnes homines, sive Barbari, sive culti sint, consuetudines ubique jungunt, & statum aliquem civilem formant, ideo imperii causas, & fundamenta naturalia non ex rationis documentis petenda, sed ex hominum communi natura, seu conditione deducenda sunt, quod in sequenti Capite facere constitui* (TP I, 7; CWS II, 505).
[18] CWS II, 83.
[19] TTP I and II; CWS II, 93, 101–2.
[20] TTP II; CWS II, 105.
[21] On the dynamic of active 'simplification' of the imagination, see Chapter 2 above. Things that the prophets imagine, like all the important teachings of Scripture, are things of the 'simplest kind', *res simplicissimas*, Spinoza writes (TTP XIII; CWS II, 257).

resistance. This logic builds a human 'world', a world of words and things as well as of institutions and laws. Through Moses' prophetic imagination, this schematising imagination is immediately politically useful for the Hebrews. This is not surprising if we understand that the imaginative power is not extrinsic to the social body, but is the very expression of its effort to persevere in being. In the case of the transition from a state of nature to a political order, the schematising imagination is inseparable from the effort that transforms the child's body into one with as much power, as Spinoza writes of the human individual, 'as its nature allows'. The transition involves transformation of the collective body as great as the constitutive connections of Habits that form its singularity allow.

The creation of institutions is, therefore, a new organisation of the social body, which the first associations of habit were not capable of producing by themselves. The imagination can evaluate what this body is politically capable of, based on the body's habits (through the actualisation of a greater power or perfection). From the most adequate solution that will allow the fullest expression of this body's forces to the one that does not, the collective imagination can use a whole spectrum of political positions for the multitude's power of self-organisation. Apart from these possible political positions (to a greater or lesser degree of feasibility), we find political utopias, operating like illusions, which can be disastrous when taken up by the multitude. This does not mean, of course, that every illusion is necessarily harmful. The Hebrew nation was formed on the illusion of a God-King. The illusion is only politically efficient (it allows for some stability of the State, though relative) if it does not brutally break with a nation's customs, the continuity of its habits. Imagination is only effectively constitutive under this condition, even in illusion. Conversely, abstract reason without the real actions of the human beings in a particular society can cause some of the worst political illusions. Therefore, 'no men are thought less suitable to guide Public Affairs than Theorists, *or* Philosophers'.[22] Spinoza notes that Moses, in contrast, 'did not make any argument in due form'.[23] The vivacity of his imagination – the very power of the collective imagination expressed in him – enables him to recognise which institutions are best. They are not the true institutions (which makes no sense) but the better ones, those produced by the multitude's desire. He produces them just as human subjects produce forms and values that are not products of nature (at least not directly) but of human imagination. They are products of imagination rather than reason.

[22] *TP* I, 1; *CWS* II, 504.
[23] *TTP* XI; *CWS* II, 242. See also *TTP* I, *TTP* II, *TTP* IV; *CWS* II, 84, 103–4, 132.

Institutions, rules and laws, therefore, cannot be explained by virtue of reason, rationality or their usefulness, even if they are both rational and useful. The productive movement of desire, in its strategic logic of active resistance, gives institutions their rationality and utility (their value), though it is not for or from them that this desire was truly born. In *TTP* XI, when Spinoza mentions God's prediction to Moses that the people would defect from divine worship after his death, he emphasises that Moses did not become 'certain of this prediction by probable reasons'.[24] Instead, he is persuaded by the present stubbornness of the people projected into the future, 'represented vividly in his imagination'. Including the laws' formation in the products of imagination, Spinoza adds:

> This is the way we must understand all the arguments we find Moses using in the Pentateuch. They're not taken from the storehouse of reason, but are only ways of speaking he used to express God's decrees more effectively and imagine them vividly.[25]

We, therefore, speak of a process of recognition, just as we do with respect to the desiring logic of human individuality. Humans produce-identify-make present the object that is the cause of their joy according to the desiring movement. Following that same movement, too, a nation produces-identifies-makes present institutions that will guarantee its security. This does not necessarily mean, of course, that this identification is an adequate one, since the object of desire cannot be its cause. The connections of imagination are therefore recognitive. That is, they produce new forms, a new hallucinatory objectification of reality. Moses, taking on his role as legislator (like prophets in general), imagines, 'Things revealed [to him] very vividly, in the way we are usually affected by objects when we are awake.'[26] The same hallucinatory and desiring process produces objects and institutions. They are more adapted to a nation's character (*ingenium*) the more they are in innovative continuity with *consuetudines* and not, like utopias, against them. Unlike the objects of human desire that, even when those objects are other human beings, cannot reach the imaginary status of final cause with which desiring wants to credit them, institutions are constituted as causes of the collective affects, and thus historically realise causal imagination. Imaginary causality becomes the real conditioning of the affects through institutions.

---

[24] See also *TTP* XVII; *CWS* II, 319.
[25] *TTP* XI; *CWS* II, 242.
[26] *TTP* II; *CWS* II, 96. See also the marginal note III of *TTP* I; *CWS* II, 91, n. 44.

In the Hebrew State, the laws and mores that give this nation its identity are juridical in character. The Hebrews will raise the expression of these very mores to a higher level of systematisation, coherence and politico-religious organisation through the constitutive imagination, through a rigorous articulation of rites and myths within which the Hebrews' existence is fully integrated. Hence, on top of old habits, they create habits that are better structured:

> Especially conducive [to promoting loyalty to their country] was the extreme training in obedience they were brought up with.[27]

> So the love of the Hebrews for their country was not a simple love, but piety. Their daily worship [encouraged] and fed this piety, and this hatred of other nations...[28]

In the constricted form of nationalism, patriotic custom becomes the very nature of the Hebrew people.[29] National identification is the very constitution of individuality and the foundation of the identity of the Hebrew person, who is, since the patriarchs, accustomed to the strict discipline of rituals and opinions that uphold their meaning and salutary value.[30] Rather than breaking from their acquired habits, the constitutive imagination produces utterly new forms, new values and a new universe of meaning by building upon the associations their habits contain. What is new could have no effective reality if it were not itself part of the history of the traces of common experience. At the same time, these traces of common experience can only become operational if they take on the different meanings that the new reality provides.

We learn from the history of the Hebrew nation that the pact from which a society comes about and is maintained is, first, a superior and novel form of association (cohesion) of the multitude's body (the multitude itself as a body) in its singular complexity (*multitudinis ingenium*).[31] Within the continuity of the associative system of the proto-political social body, new shapes of habits, organisation and meaning develop. Just like the individual body,

---

[27] TTP XVII; CWS II, 316.
[28] TTP XVII; CWS II, 314.
[29] Etienne Balibar underlines the decisive political importance of 'nationalism' in the TTP's political analysis: 'Jus–Pactum–Lex', *Studia Spinozana*, 1, 1985, pp. 131ff.
[30] TTP V; CWS II, 142.
[31] ... *qui tantum varium multitudinis ingenium experti sunt.* TTP XVII; CWS II, 298.

the collective body is a habit (a memory). This body could not do anything if it did not already have the mnemic traces through which its action and imagination are determined (along with its failure to imagine and to act). The Hebrew experienced this constraint during their first encounter with God. The covenant is a form of superior association and a continuation of the acquired habits of the multitude's body. The natural tendency of each being to seek joy as what is useful maintains the covenant, consisting in the sovereign's promises, rewards, threats and punishments, which the transfer of powers authorises. The collective body's Habit includes two dimensions of the covenant: association and obedience. Obedience to God and/or Moses is the continuation of the obedience to God and the Egyptians (and, more generally, to the dependency in which the state of nature maintains human beings), understood from the point of view of other circumstances, meanings and consequences.[32] The covenant lifted the antagonistic contradiction between the political and the religious, transforming the Hebrews' feeling of real servitude into one of illusory liberty. The principle of Habit, by virtue of which acquired habits form the system of belief, and recognitive imagination that produces new institutional forms, together constitute the basis for understanding the covenant as well as the transfer of power as a permanent consensus. They also form the theoretical basis for adequate knowledge of the singular history of a nation. For the Hebrew State, this singular history follows the instabilities and disputes that Moses' error introduced into the self-regulation of institutions, which are necessarily found in every political organisation, albeit in different forms.

2 The Covenant: From the Joy Principle to the Establishment of a Temporality and Space for the 'Nation'

The orientation of singular powers towards a certain type of transfer would not be properly understood if we didn't appreciate the role that the specific process of association of the joy/sadness principle plays in it. Spinoza places a true joy principle, understood as the objective criterion of social reproduction and its orientation, at the heart of collective life. According to this principle, the multitude's desire is always, in the best case, a desire to persevere in a joyous affect and in the conditions attached to it. A multitude thereby strives, at the same time, to remove anything that can cause sadness and, in the worst cases, to choose the lesser evil:

---

[32] *TTP* XVI; *CWS* II, 284.

For it's a universal law of human nature that no one neglects to pursue what he judges to be good, unless he hopes for a greater good, or fears a greater harm. Nor does anyone submit to any evil, except to avoid a greater one, or because he hopes for a greater good. Between two goods, each person chooses the one he judges to be greater; between two evils, the one which seems to him lesser. I say explicitly: the one which seems to the person choosing to be greater or lesser. It does not follow that things must be as he judges them to be. This law is so firmly inscribed in human nature, that it ought to be numbered among the eternal truths, which no one can fail to know. From this it follows necessarily that no one will promise to give up the right he has to all things except with intent to deceive, and that absolutely no one will stand by his promises unless he fears a greater evil or hopes for a greater good.[33]

Joy and sadness are the first strategic data that orient the dynamism of both the individual and the collective *conatus*. And we know that this orientation results from a new organisation of Habit at a higher level of corporeal complexity.

In the Hebrew State, however, the conditions attached to joy are, because of their perfect articulation, the very institutions of this State. The foundations of this social institution produced 'in the hearts of citizens a love so special that the hardest thing for them to think of would be betraying their country or defecting from it'.[34] Owed to preparation from childhood and the perfection of the institutions, no one desires what is prohibited.[35] What is denied is only the impossible, that which is beyond the imaginable or the system of meaning. What is prohibited is conflated with what the Hebrews are not, in fact, able to do. The perfect Hebrew State is the one where God's law, which appears at first as transcendent, is in fact the same as his immanent law. We can, therefore, say of the Hebrew State what Spinoza says of the right and the 'Established Practice of nature, under which all are born and for the most part live': this institution 'prohibits nothing except what no one desires and what no one can do'.[36]

The possible and the impossible have to do directly with the right of nature, which is the real power or impotence to act of each one's natural right in its singular determination. Imagination, according to which the

---

[33] *TTP* XVI; *CWS* II, 285.
[34] *TTP* XVII; *CWS* II, 313.
[35] *TTP* XVII; *CWS* II, 315.
[36] *TTP* XVI; *CWS* II, 284.

possible and impossible are defined, is thus inscribed in the historical necessity of a particular nation. This nation, because of its habits and customs, necessarily has a singular disposition of the imagination. The possible and the impossible, defined by the problematic domain of *habitus*, are therefore imaginary categories of the real constitution of history:

> For whatever man imagines he cannot do, he necessarily imagines; and he is so disposed by this imagination that he really cannot do what he imagines he cannot do. For so long as he imagines that he cannot do this or that, he is not determined to do it, and consequently it is impossible for him to do it.[37]

The logic of joy, which could have discouraged humans from work, country and God, instead expresses itself fully, in the Hebrew State, in work and piety: 'Nothing wins hearts more than the joy which arises from devotion, that is, from love and wonder together.'[38] As with the individual prejudices and superstitions that are eliminated from the State because of the institutionalisation of superstition, the principle of individual joy is entirely oriented towards service and the preservation of the State. Thus, individual joy is diverted from its seditious potential. Using the logic of joy, imagination can express its full political power and forge a reciprocal determination with it that grows stronger. It grows through a kind of reciprocal determination that goes from obedience to advantages, and from advantages to obedience. Consideration of utility and joy gives human actions their vigour and animation. The unity between the institutions and the way of life that these institutions govern – and the obedience they demand – was perfect among the Hebrews. Their effort to persevere in their being (the repetition of their habits) and their institutions had one and the same aim: their satisfaction. From this foundation in the joy-utility principle, the pact finds the strength to maintain itself and the whole of Hebrew society, because a 'contract can have no force except by reason of its utility. If the utility is taken away, the contract is taken away with it, and remains null and void.'[39] The joy principle imprints on the desire of the multitude the orientation of the continuously renewed transfer of power to God that the Hebrew people establish moment by moment, thus constituting the reality of his sovereignty and their obedience. If the utility of the pact no longer holds, if the orientation

---

[37] *Ethics* III DA 28 Expl.; CWS I, 537.
[38] TTP XVII; CWS II, 316.
[39] TTP XVI; CWS II, 286.

of the joy principle weakens or changes, sovereignty loses its power and is effaced, modified or displaced. Thus, the force of the principle of utility, 'unique' to this State, delivers the Hebrews from the individual bondage of pleasure to lead them collectively towards 'temporal prosperity, i.e., honours *or* reputation, victories, wealth, pleasures and health'.[40]

We understand that in chapter XVI, which tasks itself with identifying 'the foundations of the State', the joy principle is explicitly presented as one of the 'eternal truths that no one can ignore'. This principle appears effectively to be doubly constitutive of the pact. It both orients the transfer of power based on the associations of Habit and, following this process, it determines the outline of a new type of association between individuals. The Hebrew example, however, proves that this orientation of desire – which produces both new bonds and sovereignty – is not sufficient by itself to effectively produce the structures for regulating common life. This orientation of desire must be conveyed by the schematising (recognitive) power of the imagination (enveloped in memory) through which laws and institutions can be objectively represented within their own universe of meanings and values. This is done within a reflected order of time and by distinguishing laws and institutions as objects distinct from the reflective subject who imagines them. Imagination fits into the logic of the joy principle by reproducing it within its own hallucinatory structure, through which it gives desire an object of satisfaction. For society, this object is, first and foremost, the security that institutions must guarantee and, secondly, the conveniences or advantages that they must also generate. We can thus say that security is both the objective of the social pact and the problem that the schematising imagination must first resolve to satisfy this founding desire of the collective political body. As with the Hebrew people, when the problem of security has been almost perfectly solved by institutions, obedience and the pursuit of joy go hand in hand, leading to 'happiness'.

Let us return to the study of habitual associations to emphasise the importance of the associations with words that express the Law. They are 'arranged in such a way that they lead men to devotion' and make of the letter itself something powerful, sacred in the order of its enunciation, something which demands respect and obedience.[41]

> Words have a definite meaning only from their use. If they should be so organized that, according to their usage, they move the people reading

---

[40] *TTP* V, III; *CWS* II, 140, 115.
[41] *TTP* XII; *CWS* II, 249.

them to devotion, then those words will be sacred. So will a book written with the words organized that way. But if, afterward, the usage should be lost, so that the words have no meaning, or if the book should be completely neglected, whether from malice or because men no longer need it, then neither the words nor the book will be of any use. They will lose their holiness. Finally, if the same words should be organized in another way, or a usage should prevail according to which they are to be taken in an opposite meaning, then the words and the book which were previously sacred will be unclean and profane. From this it follows that nothing is sacred or profane or impure in itself, outside the mind, but only in relation to the mind [...] In the same way, also, Scripture is sacred and its statements divine just as long as it moves men to devotion toward God.[42]

In Hebrew, *debar Jehovah* means both 'word of God' and 'commandment' of God;[43] it is a word that demands obedience, which is the purpose of all the signs that surround and codify the life of the Hebrews, for which this word is the foundation;[44] 'and finally, the laws of the State [were rightly called] laws and commandments of God'.[45] Obedience will only be effectively obtained as a function of the regular correlation that may have been established between the arrangement of signs (images or articulate sounds that function as real signals)[46] that pronounce the law and the disposition of the body (the order of affections) and the mind towards submission or consent. This correlation is established by Habit and its associations, and reinforced by the affects of fear, hope or reasoning itself.

A single encounter is enough to form an association whose natural tendency – if it is not totally contrary to human nature – will be to repeat itself. Nevertheless, accompanied by the same affects of fear and hope and reinforced by rewards or punishments, it will require many repetitions of the law–obedience correlation, so that it develops deep roots in souls and participates in the 'nature' of those who have acquired it. It is the production of particular beings, whose perseverance in their own state blends in with the very dynamism of the *habitus* that defines the beings.[47] *Habitus*, the product and producer of history, is thus the internal law from which the

---

[42] *TTP* XII; *CWS* II, 250–1.
[43] *TTP* XII; *CWS* II, 252.
[44] *TTP* V; *CWS* II, 146.
[45] *TTP* XVII; *CWS* II, 302.
[46] *Ethics* II, 18 Schol.; *CWS* I, 466.
[47] This *habitus* can also be that of virtue: *passiones domare, sive virtutis habitum acquirere*. *TTP* III; *CWS* II, 113.

effects of external causes can be understood; it is the principle of continuity and regularity that defines the specific complexion of an individual, its *ingenium*. The *ingenium* and thus an individual's continuity and regularity can be understood from the point of view of the customs of a people, its *consuetudines*. The *conatus* itself is the problematic of *ingenium* and *consuetudines*, which asserts itself by internalising external forces, according to the logic of internal arrangements (its own schema), allowing those forces to endure by virtue of its own system. In other words, the system of *consuetudines* is neither fixed nor closed unless it always encounters the same situations, as was the case in the Hebrew State. Confronted with new situations or reinforced in its identity by encountering the same situations, the system of *habitus* defines a strategic dynamic that does not need to be explained with teleological notions.

Let me return to the connection between spoken law and obedient behaviour. Words acquire the meaning we give them through habit and repetition,[48] just as certain arrangements of words lead to certain behaviours out of habit even before they acquire meaning. Politically, this amounts to the obvious observation that conditioning is more effective when, as in the case of the Hebrew State, it is adapted to the complexion of the citizens of a particular people. Effective conditioning, then, does not contradict but obeys the general laws of human nature.

In the Hebrew State, the Law is read every seven years to the whole assembled people. The people for whom Moses wrote the Song of Songs (to teach them) are obliged to read and reread the Torah alone, constantly, with the greatest attention and the liveliest respect.[49] Their national history is naturally inscribed in people's memories by the repetition of the Psalms, which the many sing regularly with joy and fervour, according to custom. Because joy, rest and jubilation are codified, subject to order and rhythms, they transform what could be the enemy of the law, work and God into their surest support:

> To achieve this it seems to have been quite helpful that at certain times of the year they were bound to devote themselves to leisure and joy, not to obey their heart, but to obey God from the heart. Three times a year they had a feast in the presence of God (see Deuteronomy 16[:16]); on the seventh day of the week they had to stop work and devote themselves to leisure [Exodus 35:1–3]; in addition, other times were designated at which

---

[48] *Ethics* II, 18 Schol.
[49] *TTP* VIII, XVII; *CWS* II, 198, 310.

honourable acts of joy and feasts were not just granted, but commanded. I don't think anything more effective can be devised for steering people's hearts in a certain direction.[50]

This is because the pact is not only, we would say today, the structural organisation of society (in the functional and systemic articulation of its institutions), but immediately also the institution of a space and of a specific temporality:

1) The surest way, Spinoza says, for a people to be protected is 'to form a social order with definite laws, to occupy a definite area of the world'.[51] Upon leaving Egypt, no longer bound by the law of any other nation, the Hebrews were free 'to institute new laws for themselves, as they pleased, and to occupy whatever lands they wanted to'.[52] Thus, after having formed a militia, they invaded the domain of the Canaanites, and divided it into twelve lots that they randomly distributed to the twelve tribes.[53] And the land of the Canaanites became 'the holy land of the fatherland', the land of God against which the rest of the world appeared as 'unclean and profane'. The appropriation of space is therefore doubly symbolic: (i) it marks the essential difference, even the contradiction, between the Hebrew people chosen by God and other nations; and (ii) it marks the strict equality between the Hebrews. There was equality among the tribes and equality of the subjects with respect to their own chiefs: 'subjects of this State, who, with the leader, had an equal share of the lands and fields. Each one was the everlasting lord of his own share.'[54]

2) The pact allows for the formation of a human temporality. The covenant makes possible a temporality open to the future and to progress, by tearing away 'those who live as barbarians without civilisation' from an 'almost animal' life, prisoners of the moment because of their appetite for joy and the affects of the mind, 'which take no account of the future and of other things'.[55] Cooperation allows the deployment of new productive forces in the technical domain through the division of labour. It also (or thus) produces a new temporality: the productivity of the human being as a human being.

[50] *TTP* XVII; *CWS* II, 316.
[51] *TTP* III; *CWS* II, 114.
[52] *TTP* XVII; *CWS* II, 301.
[53] *TTP* XVII; *CWS* II, 305.
[54] *TTP* XVII; *CWS* II, 315.
[55] *TTP* V; *CWS* II, 144.

> Not all men are equally capable of all things, and no one would be able to provide the things which a man alone needs most. Everyone, I say, would lack both the strength and the time, if he alone had to plow, to sow, to reap, to grind, to cook, to weave, to sew, and to do the many other things necessary to support life – not to mention now the arts and sciences which are also supremely necessary for the perfection of human nature and for its blessedness.[56]

To measure this human temporality, the pact establishes an order of calendar temporality, which, among the Hebrews, is directly derived from imagined time and the universe of imaginary significations that generated the pact. Thus, for example, the week is the terrestrial expression of the temporalisation of the creation of the world. The pact puts into place a specific way for a society to experience temporality explicitly in the order of representation. Among the Hebrews, this way of experiencing temporality is found in the strict ritual repetition of activities whose meaning is based on every citizen's belief in the eternal election of his people. The rhythms that punctuate work and celebration follow the beat of the people's life whose hearts (*animos*) beat only to pay homage and submit to God.

In Hebrew consciousness, however, the cyclical temporality of the (instituted) return of the same denies the reality of the change of historical temporality in favour of God's eternity (at least in the Mosaic sense) and the eternal election of the Jews. It must not obscure the reality of the temporality that every society, regardless of the clear consciousness of the individuals who form it, produces in its making. In the connection it creates by constituting itself (by persevering in its being), the collective body produces, according to the same movement, a first reality of time. This reality is defined by the rhythms, its fast or slow pace, and the potentialities of resistance or reaction, vigour or fatigue, liveliness or languor that a society can yield. This is not merely a temporality reflected in memory, a calendar, a measure, or even in significations. Temporality is reflected in the actual duration of the perseverance, the tension or the habit-of-living of a particular society, its *dispositione temperamenti corporis*, as Spinoza said about the prophets.[57] Because this temporality expresses the *conatus*-habit, the collective body in its *ingenium*, its 'temperament', it is the actualisation of a singular essence. Owing to the perfection of their institutions, duration for the Hebrews expresses their stubbornness, constancy, endurance and the

---

[56] *TTP* V; *CWS* II, 143.
[57] *TTP* II; *CWS* II, 97.

unique courage that, in Tacitus' terms, characterises 'the complexion of this race and its irreducible fanaticism'.[58] Because of Moses' error and its consequences, it is also the duration of weariness, suspicion (towards the Levites), anger and, finally, despair: an inversion of the *conatus* into the desire to die, which led the Hebrews to break the pact with God.[59]

The immanent temporality that a society develops by affirming its existence must not be confused with the imaginary time of the calendar and of organising principles. Nevertheless, these times are closely connected, for changes in the immanent duration of affects (e.g. the discouragement of the Hebrews) are accompanied by major changes in the ordering of imaginary time and the meanings it carries. The rhythm of holiday and work is no longer respected when the decline of faith, permissiveness, luxury and laziness of the soul take over, leading to decadence and, eventually, to the downfall of the State. Spinoza underlines, however, the extent to which the collective body and 'heart' of a 'nation' cannot disappear completely, even if its members are dispersed, because the habits acquired have already deeply marked the souls for whom these habits express the pulse of life on a daily basis and remain specific to that nation and its departed state. Enveloped by the affects, this temporality exists with even greater intensity compared to the other states which, instead of pursuing a policy of assimilation, suffocate foreigners with their hatred (as was the case, with some exceptions, with the Jews).[60] Gatherings animate the nationalistic and religious sentiments and the signs of recognition within the community. When, by necessity, they are held in secret, they do so with even greater intensity. Let us remember the surprising sentence of Spinoza: 'I consider the sign of circumcision so important even in this matter that I am convinced that this one thing will preserve this nation for all eternity.'[61] Emphasising the complexity of the fabric

---

[58] Spinoza cites Tacitus in Book II of his *Histories*: *Profligaverat bellum Judaicum Vespasianus, oppugnatione Hierosolymorum reliqua, duro magis & arduo opere ob ingenium gentis & pervicaciam superstitionis, quam quod satis virium obsessis ad tolerandas necessitates superesset.* TTP XVII; CWS II, 315.

[59] TTP XVII; CWS II, 319.

[60] TTP III; CWS II, 123. Spinoza makes 'hatred' play a major political role in the constitution and the almost irreducible perseverance of the Hebrew nation – the hatred, on the one hand, that the Hebrews have for everything that is not Jewish, but also the hatred that responds to theirs, and which contributes to the reinforcement of particularism, even after the dissolution of the state. TTP V; CWS II, 142. TTP XVII; CWS II, 313–14.

[61] TTP III; CWS II, 124. In chapter XVII of the *TTP*, Spinoza underlines the role of particularisms in strengthening the nation's *conatus*: among the Hebrews, daily worship is 'absolutely contrary' to the rest of human beings (CWS II, 314); worship

that makes up the temporality of a people in its tenacity to live beyond the disappearance of its State, Spinoza immediately adds, 'if the foundations of their religion did not make their hearts (*animos*) unmanly'.[62] The difference between such conflicting affects – fluctuations or 'transitions' to greater or lesser perfection – which is at the core of the duration of the Hebrew nation shows that the *appetitus* of the multitude, as with the human individual, always affirms the full perfection and power of which it is capable, irrespective of the affects which constitute the capacity to be affected, its correlate. The capacity of a political body is determined by its institutions. The more these institutions adequately realise the unique power of the political body, the more its duration will be marked by the constancy, perseverance and courage of its citizens. If, on the other hand, these institutions only partially realise this power, the lived duration will consist of fluctuating affects, from courage to weariness and from perseverance to despair. But in both cases, this duration, understood as the immanent temporality of a given society, is the direct expression of its own dynamism. It is constitutive of the collective body, which is explained and developed through the power of Habit.

3 The Institution of Freedom

Because of the temporality of *habitus*, we can now understand two parallel remarks by Spinoza that refer to seemingly insurmountable difficulties. It is laborious to 'correct these faults and to remove the common prejudices of Theology',[63] and for a nation, 'accustomed to royal authority and held in check only by that authority',[64] to change its form of government.

> That's how it happens that the people can often change the tyrant, but can never destroy him, or change a monarchic state into another, of a different form. The English people have given us a deadly example of this truth, when they sought reasons for removing a monarch from their midst with an appearance of right. When they had removed him, they were completely unable to change the form of the state. After much blood had been spilled, they reached the point where they hailed a new monarch under another

---

and rites, before entering the temple, have 'a singular character' (CWS II, 316) etc. On this strengthening of the *conatus* in and through the consideration of its 'particularity', see *Ethics* III, 55 Schol., and Chapter 3, section 2 above.

[62] TTP III; CWS II, 124.
[63] TTP VIII; CWS II, 192.
[64] CWS II, 329. Translator's note.

name, as if the whole issue had only been about the name! The new monarch could survive only if he completely destroyed the royal family, killed the king's friends, or anyone suspected being his friend, and upset the tranquillity of peace, so suitable for generating murmurings, with a war, so that ordinary people, preoccupied with new crises, would turn its thoughts about royal murder in a different direction. Too late the people realized that the only thing they had accomplished for the well-being of their country was to violate the right of a legitimate king and change everything for the worse. So as soon as they could, they decided to retrace their steps; they did not rest until they saw things restored to their original condition.[65]

Individuals and nations are themselves specific institutions that have evolved over time. Nature does not produce obedient subjects or nations that emerge only from laws and customs. Whether religious or civil, laws are only blackened paper if no one agrees with them or makes them the content of her opinions and behaviour that define and justify her loyalty. Neither the criticism of prejudices by reason nor the political disappearance of a form of government is therefore sufficient to eliminate the complex of acquired habits and the particular forms of joy and security they bring.

As for prejudices, Spinoza says:

> But I fear my attempt may come too late. Things have already nearly reached the point where men do not allow themselves to be corrected about this, but stubbornly defend what they have embraced under the guise of religion. Nor does any place seem to be left for reason, except among a very few (few if compared with the rest), so widely have these prejudices taken possession of men's minds.[66]

The stubborn defence of prejudices is also the defence of their life in its singularity. The perseverance in one's being (*in suo esse*) and the perseverance in one's prejudices, in one's state (*in suo statu*), are one and the same thing. Because the *conatus* is the *habitus* that Churches and States have created over the centuries, fidelity to these institutions has become fidelity to oneself for the subject.[67] Temporality thus produces a structure of identity and particu-

---

[65] *TTP* XVIII; CWS II, 330.
[66] *TTP* VIII; CWS II, 192.
[67] This is how the *consuetudines* of the Hebrews became their 'very nature' (*naturam verti debuerint*, CWS II, 314) or a *second* nature. But if there is second nature (according to the Pascalian expression), for Spinoza (and Pascal) the nature of a people (its singular

larism, in and through which the *conatus* affirms itself as a fantastic power of inertia and conservatism. For this reason, despite its moments of revolution, human history, according to Spinoza, is characterised above all by its regressions to previous states. Like the Hebrew nation that, during the period of popular rule, knew how to correct its errors and return to the laws of Moses, the English people 'as soon as they could' retraced their steps to restore 'the right of a legitimate king . . . *jus legitimi regis*',[68] which, Spinoza writes, it had first overthrown under 'an appearance of right'. Whence comes this legitimacy – of the Mosaic law or of the English monarchy – if not from custom or from time,[69] which has led a people to return to it at the most difficult moments. An institution derives its legitimacy precisely from the fact that it is desired by the greatest number, from the desire of a people, that is from the very essence of this nation, insofar as it is regarded as determined to act by a certain affection.[70] The basis of legitimacy, then, is nothing other than belief in that very legitimacy, belief being understood as a movement of desire.

Is this the admission of a futile fate for individuals and nations alike, since they are unable to create something new? At first glance, one might think so, but two elements in these texts contradict this opinion:

First, despite his fear that an attempt might come 'too late', Spinoza in fact continues his fight against prejudices, 'having, he says, no reason to despair completely'.[71] At the end of chapter XIV, after having defined faith and genuine faithfulness, and having recommended that his reader carefully reread his last two chapters several times, he concludes: 'I want to ask the reader . . . to be persuaded that we did not write them with the intention of introducing any novelties, but only to correct distortions, which we hope someday, finally, to see corrected.'[72]

Second, Spinoza does not at all diagnose the retreat of the English people as a symptom of impotence, but, on the contrary, as an honest (reasonable) desire that is opposed to the illusory desire for a sudden change in the form of government.

Apart from the historical impasse that a nation seems to reach under the leadership of a monarch, according to the *TTP*, this return, taking into

---

essence) is its custom (its customs, its laws, its language); Pascal, *Pensees and Other Writings*, trans. Honor Levi, Oxford World's Classics, 2008 S 159–226.

[68] *TTP* XVIII; *CWS* II, 330.
[69] This was already Machiavelli's thesis in *The Prince*, University of Chicago Press, 1998, ch. II, 'Of Hereditary Principalities', pp. 6–7.
[70] *Ethics* III DA 1, expl.
[71] *TTP* VIII; *CWS* II, 192.
[72] *TTP* XIV; *CWS* II, 271.

account the *Political Treatise*, may also mean that a nation must find its unique path to political freedom based only on the preservation of its form of government. This is necessary to avoid the risk of total ruin or a long time lost, from the point of view of human freedom, in the revolutionary illusions of a change that is as sudden as it is radical.

In any case, Spinoza condemns as dangerous the illusion of the new, which is the root of revolutions and religious prejudices. Against this longing,[73] Spinoza argues for the return to and preservation of an earlier form of legitimate government or religion, before 'new and unfamiliar doctrines which the common people most wonder at' reduce 'faith to credulity and prejudice' and turn reasonable people into beasts or automatons.[74] Far from expressing a conservative position, the return to the Scriptures, to the true faith, as expressed in the assertion that 'each State must retain its form of government', follows from a realistic and political perspective of faith in life in its affirmation. Regardless of the political circumstances and superstitious illusions that define a society, it is never too late for human freedom. This is the thesis of the *Political Treatise*. The *TTP* insists on the inevitable resistance that human nature offers to order beyond a certain point of oppression.[75] Since the judgement of any person cannot be influenced, the political aim of a tyrant is doomed to failure. To be truly effective, so that the forms of servitude are really abolished (not only in the imagination, where humans are capable of giving servitude other names), the struggle for freedom can only be waged on the basis of forms of thought and conduct to which humans are faithfully attached beyond their passions. For people of Christian faith, this includes the structure of their faith (the Scriptures) and the form of government by which they have historically been constituted in their identity. So we have to hold together two of Spinoza's seemingly contradictory positions:

1) The instability of the multitude:

> easily corrupted either by greed or by extravagant living... Everyone knows how it goes – a disgust with the present, a craving to make fundamental changes, uncontrolled anger, a scorn for poverty – these affects lead men to wickedness. Everyone knows how much they fill and disturb men's hearts.[76]

---

[73] Ibid.
[74] *TTP*, Praef.; *CWS* II, 70.
[75] *TTP* XX; *CWS* II, 348.
[76] *TTP* XVII; *CWS* II, 299.

And 2) the deep and unconscious loyalty to institutions that leads a nation to repeat the same experiences even during its seemingly greatest upheavals, thus concealing under new names power (*pouvoir*) structures that are in fact the same as those that were violently overthrown. They do this because of the specificity of a *conatus* for which perseverance in its being (*in suo esse*) is identified with perseverance in its state (*status*).

Paradoxically, the instability of a nation can only be understood through adherence to its institutions, which, because of their imperfection, are themselves the cause of its overthrow.[77] In the religious as in the political sphere, fidelity to forms of government or to the Word of God is not the problem for Spinoza; they are not the obstacles to freedom. On the contrary, obstacles come from the external causes that make this fidelity a form of unfreedom. Spinoza's task is to know and combat these causes. In the *TTP*, he analyses the causes that turn religion into superstition. In the *Political Treatise*, he analyses the causes of tyranny. He also outlines the institutions that enable monarchy to develop its political identity, while guaranteeing the real continuity of the regime and the genuine exercise of the freedom of its citizens. Far from being contested, the loyalty of citizens, like that of religious believers, is overdetermined by the maintained legitimacy of their attachment to a form of government or religion. The new conditions of their exercise allow this loyalty to be expressed not for the purpose of servitude but for the purpose of salvation.

The paradox of the blind desire for novelty is that it can only lead to a repetition of the same but worse ... and finally, after much oppression and suffering, to a return to the old situation, the origin of rebellion. So the truly new can only develop and sustain itself on the basis of a clearly recognised and integrated earlier form. It does so in the service of a fundamentally revolutionary political project, because it is nothing other than an attempt, taking into account the specific structures of each regime, to increase the political power (*puissance*) of the multitude ... and the freedom of each as far as possible. The old inserts itself into the new, but only to strengthen it and make the change irreversible by creating new meanings. In politics, the radically new meaning is freedom, which can be said to be new from the perspective of eternity. Spinoza's political project focuses on an understanding of the essence of politics as an institution of freedom:

> From the foundations of the Republic explained above it follows most clearly that its ultimate end is not to dominate, restraining men by fear,

---

[77] *TTP* XVII; CWS II, 316.

and making them subject to another's control, but on the contrary to free each person from fear, so that he can live securely, as far as possible, i.e., so that he retains to the utmost his natural right to exist and operate without harm to himself or anyone else. The end of the Republic, I say, is not to change men from rational beings into beasts or automata, but to enable their minds and bodies to perform their functions safely, to enable them to use their reason freely, and not to clash with one another in hatred, anger or deception, or deal inequitably with one another. So the end of the Republic is really freedom.[78]

Spinoza does not change his position in the *Political Treatise*. On the contrary, this same position is radicalised by explaining the ontological basis of the political project of autonomy as the absolute affirmation of existence: freedom is actual infinity. The actual and actualising singular essence is indeed ontological power. The collective body tends towards autonomy in the historical unfolding of its forces. Autonomy itself becomes a tension towards a specific form of self-organisation of the social body. In and through this tension, a future is established, that is, the absolute affirmation of a singular existence that cannot be enclosed in the ever-present traces of Habit. Without Habit (constitutive of the body itself), the future cannot be effective in either political innovation or the repetition of the same. This is only apparent due to the historical alteration that institutions necessarily engender, of which revolutions are the most obvious symptoms. The existence of a historical collective body is always absolutely affirmed in and through institutions. These institutions either allow for an effective autonomy of this body and the subjects that constitute it, in which case Spinoza will speak of an 'absolutely absolute' affirmation of its existence, *omnino absolutum*;[79] or, they enclose the collective body within a heteronomous arrangement where illusion dominates (the foundation of the social as external to the social body), along with the domination of human by human, and the scattering of the multitude's forces, their expenditure and their contradictions.

Hence the importance of the dynamics of expectation in the collective domain as well as for the individual body, even beyond the constitution of memory, meaning and value. Expectation structures common experience as a social, political and ideological field; the field of the deployment of the imaginary is reflected in the categories of the possible and the impossible,

---

[78] *TTP* XX; *CWS* II, 346.
[79] *TP* XI, 1; *TP* V, 2; *TP* VIII, 3, 7.

according to the real power (or impotence) of the multitude to be capable or not. This field of possibility is represented in the hopes, fears, volitions, ambitions, calculations and goals of the entire community, through which it shapes its future. Common experience in turn conditions the very dynamic of expectation that first activated it, according to the same laws of association. This feedback conditioning cannot be understood as a capitulation of expectation to experience. In and through expectation, a singular essence asserts itself. It gives the present its strength and the power of potential innovation to overcome the given conditions.

We say potential innovations, because the dead ends of the repetition of the same, like those of utopia, menace desire. The main task of a human society is continually to preserve the strength of the present, so that it effectively creates a space for common life, in and through which the power of the multitude can be deployed 'absolutely'. This capacity to preserve the productive power of the present is correlated with the actualisation of the desire for democracy of which a particular people is capable. This is the power of freedom actualised, the absolute affirmation of life, and active expectation as an innovative tension *sub specie aeternitatis*. And it is the very strength of this desire, the very essence of the collective body, actively to resist external causes, illusion, and the oppression that engenders and expresses a narrowing and an impoverishment of the public realm of experience, richness and diversity of opinions.

We know Habit to be at the origin of the organisation of individual bodies. It can be considered the founding activity of the affirmation of the actual existence of all bodies, including political bodies. Thus, with Habit, Spinoza discovers the *conatus* of the multitude as a body in the realm of collective life, at the basis of the identity and temporality of a 'nation'. By Habit, I mean the power of the associative dynamisms through which the specific aptitude of the collective body is constituted, corresponding to its singular essence, the very power of the multitude. Habit is comprised of the associations through which the mores and customs of a nation are formed, through contiguity, resemblance, imitation, the logic of joy and, depending on the complexity of the collective body that is now political, the associations of the recognitive-imagination that go beyond the linked affections and the correlative affect towards the constitution of new connections. According to the productive movement of the collective desire that establishes them, these associations indicate new causes of security and peace for the whole nation. This shows the importance of the schematising imagination, the higher-level expression of the *conatus*-Habit of the collective body. Through imagination, this body can access, not only a political constitution in general, but also a particular juridico-political organisation through which it arrives at the 'absolutely absolute' affirmation of its existence.

Through historical study, grounded in the experiential richness of Scripture, Spinoza highlights a new figure of the imagination, one that is no longer only the power of illusion and fiction that was analysed in *Ethics* I, App. and in *TTP* II,[80] where he only saw in imagination the other face of a powerlessness of the understanding. Through historical study, Spinoza does not discover the constitutive nature of the imagination as a coherent solution (or instituted imaginary) in the effort of the ignorant to persevere in their being. Rather, an analysis of *Ethics* I, App. shows that a positivity is already present through the expressions of prejudice, fanaticism and superstition (the universe of meaning and value) through which humans strive to persevere in their being (something that *Ethics* III, 9 will later confirm). In this case, the positivity of imagination is useful to the ignorant who, through it, make their life of illusions and servitude cohere into a structured order of the world. But it is useless to the philosophers who, in a mathematical spirit, can lead their lives entirely in the light of truth, under the command of reason.

When extended to the political realm, however, this essentially gnoseological and ethical perspective leads to an impasse. Spinoza has to face this impasse when, in reference to the imaginary constitution of tyranny, he tries to build the rational, non-imaginary (quasi-philosophical) foundation of democracy, through an opposition between what is 'natural' and the 'artifice' used by tyrants. From this perspective, imagination only appears constitutive in the cases where humans are incapable of building their future democratically. In the appendix to *Ethics* I, the powerlessness of the understanding explains the power of the finalist imaginary horizon. Here, instead, the powerlessness of the multitude explains the imaginary institution of society. This problematic is made obsolete, despite some residual persistence, by what is practically discovered in and through the analysis of the third solution to the political problem: the Hebrew theocracy. According to the logic of finalist prejudice and superstition, not only does imagination lead naturally to the political constitution of tyranny on a mystifying basis, but imagination is also the constitutive and collective power of institutions that can be perfect and fully adapted to the desires and needs of a people. What is discovered is not only the constitutive power of the imagination, as a naturalised imaginary. We discover imagination's essential place at the very heart of the multitude's process of political self-organisation, unifying power and practical

---

[80] *TTP* II; *CWS* II, 93.

rationality. The imaginative power of the multitude thereby becomes the very essence of politics, its natural nature, so to speak. Collective imagination asserts itself as the vessel of rationality and the source of the functionality of institutions. The transition from delusional to politically constitutive imagination occurs in and through the complication of the associations that form the collective body. We can thus conceive, without contradiction, a political body that expresses an adequate practical rationality in and through its imagination: it is the very project of democracy, a society in which the multitude inhabits its own constitutive function, which remains masked and alienated in any other type of society.

Albeit with some exceptions that can appear, so to speak, outside history,[81] Spinoza's political reflection goes from the consideration of the multitude's powerlessness to its self-government, its power to self-organise, regardless of its regime-type. It is from this shift in perspective that he can 1) develop a non-abstract historical conception of the constitution of democracy; 2) ground the distinction between the autonomy or heteronomy of a society that, in either regime, nonetheless remains self-organising; and 3) clarify the Spinozist struggle through the theological-political conjuncture of its time and make the political consequences of the central chapters of the TTP legible.

The theoretical consequences of Spinoza's study of the Hebrew State go far beyond mere answers to the problems explicitly posed, and open on to a theory of the constitution of the political body, which includes a new conception of the imagination. In the TTP, the concept of the State emerges from historical study rather than from pure speculation. However, this does not mean that Spinoza breaks with an ontological conception of politics to make room for experience and history; quite the contrary. Admittedly, there is certainly a kind of break with the onto-teleological need for a transcendent foundation of society (God, reason or Nature). Yet Spinozist ontology does not serve these legitimising functions. On the contrary, it maintains singular existence as an absolute affirmation, without principle, end or model. It is an essential productive power that is fully explained and developed within a particular historical (modal) experience, through the determination of problems and their solutions.

If Spinoza also knows how to draw philosophical lessons from experience and history, it is because he never gives in to empiricism.[82] The full and

---

[81] As in TTP V; CWS II, 144.
[82] To give in to 'empiricism' would be to confuse historical experience with everyday experience, and thus not to consider the difference between the first and the second kinds

complete explanation of singular existence is always ontological for him. If 'whatever happens, happens by God's will and eternal decree',[83] the State also 'involve[s] eternal necessity and truth'.[84] To know this truth is to know the singular essence of this individual State adequately. Namely, it is to know a commonwealth by its proximate cause. Or, what is the same thing, it is to know its history, the causes that explain the social cohesion specific to this State, along with its contradictions and despairs. It is to know how this society is produced and perseveres in its being.[85] The power of God[86] is known through natural causes as the external aid for humans and for the State itself, as an individual, its *conatus*, or singular essence. In the *TTP*, the study of the Hebrew State appears as the knowledge of a singular essence. Except for the study of God in the *Ethics*, this is the only complete study in the work of Spinoza (the study of Christianity in the *TTP* is only partial).[87] We learn that the singular essence of a State necessarily involves the imagination, that a commonwealth is the power of imagination and the multitude's self-organisation, and that imagination asserts itself as the force that produces social and historical modes of being.

On the practical terrain of history, the prowess of the *TTP* leads us to discover, in the idea of a strategy of the *conatus* of the collective body, a radical Spinozist theory in the field of the political.

---

of knowledge. My use of the category 'empiricism' does not refer to any philosophical system. The category designates rather the 'general philosophical attitude' that Gaston Bachelard defined by the continuity that it establishes between 'common sense' and 'science'. Bachelard, like Spinoza, radically rejects such continuity. See *The Philosophy of No: A Philosophy of the New Scientific Mind*, trans. G. C. Waterston, Orion, 1968, foreword and chs 1 and 2; *Le rationalisme appliqué*, PUF, 1949, chs 1 and 6.

[83] *TTP* VI; *CWS* II, 155.
[84] *TTP* VI; *CWS* II, 154.
[85] *TTP* IV; *CWS* II, 126.
[86] *TTP* I; *CWS* II, 91.
[87] See Laurent Bove, 'Les raisons de l'échec de l'enseignement du Christ et la constitution du christianisme dans le *T.T.P.* de Spinoza', in *Les fruits de la dissension religieuse: fin XVe–début XVIIIe siècles*, ed. M. Clément, Travaux de l'UPRES-A CNRS 5037, Publications de l'Université de Saint-Etienne, 1998.

9

The Strategy of the *multitudinis potentia*: The Political *Conatus*

1 The Political Project of Autonomy as Absolute Sovereignty and/or the Collective Body's 'Absolutely Absolute' Affirmation

Because it is a power (*puissance*) of affirmation and resistance in every sphere, virtue is struggle. Like his ethics, Spinoza's political thought is primarily combative. And this struggle has its own (philosophical-political) strategy, adapted to time. This is the explicit approach of the *TTP*, which expands and accompanies the problems raised in the *scholia*, prefaces and appendices of the *Ethics*. The declared opponent is the theologian[1] and, in his wake, the tyrant. Beyond the concepts that Spinoza attacks, the true enemy of the philosopher is the shared universe of meaning and the structures of political domination that these doctrines entail. The universe of meaning separates societies, peoples and individuals from their own political activity and constituting power, the only true guarantors of their freedom.

The Spinozist struggle for autonomy, both political and ethical, develops on the metaphysical basis of a conception of the organisation of reality that is itself conceived as strategic in its singular modal actualisation. The concept of a strategy of the *conatus* of the collective body, or the *multitudinis potentia* (the multitude as a specific modality of political reality in its tendency to constitute itself as 'nation', 'people' or 'State')[2] places us at the centre of Spinoza's political thought as we find it in its most innovative form

---

[1] *Ep.* XXX, LXVIII [to Oldenburg]; CWS II, 13, 459. On the radical antagonism between the philosopher and the theologian, see André Tosel, *Spinoza ou le crépuscule de la servitude*, Aubier, 1984, ch. 1.

[2] *TP* II, 17.

in the *TP*.³ We find a perfect analogy in the *TP* between the individual body and the collective body: their common pursuit of preservation and affirmation follows the logic of causality inherent in singular beings. The analogy has implications that make this unfinished work the most radical theory of the strategy of the *conatus*. Thus, reading the *TP* confirms and clarifies the innovative theoretical consequences of the historical study of the *TTP*.

Spinoza's political thought is first, as we said, struggle. To say that this struggle is a fight for freedom would be correct. However, it is somewhat trivial if we do not add to Spinoza's definition of freedom a dynamic of 'free necessity', which, we know, corresponds to the absolute affirmation of an existence, its infinity in act.⁴ This definition of autonomy (the human individual acting according to causes 'which can be understood through the laws of his nature alone') can also be applied to the political:

> Like man, a Commonwealth will also be the most powerful and the most its own master, if it is founded on and directed by reason.⁵

And the basis of reason is nothing other than the power of the multitude. Thus, free necessity is first that of *multitudinis potentia*, organised as a body politic,⁶ as far as possible by its 'absolutely absolute'⁷ affirmation. Its self-affirmation is, at the same time, the specificity of its political question and its project of a radically autonomous self-constitution. But the free necessity of the body politic also implies the free necessity of the citizen-subjects who assert their own freedom in and through that of the State. For, paradoxically, civil liberty correlates with the absolute affirmation of the State, its 'absolute sovereignty'.⁸

By taking the ideal of political rationality of his contemporaries to its logical conclusion (this is, the political meaning of absolute rationalism),

---

³ Antonio Negri, following the work of Alexandre Matheron on the relationship between politics and the passions, has masterfully enlightened us on the constitutive logic of the state from the point of view of the 'power of the multitude'; see *The Savage Anomaly: The Power of Spinoza's Metaphysics and Politics*, University of Minnesota Press, 1991.
⁴ TP II, 7; TP II, 11.
⁵ TP III, 7; CWS II, 520. See also Paolo Cristofolini, 'Esse sui juris e scienza politica', *Studia Spinozana*, 1, 1985, pp. 53–72.
⁶ *Nam Civitatis Jus potentia multitudinis, quae una veluti mente ducitur, determinatur.* TP III, 7.
⁷ TP XI, 1.
⁸ TP VIII, 3.

Spinoza attempts to overcome two great contradictions that pervade both political thought and reality. The first contradiction is between the freedom of citizens and the authority of the State included in the absolutist perspective of his time: the authority of the State seemed to be able to prevail only against the freedom of the citizens. The second contradiction is between the pre-political freedom of the multitude and the authority of the State, which establishes a latent state of war in society. The authority of the State de facto leaves an 'untamed' freedom that the multitude can only express rebelliously.

Because of their inner connection in the dynamic process of their constitution, Spinoza grasps the absolutism of the State and the freedom of citizens together. The freedom of citizens is contained in the 'absolutely absolute' affirmation of the power of the multitude that defines the right of the sovereign.[9] On the verge of the body politic's fracture, through the revolutionary use of the right of war (an insurmountable limit in a true democracy), Spinozist political reflection leads us to a new figure of citizenship through the self-constitution of the multitude as an autonomous-strategic 'subject' – a figure of citizenship limited by the double tension of natural/civil law and obedience/resistance.

In the *TP*, Spinoza repeatedly describes the State (*imperium*) as an individual (an individual of individuals) and compares it to a human individual. First in *TP* III, 2, where the term *multitudo* (which already appears in *TP* I, 5 and II, 17, where Spinoza defines the law of the State by the *multitudinis potentia*) refers to the collective body politic (or the body of the State when the multitude is governed with order, as opposed to the *inordinatae multitudinis*),[10] organised like a *humano corpori*.[11] This amounts, according to the expression of *TP* III, 2, to the body of the State being 'led as if by a single mind'. Let us not deceive ourselves about this last phrase (*multitudinis quae una veluti mente ducitur*), which seems to invite the illusion of dualism according to which the mind guides the body. The mind here is in fact nothing other than the social body in its political self-organisation, even if under certain conditions this organisation seems to be intolerable for a large proportion of the individuals who make up this body.

It is legitimate, then, that 'in the civil State, all the citizens collectively ought to be considered just like a man in the state of nature'.[12] All bodies

---

[9] *TP* II, 17.
[10] *TP* VIII, 19.
[11] *TP* X, 1.
[12] *TP* VII, 22; *CWS* II, 555.

arise according to the same causal logic (namely that of the present and actualising essence of modes), whether they are bodies of human individuals or of States. What consequences can be drawn from the Spinozist conception of the political individual as a body? It means, *first*, that the body politic is defined by a multiplicity whose elements are stabilised by a certain relation of movement and rest (its *facies civitatis*);[13] *second*, that this body has the capacity to affect and to be affected (to affect bodies other than itself and to be affected by them; to affect and be affected by the bodies that form it); *thirdly*, that this complex body, like the human body, has a constitutive power to link affects; *fourthly*, that because of its complexity, this body must also be able to be thought of as a practical subject; the question of its becoming-cause, its autonomy, arises, as it does for the ethical subject.

First, the State (like the human individual defined as a practical subject) always acts according to an end, namely the utility it seeks. The purpose for which an individual acts is nothing other than her appetite,[14] but this, like the power of the body politic, is reflected in a teleological structure that defines the ends and reasons for which that State exists and acts. As with the human individual, the ends and reasons of the State can be rather imaginary because of ignorance of the real causes that determine one to act.

The State can be defined teleologically on three levels of meaning:

1) There is first of all a real aim of the State, inherent in its existence, 'which is nothing other than peace and security of life',[15] and towards which 'a free multitude, guided more by hope than by fear', strives.[16] This is the very aim of the State:[17] to advocate for the State is thus to advocate for a structure of coexistence which, because of its difference from the state of nature, must guarantee greater security. A State aims to lead people as far as possible along the path of reason and thus to transform the striving for security into a striving for freedom.[18] But when the State is imposed on a defeated population by the right of war, the very purpose of the State is inverted into a no less real servitude of the people:

> The end of a State someone acquires by the Right of war, then, is to be master; it has slaves rather than subjects. When we attend to the general

---

[13] *TP* VI, 2.
[14] *Ethics* IV, Def. 7.
[15] *TP* V, 2; *CWS* II, 529.
[16] *TP* V, 6; *CWS* II, 530.
[17] Just as there is a 'real end' to laws, *TTP* IV; *CWS* II, 126.
[18] *TTP* XX; *CWS* II, 346.

right of each State, there is no essential difference between one created by a free multitude, and one acquired by the right of war. Still, we've shown that each has a very different end. Furthermore, the means through which each State must be preserved are very different.[19]

2) There is also an imaginary goal that each one predicates of her own community, such as the founding narratives about the existence of a 'nation'. The Hebrews, for example, see themselves as 'children of God', members of a chosen people.

3) Finally, there are the partial and cyclical goals that a State pursues in each situation, according to the real and imagined goals that are peculiar to it, but also according to its immediate interests. In this last sense, we will say that the State, like a human individual, has the structure of a practical subject.

Like every individual in the state of nature, the State – that is, a collective power exercised through its institutions and its leaders – acts according to what it considers useful to itself. Following the movement of its desire (power), it assigns values that are its own: what is good or bad for the State, just or unjust; it creates laws, interprets them for each case, and so on.[20] So the State exists by enforcing its own laws, by establishing its own meanings and values, by building its own world through its laws, decrees and decisions.

> This right, which is defined by the power of a multitude, is usually called Sovereignty. Whoever, by common agreement, has responsibility for public Affairs – that is, the rights of making, interpreting, and repealing laws, fortifying cities, and making decisions about war and peace, etc. – has this right absolutely.[21]

The structure of the State is thus inextricably linked to 'the direction of a sovereign'[22] and Spinoza compares this to 'the mind of the State, by which everyone ought to be guided'.[23] The practice of the State is thus teleological in nature. It involves (or presupposes) a practical reflection which, as politicians know only too well, is an understanding of the power struggles and interests of each. States are 'related to one another as two men are in the

---

[19] TP V, 6; CWS II, 531.
[20] TP IV, 1.
[21] TP II, 17; CWS II, 514.
[22] TP III, 1; CWS II, 517.
[23] TP IV, 1; CWS II, 525.

state of nature',[24] as natural enemies.[25] The alliances that maintain peace between them exist only on the condition that the reasons that bound them together remain: fear of harm or hope of profit. As soon as these reasons disappear, each retains its own right, limited only by its power:

> That's why each of the allied Commonwealths retains the right to look out for itself, and why each of them strives, as far as it can, to get beyond fear, and hence, to be its own master. That's also why each of them strives to prevent the other from becoming more powerful. So, if any Commonwealth complains that it has been deceived, it can't condemn the good faith of the allied Commonwealth, but only its own foolishness, because it entrusted its own well-being to another Commonwealth, which was its own master and for which the well-being of its own State is the supreme law.[26]

Therefore, the only real misdeeds of States – just like those of individuals in the state of nature – are harms against themselves,[27] that is, errors in strategy:

> The Commonwealth sins, then, when it does, or allows to happen, what can be a cause of its ruin. We say then that it sins in the same sense in which Philosophers or Doctors say that nature sins.[28]

This tendency, indispensable in any civil society, to how things should be and what must be done (what is useful for them) defines 'the will of the Commonwealth' and 'must be considered the will of all'.[29] It explains that the first powers (*pouvoirs*) a society establishes – the first expressions of the 'Right of a State, of the supreme powers'[30] – are those of governance, orders or *mandata*. It is about governing and being obeyed, and thus about oppression. It is also about punishing those who do not obey the directives of the *summa potestas*:

> Where men have common rights, and all are led as if by one mind, it's certain (by §13) that each of them has that much less right in proportion as

---

[24] *TP* III, 11; *CWS* II, 522.
[25] *TP* III, 13; *CWS* II, 523.
[26] *TP* III, 14; *CWS* II, 523.
[27] *TP* II, 18.
[28] *TP* IV, 4; *CWS* II, 526.
[29] *TP* III, 5; *CWS* II, 519.
[30] *TP* III, 2; *CWS* II, 517.

the rest of them together are more powerful than he is – that is, he really has no right over nature beyond what the common right grants him. For the rest, whatever he's commanded to do according to the common agreement, he's bound to carry out – or (by §4) is rightly compelled to do.[31]

This is the extension of the state of nature, with the essential difference – which defines the teleological structure of the State as a practical subject – that in civil society all strive (or 'will') for the same thing to be done or avoided: '[for] everyone fears the same things: for everyone, there is one and the same cause of security and principle of living'.[32] As a practical subject, the State can define itself through the associative principles that make up its relational and social fabric, through the natural laws that comprise its law or natural power (*puissance*).[33] These are the constitutive laws of imitation that belong to the primitive (pre-political) social body: the laws of Habit that form collective memory, language and mores; the joy principle that gives associations their orientation.

These principles and their consequences are ultimately reflected in the State as a practical subject, in the form of the institutions and laws that it deploys according to the instrumental logic of ends and means. The role of the schematising and recognising imagination really gives society its status as a practical subject:

> Since all these activities, as well as the means required to carry them out, are matters which concern the whole body of the State, that is, Public Affairs, it follows that Public Affairs depend only on the governance of whoever has the supreme authority. It follows that only the supreme power has the Right to judge each person's deeds, to require each person to account for what he's done, to punish offenders, to settle disputes between citizens concerning the law, and to set up people knowledgeable in the laws, who will administer them in its place. In addition, [the supreme power] has the right to organize and use all the means of war and peace, to found and fortify cities, to assemble soldiers, to assign military offices, to command what it wants done, to send and receive ambassadors for the sake of peace, and finally, to levy taxes for all these purposes.[34]

---

[31] *TP* II, 16; *CWS* II, 524.

[32] *TP* III, 3; *CWS* II, 518. On the first two aspects – governmental and judicial – of the constitution of power, see *TP* III, 2–8.

[33] *TP* II, 4; *CWS* II, 508.

[34] *TP* IV, 2; *CWS* II, 525–6.

As a strategy of the explicit power (*pouvoir*) directing society, the strategy of the *conatus* of the body politic is thus deployed from the perspective of the practice of sovereignty: to command and to punish. But it is only from the standpoint of the constitution of this sovereignty and its dispositions that determine the elaboration of law in civil society that the degree of rationality (or adaptation) of the overall strategy of the State can be understood beyond the conscious reasons of the sovereign himself. If we can speak of a strategy of the *conatus* peculiar to civil society, it exists in relation to the constitutive self-organisation of sovereignty in the State, according to a logic of active resistance to dissolution. The *conatus* resists dissolution when confronted with enemies from outside or with internal forces of dissolution. The institutions, laws and decisions thus appear as particular solutions that a body politic reflects and produces according to how it has been able to pose the problems of its real relations that arise in them and through them, and thus in the effort that this body makes to persevere in its being. The problems posed are always particular articulations peculiar to individuals, according to the laws of imagination already contained in the specific structures of a given society.

We see that the relations (from which the specific problems of a society arise) at the heart of the subjectivation apparatus of the body politic are shaped by a different logic. The other logic is deeper than, and even presupposes, the teleological logic of explicit strategies proper to the practical subject. It is a causal logic of the power (*puissance*) of affirmation and resistance, which consists in the connection of all bodies through the power of their common persistence. It is also a power of imagination and constitution, because the singular being or the *conatus* of this collective is affirmed according to the laws of imagination, which is nothing other than the power of the multitude. This force – the absolute affirmation of all existence or infinity in act – is also the strategy (without a specific goal) of political *conatus*. According to this force or strategy, each thing (people or State) affirms itself as perfectly as possible, and draws the consequences of its own being at every moment in relation to the affects that determine the multitude's capacity to be affected as a body politic. This political analysis radicalises the metaphysical analysis in a materialist way, because here the essence of the political modal reality (the State) is quite explicitly a historical product. For what else are the specific relations between movement and rest of a society – its specific capacity to affect and be affected – if not products of Habit? In the analysis of political modality, the total identification of the *conatus* of the collective body with its *habitus*, the product and producer of history, emerges clearly. This identification appears ontologically as the pure immanence of the strategy of the collective body in its affirmation.

Actual infinity, the absolute affirmation of existence, is the self-organisation of political modality without principle or end. Of course, freedom is a goal for the political project that strives for autonomy. From the point of view of this project, 'the end of the Republic is really freedom'.[35] However, before it is a goal for a subject, freedom is the real movement of self-organisation of political reality, its inner necessity, and its essence as a power of affirmation, resistance and constitution. The project of autonomy implies that actual infinity can be politically organised with freedom as its goal, because freedom is its very essence.

Beyond any technical illusion of organisation, we find two levels of strategy of the *conatus* in the ethical realm for the politician. The seemingly transcendent second level of the project is always the effect of the first: the immanent movement of the constitution of reality. The political project of autonomy turns with the strategy of immanence, of which it is the effect, in a circular process of accumulation of forces. The tension from essence to existence, according to a perfect strategy of *multitudinis potentia* in its 'absolutely absolute' assertion, abolishes the State as a structure of domination in favour of the 'absolute State' as an assertion of its freedom.[36]

Habit is the organisation of the body politic in and through the pull of actual infinity. We know that the collective as a body is always-already organised through acquired habits of the pre-political or politically organised social body: 'So by nature men desire a civil order. It can't happen by nature that they'll ever completely dissolve it.'[37] This means that even without the State, people cannot escape the *consuetudines*, the customs, the common habits of thought and action that define the human condition, their *ingenium*. And this makes the question of *consuetudines* a political question. This is clearly stated at the end of the introduction to the *TP*:

> Finally, because all men everywhere, whether Barbarians or civilized, combine their practices and form some sort of civil order, we must seek the causes and natural foundations of the State, not from the teachings of reason, but from the common nature, or condition, of men, which I've decided to do in the following chapter.[38]

---

[35] *TTP* XX, 12; *CWS* II, 346. Translator's note.

[36] As Antonio Negri rightly says, 'the infinite is now given as the organization of human liberation', that is, his perfection (or power); *Savage Anomaly*, p. 156.

[37] *TP* VI, 1; *CWS* II, 532.

[38] *TP* I, 7; *CWS* II, 506. The example of the Aragonese, who, having been liberated from the Moors, decided to give themselves a king, is symptomatic in this sense; and one understands the homage which Spinoza pays on this occasion to the Pope, who advises

Socially, infinity in act necessarily lies in a certain *habitus* that determines the singular essence of the State, or, more precisely, in which the essence of the State is self-determined. This occurs in and through a certain relationship of movement and rest, together with the capacity of the collective body to affect and to be affected. The *conatus*-Habit is thus immediately *habitus* as *conatus*. The imagination sets boundaries that are not limits. The determination of the being is its very affirmation. The specific *habitus*, the dynamic structure of a particular collective body, determines the realm of possibilities in and through which the body exercises its effort to persist in its being. Through *habitus*, possibilities for the future are dynamically structured, in a fully organised yet unpredictable way. The *conatus* of the collective body, which does not unfold arbitrarily, nevertheless does not contain its future in germinal form. As a product, the *conatus* of the collective body constitutes itself to the extent that it asserts itself in the process of self-organisation, under the determination of the external causes that act upon it but also through it. As productive forces, *appetitus* and *cupiditas* are in it, in the present of its duration, constructing the future according to strict necessity. The adequate idea of society (as an 'infinite' and 'perfect' idea) is not only a true idea that the human subject, the political philosopher, can present as knowledge of a particular society. It is the movement of reality itself in its 'absolutely absolute' affirmation of political modality. The political project of autonomy that a society, a people, can give to itself is the direct expression of the *cupiditas* of the self-organisation of the body, a desire that is self-aware. It is also the supreme affirmation of a rationality born of the collective movement, born from its power of affirmation and resistance: its perfection. Rationality, perfection, liberation and the power of the multitude go hand in hand.

The rationality of the collective body – its perfection and power of liberation – depends on the effective capacity of the multitude to organise itself, without losing power through the neutralisation or exclusion of an important part of its constitutive elements or through the sterile confrontations of its forces. If its organisation expresses the 'absolutely absolute' affirmation of the collective body, then politics is the domain of freedom. Not as a mere state, but as the real movement of the constitution of the real as infinite in acts, as eternity, which are then the duration of the actual freedom of the State and its citizens. Infinity and eternity are affirmed in

them 'not to choose a king unless they had first established customs both equitable and consistent with the people's mentality', *ingenio gentis consentaneis* (TP VII, 30; CWS II, 561).

the duration of the social body, which means that they are the very forces of history. Forces that are necessarily always determined – this duration, history, belongs to the dynamics of *habitus* – and are deployed at the level of the immanence of the strategy of political modality.

Whether they are adapted to the situation they purport to control, whether they are decided by the king, by a select few, or by the whole multitude, the conscious and ostensibly transcendent strategies of the State are the effect of the real and immanent movement of the constitutive affirmation of Nature itself in its singular affections. They contain solutions that life in its affirmation, as the infinite power to act and think, imagines and realises (they are the same thing) without pursuing a goal, depending on the contexts of contradictory power relations in and through which they are deployed. These contradictory forces are life itself as *natura naturata*. The *conatus* of the State, through which this body begins to exist,[39] therefore envelops an essential imaginary that, like desire itself, lacks nothing. It is an imagining of nothing other than absolutely positive power, *natura naturata*, through which it constitutes and establishes a naturalised imaginary characteristic of a particular society, with its own prejudices, language, beliefs, customs and laws, by which its identity or singular individuality is defined: its *ingenium*.[40] Instituted society is thus the product of the essential *naturans* imaginary, the ordering power of the *conatus*. It is the power of collective corporeality that the multitude deploys in its actual existence by virtue of the determination of the laws of the imagination. For *naturans* imaginary is nothing other than the capacity, the very power of the collective body to bind and organise its affections according to the natural laws of the imagination. We find for the collective body the equivalent of Habit for the individual body, and the essential problem of its autonomous becoming; this is the political project itself. But in the political realm, Habit generates and

---

[39] *TP* II, 2.

[40] In the process of singularisation of a people, *TTP* XVII seems to give little importance to the language. Although with laws and customs language defines a nation, Spinoza adds, *& ex his duobus, legibus scilicet & moribus, tantum oriri potest, quod unaquaeque natio singulare habeat ingenium, singularem conditionem & denique singularia praejudicia*. *TTP* XVII; *CWS* II, 316. The *Compendium Grammatices Linguae Hebraeae* allows us to qualify this assertion; see the expl. of XIII, 134, Gebhardt, I, p. 344; the commentary by Geneviève Brykman, *La Judéité de Spinoza*, p. 123; and the recent book by Pierre-François Moreau, *L'expérience et l'éternité*, PUF, 1994 [*Experience and Eternity in Spinoza*, trans. Robert Boncardo, Edinburgh University Press, 2021], particularly chapters 2 and 3 of the second part devoted to language and the passions. I can only regret not having been able to consider, in my analyses, this major book published after the conclusion of my own study.

explains capacity. The actualisation of the essence is its self-constitution in and through existence.

The real and novel political problem that Spinoza raises in the *TP* is not just the traditional problem of which regimes are best, because they are most stable and would be most effective in providing security and peace. It is rather the problem of the real, historical conditions of possibility for the emergence of an organisation through which the social body would attain a real autonomy that would correspond to an appropriate strategy – a strategy according to which the emergence of a collective body as a subject would no longer be a quasi-automaton subject to the *a priori* goal of the established imagination, and whose reflexivity and rationality are deeply rooted in a functionality that is sometimes effective but always blind to its own nature. The production of a new subjectivity that, like ethical subjectivity, is defined by a critical reflexivity in relation to its own functionality and a constitutive will that is self-aware frees itself from a superstitious relationship to the law that is imagined as external and transcendent. It is also a question of autonomy. Autonomy is expressed in the capacity of the body politic to generate active affections and actively to combine these affections according to the order of their productivity *sub specie aeternitatis*. Or it exists according to the real movement of the production of the Real, which would then be produced in God in the same way as it is in the mind (whose object is the body). It would be the adequate idea of the same body.

This, however, would suppose a condition that the reality of the body politic seems at first sight to make impossible, for this condition opens up a theoretical contradiction in Spinozist philosophy: the State as an individual seems to have the capacity to produce adequate ideas, to really think, but the essence that constitutes and defines it is the power of the imagination. The discussion of the kinds of knowledge reminds us of the crucial break between the first kind of knowledge, the imagination, and the second and third kinds of knowledge, reason and intuition, which for Spinoza are the only ones capable of producing adequate ideas. Moreover, in the *TP* Spinoza does not propose an axiom corresponding to *Ethics* II, 2, 'man thinks'. It should also be noted that if the capacity for adequate knowledge were possible for the State, Spinoza would not have ruled out, in the very first lines of the *TP*, the philosophers' dream of 'governing a republic' to promote – as an even more utopian horizon – a philosophers' State! The goal or function of the State is not to be the theorist of its own constitution, even a Spinozist one. Not to mention that such a perspective presupposes access to a global wisdom of the collective body modelled on human individuality, which at that moment renders the State useless as a power of control and oppression, something

Spinoza would never consider. The problem of a real autonomy of the body politic, of an adequate strategy for this body, thus seems to lead to a dead end by stumbling over the problem of the necessary (simultaneous) correlation of adequate ideas and active affections in autonomy.

But perhaps it is necessary to free ourselves from the now cumbersome model of human individuality, to understand political individuality in its particularity, in order to discover there the new problematic of the practical relations of imagination and reason that it forces us – beyond the theoretical aporia – to think.

The political position of Spinoza, from the *TTP* to the *TP*, is that reason is born of number. Just as there is a Spinozist ethics of quantity, there is also a Spinozist politics of quantity. If we know that in the ethical realm, the great quantity of forces, experiences and relations that an individual body has accumulated or acquired (leading to a greater capacity to affect and to be affected) corresponds to the true ideas that the idea of that body (the mind) can produce, what does a greater capacity of the collective body look like in the political realm? First, it means that the absolutely absolute affirmation of sovereignty can only be realised by the entire multitude that constitutes the collective body.[41] Secondly, it means that the affirmation of an all-the-greater degree of rationality (power and perfection) in the body politic is the product of a democratic movement in which the greatest number of citizens, and, if possible, the entire multitude, participate.[42]

In the realm of collective practices, according to Spinoza, the human imagination produces both the real and the rational. Rationality here derives not from the form or content of the idea, but from the constitution of the mind itself. The mind of the body politic is nothing other than the legal and political organisation in action, which this body, in its effort to affirm and preserve itself, has been able to give itself in a strictly immanent way. The mind of the body politic is the practical rationality of the organisation of the body politic itself. In this practical sense, we can speak of an adequate idea of this body when, like the adequate idea in God, it is affirmed in and through its institutions in an absolute and perfect way. This does not presuppose, as in our first hypothesis, that the individuals who constitute this body have themselves become sages or philosophers. Rather, under the compulsion of institutions – either as freely obeying subjects or as subjects determined by hope and fear – they are effectively made to act rationally, both individually and in their management of the State.

---

[41] *TP* VIII, 3.
[42] *TP* VII, 4; *TP* VIII, 6–7; *TP* IX, 14; *TP* XI, 1.

On the other hand, if the multitude – this is the most common case – has not been able to 'achieve unity within [itself]'⁴³ and has transferred its right to a single person responsible for its management, the logic is the same. In this case too, the body politic has given itself an organisation in an immanent way and, at the same time, enforces its right through the figure of the king. Through this monarchical institutional mediation, however, the State has lost its character of absolute absoluteness. The rationality of its decisions, which exists insofar as the collective body maintains a certain unity, is thus diminished. Since the force of the imagination of the multitude is now exerted only under the individual figure of the king, its rationality is reduced to the opinions and interests of one person and those who surround that person.⁴⁴

The absolutely absolute affirmation of the existence of a body politic, its autonomy and its perfect strategy, is expressed in the maximum (though never total) reduction of the gap between the power of the imagination of the multitude (*naturans*) and the imaginary of the institutions (*naturata*). This happens when whole sections of the population are no longer condemned to a sterile inertia or (worse) to a necessarily subversive and depleting logic, as is sometimes the case in a tyrannical regime and always in an aristocracy. The closer a State approaches the 'absolute State', the less it fears the causes of revolt and thus offers its subjects a maximum of security:

> For the greater the right of the supreme power [*pouvoir*] is, the more the form of the State agrees with the dictate of reason (by iii, 5), and consequently the more suitable it is for preserving peace and freedom.⁴⁵

If society deprives itself of political power (and thus of rationality) and reduces itself to passive obedience – which in most cases will backfire into a revolutionary reaction – it cannot have access to this 'absolute right'.⁴⁶ It cannot fall back on its perfect strategy, on its maximum capacity to determine, manage and rationally solve the problems it faces. As in the ethical realm, the body capable of autonomy is a body superior in strength, whose forces are neither neutralised, nor wasted, nor turned against itself, but rather actively deployed in and through institutions that are the direct expression of its self-organisation, its self-development.

---

[43] *TP* VII, 5; *CWS* II, 547.
[44] *TP* VI, 4–5; *CWS* II, 533.
[45] *TP* VIII, 7; *CWS* II, 568.
[46] *TP* V, 2.

The real dimension of the political problem is above all its anonymous and quantitative collective dimension, a dimension of the *multitudinis potentia* and the natural imaginary (its essence) contained in its implicit constitutive activity. In Spinoza, we know that there is the distinction between direct explicit power and indirect implicit power.[47] This distinction tends to disappear in two regimes that are diametrically opposed from the standpoint of individual freedom and the nature of the State: the Hebrew State and the democratic State. We know that, in the Hebrew State, the erasure of distinction leads to a total automation of individuals who only want what is permitted and no longer like what is explicitly forbidden. Therefore, the commands and threats of an explicit power are ultimately useless. In this first case, the real self-restraint inherent in the constitution of every society is so well integrated that it goes completely unnoticed, so that in the depths of servitude the feeling of total freedom ultimately prevails. This is a perfect model of the absolute heteronomy of society and individuals that a perfect Hebrew State could have achieved. Indeed, this model would have completely absorbed the human subject, the power to think and imagine, into the automation of the social subject. Reflexivity and will would have been at the service of the individual's adaptation to the society into which she was born, and which trained her from childhood to adapt perfectly. This is the degree zero of critical reflexivity, the absence of human subjectivity, and we can say, ultimately, the absence of politics, understood as the human endeavour to manage collective existence with lucidity.

What would this look like in a democratic regime? Note, first, that in the comparison between a practical political subject (as a society) and an individual ethical subject, the political subject has an advantage. The individual practical subject cannot be understood as a subject of knowledge or even as a subject of desire since both effective knowledge (adequate ideas) and affirmation of desire (*conatus*) are developed prior to the subject form. Nevertheless, the practical subject of the collective body can be identified with the collective *conatus* under certain conditions.

If the multitude, which holds political power (and without knowing it, uses it implicitly and explicitly, even to its detriment), can produce an organisation through which this power can effectively assert itself without escaping its control, the multitude will assert its 'absolute right' as a subject. Democracy is this explicit institution of the multitude as subject that decides what counts as a problem and how it should be addressed. The multitude is the subject in and through which the body politic is constituted. In contrast

---

[47] *TTP* XVII.

to the individual subject, the most important aspects take place within the practical political subject form, or even entirely within this structure, because the democratic project is the collective will to consciously decide the future of society, its becoming and meaning, direction and significance. Where there are unconscious mechanisms of passions and interests that lead the multitude to blindly decide in favour of this or that direction, democracy establishes the people as a subject, as an instance of reflection, of confrontation between opinions, of dialogue, and finally as an instance that decides knowingly. The autonomy of the body politic is the institutional and historical beginning of the constitutive power of the multitude as a power of reflection and decision making. This means that the popular subject, the subject of a rational strategy, must take the place of the automatisms imposed by the institutionalised imagination (for example, religious authority).

In the human individual, understood as a subject, reason determines the practical subject to act rationally. But this 'dualistic' perspective is indeed challenged when we understand subjectivity as a process of singularisation and/or as the becoming cause of modality, beyond the subject form. In a democratic society, the popular subject determines itself to act rationally. What is rational is no longer the product of the determination of the practical subject by reason, but rather the product of the subject itself according to its confrontations, exchanges, deliberations, inner dialogues and finally its decisions. While, for the human individual, the subject form is always an *effect*, for the body politic, the multitude (whose power is constitutive) can be understood as the real subject of both the matter and the form of political reality, of the State itself in its singular organisation (which is nothing other than its own right or power). The *conatus*-imagination through which the multitude asserts itself by constituting itself as a political body is thus the real subject of the constitution, which only functions at its optimal level of actualisation in democracy when the assembled people deliberate and decide on their own future. We could add that it functions at its optimal level and with the greatest operational efficiency when the democratic assembly is the place of confrontation between the opinions of citizens prepared for this practice of active subjects, which can only be carried out by democratic society itself and which leads people as far as possible along the path of reason.

Outside democracy, people – who never cease to be subjects, even if they are not conscious of themselves – are dominated by an imaginary that is always-already constituted, which defines reality and thus imposes on the multitude the ways of its constitutive (passive) activity. We call this alienated or heteronomous self-organisation. The rise of the multitude as a decision-making authority, as an explicit subject of the governance of society, cannot be understood as the emergence of a State that would be more static because it is more perfect. On the contrary, it is the adequate expression of the real movement through which a society organises and produces itself in institutions. The democratic State is thus the reality of a concrete situation in and through which a people increasingly takes the place of political decision. It thus reverses the relationship of servitude imposed by passive affections and the established imaginary. The reversal of the relation of servitude implies the establishment of a different relation between clarity and illusion, between what is actually conscious – an idea of the true idea – and what is only prejudice and superstition. At the same time, this implies a different relationship of the people to itself and to the reality of its political power, desires and needs. This is not simply a consciousness (or an increase in consciousness), but an effective knowledge, corresponding to a real movement in the history of a people, to the accumulation of power that could tear it from the shackles of the naturalised imagination and the oppressive forces that were legitimised by it. By transforming the passive affections of its habits into active forces of freedom, the people wrests itself from the fate of the repetition of acquired habits.

Democracy, like wisdom, is not so much a particular State as much as it is the real movement by which a society ceaselessly tears itself out of a state of bondage by passing to a greater perfection. The democratic State must both express and promote this liberation movement. It is at the same time a movement to realise, constitute and affirm the unique nature of the body politic. The stability of the institutions of this State rests on the dynamism of the people that produced them, on their capacity to act and resist any aggression against their sovereignty (whether that aggression comes from outside or from within). The stability of democratic institutions depends, paradoxically, on their willingness to be rationally criticised, and thus on their willingness to change according to the needs and desires of the people, to organise themselves in ever more perfect ways, in ever more adequate adaptation of the strategy of affirming the collective body. Stability, like the reality of democracy, lies in the endless dynamic of self-perfection that is part of the *multitudinis potentia*.

If the realisation of the power of the multitude could be total, if the whole of the *naturans* imaginary were to pass into the naturalised (institutions, customs, laws), if the essence of the political were thus to become the existence of a particular State, this would mean 1) that the transformation of imaginary power into rational strategies would itself be total, and would lead to the extinction of every element of particularity that defines the identity of a nation (its own prejudices, its particular customs, etc.); and 2) that the particular temporality of this State (as absolute subject) would be nothing other than the duration of eternity itself, in the perfect identification of the order of its production with what is formed in God: its adequate idea.

These two consequences are absurd from the point of view of the letter and the spirit of Spinozism. They involve two ideas that Spinoza rejects: 1) the idea of a society composed exclusively of philosophers, which has absolute knowledge of itself as an absolute subject (a perfect identity of the subject and the object of knowledge); and 2) the idea of an end of history (a halt and a goal), which would be the final reign of reason, both for society and for humanity.

We have already seen that this would result in the State becoming useless and all institutions being dissolved, something that Spinoza's ethical and political realism could never have intended. Indeed, 'as we've said, men are by nature enemies – and however much they're united and bound by laws, they still retain their nature'.[48] We can add that these laws, however perfect, can never abolish this antagonism. The passions cannot be eliminated even in a democratic society, for they are the relational basis of the primitive social body and the very condition for the integration of bodies into a collective social body. Social transparency (the rationality of the social body) is a constantly renewed effort whose unattainable limit (the identification of essence and existence) is by no means a limitation, but, on the contrary, the very condition of this effort and of the possibility of a history of societies.

However, the idea of the absolute State as a subject whose rational strategy has reached the highest degree of perfection (and political reality) remains essentially valid if one does not consider the rational subject as a closed state, but only as the real movement of the multitude in its persistent and renewed desire for autonomy. It is through this movement of political power in its absolute affirmation that the people, by organising its contradictions and its passions, can truly assert itself as a subject. The people can endow the practical subject structure of the body politic with its constitutive power. For the sage, the full 'flourishing' of sovereignty is not achieved by restraining 'our lusts; on the contrary, [it is] because we enjoy [this virtue, that] we are able to restrain them'.[49] It is thus precisely the practice of democracy, its ever more powerful development, that transforms the power of the *naturans* imagination of the body politic into an ever higher productive power of rationality. It is the same logic of the accumulation of forces that we have already noted

---

[48] *TP* VIII, 12; *CWS* II, 570.
[49] *Ethics* V, 42; *CWS* I, 616.

for the ethical subject. *Ethics* IV, 20 can thus be reformulated as follows: the more a State strives to seek what is useful for concord and peace, in order to preserve its being, and the more it has authority, the more it is endowed with power (*puissance*) (or right, or what amounts to the same thing, the greater the power with which it is endowed to act autonomously according to the laws of its own nature);[50] and, on the contrary, to the extent that this State fails to preserve what is useful, its being, its right, diminishes (and thus it is doomed to heteronomy). The subject of autonomy, then, is not the power (*pouvoir*) of a sovereign conscience against desire. Rather, it is desire itself (the multitude as Desire) that exercises authority as reason, towards the endless work of liberation from that which resists its absolute sovereignty in the social body as subject.[51] This work is the very practice of democracy, the teaching of science, moral education, and the constant struggle against prejudice, superstition, intolerance and fanaticism.

With the cycle of accumulation between the *naturans* and the *naturatum* we find the distance (without which this cycle would be impossible) already established in the human individual between the organic body and the desiring body, between the body of established society and the natural body of the institution. This is the necessary, unsurpassable gap of the paradoxical relationship by which an individual, like a society, is produced in and through organisation. Apart from the order of thought and the production of the adequate 'absolute' and 'perfect' idea, this organisation cannot radically realise itself in the infinity of its immanent cause, but it can realise itself there in an 'absolutely absolute' way without contradiction. Just as a body is not alienated by its organisation when its health is confirmed by the perfection of its organisation, so a body politic is not alienated by its institutions when they effectively ensure concord and peace within it. If there is aliena-

---

[50] *Ethics* IV, 35 cor. 2.

[51] Except for the Monarchomachs (to whom we will return), before Spinoza the dominant idea of sovereignty (and absolute sovereignty) is related to the idea of the sovereign's political domination over the 'savage' multitude and over its natural power. The caveat is to make this domination 'absolute', to give the sovereign unlimited control (even over hearts: Hobbes, Richelieu). Spinoza unshackles the idea of absolute sovereignty from the phantasmic idea of an unlimited mastery of the multitude, to assert absolute sovereignty in an immanent logic of the autonomous self-organisation of the collective body. Sovereignty-autonomy versus sovereignty-mastery, such is the dyad opened by Spinoza; and it is only according to the first that the idea of 'absolute' sovereignty does indeed find its rational fullness of meaning. But the latter, far from giving in to the fantasy of unlimited mastery, on the contrary affirms the self-limitation of the multitude, and thereby the self-mastery that is the main guarantee of the freedom of citizens and of stability of the State.

tion, it is indeed found in this relation, but since it expresses the movement of the self-affirmation of the social *conatus*, its radical positivity, it is not the relation itself that alienates. Alienation, conversely, is the result of a society's inability to combine all its forces. This leads to a political organisation whose rationality diminishes, as does the right or power to guarantee concord and peace.

The real self-restraint that arises from the relationship between the *naturans* and the *naturatum* must not be confused with the alienation according to which a society is separated from its own forces. The alienated (heteronomous) society, which misunderstands itself as self-organising, cannot recognise its own self-limitation because of this fact. If it recognises a limit, it is in the form of an entity that society appears to be external and transcendent to its own activity (Nature, reason, God). As in the case of a perfect theocracy, it may also tend, through education from childhood, to erase the sense of limitation in its subjects and even rid them of it altogether. Thus, for those who would only desire what is allowed and for whom what is prohibited no longer has any temptation, to obey Nature, reason or God is to be free (or to think oneself free).

A truly free society recognises its own limits with complete clarity, in the very act by which it is founded. It establishes its own criteria for determining good and bad, just and unjust, without anything outside itself ever being able to guarantee the truth of what it posits as true, the justice of what it considers right, or the validity of what it prescribes as good. Since a true idea involves knowledge of its own standard, a democratic society knows that it is *index sui*, autonomous. A democratic society knows that it can and must rely only on its own strength, that its only guarantees are, first, its ability to regulate itself, to create for itself those institutions, which (at best) guarantee the rational behaviour of the social body by preventing excessive passions. The passion for freedom that underlies democracy is the only exception, since it cannot, by nature, be excessive. Secondly, its other guarantee lies in its capacity to shape the minds of its subjects, to instil the democratic spirit in the hearts and mores of a people: the ultimate function of education.

Although the first institutional point is of great importance, Spinoza knows only too well that laws are rarely effective when social passions are unleashed, and that in the face of the anti-democratic zeal of a section of the population, we must rely not on institutions, but on the power of the multitude to defend them. This resistance – the natural law against the law (and logic) of war enacted by the rebels – will be proportional to the desire of the 'masses' for democracy, for freedom and equality as common objects of love. This law 'which is defined by the power of the multitude'[52] takes precedence over the law instituted as a representation. The effective power of the multitude takes precedence over institutions, which (like ideas) are only functional and adequate if they are not disconnected from their cause. Otherwise, institutions are nothing more than abstractions or ink stains on a piece of paper, that is, traces of impotence. For Spinoza, freedom is not affirmed and defended from the point of view of institutions and their legitimacy. Rather, freedom is affirmed and defended from the point of view of the power of the movement of reality that produces institutions. This is an ontogenetic view that belongs to the law of nature (power) rather than to the law of authority.[53] This brings us back to our first reflections on obedience.

2 Resistance Makes the Citizen

Obedience is central to any society. Yet we cannot equate the state of the obedient subject of a free republic with tyranny! The human individual is natively powerless and maladjusted, and all her efforts are aimed (in and through representation) at adapting herself to the world, or at adapting the world to herself by constituting it. In a politically organised society, the society itself builds the conformist, obedient, social individual. In a tyrannical State, the sovereign wants this conformity to be perfect. But, except for barbarians, who are completely without reason, and under exceptional conditions, this construction of automata remains an ideal but contradictory limit of obedience.

Since automation is the sign (and the result) of an integral transfer of an individual's natural right to the sovereign, it is ideal only in appearance, and, as we shall see, is impossible. It is contradictory because it is difficult to speak of obedience when the automation of the subject is total. Can we still speak of a human subject at all? Does not the animal act with an expanded consciousness of its actions or even without consciousness at all, in the same

---

[52] TP II, 17; CWS II, 514.

[53] On the repetitions of the terms *jus* and *lex* in the TP (clearly in favour of *jus* – 335 against 84), see Pierre-François Moreau, 'Spinoza, nouvelles approches textuelles', *Raison présente*, 43, Paris 1978. On this, see also Negri, who contrasts right with law as *potentia* with *potestas*, *Savage Anomaly*, pp. 190–1. The constitutive power of the multitude thus triumphs over the formalism of the law. But we must also understand (which Negri does not say) that the law itself, in the imaginary representation of the juridico-political sphere, is the necessary mediation of the power of the multitude in its affirmation and the symptom of its present condition.

way and in perfect adaptation to its conditions of existence? It seems not. First, obedience is 'a constant will (*constans voluntas*) to do what by law is good and what the common decree says ought to be done'.[54] It thus implies a relation to an explicit external law and thus a 'will' of the social subject to submit to this law or to circumvent it, depending on her relationship to reality, which is distributed in a field of 'possibilities'.[55] Secondly, the human subject is defined by her use of reason, not as a capacity to adapt (animals also have this kind of reason), but as a capacity to judge what is true and false, just and unjust, good and evil. Thus, she can determine her actions depending on the representation of a law that her will may or may not follow, a law that takes on a reflected meaning and value for the subject in relation to her.[56]

Spinoza is not Hobbes. For Hobbes, when the human subject's practical rationality is ideally (that is, adequately) employed for its own ends, it is identified with the subject as an obedient automaton. For Hobbes, who remains a prisoner of the idealist problematic of *praxis* that Spinoza criticises at the beginning of the *TP*, the perfect use of reason lies in the perfect expression it can produce through the calculation of her interest, properly understood. The complete reduction of reflection to a natural law necessarily points to the proper utility of a given thing, which by its nature cannot conflict with the advantage of the sovereign.[57] Natural law, which Hobbes postulates to lie at the heart of human nature and by which subjects can become perfect automata through reason, renders the State useless. This is the limit and contradiction inherent in any notion of total political obedience (and/or the unlimited domination of power) conceived as an inner submission that must not be confused with the full consent of the mind as an activity and outcome of rational and critical reflection. In Hobbes, the social success of the thinking subject consists precisely in her disappearance into automation. The rational subject is the functional subject, the automaton completely subjected to the ends of sovereignty, whose strategy (or teleology) is even more perfect when it is adapted *a priori* to its political

---

[54] *TP* II, 19; *CWS* II, 515.
[55] *TTP* IV; *CWS* II, 126.
[56] This has been well explained by Etienne Balibar in 'Jus–Pactum–Lex', *Studia Spinozana*, 1, 1985, pp. 123–4.
[57] See Alexandre Matheron, 'Spinoza and the Breakdown of Thomist Politics: Machiavellianism and Utopia', in *Politics, Ontology and Knowledge in Spinoza*, Edinburgh University Press, 2022; André Tosel, 'La Théorie de la pratique et la fonction de l'opinion publique dans la philosophie politique de Spinoza', *Studia Spinozana*, 1, 1985, pp. 194–5.

conditions of existence. Hence, in Hobbesian society, the importance of political education, which must convince subjects of the truth of Hobbes's political science and reduce the public space of diverse expression to one of propaganda. To convince or to educate in Hobbes, from the Spinozist point of view, is to restrict:

> Anyone who wants to introduce a sound doctrine has to be in with the Universities [*Academiae*]. That is where the foundations of civil doctrine, which are true and truly demonstrated, have to be laid; after the young men are steeped in them, they can instruct the common people in private and in public. The more certain they are of the truth of what they teach and preach, the more vigorously and forcefully they will do so. For as everyday exposure has given current acceptance to propositions which are false and no more intelligible than if you took words by lot from an urn and strung them together, how much more would men imbibe true doctrines conforming to their own understanding and to the nature of things, if they were similarly exposed to them. I hold therefore that it is a duty of sovereigns to have the true Elements of civil doctrine written and to order that it be taught in all the Universities in the commonwealth.[58]

Whether through the 'reasons, clear and strong' of 'science' (Hobbes) or the word of God (Moses and the Hebrew State), through pedagogical 'talent' and rational persuasion or the systematic training that leads to superstitious submission, when truth imposes itself on subjects in an institutional, domineering and transcendent way, the political subject of obedience is reduced to the state of an automaton.

When the subject's reflection is functionally and politically automated, her consciousness is thoroughly illusory in its perfect social adaptation, and her reason is reduced to instrumental use. The subject's self-perception is the site of a fundamental misunderstanding of her own functioning, even – or especially – when nurtured by the political science of Hobbes. Functionalised reflexivity stems from a strategic logic of the social subject that is itself not adequately reflected. The constitutive reflexivity of ethical subjectivity, on the other hand, is a reflection on a thoughtless functional reflection. Apart from the illusion, which can certainly multiply the contradictory standpoints of opinions, critical reflection can only take place from the true stand-

---

[58] Thomas Hobbes, *On the Citizen*, trans. R. Tuck and M. Silverthorne, Cambridge University Press 2003, II, XIII, 9, pp. 146–7.

point of the adequate idea of the human *conatus* in its ordering, imaginative and strategic nature.

On the opposite side of the practical subject of obedience, then, we find the ethical subject whose object of desire (endowed with meaning and value) is truth. Certainly, we can only very improperly 'call a rational life obedience'.[59] The ethical subject is not an obedient subject, but only a social subject confronted with the laws of a particular society. The subject of a free republic, on the other hand, like the ethical subject, is defined by her reason and power of judgement. And in the citizen *par excellence*, her power is critical reflexivity. Also,

> if someone shows that a law is contrary to sound reason, and therefore thinks it ought to be repealed, if at the same time he submits his opinion to the judgment of the supreme power (to whom alone it belongs to make and repeal laws), and in the meantime does nothing contrary to what that law prescribes, he truly deserves well of the republic, as one of its best citizens . . . *ut optimus quisque civis*.[60]

It is this specifically human subjectivity that Spinoza, in contrast to the reflexivity of functionality, sees as incompressible.

> For example, no one can surrender his ability to judge. For what rewards or threats can induce a man to believe that the whole is not greater than its part? or that God does not exist? or that a body which he sees to be finite is an infinite Being? or to believe absolutely anything else contrary to what he thinks or is aware of? Similarly, by what rewards or threats can a man be induced to love what he hates or to hate what he loves? In this category we may put those things which human nature so abhors that it considers them worse than any other evil, as that a man should act as a witness against himself, that he should torture himself, that he should kill his parents, that he should not strive to avoid death, and the like, which no one can be induced to do by rewards or threats.[61]

---

[59] *TP* II, 20; *CWS* II, 515. Here again Spinoza's opposition to Hobbes is radical. Teaching, even the truth, is nothing else for the author of *Leviathan* than a 'sign of our obedience'. For Spinoza, teaching is an act of pure independence that is done 'at the risk of one's own resources and reputation' (*TP* VIII, 49; *CWS* II, 588. See also *Ep*. XLVIII [to Louis Fabritius]).
[60] *TTP* XX, 15; *CWS* II, 347.
[61] *TP* III, 8; *CWS* II, 520.

This is the irreducibility of a power or an absolute right that resists any transfer:

> No one will ever be able to transfer to another his power, or consequently, his right, in such a way that he ceases to be a man. And there will never be a supreme power who can get everything to happen just as he wishes.[62]

Even in the Hebrew State, which came as close as possible to a complete automation of the subject of obedience, Moses, and thus the law, could not escape criticism:

> But whatever ingenuity has been able to achieve in this matter, it has never reached the point where men do not learn from experience that each person is plentifully supplied with his own faculty of judgment and that men's minds differ as much as their palates do. Though Moses had gotten the greatest prior control of the judgment of his people, not by deception, but by a divine virtue, with the result that he was believed to be divine, and to speak and do everything by divine inspiration, still he was not able to escape murmuring and perverse interpretations. Much less are other Monarchs able to do this. If this were conceivable at all, it would be in a monarchic State, not in a democratic one, where all the people, or a great many of them, govern as a body. I think the reason for this is evident to everyone.[63]

Criticism coming from an obedient subject is neither always strictly rational (quite the contrary) nor always free from seditious thought (whether explicit or implicit). In its origin, at the heart of superstition, criticism is but an expression of the multiplicity and inconstancy of illusions that flatter the human mind.[64] However subject to the meanings it seems to deny, Spinoza regards this capacity to 'judge all things'[65] as a 'natural right' that the State cannot suppress without putting itself in danger. In its extreme variety, as in its nature, 'freedom of judgment is' therefore 'undoubtedly a virtue'.[66] It is both an inherent power of human nature and the foundation of the absolute

---

[62] *TTP* XVII, 2; CWS II, 296.
[63] *TTP* XX, 5; CWS II, 345.
[64] *TTP*, Praef.
[65] *TTP* XX.
[66] CWS II, 349. Translator's note.

State whose freedom (in its diversity of expression) constitutes its very substance.[67] This 'natural right, *or* faculty, of reasoning freely, and of judging concerning anything whatever',[68] can indeed only belong to a conquest and a historical production – that is, if by freedom one understands not only the relative independence of one's prejudices from those of the sovereign, but the actual power to judge the law from the standpoint of reason. Hence Spinoza's admirable reply to those who foolishly despise the multitude,

> who think the vices common to all mortals belong only to the plebeians. Finally, it's no surprise that 'there's neither truth nor judgment in the plebeians' when the rulers manage the chief business of the State secretly, and the plebeians are only making a guess from the few things the rulers can't conceal. To suspend judgment is a rare virtue. So, it's sheer stupidity to want to do everything in secrecy, and then expect the citizens not to judge the government's actions wrongly, and not to interpret everything perversely. If the plebeians could restrain themselves, and suspend judgment on matters they know little about, or judge things correctly from scanty information, they would be more worthy to rule than to be ruled.[69]

The construction of the State subject *par excellence* can thus only be the result of institutions and education. It is a historical task to enable the State to achieve its own end, which is not domination but freedom. Its task is not to produce (more or less regulated) automatons but real human subjects capable of building together a society of harmony and peace, an autonomous society in which all citizens participate effectively in the political constitution.[70] The dynamics of life in its affirmative essence and in its fierce resistance to all forms of oppression confirms this: humans cannot long be kept in the state of brutish animals or automatons. '[T]he more the authorities try to take away this freedom of speech, the more stubbornly men will resist', with the same vivacity that resists sadness in all, for 'the greater the Sadness, the greater the power of acting with which the man will strive to remove the Sadness'.[71] Tyranny, like sadness, is fundamentally opposed to nature . . . unless it indirectly causes some joys through the sad paradox of servitude. We already know that 'bad' joys trap the subject in her helplessness

---

[67] *TTP* XX.
[68] *TTP* XX; CWS II, 344.
[69] *TP* VII, 27; CWS II, 558–9.
[70] *TTP* XX.
[71] *Ethics* III, 37 Dem.; *TTP* XX; CWS II, 515, 349.

and prejudices.[72] The *TTP* teaches us that 'the greedy, the flatterers and other men without moral force, for whom the supreme salvation consists in contemplating crowns in a casket and having their stomachs too full',[73] will offer no resistance and will live 'in contentment and happiness … blooming of their almost animal nature'.[74] The only resistance will come from those 'whom a good education, integrity of character, and virtue have made more free';[75] those who have been prepared by historical and social circumstances for such resistance by loving truth and freedom above all else, and who, thereby, in order to defend the values to which they are intimately attached (because they constitute the meaning of their existence), will not fear death.

Spinoza claims that 'the most natural state', which consists in the free exercise of judgement and speech, is a historical product. So,

> people who know themselves to be honourable don't, like criminals, fear death or plead to be excused from punishment; they're not tormented by repentance for a shameful deed; on the contrary, they think it honourable, not a punishment, to die for a good cause, and glorious to die for freedom. What kind of precedent is established by the death of such men, whose cause those lacking in spirit and weak-minded know nothing about, whose cause the seditious hate, whose cause the honourable love? No one can take any example from this death, except to imitate it, or else to be a flatterer.[76]

The philosopher, like society as a whole, is thus charged with the task of educating 'men of fortitude' (*viros ingenuos*)[77] out of love for truth and freedom: citizens capable of outrage and resistance against all powers of oppression and inhumanity. Such citizens are able, by their righteousness and courage, to evoke the admiration of the people and the shame of tyrants. Moreover, by their example they arouse the indignation of all and bring down ambition and fanaticism. The political task of the philosopher, like that of society as a whole, is thus to produce a loving subject whose object and source of joy is truth and freedom. This subject derives its meaning and value from desire, which constitutes truth and freedom as the object of love

---

[72] *Ethics* IV, 59 Dem.
[73] *TTP* XX; CWS II, 349.
[74] *Ethics* III, 57 Schol.; CWS I, 528.
[75] *TTP* XX; CWS II, 349.
[76] *TTP* XX; CWS II, 351.
[77] Translation modified. *TTP* XX; CWS II, 350.

and the cause of joy. Truth and freedom, however, are only recognised in the realm of the imaginary as object, cause, value and meaning. They can be desired by a subject only as value and meaning, as *bona causa*, which are nevertheless 'good' and 'cause' only according to the movement of desire directed towards a thing by constituting it. The process of the imagination is also one of loving recognition.

That freedom and truth can be objects of investment of desire for people indicates that they are not simple abstractions. Rather, they are values constitutive of ordinary life, a 'truly human' life, a truly human *habitus*, which gives them a powerful joy, superior to all other joys, and an even stronger passion to live freely loving the truth. Crucially at stake within any society, then, is education. Because it is dangerous to seek to regulate everything through laws, education occupies an essential place in a free republic:

> Anyone who wants to limit everything by laws will provoke more vices than he'll correct. What can't be prohibited must be granted, even if it often leads to harm.[78]

How can we reduce this 'price' of freedom as much as possible? Freedom itself offers the means to fight against its own harmful consequences. Grounded in adequate ideas and critical reflection, teaching that works within the domain of the exercise of freedom instituted by the State is open to the expression of the most diverse opinions and to the formation of free public opinion. Philosophy must, thus, 1) defend – and, we should say, produce – this open field of the diversity of ideas, without which it would not itself be possible. Because 'a thought is limited by another thought',[79] the political problem, for both bodies and ideas, is a problem of the space to be produced, liberated and defended. The historical necessity of ideological struggle is to conquer new terrain for thought. Hence, also the need for strategy, a term that refers to a conquest of space, the public space of the free expression of opinions. 2) Philosophy must develop at the heart of this same field, necessarily traversed by contradictory forces (because it is the ground of confrontation of opinions and interests), singular forces of analysis, criticism, resistance and indignation. It must face those who wish to reduce the space for the social expression of opinions to the closed field of their superstition alone, to degree zero of critical reflection, the most favourable ground for the formation of an automaton subject.

---

[78] *TTP* XX; *CWS* II, 328.
[79] *Ethics* I, Def. 2; *CWS* I, 408.

The dynamism of an adequate strategy of *multitudinis potentia* presupposes the existence of this double necessity within the State: the free expression of opinions that must lead to a consensual decision with the help of institutions. It leads to teaching that does not allow the confrontation of opinions to drift into confusion and ultimately to the powerlessness to decide and act. The critical educational enterprise must neutralise the forces that want to suppress the free confrontation of opinions, strengthen the love of freedom and the reasoning skills of everyone, and accelerate the process of building the most suitable solutions.

For Spinoza, the necessary formation of this critical public opinion, which in a sense must occupy and defend the (possible) space of freedom that the law leaves free (against the forces of ambition and fanaticism that demand laws and sanctions solely for the benefit of their sect and their interests), is the sign of the primacy of real power – the balance of power that permeates the multitude – over the law (which is ultimately only the institutionalised expression of these relations). The human future, a society that a philosopher might prescribe, can only be prepared by our powers of indignation, perseverance, courage and love: by the power of the 'example' of the 'free man' who, in the face of tyrannical rule, in complete agreement with himself and at the risk of his life, opposes honesty to deceit, pride to adulation, justice to corruption, honour to cunning, reason to violence, and finally the glory offered by the struggle for freedom to the 'shame' of the ruler corrupted into a tyrant.[80] Shame (*pudor*) – 'a Sadness, accompanied by the idea of some action [of ours] which we imagine that others blame'[81] and that, like repentance, 'depends chiefly on education'[82] – is a necessary affect in the constitution of the subject of obedience. For it is also shame that a subject must be able to feel when she disobeys orders worth obeying, and when she obeys unworthy orders which are a disgrace to the sovereign and provoke indignation. Indignation, then, corresponds to the shame involved in accepting a situation that is contrary to human nature, as expressed in the indignation and resistance of the most honest citizens who face it. Only when people with proud souls and independent character obey the laws with the full consent of their minds is society on the road to freedom. This, however, is a necessary but not a sufficient condition, for sometimes it is tactically more advantageous for freedom to allow itself to be conquered, to obey the tyrant outwardly, than to rebel at the most inopportune moment. The task of philosophy, then, like that of the free

---

[80] *TTP* XX.
[81] *Ethics* III, DA 31; CWS I, 538.
[82] *Ethics* III, DA 27 expl.; CWS I, 537.

republic, is not to produce obedient subjects adapted to a given society, but to train people who can resist the constraints which both the State and the various sects seeking supremacy wish to exert on their minds. It must produce people who are able to resist. Education, then, must both extend the function of the State and give citizens the power to resist it.

For Spinoza, the State, like the law, has not only the function of commanding and punishing, but also the function of encouraging people on the path to freedom and reason, so that 'their minds and bodies [perform] their functions safely'.[83] The pedagogical function of the law extends the education that a State must provide for its citizens. Although Spinoza presents the law as a substitute for reason – and as a means of constituting it in individuals who are unable to develop it in the state of nature – he is cautious about the education that a State can directly regulate:

> Academies supported at the expense of the State are instituted not so much to develop native abilities as to keep them in check. But in a free Republic both the arts and the sciences are cultivated best if permission to teach publicly is granted to anyone seeking it, at the risk of his own resources and reputation.[84]

If the law as such (apart from its rational content, which may be at odds with its function) structurally plays a liberating role, the State as an educational enterprise is, in contrast, a coercive force. Both the *TP* and the *TTP* praise the diversity of opinions and teachings as a public space for the freedom of expression, where education can be exercised from the standpoint of reason. In contrast to the natural tendency of the doctrine of a particular Church or State to produce its own subject of obedience (even a 'rational' subject in the Hobbesian sense), this education creates a subject of society in general, that is, independent of its content, and about which this subject can reflect, criticise and even (in a democracy and with her fellow citizens) change. This education, however, produces a *habitus*, a reflex to resist any form of automation (subjugation) that trains people without their knowledge to fight for their servitude as if it were their salvation, and typically leads them into such blindness that they forget their human nature. The habit of examining, listening to others' opinions, considering and thinking critically is the *habitus* of freedom.[85]

---

[83] *TTP* XX; *CWS* II, 346.
[84] *TP* VIII, 49; *CWS* II, 588.
[85] ... *passiones domare, sive virtutis habitum acquirere*. *TTP* III; *CWS* II, 113.

Spinoza praises the educational function at the heart of a free republic.[86] The *TTP* is not a party programme to rally citizens behind a new opinion. Its purpose is not to educate citizens, but to prevent them from being imprisoned against their will. In a free republic, the best education is an ethics of resistance.[87]

But this cannot be abstract, detached from the culture of a particular nation, detached from its history. Since honour, envy, shame and repentance are also products of education,[88] the question of mores must be understood for Spinoza as a political question. This perspective sheds light on Spinoza's struggle, which is at the centre of the culture of his time. The struggle is based on a paradox. If one grounds the formation of the absolute subject of obedience in the love of freedom and thus in the impossibility of a complete transfer of agency from the individual to the State, one affirms, by virtue of this constraint, an 'absolutely absolute', autonomous subject-State. The complete transfer of the individual's agency to the State is impossible because the subject's right to critical reflection – her ability to resist the logic of unlimited submission to the State – is incompressible. Spinoza calls this impossibility 'natural', but it must nevertheless be inculcated and taught. In short, it must be historically produced.

The strategy *par excellence* of the political *conatus*, or *multitudinis potentia*, is understood as the free and necessary movement of the self-constitution of society as a body, when this movement has its origin in the real and plural exercise of the freedom of judgement and speech of its subjects. The power of the multitude is the positive condition for the constitution of law, its actual and actualising productive essence. Indeed, the law is the power of the majority only because it *de facto* constitutes this majority in its actual power.[89] The constitution of the juridical-political body is not initially the result of a contract between individuals who are supposed to be free and act voluntarily (even if the idea of the contract remains only a historical project corresponding to the formation of an autonomous subject). It is a physical, quantitative, consensual, historical process through which the always-already social body of the multitude passes to a higher organisa-

---

[86] *TTP*, end of XX.

[87] 'The constitution of a *habitus* of justice and charity', to use the expression of Henri Laux (*Imagination et religion chez Spinoza. La potentia dans l'histoire*, Vrin, 1993, p. 210), is part, for me, of an ethics of resistance. See Laurent Bove, 'Enseignement du Christ et résistance dans le *T.T.P.*', in *La Bible et ses raisons*, publications de l'Université de Saint-Etienne, 1996.

[88] *Ethics* III, 55 Schol.

[89] As Antonio Negri writes in *The Savage Anomaly*.

tion, according to a logic of self-affirmation that resists the external[90] and internal[91] forces that seek to dissolve it. The process belongs to the collective itself, as a multitude, in its majoritarian constitution, its collective majority and political self-organisation. The majority is not that of a political party or a governing coalition. Rather, it is the consensual majority that constitutes the very existence of the social body, its persistence in being. The obedient majority, the majority of consent, can tend towards a true majority of the contract in a society where this consent attains a rational self-consciousness corresponding to the free exercise of the will of all. The contract is nothing other than the 'name' of the critical, reflected, willed consent through which subjects individually and collectively reappropriate their singular histories. Through this operation, the collective subject (as *cupiditas*) tends to fully occupy the practical-subject structure of the State. It strives to achieve the harmony of essence and existence through which it affirms its absolute sovereignty. Therefore, the definitions of 'just' and 'unjust' correspond to the definitions of 'legal' and 'illegal'. The just and the unjust are only conceivable within the State.[92] They represent open values, historical achievements. It is not positivism (as with Hobbes), but rather the understanding of civil law as the power of the multitude.

The tension inherent in democracy is more perfect – absolute – because it is constituted according to a critical consensus on the borderline between obedience and revolution. The more democratic a State is, the more it constitutes itself at the extreme limit of its own possible destruction. And precisely because it is so perfect, destructive turmoil is all the less to be feared. Conversely, the less democratic a State is, the more it moves away from the theoretical limit at which obedience might enter a crisis (especially among the best, because their resistance to the established imaginary, their critical minds and their love of freedom and justice are so strong), and paradoxically, the more prone this State is to sedition and crime. Democracy – the real movement that constitutes collective reality as freedom or autonomy – thus lives from the power of critique and resistance against the established society, its established imaginary and/or its own logic of subjugation. This means that democracy, like any State, cannot be defined only by institutions or a particular organisation (that is, a legal-political State that necessarily includes its own structures of subjugation or power). It is essentially dynamic, or rather, democracy is the dynamic and contradictory essence of collective

---

[90] *TP* II, 15.
[91] *TP* VI, 2, 3, 6.
[92] *TP* III, 5.

reality. It explicitly affirms conflict as the very modality of existence: the confrontation between forces and opinions, between established power and dissenting opinions, between the logic of power and the logic of the multitude (although *a priori* there is no good democratic side to contradiction!). What Spinoza writes about cities in a non-centralised aristocratic State also applies to human individuals, who, as we know, 'are by nature enemies, so that they retain this nature even when they are united and bound by laws':[93] 'It does not matter' that every

> city consults its own interest and is jealous of the others, they frequently quarrel with one another and waste time arguing. Some will remind us of the saying 'while the Romans deliberate, Saguntum is lost.' On the other hand, when the few decide everything, simply on the basis of their own affects, freedom and the common good are lost. For human wits are too sluggish to penetrate everything right away. But by asking advice, listening, and arguing, they're sharpened. When people try all means, in the end they find ways to the things they want which everyone approves, and no one had ever thought of before.[94]

By praising exchange and, above all, resistance and discord, Spinoza rediscovers constitutive power after Machiavelli's *Discourses on Livy*.[95] Democracy as an absolute affirmation of the power of the multitude is a positive power of openness and movement. As an adequate idea of political life, it is an open truth about (and in) an infinite history. As a process, it is the very essence of the social in its necessary historicity. It is the open process of adequacy (of essence and existence) in constant progress, by virtue of an infinite perfection. The self-organisation of collective reality as a 'subject' in and through history is this open process of exchange, resistance and contradiction. Democracy as a movement towards the realisation of freedom never ceases, except – like revolution itself, to use Saint-Just's beautiful expression – 'at the perfection of happiness', when all obstacles to the full development of ordinary life have been overcome, when all the human power of the collective body is fully developed, without abandonment or loss.

---

[93] TP VIII, 12; CWS II, 570.
[94] TP IX, 14; CWS II, 594.
[95] *Discourses on Livy*, Book I, chs III–IV.

3 Resistance as a Sovereign and Eternal Right

The power of resistance is at the heart of history and democracy. In what sense is this power also a 'right'? Let us first note that the key events in the elaboration of the concept of the 'right of resistance' are simultaneously theological and political: the Peasants' War in Germany, the Dutch War of Liberation against Catholic Spain, Saint-Barthelemy in France ... and finally – although the century is almost over and John Locke's *Second Treatise* dates from 1690 – the English Revolution.

3.1 The Ephors' Right of Resistance: From the Monarchomachs to the Political Treatise

At the beginning of the sixteenth century, in contrast to the theory of the divine right of kings – for which the writings of St Paul served as a basis[96] and to which Luther remained faithful[97] – Thomas Müntzer invoked a heavenly 'natural right' to justify the rebellion of the peasants against their lords, which was not respected by the rulers.[98] The theocratic spirit of Müntzer's preaching and theology remains essentially archaic despite its actual rebellious power. The idea of a right to resist tyranny will only take on a new consistency and meaning with the more secular spirit of the contract.

Indeed, a few decades later, because of contract theory, some provinces of the northern Netherlands legitimised the proclamation (22 July 1581) of the forfeiture of the sovereignty of the King of Spain over the Batavians with the right to resist the tyrant (in this case Philip II). Because of the

---

[96] The text referred to is, of course, the Epistle to the Romans 13:1–7.
[97] See H. T. Lehmann and J. Atkinson, eds, *Luther's Works*, Volume 45: *The Christian in Society*, 2, Fortress Press, 1962. Calvin's position is in principle the same, albeit with significant nuances, since Calvin legitimises resistance to the tyrant when there are 'Magistrates Constitute for the defense of the people to curb the excessive greed and license of the Kings, as formerly the Lacedaemonians had those they called Ephors...'. *Institutions of the Christian Religion*, p. 782 of the ed. of 1541 reprinted under the direction of Abel Lefranc. On Calvinism and the right of resistance to the State, see L. Arenilla, who studies Calvin's position in 'Le calvinisme et le droit de résistance à l'État', *Annales: Economies, sociétés, civilisations*, 22.2, 1967, pp. 350–69 (pp. 360–6).
[98] See Ernst Bloch, *Thomas Münzer als Theologe der Revolution*, 1855. Let us note how much Spinoza mistrusts those who invest themselves as 'accredited defenders of religion' (*TP* III, 10). This position is already that of Hobbes, who refuses any legitimacy to the theological reference that gives a right of resistance to the prince, *Leviathan*, ch. 21. On this question, see Pierre-François Moreau's analysis, *Hobbes: Philosophie, science, religion*, PUF Philosophies, 1989, pp. 78, 95, 102–3.

same principle and against the background of 'natural law', Hugo Grotius can write that it is right to fight a king 'who acknowledges that he is an enemy of the whole people, [and precisely by doing so] renounces his kingdom'.[99] But the concept of a 'right of resistance' had previously been coined, especially in the writings of the Huguenots after the St Barthelemy massacre. Among the many writings of those whom William Barclay would call 'Monarchomachs',[100] the *Vindiciae contra tyrannos* (dated 1579) by Philippe Du Plessis-Mornay (adviser to the Prince of Orange and to the rebels of the Netherlands) is undoubtedly the first to clearly express a theory of the right of resistance that is part of an explicit philosophy of the social contract. Without questioning the fundamental authority of divine right, Du Plessis-Mornay writes:

> We read two kinds of covenants at the coronation of Kings: the first between God, the King, and the people, that the people would be a people of God; the second between the King and the people, that the people would faithfully obey the King, who would command justly.[101]

The sovereign is bound by a double contract that bases his legitimacy not only on the will of God but also on the people. The people exchange their obedience to the sovereign for his obligation to protect them, to guarantee them security and, in general, to work 'honestly' for the common good.[102]

---

[99] This is, however, according to Grotius, an exceptional case; Hugo Grotius, *The Rights of War and Peace*, ed. Stephen C. Neff, Cambridge University Press, 2012, Book I, ch. IV, 11, p. 73. On the political theories of the Calvinists in the Netherlands at the end of the sixteenth and beginning of the seventeenth centuries, see Ch. Mercier, 'Les théories politiques des calvinistes dans les Pays-Bas', *Revue d'histoire ecclésiastique*, 29, 1933, pp. 25–73. On the different stages of the liberation process and the accompanying legal-political justifications, see especially pp. 28–36.

[100] William Barclay, *De regno et regali potestate, adversus Buchananum, Brutum, Boucherium et reliquos Monarchomaquos*, 1600.

[101] Translator's note: the text of the *Vindiciae contra tyrannos* was translated into French in 1581 under the title *De la puissance légitime du prince sur le peuple et du peuple sur le prince*. A facsimile reproduction of this translation was produced by Droz, 1979. Bove quotes from this edition, and I translated directly from the French.

[102] For 'no man was ever born with a crown on his head and a sceptre in his hand, that no man can be king by himself, or rule without a people; and that, on the contrary, the people can be a people without having a king, and long before they had kings, it is very certain that all kings were first instituted by the people', *Vindiciae contra tyrannos*, p. 102. Note that it was Du Plessis-Mornay who was commissioned by the States General of the Netherlands to present to the Diet of Augsburg the right of the States to depose Philip II, on the legal basis of a breach of treaty for which the King

If the king breaks this contract, he loses his legitimacy, betrays both God and his people, and thereby provokes the righteous resistance of his subjects, who, when a king becomes a tyrant, have not only the right but also the 'duty' to revolt. It is a duty to sanction the abuses of a king who has rebelled against God by becoming a traitor and a tyrant! In this sense, even insurrectionary resistance is not revolutionary in the social contract theory on which it is based; on the contrary, it is essentially conservative. Social contract theory legitimises resistance to the tyrant by reversing the roles. The people and their right to resist (a true divine right), even their right to assassinate the tyrant, become the true guarantors of the monarchical order desired by God. And this guarantee, writes Du Plessis-Mornay, must be constitutional. Against madness and tyrannical treachery, popular revolt is a defence of stability, an attempt to return to the old, legitimate order. The right to resist is part of a logic of conformity, an attempt to restore the order (divine and human) established by the contract willed by God and unlawfully violated by the tyrant. It is a recourse to a principle that – like the divine right of kings and those who worship it – exists only in the theological-political imagination of the Monarchomachs!

But that does not prevent this principle from having very real implications. A true political realism emerges from these considerations when a politician such as Johannes Althusius (in chapter 38 of his *Politica methodice digesta*) develops a detailed theory of the constitutional practice of the right to resist.[103] We are, it seems, very close to Spinoza. For Althusius, it is not so much a matter of justifying or legitimising the right to resist morally or legally (although that is also the point), but rather of 1) really conceiving the right to resist as an inescapable phenomenon of 'consociation'[104] that

and his agents were solely responsible. See the commentary by Mercier, 'Les théories politiques des calvinistes', pp. 48–51.

[103] Chapter 38, titled 'Tyranny and its Remedies', did not appear in the 1603 and 1610 editions of *Politica*. It was added to the 1614 edition. This chapter has been translated into French by Marie-Héléne Belin and published in *Philosophie*, 4, November 1984, pp. 13–68, and was preceded by the translator's introduction entitled 'Souveraineté et droit de résistance', pp. 3–11. The French citations of Althusius are based on this translation. For a more detailed discussion of Althusius' position, see Laurent Bove, 'Spinoza et la question de la résistance', *l'Enseignement philosophique*, 5, May–June 1993, pp. 3–20.

[104] 'Consociation', in Belin's translation, from Althusius' creation *consociatio*, expresses the organic constitution of the social and political body. Belin writes in her introduction, 'I prefer "consociation" to "association" because it better captures the idea that, in Althusian political thinking, community comes first' ('Souveraineté et droit de résistance', p. 10, n. 15).

corresponds to the popular character of sovereign power and to the absurd (impossible) character of tyranny as a desire for unlimited rule; and 2) really constituting it in terms of a constitutional right as participation in sovereignty and its exercise. According to a logic of checks and balances, it is necessary to institutionalise the right to resist to save society from the state of war into which the tyrant has plunged it. For 'it is wiser and more prudent to prevent and avoid the danger than to try to push it back through an act of resistance. It is better to prevent than to be warned, and better to apply the remedy before the tyranny is complete and incurable.' This is the practical conclusion of Althusius.[105]

As a thinker of sovereign power, which is an inalienable property of the multitude, Spinoza is part of this political lineage. The *multitudo* is the specific modality of political reality constituting itself, in its tension, as a 'nation', as a 'people' or a 'State'.[106] Above all, the Althusian concern for checks and balances seems to follow the same logic of constitutional construction in the *TP*. Indeed,

> For [a State] to be able to last, its affairs must be so ordered that, whether the people who administer them are led by reason or by an affect, they can't be induced to be disloyal or to act badly.[107]

That is, the 'administrators' of the State cannot become 'dominators' of the State.[108] This healthy limit to which the administration of the State must be subjected lies in the various institutionalised forms that make possible the effective exercise of a right of resistance or opposition on the part of those who do not exercise power directly but who nevertheless 'possess' sovereignty:

> it's been necessary to set up a State, so that everyone – both those who rule and those who are ruled – does what's for the common well-being, whether they want to or not. That is, it's been necessary to set it up so that everyone is compelled to live according to the prescription of reason, whether of his own accord, or by force, or by necessity.[109]

---

[105] *Tyranny and its Remedies*, p. 68.
[106] TP II, 17.
[107] TP I, 6; CWS II, 506.
[108] See already in TTP XVII.
[109] TP VI, 3; CWS II, 532

But it is especially important to beware of rulers, and therefore they must first be muzzled:

> This happens if the affairs of the State are so arranged that nothing which concerns the common well-being is committed absolutely to the good faith of any one person. For no one is so alert that he doesn't sometimes lose focus; and no one has such a powerful and unimpaired mind that he is not sometimes broken down and apt to be overcome, especially when the greatest strength of character is needed. It's folly to require of someone else what no one can ask of himself, that he look out more for others than for himself, that he not be greedy, or envious, or ambitious, etc., especially when every day he has the strongest incentives to all the affects.[110]

When considering a monarchical regime and its ability to maintain concord and peace (which is possible after a Spinozist reform of a democratic nature), compared to a so-called 'absolute' monarchy which, contrary to what is believed, leads the sovereign to a regime of almost total heteronomy (in which he no longer subjects only to 'his own right') and the subjects to the wretched condition of slaves[111] – Spinoza observes:

> it's not at all contrary to practice for these laws to be so firmly established that not even the King himself can repeal them [. . .] And nowhere that I know is a Monarch elected absolutely, without any explicit conditions [. . .] If everything depended on the inconstant will of one man, nothing would be firmly established. If a Monarchic State is to be stable, it must be set up in such a way that everything is done, indeed, only according to the King's decree, i.e., that all law is the King's will, as it has been made known, but that not everything the King wills is law.[112]

To avoid a tyrannical slide of the monarchical State, the army of the kingdom must primarily consist of 'only [the] citizens, without exception, and not [any] others'.[113] An armed people above all, by the constant presence of its strength, demands and guarantees the loyalty of the king and the good exercise of the power for which the people have elected him. Armed 'citizens [remain] their own masters and protect their freedom'.[114]

[110] Ibid.
[111] *TP* VI, 8; *TP* VII, 14, end.
[112] *TP* VII, 1; *CWS* II, 544–5.
[113] *TP* VI, 10; *CWS* II, 535.
[114] *TP* VII, 17; *CWS* II, 552.

On the other hand, it is necessary to form a large assembly of citizens:[115]

> [Their first duty is] to defend the fundamental laws of the State and to give advice about the things to be done, so that the King may know what he must decree for the public good.[116]

So much so that the king, who had to choose among the opinions of the assembly, could not choose the minority opinion without having the people against him and risking rebellion, let alone deciding according to his own opinion against the advice of the whole assembly.[117]

The power of constitutional and armed resistance to tyrannical logic must be introduced in the reformed monarchical State so that

> the King is led by a fear of the multitude, perhaps to bind the greater part of the armed multitude to himself, or led by a nobility of spirit, to consult the public advantage, either he'll always endorse the opinion which has the most votes, i.e., (by §5), which is more useful to the majority, or he'll be anxious to reconcile, if possible, the inconsistent opinions brought to him, so that he draws everyone to himself. He'll direct all his energy to this end, so that they'll know by experience what they have in this one man, as much in peace as in war. Indeed, when he most looks after the common well-being of the multitude, he'll be most his own master, and will have the greatest control.[118]

As an example, Spinoza cites the Aragonese who, on the advice of the Pope, established 'a supreme council which would be an obstacle to the kings, as the Ephors were in Sparta, and would have an absolute right to settle quarrels which arose between the King and the citizens'.[119] With the reference to the law of the Ephors of Lacedaemon, we are as close as possible to the problem of the right of resistance as expounded by the Monarchomachs,[120] and

---

[115] *TP* VI, 15–30.
[116] *TP* VI, 17; *CWS* II, 537.
[117] *TP* VII, 5.
[118] *TP* VII, 11; *CWS* II, 549.
[119] *TP* VII, 30; *CWS* II, 561.
[120] The Prince of Orange also referred in his Apology to the law of the Ephors of Lacedaemon in response to the proscription promulgated against him by Philip II. Addressing the States General, the Prince of Orange declared that it was up to them and the great vassals of the kingdom to 'serve our dukes as the Ephors served their

all the more so because Spinoza has previously legitimised a right of ministers to disobey the orders of the monarch on the basis of the foundations of the State being 'the eternal decrees of the king'. This right of resistance is based on the incompatibility of these decrees with the fundamental laws of the State:

> For the fundamental principles of the State must be regarded as the eternal decrees of the King. Indeed, his ministers obey him completely if they refuse to carry out any commands he gives which are inconsistent with the fundamental principles of the State.[121]

It is the right (and duty) of the *optimates*.[122]

Despite their practical (and historical) proximity, the interest of Spinoza's position *vis-à-vis* the right of resistance lies less in how it resembles the problematic of Althusius (and, moreover, that of the Monarchomachian Protestants) than in how it differs from it.

3.2 The Right of War and the Collective Body's Active Resistance Strategy

The 'physical' Spinozist consensus that is constitutive of ordinary political life is not in reality a legal-moral contract between the people and the sovereign (even if it is imagined as such). If there is a consensus – the *de facto* obedience of subjects to the sovereign – it is only because the material conditions for obedience are presently met, and strong enough to induce subjects (voluntarily or by force) to obey or merely to submit:

> [W]hen certain circumstances are present, the subjects respect and fear the Commonwealth, and [...] when those circumstances are absent, this fear and respect are destroyed. When they're destroyed, so is the Commonwealth itself. So for the Commonwealth to be its own master, it's bound to maintain the causes of fear and respect. Otherwise it ceases to be a Commonwealth.[123]

---

king in Sparta, hold the royalty firmly in hand of their prince and make serve rightly whoever contravenes his oath'. See Mercier, 'Les théories politiques des calvinistes'.

[121] *TP* VII, 1; *CWS* II, 544.
[122] Translator's note: I decided to retain this technical term in the original Latin.
[123] *TP* IV, 4; *CWS* II, 526.

And certainly, from this consensual standpoint – whose material conditions of possibility must be renewed and maintained at every moment – Spinoza is above all the direct heir of Etienne de La Boétie. The author of the *Discourse on Voluntary Servitude* underlines, beyond any social contract theory, how the sovereign power of the multitude confers authority and power on the ruler on an instantaneous, consensual basis, which can also be withdrawn instantaneously. Obedience ceases as soon as the will to serve ceases (and, it should be added, as soon as the material and 'affective' conditions for accepting that submission cease to exist).[124] This replacement of the legal figure of the contract by a (punctual and material) consensus leads Spinoza to draw quite different consequences from the question of the right of resistance. He draws consequences that contradict the tradition of the Monarchomachs, leading him to develop a completely new political philosophy of resistance.

For the Monarchomachs, the king declares war on his own subjects by breaking his promise. So it is the king who opens the 'state of war' and turns his subjects into 'enemies'. The citizens (more precisely, the *optimates*) can and must respond to this aggression from a legal point of view (contract) and by virtue of the legitimacy (promise) of a 'right' that has its origin in the fundamental constitution of the State and whose essence is both legal and moral (even theological): resistance is both a right and a duty.

For Spinoza, on the other hand, the king's tyrannical logic cannot be understood in terms of a breach of contract or a violation of morality if he does not keep his word. Tyranny can only be understood in terms of the laws of the material conditions and the affects (desires and wills) governed by these laws. The logic of the desire to dominate tends in its unfolding (and the necessary blindness that accompanies it) to push the sovereign beyond the physical limit of what is presently tolerable for the subjects, due to their own ways of being affected, resulting from the laws of human nature in general and from the specific prejudices of a nation, its attachment to certain rules, values and so on. In this way, the tyrant's desire to dominate provokes the breaking of the consensus for (and by) the subjects, the limits varying according to time and place. But it is the subjects who initiate the

---

[124] I would need to cite a lot more of Etienne de La Boétie's *The Discourse of Voluntary Servitude*. Nevertheless, reminiscent of La Boétie, Alexandre Matheron quite rightly explains the transfer of power in Spinoza as something that, strictly speaking, does not exist. 'Spinoza et la problématique juridique de Grotius', *Philosophie*, 4, November 1984, pp. 87–8. See also, by the same author, 'La fonction théorique de la démocratie chez Spinoza et Hobbes', *Studia Spinozana*, 1, 1985, esp. p. 270, on Spinoza's philosophy of society.

state of war based on a right that is their natural right, a 'right of war' that consists solely in the effective power to resist tyrannical violence and to protect themselves by all available means. Physical or logical necessity is, therefore, for Spinoza, the objective and amoral characteristic of the process of resistance:

> For the rules and causes of fear and respect the Commonwealth is bound, for its own sake, to observe don't concern the civil Law, but the Law of nature. By §4 they can't be defended by the civil Law, but [only] by the Law of war. The only way the Commonwealth is bound by them is the way a man in the state of nature is bound to take care not to kill himself: to be able to be his own master, or not to be an enemy to himself, he must take care not to kill himself. This care, of course, is not obedience, but freedom of human nature.[125]

In the state of nature, people do everything to preserve themselves and cannot act against the preservation of their own existence. For these very reasons, sovereignty cannot be exercised absolutely, against laws (or against the foundation of the State) to which the majority of the people have historically adhered. Indeed,

> if that's the nature of these laws – that they can't be violated unless the strength of the Commonwealth is at the same time weakened, i.e., unless the general fear of most citizens is at the same time turned into indignation – by that very fact [of political weakness arising from general indignation] the Commonwealth is dissolved, and the contract is inoperative. So the contract is defended, not by the civil Law, but by the Law of war. So the sovereign is bound to observe the conditions of this contract for no other reason than a man in the state of nature is bound to take care not to kill himself, if he's not to be an enemy to himself.[126]

There is a tension between the *multitudinis potentia* (its self-preservation instinct) and the exercise of sovereignty that can become antagonistic. The power of the multitude is *de facto* a power of resistance to the exercise of sovereignty. The state of war is always latent at the heart of civil society and becomes explicit when the multitude experiences the exercise of sovereignty as an aggression: 'the King can't be deprived of his power of being the master

---

[125] *TP* IV, 5; *CWS* II, 527.
[126] *TP* IV, 6; *CWS* II, 528.

by civil right, but only by right of war – that is, his subjects are permitted only to repel his force by force'.[127] Consensus is thus broken not because of the legitimacy or legality of a right or even a duty, but because the situation has become physically and/or emotionally unbearable, because it is experienced with indignation, anger and outrage: there is a physical rift in the social fabric caused by violently opposed tensions.[128]

The act of resistance no longer concerns only those who have the right and the (constitutional) duty to revolt. It concerns all persons for whom the tyrant's misdeeds have turned 'fear and respect', which subjects normally have towards the sovereign, into 'indignation'. Beyond the legal quibbles with the Monarchomachs, and especially beyond the historical end of their political imagination, Spinoza unequivocally affirms that political sovereignty, by its very nature, belongs absolutely to the multitude. Sovereignty does not belong to this 'people', which is ultimately reduced to its representatives, or more precisely to those who have historically replaced them to the point of posing as its 'natural' representatives, but to the multitude itself, which by virtue of its natural power, its absolute and inalienable right to self-organisation, inherently possesses sovereignty.

In contrast to the legalistic illusion of Monarchomachs (even if it is weakened again in someone like Althusius by the precise practical regulations), Spinoza, on the other hand, claims that 'laws alone, taken by themselves, are powerless',[129] and that they 'don't really bind the sovereign'.[130] Laws are binding on the king or on those who administer the State only if they are accompanied by the control of an armed people and a powerful popular assembly to enforce them, as in the reformed monarchy in the *Political Treatise*. Hence the importance of the constant 'vigilance of the multitude' (*multitudinis vigilantia*),[131] which must be drawn like a *dictatoris gladius perpetuus* over the heads of those in power who are driven to tyranny by their ambition.[132] The only law to which the monarch can submit is the effective power of the people – their will and their power – to enforce compliance with the rules to which he is subject. And only under the threat of his own death – that is, the martial law that the multitude has to 'deprive him of

---

[127] TP VII, 30; CWS II, 562.
[128] This formulation comes from Antonio Negri, who in the conclusion to *The Savage Anomaly* speaks of a 'physics of resistance' underlying political constitution.
[129] TP VIII, 19; CWS II, 572.
[130] TP IV, 6; CWS II, 528.
[131] TP VIII, 4; CWS II, 567.
[132] TP X, 2; CWS II, 598.

his power'[133] – can he run the state rationally and in terms of the 'common good'.[134] If these material conditions (the separation of powers) are not met, the right of the sovereign goes so far – it is the state of nature! – that he too has the power to be effectively feared and respected and thus to win the obedience of his subjects. The only factual limit to the exercise of sovereignty is the resistance (also factual) of those for whom 'the laws of the State [are] worse than any evil'[135] and who break the consensus at the risk of their own lives. But with the life of the State, the sovereign, who has become a tyrant, exposes his own life to death. Following the logic of natural law, Spinoza treats the prince's 'treason' in terms of misconduct not only in state affairs but also in his own affairs. The ambition for domination leads the king to forget all 'prudence' (*quae sane cautio*)[136] and commit a fatal strategic error that arouses 'general hatred'[137] against him and causes his own downfall. Since he is not bound by any law, we cannot say (as the Monarchomachs do) that the ruler 'can sin'.[138] There is no sin or guilt except strategically, that is, against himself.[139] The lesson is Machiavellian and no longer that of the Monarchomachs.

On the one hand, the actions of the body politic and/or the actions of the sovereign and its (possible) logic of self-destruction (tyranny) can only be seen as absurd by natural law and in view of its own strategy of *conatus*. Indeed, tyranny develops a radically contradictory logic of self-affirmation. Strictly speaking, it is just as impossible to be a tyrant 'as to be and not be

---

[133] *TP* VII, 30; *CWS* II, 562.

[134] Spinoza has Machiavelli in mind, who writes that 'men never do any good unless by necessity' (*Discourses on Livy*, trans. Harvey C. Mansfield and Nathan Tarcov, University of Chicago Press, 1998, p. 15). Indeed, 'so great is the ambition of the great that it soon brings [a city] to its ruin if it is not beaten down in a city by various ways and various modes' (*Discourses on Livy*, p. 80). Mere trust in the good faith of rulers is folly and an obstacle to freedom (*TP* VI, 3). On the contrary, the people's distrust of those in power (or rather the caution that requires the necessary clarity for self-preservation: 'to be armed' for Machiavelli or 'to be on guard' for Spinoza) is a fundamental value of freedom and democracy; it is a recurring theme in the *Discourses*, recalled in the *Political Treatise*. On the 'theoretical importance of vigilance', see Geneviève Brykman, *La Judéité de Spinoza*, Vrin, 1972, pp. 95–7.

[135] *TP* III, 8; *CWS* II, 520.

[136] *TP* IV, 5.

[137] The expression is from Machiavelli in the *Discourses*, Book III, ch. VI. It fits perfectly with what Spinoza means when he speaks of 'measures which arouse general indignation' (*TP* III, 9) since, as *Ethics* III teaches us (in DA 20), indignation is 'Hate towards someone who has harmed another'.

[138] *TP* IV, 5.

[139] *TP* II, 18; *TP* IV, 4.

at the same time',[140] because to suppress the object of tyranny (civil society itself) is also to suppress oneself.

On the other hand, citizens can keep those who run the State within the bounds of the law by martial law (their power of effective resistance) rather than by contract. The right of resistance is basically the natural power of the multitude itself: it is their right of war, and this right always remains a right of war, even if it is partly found in institutions, in the form of a right of resistance and legal expressions. The institutionalised right of resistance, as we have already said, is effective only through the force (the right of nature) that makes its exercise possible. Spinoza believes that politics (the organisation of ordinary life) is the continuation of war by other means – so teaches the 'very wise Florentine'.[141] Remember his reply to Jarrig Jelles:

> As far as Politics is concerned, the difference you ask about, between Hobbes and me, is this: I always preserve natural Right unimpaired, and I maintain that in each State the Supreme Magistrate has no more right over its subjects than it has greater power over them. This is always the case in the state of Nature.[142]

Spinoza thus replaces the contract of the Monarchomachs with the confrontation between natural rights, which forms the core of civil society and the material basis of consensus. On the one hand, there is the logic of the natural right of the sovereign, which turns against its own preservation when it becomes domination. On the other, there is the logic of the natural right of the multitude, which inalienably possesses sovereignty and power and which, through its power of resistance, unfolds the strategy of active resistance of the social body against any logic of (self-destructive) domination, through which this same body affirms its own (essential) aspiration to autonomy (*ut sui juris esse possit...*).

3.3 Benevolence and Indignation: The 'Affects' of Resistance

In the becoming-autonomous-subject of the human individual that is characteristic of the ethical enterprise, we can recognise the starting point of the resistance movement (that is, the focal point from which – in and through which – the reversal of the process of destruction takes place). It takes place

---

[140] *TP* IV, 4; *CWS* II, 527.
[141] *TP* X, 1; *CWS* II, 596.
[142] *Ep.* 50 [to Jarig Jelles]; *CWS* II, 406.

in accordance with the dynamics of active resistance to sadness,[143] in an affect that Spinoza calls 'benevolence' and defines as 'a Desire to benefit one whom we pity'.[144] For the collective individual, the process of destruction is both arrested and reversed in and through 'general indignation' (*plurimi indignantur*),[145] or 'the indignation of the greatest part of an armed multitude'.[146] Indignation initiates the quantitative process of the reorganisation of collective life.

At first glance, it may seem that Spinoza sees – in the rupture of consensus through the effect of tyranny but adopted by its subjects according to the logic of martial law – an explosion of the collective body, whose individual components (the subjects) would thus be relegated to the state of nature, dispersed, atomised. Revolt would, then, be, as with Aristotle, only the reverse expression of the disorder of tyranny.[147] Through the action of general indignation, we do not witness the dissolution of this body, but rather its reorganisation according to a dynamic of active resistance, a strategy of the social body's *conatus*. Against the domination and the heteronomous logic of the collective body installed by the tyrant,[148] the resistance movement of the multitude expresses the opposite tendency towards autonomous self-organisation. For the body politic, the tyrannical logic is the very process of its self-destruction, its suicide, according to a strategy that tends towards the degree zero of rationality. The logic of resistance of the multitude is the reverse process by which the collective body defends and asserts itself, according to a process of self-organisation whose degree of rationality is greater the more the reorganisation corresponds to a democratic logic of autonomy:

> For the greater the right of the supreme power is, the more the form of the State agrees with the dictate of reason (by iii, 5).[149]

The more sovereign power approaches absolute sovereignty – the 'rule which occurs when the whole multitude rules'[150] – the more the State agrees

---

[143] *Ethics* III, 37 Dem.; CWS I, 515.
[144] *Ethics* III, DA 35; CWS I, 539.
[145] TP III, 9.
[146] TP VII, 2; CWS II, 545. See also IV, 2 and IV, 4, where indignation is always that of the 'greatest part of the citizens'.
[147] *Politics* III, 1312 b 18ff.
[148] TP VI, 8; TP VII, 14 end.
[149] TP VIII, 7; CWS II, 568.
[150] TP VIII, 3 end; CWS II, 566.

with the dictates of reason. The question of resistance thus leads to the great political problem of the autonomisation of the social subject and the strategy of the *multitudinis potentia* in and towards its absolute affirmation of existence.

The dissolution of the collective body is, indeed, the work of the tyrant, the destructive effect of his domination. If we consider the destruction he wreaks on human and social relations, the tyrant turns society into a desert, turns every life into a solitude, and the human community into a 'flock'.[151] The subjects break with this quasi-animal life by rebelling and restoring 'a human life' through their resistance: '[a life] defined not merely by the circulation of the blood, and other things common to all animals, but mostly by reason, the true virtue and life of the Mind'.[152]

Resistance already involves reason and virtue. For general indignation is explained by the principle (inherent in common human life, never to be entirely dissolved) of the longing for security (the 'proper utility' of the collective body, which corresponds to the joy principle on an individual level) and resistance to the destruction associated with it: this desire is 'honest', reasonable.[153] In the resistance that every being puts up to everything 'that can take away its existence' (its own principle of security), we find the same affirmation of the power of the composition and organisation of bodies that constitutes the real continuity of the 'virtue' of the body politic. We also find it in the unfolding of peace and freedom or 'general indignation' against the absolute assertion of freedom as the essence of the State, which is best expressed in a democracy that is *omnino absolutum imperium*.[154] Spinoza identifies this power with the absolute affirmation of the power of the multitude. The strategy of the collective body's active resistance is thus directly inscribed in an ontology of the absolute affirmation of all existence. And the systematic order of reason is already expressed in this power of resistance and affirmation.

Indignation is the sign of this reason, of virtue in reconstruction. Like pain, it shows that the injured part is not yet rotten, a will to heal is present: virtue fights. General indignation in a sick body politic is a sign of the restoration of collective health. Like the benevolence that comes from pity,[155] however, indignation for Spinoza is first a passive affect, and, since it is an

---

[151] *TP* V, 4.
[152] *TP* V, 5; *CWS* II, 530.
[153] *TTP* III.
[154] *TP* XI, 1; *CWS* II, 601.
[155] *Ethics* III, DA 35; *CWS* I, 539.

affect of hatred, it is obviously one of the most negative. Indignation, writes Spinoza, is hatred of 'someone who has done evil to another'.[156] But there is already something positive underlying this hatred: the relationship of identification, of similarity, even of love, which we feel towards our fellow human beings necessarily leads us, because we suffer from the same things, to try to alleviate them. 'As far as we can, we strive to free a thing we pity from its suffering.'[157] Benevolence realises the resistance movement. *Ethics* III, 27 Cor. 3 Dem., referring to *Ethics* III, 13, clearly shows (as we have already seen) that we act to come to the aid of our fellow human beings, according to a genuine dynamic of resistance to sadness (in ourselves and in others with whom we identify). We act to regenerate life in ourselves, in and with others. This is virtue. In this same demonstration, Spinoza shows how much this movement of resistance and liberation (this desire) necessarily involves the desire to destroy the cause responsible for the pain of our fellow human beings:

> Whatever affects with Sadness what we pity, affects us also with a like Sadness (by P27). And so (by PI 3) we shall strive to think of whatever can take away the thing's existence, or destroy the thing, i.e. (by P9S), we shall want to destroy it, or shall be determined to destroy it. And so we strive to free the thing we pity from its suffering.

But what is indignation if not the same desire to destroy that which has injured another? Which is to say, that it is the exercise of the virtue of benevolence, when it is not confined – as it necessarily is according to Spinoza – to the treatment of the effects (the consolation of our fellows), when it attacks the cause of the pain itself. In this destruction, however, to relieve the other of his misery, there is expressed a 'will, or appetite to do good',[158] to restore life. It is no longer merely a will to destroy the cause of pain (according to a partial image). If we consider that we also find some tools in this effort – such as the memory of 'everything that takes away the existence of this thing' (from a political point of view, the memory of freedom, peace and security), that is, ideas (and/or affects) that are incompatible with the existence of the tyrant – then we can really see the exercise of virtue in collective indignation.

The resistance of the multitude is explained by the power of the affirmation of life and not by the powerlessness expressed in the feelings of

---

[156] *Ethics* III, DA 20; CWS I, 536.
[157] *Ethics* III, 27 Cor. 3; CWS I, 509.
[158] *Ethics* III, 27 Cor. 3 Schol; CWS I, 509.

pity and hatred. As a constitutive affirmation, benevolence in indignation – in and through resistance to sadness – turns against the affects of pity and hatred that exhaust life. Just as the ethical process of subjectivation is a real movement of resistance and love, benevolence in indignation is, at the heart of servitude, a centre of freedom and virtue in and through which the self-organising power of the collective body asserts itself. In and through the solidarity and liberatory dynamic it generates, indignation is a remedy that the collective body produces and applies to itself to restore the social fabric. Indignation is the very process of self-defence and self-healing. The rage of outrage is, therefore, accompanied by joy: an essential joy ('self-contentment') through which the collective body experiences and contemplates the increase of its capacity to act, the rebirth of its 'health' by those who collectively resist. It is a joy that is inseparable from natural love for oneself, that fundamental affect from which all resistance grows, and, with it, active hope. The multitude becomes an autonomous subject through generalised indignation. The dynamics of collective (political) subjectivity as a process is elaborated through resistance to domination. In indignation, the act of resistance already contains the dynamic of joy, which is intensified in and through the political institution of freedom, which is the fullness of the collective body's natural love for oneself.[159]

3.4 From the Resistance of the Best to the Indignation of All: Machiavelli, La Boétie, Spinoza

To think about politics and sovereignty according to the self-organising dynamics of the multitude, from active resistance to domination to the affirmation of its autonomy (the absolute affirmation of its existence and its right), means often observing, in the light of historical experience, the failure of these efforts, which are generally committed to a logic of heteronomy.

---

[159] According to Spinoza, the entire teaching of Christ (and of Holy Scripture) consists in this commandment: 'Do unto others as you would have them do unto you, for this is the sum of the Law and the Prophets' (Matthew 7:12). From the point of view of the logic of affects, this is a teaching of resistance (see Bove, 'Enseignement du Christ et résistance dans le *T.T.P.*'). On the contrast between Spinoza and Hobbes, who inverts the relationship of participation in justice and charity into one of obedience, thus opening up the possibility of the right of resistance, see Jacqueline Lagrée, who, without drawing the conclusions that I do (that is not her intention), sets out very clearly the difference between the two problematics of Spinoza and Hobbes in relation to the evangelical principle. *Le Salut du laïc*, Vrin, 1989, ch. 7, pp. 89–90.

We know that the actual autonomy of the body politic, like individual wisdom, is as difficult as it is rare; we know the reasons for these difficulties. Even when freed from any explicit political rule, the multitude remains a prisoner of its prejudices, habits and customs. As we learned in *Ethics* I App., according to the commonly shared logic of the imagination, people are naturally led to a teleological account of the world in which the monarchy of divine right is the finalist superstition realised in political reality. It is logical, then, that despite the great dangers involved in this decision, and despite the affirmative character of the collective body, 'experience' shows and teaches us that the 'masses' 'on the contrary' want to 'transfer all power to one man' in the interests of peace and harmony![160]

Let us consider, again, the instructive example of the Aragonese. This is a people who freed themselves from the slavery of the Moors through struggle. They had to experience their strength of self-organisation, initiative and decision in that struggle ... and, having achieved victory, they nevertheless decide to give themselves a king. Could the desire for servitude be a *causa sui*? Certainly not. Such an answer is absurd for Spinoza. Moreover, the same example shows that the Aragonese – because of the real possibilities of living freely that they actualised, and despite their (seemingly insurmountable) desire to elect a king – were able, with a good constitution and the (armed) will, 'to take up arms against any force by which anyone tries to invade the kingdom to their disadvantage, even against the King himself and any future prince who might be his heir if he invades (the State) in this way'.[161] In this way, they were able to preserve their freedom 'for an incredibly long period of time'. Servitude is not inevitable. The path to a people's liberation, however narrow, is always present in the terrain of possibilities that constitutes their history.

Historically, the path to liberation is initially known only to a minority, through the resistance of a 'very small number' (*paucissimos*) of citizens to the forces that subjugate mind and body: this is the thesis of *TTP* VIII,[162] itself based on experience. Spinoza's political treatises are addressed to these few sparks of light and resistance in the context of the theological-political domination of his time. They address the 'very few' who stand out from the masses by virtue of their education and strength of character, those most likely to remember freedom and hear its call. Spinoza does not write for anonymous and vague, abstract reasons. Rather, he writes for individual

---

[160] *TP* VI, 4; *CWS* II, 533.
[161] *TP* VII, 30; *CWS* II, 562.
[162] *TTP* VIII.

subjectivities determined in and by the theological-political context of the time and who, because of their contemporary resistance to the logic of domination, can benefit from hearing a discourse of liberation.

So we must again invoke the legacy of Machiavelli and Etienne de La Boétie – the 'ever shrewd' Machiavelli who, as the author of the *TP* puts it, 'gave very good advice' to protect a liberty[163] that triumphs only when it is desired. When he deals with 'conspiracies' in chapter VI of Book III of the *Discourses*, Machiavelli sees the main motive that leads citizens to conspire against a prince in 'the desire to free one's own country from slavery'. This motive is irresistible:

> [A tyrant can only] guard himself from this humor [by] laying down the tyranny. And because no one is found who does this, few are found who do not come out badly.[164]

The Discourse on Voluntary Servitude is of the same kind.[165] 'Freedom', La Boétie writes, 'arouses [valour] in the hearts of those who defend it';[166]

> There are always a few, better endowed than others, who feel the weight of the yoke and cannot restrain themselves from attempting to shake it off: these are the men who never become tamed under subjection;[167]

> These are the ones who, having good minds of their own, have further trained them by study and learning. Even if liberty had entirely perished from the earth, such men would invent it. For them slavery has no satisfactions, no matter how well disguised.[168]

When these heroes, who see 'their country in evil hands', approach 'their task with a firm, whole heart and sincere intention', none of them fail.[169]

---

[163] *TP* V, 7; CWS II, 531.
[164] *Discourses on Livy*, Book III, ch. VI, p. 220.
[165] On the kinship between Etienne de La Boétie and Machiavelli, see Claude Lefort, 'Le nom d'Un' in the Payot edition of *Discours de la servitude volontaire*, 1978, particularly pp. 284ff.
[166] Etienne de La Boétie, *The Politics of Obedience: The Discourse of Voluntary Servitude*, trans. Harry Kurz, Ludwig von Mises Institute, 2015, p. 45.
[167] Ibid., p. 60.
[168] Ibid., pp. 60–1.
[169] Ibid., p. 61.

The whole of *TTP* XX famously praises these 'proud' and rebellious souls, these people 'who have free and unbiased judgement', who 'love the virtues and the arts'.[170] Spinoza distinguishes them from those who have been corrupted by tyranny and subjected to the rule of 'deceptions', whose 'highest good consists in contemplating the money in their coffers and having bloated bellies', and whose greed, the hope of a fraudulent fortune (under the protection of the tyrant), drives them to flattery and 'shameful treachery'.[171] It is true that

people easily become cowardly and servile under tyrants,[172]

The most intelligent and understanding among them would not have left his soup bowl to regain [liberty][173]

all those corrupted by burning ambition or extraordinary avarice rally around him and support him in order to get a share of the spoils and make themselves petty chieftains under the great tyrant;[174]

These wretches see the glittering treasures of the despot and are dazzled by his splendour. Attracted by this splendour, they approach without realising that they are approaching a flame that will inevitably burn them.[175]

Machiavelli, La Boétie, Spinoza: all three proclaim the exemplarity of the virtue of resistance. It is a virtue that can only spread and eventually triumph, even if the heroes meet death. In battle, the virtue of the 'few' demands further virtue, and virtue demands victory. According to the mimetic basis of the dynamics of affects, we necessarily pass from the indignation of the best to the indignation of all.[176]

Certainly, experience and reason seem to show that it is as 'impossible to preserve the common people from superstition as from fear',[177] for they are the best supports of tyranny (present or future). And we cannot (and should

---

[170] *TTP* XX; *CWS* II, 349. Translator's note.
[171] *TTP* XX; *CWS* II, 349.
[172] La Boétie, *The Politics of Obedience*, p. 62. Translation modified.
[173] Ibid., p. 65. Translation modified.
[174] Ibid., p. 73. Translation modified.
[175] Ibid., p. 78. Translation modified.
[176] *TP* X, 8.
[177] *TTP*, Praef.; *CWS* II, 75. Translator's note.

not) address ourselves to the non-philosophers, for whom the reading of the *TTP* would only lead to 'trouble through a perverse interpretation'. That is, it would lead to the persecution of 'others who wish to philosophise more freely' and for whom 'this work will be extremely useful'.[178] Indeed, it is not possible to debate with a tyrant, nor is it conceivable to reform tyranny peacefully: 'His subjects can repel his violence only by violence.'[179] We also know that, unfortunately, it is not enough to eliminate the tyrant to free oneself from domination.

Machiavelli and La Boétie, like Spinoza, know that it is often as useless as it is dangerous to 'touch incurable wounds',[180] but they also affirm even more strongly that this clarity must neither prevent the struggle nor make us forget the goal. Since 'a few' are always able to listen and resist, there will never be 'reason to despair completely'.[181] There is always a path to liberation, narrow though it may be, which, under favourable circumstances, can open up to anyone. It is the task of philosophers and people of vision to ensure that the overthrow of the tyrant is not in vain. But the tension of autonomous self-organisation of the *multitudinis potentia* is already at work in the resistance of a few. We must lean on them. Their power of freedom and peace is already unfolding in the struggle and must be protected for the future. This resistance cannot in any way be considered a martial value, even if it produces heroes. Resistance is essentially active through the values it represents. Resistance is a desire and thus underlines the value: a 'yes' to life, to human solidarity, to freedom and to peace. In principle, resistance is fundamentally anti-nihilist. Logically, it cannot be the bearer of domination and death, unless it involves lies and evil intentions. If this is the case, it betrays itself. In that case, we might as well return to a 'legitimate government'.

Spinoza's strategy of political liberation is based on the resistance of those (individual and/or collective) subjectivities that actively oppose the inhumanity and degradation of subjugation (the producers of slave herds) with a human singularity that brings with it, here and now, the political hope of freedom. These singularities, which already resist the rule of servitude in the present, which is also a rule of loneliness, hatred, lies and perfidy (the corruption of the 'good faith necessary for a Republic'),[182] create benevolence

---

[178] *TTP*, Praef.; CWS II, 185.
[179] *TP* VII, 30; CWS II, 562.
[180] La Boétie, *The Politics of Obedience*, p. 50. See Machiavelli, *The Prince*, ch. III, where we can find similar wording.
[181] *TTP* VIII; CWS II, 192.
[182] *TTP* XX; CWS II, 349.

and love, good faith, freedom of communication and speech, with the desire to know, act and live together. The great political significance of the central chapters of the *TTP* becomes clearer. They convey the politically liberating significance of the doctrine of love for one's neighbour, based on the essential ontological trust that life maintains with itself through its multiple forms (its political modality). Are these passages idealistic? Apolitical, individualistic, even elitist? Quite the contrary. Spinoza, from his own standpoint, tries to maintain the fighting spirit of Machiavelli and La Boétie. Theirs is the standpoint that defends the 'masses'. From the resistance of a few – a real crucible of the collective body's autonomous self-organisation – to the liberation of all, this is the political meaning (and the historical direction) of the Spinozist project. Spinoza realises the articulation of ontology and history through the concept of resistance.

The paradox of the concept of resistance can be seen in its historical development. This concept was forged from the sixteenth to the seventeenth centuries in a practice of real historical change, and yet it was reflected in a conservative ideology of the Restoration based on the key concepts of natural law and contract. From the perspective of the *multitudinis potentia*, Spinoza shatters the theologies of law, right and State (whether based on the myths of natural law or the contract). Beyond the theatre of theological-legal representation and the 'appearance of law' with which revolt, even regicide, is to be justified in the imagination,[183] Spinoza affirms the absolute and real fact of the sovereign and eternal right to resist, understood in the constitutive dynamic of the affects of the body of the multitude, its strategy of active resistance, its absolute affirmation of existence. Breaking with the imaginary of natural law and contract, Spinoza transforms the concept of resistance into the concept of the possibility of history. But the concept of the possibility of the emergence of a singular subjectivity (as a process) and the place of the self-constitution (and understanding) of sovereignty also emerges from the point of view of the dynamics of the power of the multitude. The project of a political Spinozist philosophy is to ground both the stability and the flourishing of the collective body in the principle of resistance: that is, the nature of the collective body as tension from/to autonomy, the expansive fullness of *cupiditas*. If 'obedience makes the subject',[184] then chapter XX of the *TTP*, which praises the resistance of the 'best' – and the entire *TP* with its democratic bias in favour of checks and balances – teaches us above all that resistance makes the citizen. The act of resistance cannot

---

[183] *TTP* XVIII.
[184] *TTP* XVII; CWS II, 297.

only appear as an act of preservation. Resistance is also the act through which human reality and its ethical and political dimensions emerge in their essential historical sociality, along with the new meanings that accompany this constitution of the imagination.

Conclusion
Strategy and Infinity

In the political as well as in the ethical spheres, the philosophical project of Spinozism is to bring us ever closer to the real movement of the self-production of the Real. As a naturalist philosophy of *causa sui*, Spinozism is also the philosophy *par excellence* of the real movement through its radical immanentism: which is to say, it is a philosophy of substance. For 'substance' is the self-normative, self-organising, self-constituting movement 'without principle or end' that takes place in infinitely many ways in (and according to) an infinity of things. This dynamic reality (in its causal complexity), for both individuals and nations, bodies and ideas, is freedom, because freedom is movement.

Prior to the question of the factual finitude of the human landscape and the systems of order in and through which they are necessarily established and maintained, it is a question of grasping the real movement of the self-production of substance in its substantial infinity; before life, refracted in the theatre of passive affections, becomes a dream. The Spinozist imperative, in ethics as well as in politics, is therefore Machiavellian: it is a 'return to the principle'. It is certainly not a conservative return to a putative 'natural order', or to a life that would organise its materiality prior to modality. Rather, it is a return to the principle as a self-normative, self-organising movement, a law of nature that we find as much in the power (*puissance*) of ideas as we do in the power of bodies and the power of the multitude. Substance is a model of autonomy for ideas, humans and peoples.

The *Ethics* ends with a clear contrast between the *vera animi acquiescentia* of the wise, which exists according to the inner logic of their 'free necessity', and the 'restlessness' of the ignorant, which is tossed about by external causes. This opposition is neither that of motion and rest, nor that (in some ways closer to the truth) of the productive affluence of desire and its opposite, impotence and unproductivity. The real opposition is between a happy and balanced productivity (in and through 'the power of God') of the real movement of the Real in its autonomy (in which the philosopher in her becoming participates, with all her unique causal power in the alignment that has taken place between her essence and her existence) and the heteronomous movements of the ignorant. The ignorant also participate in the reality-generating processes, but through representations, imaginative ideas and fantasies. If they can console themselves – by constructing an order of the world, as they do with the finalist prejudice – they end up also depleting their life, wasting it, thwarting it and even turning it against themselves in a blind process of self-destruction, all while believing they are promoting life. The greatest misfortune of the ignorant is their own ignorance and, above all, their ignorance of themselves.

Strictly speaking, the movement of life in the person subject to illusion certainly has no less reality than it does in the life of the sage. And every being is in absolute proximity to being, according to its own perfection. No process of individuation enjoys a privilege over another. In the world of substance, there are neither models, nor copies, nor hierarchies: equality is ontological. Spinoza, however, emphasises how much the wise person is worth, how supremely desirable her life is, and how powerfully she rises above the ignorant person. This means that the wise predominate in the autonomous quantity of movement that generates real presence to self, others, the world and God. They have more presence and knowledge, since 'the power of natural things, by which they exist and have effects, is the very power of God . . . *ipsissima Dei sit potentia*'.[1]

To generate an adequate idea of one's affects is also to generate this presence in the Real, that is, presence for oneself in becoming and, in the same movement, presence for God (Nature), others, the world. . . Singularity is the very process of becoming subject. In contrast, the ignorant person, almost completely dominated by external causes, is at nearly degree zero of real presence and singularity. For them, the relationship with the real (with oneself, others, things and God) is (almost) completely mediated by imagination, so that presence, here in the realm of hallucination, is what shields and hinders Reality. Paradoxically, the incessant restlessness of the ignorant, and the multiplicity of ways in which they encounter external things, form a fantastic force of inertia and solitude. The ignorant are almost entirely disaffected. This expression is to be taken literally, since it is a matter of the virtual loss of self-affection, the loss of the unique and definitive bond through which we experience all the richness of nature, from the love of ourselves to the intellectual love of God, *sub specie aeternitatis*, from the standpoint of

---

[1] *TP* II, 3; *CWS* II, 507.

our uniqueness. It is the loss of the unique reality that they 'are' and *vis-à-vis* the reality that they 'live'. This pathological withdrawal from reality is its ordinary state of existence. In this 'forgetfulness' of God (the theological expression must be naturalised here), the movement of life in them (and not through them) manifests itself as so many maladaptive reactions to the affirmation of existence, which, however, paradoxically expresses itself in the inadequacy and at the limit of modal dispersion.

In the ethical inscription of life – becoming a subject is a possible 'project' rather than a teleological necessity – the real movement signifies the power of God and/or of oneself in one's singularity. With the third kind of knowledge, this real movement is the direct intuition of one's own power in its complex logic of self-constitution. Thus, from the third kind of knowledge arises 'the highest satisfaction of the mind that there can be'.[2] The one who knows things through this kind of knowledge attains the highest human perfection and consequently the highest joy, which accompanies the idea of oneself, one's virtue, 'and consequently the idea of God'.[3] In accordance with herself and/or with God, the sage loves herself as she loves God, with an intellectual love within the highest satisfaction that can be known. Ignorance, in contrast, is the rule of separation and the almost total 'ignorance of oneself, God and things'.

Faced with the universal experience of human profligacy and the adequate knowledge of its causes, the entirety of Spinoza's thought is marked by this radical opposition, and by the ethical-political resolve to lead human reality as far as possible towards its sovereignty, or, to say the same thing, towards the wisdom that is 'the eternity of uninterrupted and sovereign joy' by promoting the productive forces of clarity, freedom, sociability and happiness. Human sovereignty – the eternity of joy in the unique union of the mind with all of nature – is mentioned at the beginning of *TdIE*, and explains the whole work. In a nature of which humans are only a tiny fragment, a finitely existing form, without which nature can (could and will) very well do without imperfection or privation, and whose happiness or unhappiness is indifferent to humanity, the important project is to build a 'human' world.

Thus, the 'absolute affirmation of existence' is indeed the 'supreme truth from which all doctrines derive',[4] regardless of whether it is the absolute

---

[2] *Ethics* V, 27; CWS I, 609.
[3] *Ethics* V, 32 Dem.; CWS I, 611.
[4] Based on the remarks of Victor Delbos in *Le problème moral dans la philosophie de Spinoza et l'Histoire du spinozisme*, F. Alcan, 1893, repr. Presses de l'Université de Paris Sorbonne, 1990, ch. 10, p. 200.

affirmation of the human individual (her simple effort to survive the development of bliss) or the absolute affirmation of the collective body, from a fragile primitive union to the fullness of solidarity in freedom. The absolute affirmation of existence – the real and self-normative movement of the Real, 'substance' as the positing of present infinity, the movement without interiority or lack – is a multiple affirmation or an affirmative multiplicity. At the same time, it is a movement without purpose. It is the task of the people with the most foresight to ensure that the affirmation of the substance in and through which we are what we are does not crush the affirmation of human existence.

Grounded in the active resistance through which everything opposes its own annihilation, the affirmation of life in the multiplicity of its forms, bound up in the contradictory complex of existences (and there are only existences), necessarily unfolds as a 'strategy'. Where there is resistance, there is strategy. There is necessarily always resistance and strategy ... or death. This means that, strictly speaking, resistance is not a figure of negativity; it is not reactive.[5] From the perspective of the eternal and always unique alliance between knowledge and the love of God, we resist. We affirm absolutely our existence, however minimal and unconscious our resistance may be, either from the perspective of our present infinity or from the perspective of our eternity.

According to the laws of Habit, the joy principle, imitation in benevolence, indignation, the pursuit of glory or domination, the universal basis of this active resistance explains the formation of an organisation (to a certain degree of rationality) of the political body, starting from the precarious associations of the 'free' affects. But all bodies in general, whatever their nature, organise themselves in their rationality in and through the resistance of their associations to the attacks of external forces. And these same bodies, depending on their degree of associative complexity, develop more or less sophisticated strategies. They range from the minimal but already rational strategy to the first complex bodies that can only assert themselves

---

[5] With Descartes we can say that resistance is as reactive as the joy that accompanies it. For him, this is symptomatic of the primacy of the obstacle, the work that our 'power' must do to enjoy in victory the efficacy of its perfection. There is, then, no joy – or titillation – except in function of the consciousness of this perfection, which is proven and experienced only in a victorious confrontation with the obstacle. And this self-satisfaction will be all the greater, the greater the obstacle to be overcome and the dangers involved. See on this subject Alexandre Matheron, 'Psychologie et politique: Descartes. La noblesse du chatouillement', in *Anthropologie et Politique au XVIIème siècle*, Vrin, 1986, pp. 35–6, 43–5.

absolutely or disappear, to bodies whose associations are richer and which, like human bodies (and, by analogy, political communities), are able to feel joy or sadness and to recognise the cause of these affects. A collective body, following the same process, can develop and introduce rules, conducive to the affirmation of its life, and condemn individuals, according to the logic of the practical subject. These bodies exhibit an essentially loving behaviour, from which will follow their 'happiness' – their individual capacity to rise to an ethical strategy in the adequate knowledge of causes, their collective ability to adequately solve the problems that the community has been able to pose; as well as their 'unhappiness' – their individual submission to false problems, to strategies of self-love and pride, or collectively to the tyrants' destructive strategies.

Spinoza leads us to a dynamic ontology of the problem. Every body – society or organism – poses a problem through its affirmation. Its specific organisation proposes a particular solution, which, by adapting to it, accommodates the problem posed, without ever extinguishing the constituent question inherent in its own perseverance. According to the abstract scheme of an individualistic strategy of consciousness, in the constitutive process the real movement does not go from the field of possibilities (hypothetical actions) to the final reality of choice, decision and execution. There are neither hypotheses, nor fields of possibility, nor *a priori* decisions in nature, society or history. There is only the strict, complex necessity of the productivity of reality. Nature proceeds in each individual by determining the problems and the necessary avenues of solutions: in its confrontation with the multiplicity, not of possibilities but of real forces presently at work, within and outside of it, with which it composes itself but which it also resists.

In contrast to the illusions of consciousness, problems do not arise from themselves, nor, strictly speaking, do they arise from the obstacle with which they are often confused.[6] The problem is not the data encountered in an experiment. It is a product of the power of affirmation of any being (individual or society) in its complex dynamic articulation with reality. The problem as a real object is thus the affection of which a body is capable, and, at the same time, the idea of that affection, through which that body is affirmed together with the problem it faces. Since it is necessarily bound up in a complex of power relations, affirmation is the constitutive activity of resistance. The nature of affirmation is, therefore, to problematise the real, to

---

[6] On the need to clearly distinguish the 'problem' from the 'obstacle', as well as from the 'negative' which is only the shadow and the illusion of the problem, see Gilles Deleuze, *Difference and Repetition*, Columbia University Press, 1994, pp. 235, 244

constitute it as a problem, and, in the same gesture, to produce the paradigm of a solution corresponding to this situation. This is the real movement of the real into a singular affirmation, the strategic and hermeneutic dynamic of the *conatus*.[7]

Where there is resistance and strategy, there is necessarily rationality. Strategy has no prescribed goal or end. It is the movement of rationality in the making. The present infinity is, therefore, a power of resistance and rationality. The infinite is reason itself in the multiplicity of its affirmations, and the strategy of active resistance is the real process of the emergence of the Real and of reason. In its various degrees of rationality (defensive/affirmative self-organisation of modality), infinity affirms itself and struggles (it is virtue itself). It thus always preserves the possibility (however minimal) of a path (however narrow and difficult in practice) for the becoming-human subject of the affirmation of power that applies equally to humans and States. Enlarging this path of freedom and wisdom as far as possible is the human project par excellence.

The dynamic of resistance and the associated strategy of (individual and collective) *conatus* ultimately explain the imaginative formation of a teleological order of the world and the resulting (theological-political) systems of life as the solution to a problem that necessarily precedes and produces it. We have emphasised an imaginative conception of order, which is both a vital necessity and the source of a paradoxical connection to what destroys us (prejudice, superstition, and the institutions that support them). The same imaginative conception of a world order, freed from its superstitious content in favour of an imaginary content that is adequate to its inherent vital necessity, could become the adequate solution of salvation adapted to the ignorant. Such is the strategy of the *conatus* that the *multitudinis potentia* has long been trying to work out. The Old Testament points to this doctrine. Christ the philosopher rationally elaborated the teaching in its effective simplicity. Experience (of the multitude) and reason (of the

---

[7] The application of the geometrical method does not mean that the question of the 'problem' and its position is settled. But the anti-theological (and/or) anti-teleological ontology that this application evokes (and for which it is made) opens Spinozist philosophy – in its confrontation with politics and history (this is the *moment* of the *TTP*) – to a strategic logic of *conatus* (and/or *potentia*) that is that of the constitution of problems and cases of solutions. And perhaps there, behind the 'geometrical mode' but at the heart of the work, we should see a philosophical elaboration peculiar to the 'experiential mode' that is discovered and systematically explored in the recent work of Pierre-François Moreau, *Experience and Eternity in Spinoza*, trans. Robert Boncardo, Edinburgh University Press, 2021.

few) have been trying vigorously to recover and reproduce this lesson ever since.[8]

Affirmation of an adequate idea is not independent of the logic of resistance. The true idea paves the way to its autonomous affirmation, both against and with imaginative ideas. Just as in the realm of bodies, a thought is always limited by another thought. Because there is no singular thing in nature that cannot be destroyed by another that is stronger and more powerful, there is also resistance and strategy in the realm of ideas.

The great challenge of thought lies neither in reflection nor in the choice of solutions, as consciousness mistakenly believes. Rather, it lies in the choice of the problems themselves, in our ability, our power to problematise the real adequately, and thereby to elevate ourselves to its truth. This holds both within an epoch – in the space of public opinion, which makes it historically more or less possible to express the truth – and within the mind of every human being. In the case of someone's mind (which, of course, always includes the conditions of her epoch), we must emphasise the extent to which certain inadequate ideas can form such a firm structure of imagination in each person that it leaves no room for the emergence of a true idea (for example, when the finalist prejudice has become an official superstition, elevated to the rank of a 'true world-view').[9] We must emphasise how, in

---

[8] I continue these reflections in 'Enseignement du Christ et résistance dans le *T.T.P.*' in *La Bible et ses raisons*, collective work of the UPRES-A; see Henri Laux, who systematically examines the transition from superstitious religion to a liberated world of imagination: Henri Laux, *Imagination et religion chez Spinoza*, Vrin, 2002.

[9] This, as we know, is the case with the 'subjects' of the Hebrew theocracy. Note that Spinoza never refers to Athenian democracy in his historical examples. And perhaps he reserved this analysis (but nothing suggests it and his culture does not seem to lead him to it) for chapter XI of *TP*, an analysis that could thus have been the 'counterpart' to the *TTP*'s theoretical-historical chapters V and XVII on the Hebrew State. The symmetry would have been perfect between the affirmation of democracy (in theocratic form) among this barbarian people, who despise philosophy and live in radical autarky to protect what they consider their unique singularity, and the affirmation of democracy among the people who also invented mathematics and philosophy and who live their radical singularity – as Pericles explains in his eulogy to the victims of war (see Thucydides, *History of the Peloponnesian War*, ed. M. I. Finley, trans. Rex Warner, rev. edn, Penguin Classics, 1972, book II, chs XXXV–XLVI) – in its 'openness' to the whole world and without any *xenēlasía* to the strangers welcomed on to its soil. And this confrontation would have been instructive for us, because if Spinoza, with the perfect Hebrew State, made us reflect on the extreme theological-political conditions of the impossibility of the development of individual reason, this confrontation with Athenian democracy would have made us reflect, conversely, on the positive conditions for the possibility of the development of reason, as they

any human mind, adequate ideas themselves can only be developed from the affects of the body – which is to say, necessarily from inadequate ideas – and this development can only be understood by virtue of the strategy of active resistance to sadness, which forces the mind to think about what and why certain bodies fit, or do not fit, the body whose idea it is. The emergence of a true idea is, thus, also part of the strategic logic of active resistance and of the continuous reinforcement of joy in the increasingly rational organisation of modality, in a dynamic of the emergence of reason as 'cause'. This is the ethical project. But this becoming-cause of human reason will never emerge definitively from the realm of the imagination. Thus, the tension, indeed the contradiction within us between adequate and imaginative ideas, will necessarily always remain. In addition, the adequate idea in the human subject is necessarily always accompanied by its imaginative counterpart: a non-adequate cognition of the adequate idea, which entails cognition of the true idea. Although under certain conditions it can support the emergence of new truths, this 'consciousness' can also act as a real obstacle to the progress of the human mind. Like bodies, ideas resist their own extinction, whether they are true or false.

Following the affirmative logic of the adequate idea it expresses, the philosophical project of clarifying problems is articulated and sustained by this singular power of infinity, resistance and rationality. The real movement of the Real in its autonomy opposes this force (presented as irreducible) to (the imagined ordinary) death, the negative destiny of human desire. But this opposition is a divided one since one and the same movement produces the ideas in and through the effort that every being makes to persist in its being and, at the same time, opposes the same ideas when they turn against the very affirmation that produces them (according to the logic of the paradoxical connection).

Both the actual and the actualising singular essence of an individual forms in and through this resistance, as the complex process of the causality of a particular mode in its affirmation (constitution). Its *conatus* is nothing other than the process through which each individual is produced and (re)produced in its actual existence, by virtue of an effort of absolute affirmation. For 'the same power [things] require to begin to exist, they also require to continue to exist'.[10] As in Plato's *Republic*, political analysis leads us to read in bold letters what is very difficult to discern at the level of

---

are necessary in every republic and at every time, and as they are presupposed in the exercise of our thought itself, which carries within it the memory of its origins.

[10] *TP* II, 2; *CWS* II, 507.

singular human essences. Singular causality as essence is the process through which each being, in its history, with its strategy of active resistance, strives to affirm its being absolutely. By considering the nation to be 'like' the individual, Spinoza's political analysis effectively guides us to an explicitly historical conception of singularity, with a dynamic (and ontological) connection of the particular to the universal, the finite to the infinite, history to eternity.

Conatus sive Habitus is the philosophical output of the study of the Hebrew State. Due to the accidents of fate, the historical conditions from which one has benefited, a human being can make the power of reason effective. And a people can make its power of autonomous self-organisation in the political form of democracy. Thus, one can be the 'adequate cause' of their life in most of their actions. Neither every human being nor every people is destined to become master of their own destiny. . .

Certainly, essential singularity cannot be reduced to the particularities of modes. The *habitus* of the body (individual or collective) also struggles against the *habitus* of deep-rooted habits to assert a higher degree of perfection, a higher degree of reality and modal existence, according to new associations among affections. The highest perfection is the highest degree of rationality and/or singularity, which is also the tendency in and towards the perfectly autonomous strategy of *cupiditas*. Therefore, the others are always and necessarily fought from the point of view of new particularities. Historical production, the *habitus-ingenium*, is itself the productive force of history. This dynamic of *habitus* belongs to singularity. The play of contradictory forces, depending on the *aleas* of fortune, involves a mode in a process of infinite perfection and active resistance to everything that stands in the way of its unfolding. This is the becoming-singular (the becoming-wise) of the human mode, whether it is individual or collective. As Engels later put it, there is 'the uninterrupted process of becoming and of passing away, of endless ascendancy from the lower to the higher',[11] of this transformation of the 'infantile body' to the constitution of a being possessing 'a Mind which considered only in itself is very much conscious of itself, and of God, and of things'.[12] This higher becoming-singular is also a becoming-adequate cause, understood as a process of subjectivation in the practical subject form. If this process is political in nature, however, it tends to be completely invested by the power of the multitude in its affirmation. *Perseverare in suo esse* means

---

[11] Friedrich Engels, *Ludwig Feuerbach and the End of German Classical Philosophy*, trans. Austin Lewis, Origami Books, 2020, p. 12.
[12] *Ethics* V, 39 Schol.; CWS I, 614.

singular productivity in contrast to perseverance *in suo statu*, which is the conjunctural preservation of particularity, a real power of imbalance, revolution and constitution.

Spinoza's project: not to get into a position of power (*pouvoir*) or domination over oneself, over others, over the world, by virtue of the deceptive signs of representation and the blind strategy of self-love in its quest for domination. But, above all, to know human nature and its laws, to prevent a human being from building her own unhappiness on this illusion of external domination (characteristic of the practical subject). Thus, the intrinsic and unique necessity of *cupiditas* is affirmed as far as possible in the becoming of the autonomous subject, conscious of her own standpoint and uniqueness.

The point is nothing other than becoming 'eternal in our place', as Goethe, a reader of Spinoza, understood well, but which, by virtue of 'nature and the common condition of men', is as difficult as it is rare. Although it belongs to us alone from eternity, this place is a real fortress from which we are nevertheless always partially separated, excluded and banished. It is our human condition, which we must reconquer and defend, again and again, with the most adequate means. *Perseverare in suo esse* is also this: rediscovering and/or producing, in the clarity of truth, the singular relationship of trust, knowledge and love that both envelops and develops an entire life in its essential affirmation. And this 'relationship' has degrees that correspond to our own process of singularisation.

Trust implies neither renunciation nor submission to a superior order, and is far from enclosing us in a metaphysical system that subjects us to its truth for all eternity. Spinoza invites us to free ourselves from the fiction of order and meaning that the *conatus*, in its strategy of survival, necessarily constructs in the imagination. We are freed to take over the explicit self-organisation of human life in an autonomous and determined way. Trust is the dynamic process of self-organisation, contained in the 'eternal covenant of God's knowledge and love', which the world misunderstood or repressed in its various theological-political pacts with God, gods or their representatives (in an imaginary constitutive of history), until Christ explicitly taught it. We constitute ourselves (individuals as well as nations) in our singularity (in our place) in and through this covenant *sub specie aeternitatis*. This occurs in the self-affection, with and through the active forces of nature, which confirm themselves in one and the same movement of universal self-constitution within and beyond us, in infinitely many strategies of singular individuation. Trust, then, is that absolute and always singularly determined bond that a being has with itself. In each being, the eternal affect of itself through itself, the necessary relation to itself (and/or the Real in its universality), the very power (*puissance*) of love for itself in and through the intellectual love of God, is that through which each affirms itself and resists everything that stands in the way of this affirmation. *Quare hoc aeternum foedus Dei cognitionis & amoris universale est.*[13] Being, the singular essence, is precisely this 'alliance'. And the constitutive resistance of each being is affirmed by this trust, an eternal bond of cognition and love, that every being maintains with nature, according to their own degree of complexity and consciousness.

In the human mind, confidence is the very substance of the 'will'. The mind cannot doubt itself; this is an absurdity for Spinoza. In the absolute affirmation of the idea, how could a mind really think that it does not think! An intangible certainty necessarily accompanies the mind's effort to persist in its being: its 'will' is its asserted confidence. As Spinoza writes to William Blijenbergh, the fruits we draw from our natural capacity for knowledge, 'if even once . . . false', can make us happy.[14] We find both our greatest perfection and our greatest satisfaction in our natural capacity for knowledge. We must, therefore, use our intellect with complete certainty, for our intellect is the confidence that the thinking being has for itself. There, as Alain writes, is 'our human position', 'where the immensity of things gathers into a well-determined existence',[15] and from where we can resist the repeated assaults of the universe that come from suffering and oppression, as well as from the delirious prejudice, wickedness and hatred of our fellow human beings. The only 'real position' for anyone is not to leave 'this place of understanding, which is strictly determined by our living body', and is thus historically situated, but to hold fast to this 'singular position'.[16] The real process of singularisation (subjectivation) is the very process of existence: arming ourselves with virtue, reclaiming our place when (this 'when' is the condition that is necessarily separate from all existence) we have moved away from it. . . Singularity is the historical dynamic of this movement back to this singular position. Our real position is this readiness to fight.

In the process of *Habitus*, we experience this confidence and active resistance in our own bodies, in which the tension of *cupiditas* (or *appetitus*) is expressed. This is life's active expectation of itself in the process of singular subjectivation.

---

[13] 'This eternal covenant of the knowledge and love of God is universal.' *TTP* III; *CWS* II, 123.
[14] *Ep.* XXI [to Blijenbergh]; *CWS* I, 376.
[15] Alain, 'Souvenirs concernant Jules Lagneau', in *Spinoza*, Gallimard, 1986, pp. 163, 164.
[16] Ibid., p. 164.

For the collective body, self-confidence is above all confidence in its own imagination, fidelity to its laws and customs (its self-love). But even more profoundly – and this is what democracy explicitly expresses – the essential confidence that the collective body has in itself is confidence in its own power of imaginative institutionalisation, confidence in the affirmation of the *multitudinis potentia*. Beneath all self-love and trust in its ontological principle, democracy rediscovers the essential relationship of the collective body's love for itself, the love of its own acting power, the joy of communicating, deliberating, deciding and building the future together: love of its freedom. For the philosopher who knows all this, trust in the self-organising power of the multitude is precisely trust in the rationality of the collective body in the process of its constitution (and/or reconstitution). Inseparable from being in its absolute affirmation, trust is thus the 'fuel'. In body as much as in thought, trust is the very dynamism of the intellectual love of God in the infinite infinity of singular 'alliances' of love for oneself. It is the endless process of singularisation.

The ultimate truth of Spinozism is *amor sui sive causa sui*: a radical and always singular ontology of trust – a trust that must be, at the same time, recovered (since, like our place, it has been there for all eternity) and produced (since eternity exists in and through its unique and historical affirmation). In the affirmation of the *multitudinis potentia*, and prior to all bondage and perseverance in a particular state, Spinoza discovers the never-ending promise of freedom in the inner confidence in the adequate idea (*verum index sui*), which exists in all bodies, those of human beings and those of nations.

Living out this trust that constitutes our being (a singular, dynamic and multiple alliance with the universal-Real in its self-constitution) entails feeling completely alien to this other imagined life in the process of appropriation, exhausted by the strategies of self-love and pride. This estrangement allows us to increase, test and actively defend one's own singular power of acting, free from the blinkers, illusions and values of the subject in love. The actual principle of our singular affirmation and our liberation lies in this distance from oneself (as self-image). The affective lack of interest in images – not for their own sake and the power of imagination they express, but as obstacles, substitutes and fixations of thought and life – has no strength equivalent to the interest we have in knowing them. Notwithstanding the disruptions of power that images produce, our interest lies in loving and affirming the life that produces them (and which they produce). For the 'return' to the ethical-political principle of life as real movement does not open a dualism that would equate this enterprise with a devaluation of the world and its images. The philosophy of the real movement is also a theory of the constitution of the Real itself in its imaginary dimension. It is a theory of the positive reality of images, not only on the gnoseological level, but also on the practical level of common perception and the constitution of the human world, the formation of a world of 'things', 'objects' and 'subjects'. Above all, it is a theory of politics and history, the formation of languages, customs, institutions and laws... Far from being devalued, at the centre of Spinoza's dynamic ontology is imagination, understood as the power inherent in people and the multitude in their affirmation, the collective process of constitution. A labour of invention and imagination, the real movement in its recursive cycle is a creative movement: the future is created in and through imagination.

The sage experiences the creative presence of the world in its pure affirmative necessity, beyond which exist only the established consequences of our *cupiditas*, whether negative or positive for the affirmation of human life.

A later thinker such as Schopenhauer, who, wanting to take the abstract (non-) standpoint of a spectator God (in his absence), and abandoning the standpoint of singularity (or self-affection as ontological trust), inevitably meets only with indifference, boredom and despair. Spinoza, on the contrary, discovers the happy and eternal knowledge and love of God with the infinite multiplicity of the Real, and the universal communication of actual, singular essences in their own process of production and complication. This complication is the very movement of the Real in its recursive cycle. It is, in the infinite infinity of its individuation strategies, the complex logic of the *causa sui* and the absolute affirmation of existence in each mode.

From the dynamic point of view of singularity, then, the wise Spinozist enjoys the actuality of (and in) necessity, from which she draws her own strength beyond the fears and hopes of a life bound to the represented order of time. For this necessity without hope, without principle or end, is her own eternity, her trust, and her essential loyalty to life.

We do not, however, draw any optimism from this confidence. The world has no mercy for anyone, and we will inevitably be its victim. *Ethics* IV, Ax. is the bloody mathematical axiom that rules the destiny of finite modes, fatally doomed to the misfortunes of compulsion, separation and ultimately death ... while the happiness of blessedness, like that of political freedom, is a human exception, isolated, transient, concerning 'only a very few (compared with the whole human race)'.[17] This shows how much Spinozist confidence cannot come at the expense of clarity and vigilance, quite the contrary. For the sage as much as for the State, the absolute affirmation of

---

[17] *TTP* XV; *CWS* II, 282.

existence is inseparable from armed confidence. Confidence is nothing other than the dynamic of arming the sage 'with knowledge and love' and arming the State with good democratic institutions, checks and balances, and a strong defence against external enemies. But the sage, like the State, lives with even more confidence and freedom insofar as her vigilance and strategic acumen is sharper. Both rationality and vigilance grow with confidence. Spinoza quotes the Proverbs of Solomon on this subject: when 'knowledge shall enter into your heart, and wisdom shall be pleasant to you, then your providence [*mezima* means, as Spinoza notes, thought, deliberation and vigilance] will watch over you and prudence will guard you'.[18]

Spinozistic confidence is the opposite of the optimist's blissful stupidity. The armed confidence of the sage certainly assuages all fears (even those of death). But, due to its lucidity and its armour, the sage's confidence also eclipses all illusions, even illusions of unlimited mastery (self-love and pride) we might believe we have over our own destiny, thanks to our reason. We also learn from Proverbs, 'No wisdom, no understanding, no counsel can avail against the Lord' (21:30).

True, death is nothing, and there is only life. But all beings are condemned by life to necessary disappearance. They are shattered and dispersed by the fact that the absolute affirmation of nature occurs in and through them, without ever having experienced or even conceived of true bliss. This is the fate of almost all, since most have had to suffer 'a thousand evils'. Thus, Spinoza writes bluntly to Henri Oldenburg: 'I deny that . . . all men ought to be blessed.'[19] Misfortune is the most common lot.[20]

---

[18] *TTP* IV; CWS II, 137.

[19] *Ep.* LXXVIII [to Oldenburg]; CWS II, 480.

[20] The world is mathematically inhuman, and it is humans who are most terrible to themselves. Spinoza is thus furthest from Leibniz, whose (fragile) confidence asserts itself against the innocence of the Real in its autonomy, against the free necessity of God in the meshes of the net of universal harmony – a confidence of weakness that does justice to the world only through the imaginary mediation of its ordered representation. Leibniz is afraid of the world, just as he is afraid of Spinoza and the inhuman truth revealed by mathematical proof; an intolerable truth that Leibnizian pusillanimity will reduce in favour of what is desirable to him. In Leibniz, the desire for order and meaning will be stronger than science. Christian desire will take the place of courage for truth. Unable to rise according to the immanent logic of the Real against this armed confidence of the wise Spinozist, Leibniz constructs an arsenal of external reasons to give confidence to the common person, which are so many symptoms of his own anxiety in the face of the Real and Spinozism. See Georges Friedmann, who stresses that 'Before God, Leibniz postulates the "better" that God compels. In this we see neither a sign of fundamental optimism nor a sign of trust in God. On the

The misery of finitude, yes, but also the unhappiness that individuals, like nations, in their ignorance and their impotence inevitably produce for themselves, while following the necessary laws of their affects, the logic of their opinions and mores, though they seek only to be happy: see Solomon, Calderon, Spinoza. For individuals as well as for nations, 'there is no unhappier state ... *conditionem miseriorem*', no more tragic fate, than when they run towards their own loss, even though they are endowed with excellent dispositions. The imaginary and yet strategic constitution of human reality in its history is, from this point of view – namely, the point of view of illusions, false problems and maladjustments – a formidable apparatus for the (deferred) self-destruction of life.

From the perspective of the practical subject determined by reason – an immovable observer of universal necessity in its life-destroying manifestations, in that fixed point of division from oneself where the power of wisdom grants no complacency to this external perspective we have on the world – there is a tragedy peculiar to Spinozism. Without sadness or drama, but in full lucidity, in the face of the endless turmoil of reality and the blind strategies of individuals and nations, there remains the scarcity and brevity of joy. A relationship with the world in the image of its necessity is certainly a 'true' but nevertheless an abstract relationship. It cannot be the 'adequate' and real relationship that the sage maintains in her singular affirmation of Nature in its universality. But because it robs us of any projection of value, because it robs reality of any illusion, because it is momentarily removed from the unique dynamic of resistance and affirmation, because it does not benefit from the enjoyment of the present, this abstract but lucid perspective offers to the eye of reason a spectacle of the world that could only inspire fear if it were not for the great command of the sage who bears it.[21]

But the real movement of the Real invites and leads us in a certain and determinate way to be entirely an actor (our real position) rather than

---

contrary, Leibniz seems to distrust God himself.' *Leibniz et Spinoza*, Gallimard, 1962, p. 315. Cf. also Gilles Deleuze, who remarks, 'How strange Leibniz's optimism is', but deduces from it that the principle of the best is there to save the freedom of God, to the detriment of that of humans. *Le Pli. Leibniz et le Baroque*, Minuit, 1988, pp. 92–4. The two approaches do not seem contradictory to me. For a stimulating comparison of the philosophies of Leibniz and Spinoza, see Elhanan Yakira, *Contrainte, nécessité, choix. La métaphysique de la liberté chez Spinoza et chez Leibniz*, ed. du Grand Midi, 1989.

[21] Spinoza attaches great philosophical value to the view of Ecclesiastes, for he makes of Solomon the (already Spinozist) 'philosopher' of the Old Testament, *TTP* II; *CWS* II, 107.

a spectator (hypnotised by the tragic image of necessity). The Spinozist philosophical enterprise is to put up a fight rather than to rest.

Da ma lemaala mimekha. Where the traditional exegesis of the *Pirkei Avot* (ch. II, 1) instructs us to 'know what there is above you', Spinoza's reader encounters instead – in a translation that still respects the Hebrew grammar – the Good News and its ethical-political plea to 'know that what is above you (and determines things) comes from you'.

Index nominum

Augustine, Saint, 72n, 144n
Alain, 99n, 269
Alquié, F., 130n
Althusius, 239–40, 246
Althusser, L., 148n
Appuhn, C., 47n
Arenilla, L., 237n
Aristotle, 2, 8n, 34, 72n, 249
Aron, R., 117n

Bachelard, G., 128n, 203n
Balibar, E., 184n, 225n
Balling, P., 43
Barclay, W., 238
Belin, M.-H., 239n
Bernard de Clairvaux, 72n
Bloch, E., 237n
Bloch, O., 126n
Blijenbergh, G. De, 28n, 54, 269
Bordoli, R., 36n
Boss, G., 17n
Bouwmeester, J., 13n
Boxel, H., 123
Brehier, E., 20n
Breton, S., 113n
Brykman, G., 154n, 214n, 247n
Burgersdijk, F., 142n

Calderón de la Barca, 273
Calvin, J., 237n
Canguilhem, G., 117n
Cavailles, J., 117n
Cicero, 72n

Comte-Sponville, A., 117n
Cristofolini, P., 205n
Curley, E., 31n, 67n, 73n, 166n

Delbos, V., 120n, 261n
Deleuze, G., 124, 263n, 273n
Democritus, 123
Desanti, J.-T., 167n
Descartes, R., 2, 262n
De Deugd, C., 36n
de Vries, S., 38
Du Plessis-Mornay, P., 238–9

Engels, F., 267
Epicurus, 103n, 123

Fabritius, 227n
Foucault, M., 28n
Freud, S., 26, 45n
Friedmann, G., 272n

Gilbert, F., 8n
Goethe, J. W., 268
Goyard-Fabre, S., 147n
Grotius, H., 238
Gueroult, M., 2n, 36n, 39n, 47n, 50n, 96n, 132n, 136, 142n

Heerebord, A., 142
Hobbes, T. 85, 87, 106n, 225–6, 227n, 235, 237n, 252n
Huan, G., 8n
Hudde., 122n, 129

Huizinga, J., 167n
Hume, D., 17n

Jelles, J., 34n, 38, 248

Klever, W., 108n
Kojeve, A., 121n

La Boétie, E. de, 147n, 244, 254–7
Lacan, J., 1n
La Forge, 36n
Lagrée, J., 252n
Laux, H., 234n, 265n
Laplace, P. S., 128n
La Placette, J., 124n
Lefort, C., 254n
Leibniz, G. W., 44n, 125, 272n
Levy-Valensi, A., 130
Locke, J., 237
Lucretius, 123–4
Luther, M., 237

Macherey, P., 28n
Machiavelli, N., 8n, 10, 196n, 236, 247n, 254–7
Maimonides, 128n
Malet, A., 145
Matheron, A., 33n, 35n, 67n, 111n, 159n, 225n, 244n, 262n
Matthew, Saint, 252n
Mercier, C., 238n
Mignini, F., 38n
Misrahi, R., 17n, 73n
Moreau, P.-F., 126n, 214n, 224n, 237n, 264n
Mugnier-Pollet, L., 167n
Müntzer, T., 237

Negri, A., 205n, 212n, 224n, 234n, 246n
Nizan, P., 97n, 126n

Oldenburg, H., 38, 129, 138–9, 204n, 272
Orange, William Prince of, 242n

Paul, Saint, 72n, 237
Pascal, B., 195n
Pericles, 265n
Philip II, 237
Philo, 130
Plato, 10, 12, 266

Quintus Curtius, 159

Rice Lee, C., 176n
Richelieu, 222n
Robin, L., 126n
Rousset, B., 4n, 20n, 36n, 134n

Saint-Just, 236
Solomon, 272
Schopenhauer, 271
Schuller, G.H., 32n, 54n, 132, 138
Shirley, S., 73n

Tacitus, 193
Terence, 102n
Thomas Aquinas, 2n, 4n, 72n
Tosel, A., 115n, 176n, 204n, 225n
Tschirnhaus, E. W. De, 129
Thucydides, 265n

Vernière, P., 124n

Weber, M. 85n
Wilson, C., 85n
Wolfson, H., 34n, 36n

Yakira, E., 273n

Zac, S., 122n

EU representative:
Easy Access System Europe
Mustamäe tee 50, 10621 Tallinn, Estonia
Gpsr.requests@easproject.com

www.ingramcontent.com/pod-product-compliance
Lightning Source LLC
Chambersburg PA
CBHW050211240426
43671CB00013B/2290